INUBAKA

CRAZY FOR DOGS

11

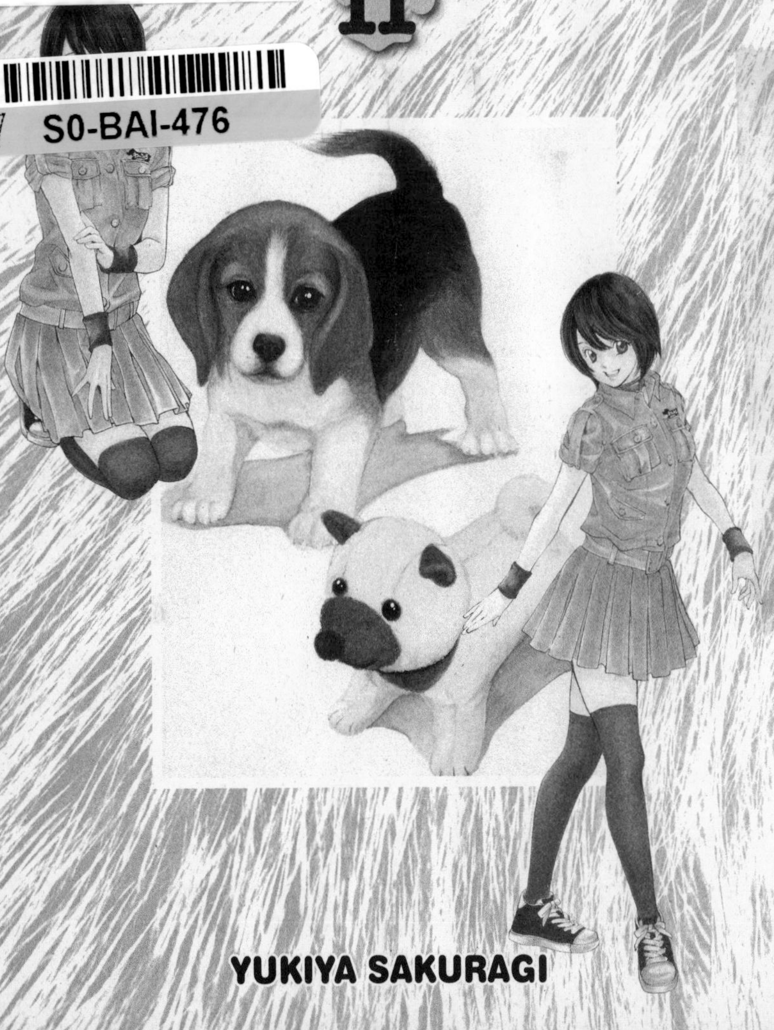

YUKIYA SAKURAGI

Contents

Story thus far

Teppei is the manager of the recently opened pet shop Woofles. He intended to breed his black Labrador Noa with a champion dog, but instead Noa was "taken advantage of" by an unknown and unfixed male dog!

The unknown dog's owner was Suguri Miyauchi and her dog was a mutt named Lupin. Suguri is now working at Woofles to make up for her dog's actions.

Suguri's enthusiasm is more than a little unique. She has eaten dog food (and said it was tasty), caught dog poop with her bare hands and caused dogs to have "happy pee" in her presence. Teppei is starting to realize that Suguri is indeed a very special girl.

Rumors have started to spread that a company is opening a new pet shop named "WAN KAW" right across the street... Show Kaneko, the main Woofles' store manager, suggested that Teppei hire more staff as a way to compete with the new store. Ryusuke Mikage is hired to join the team. He appears to be a hardworking guy who approaches every task diligently, but he's hiding a secret! He secretly works for Hibino, the general manager of "WAN KAW." From information Mikage gathers, Hibino realizes Suguri has special talents and plots to entice her out of Woofles! But that plan couldn't fool Woofles regular Chizuru!

CHARACTERS

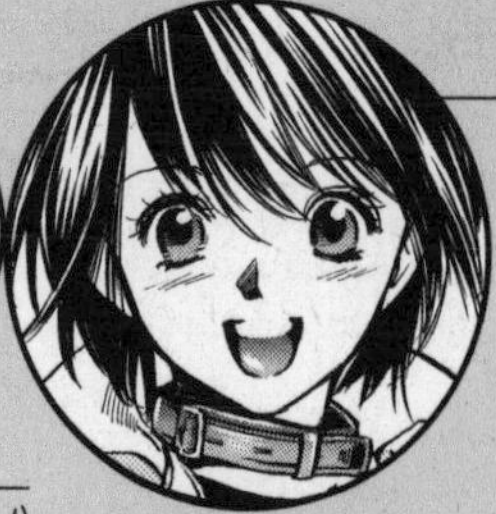

Suguri Miyauchi

She seems to possess an almost supernatural connection with dogs. When she approaches them they often urinate with great excitement! She is crazy for dogs and can catch their droppings with her bare hands. She is currently a trainee at the Woofles Pet Shop.

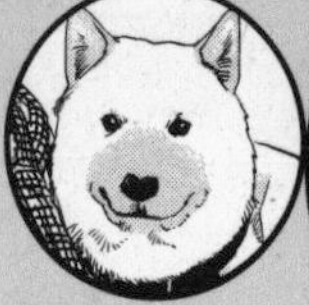

Lupin

♂ Mutt (mongrel)

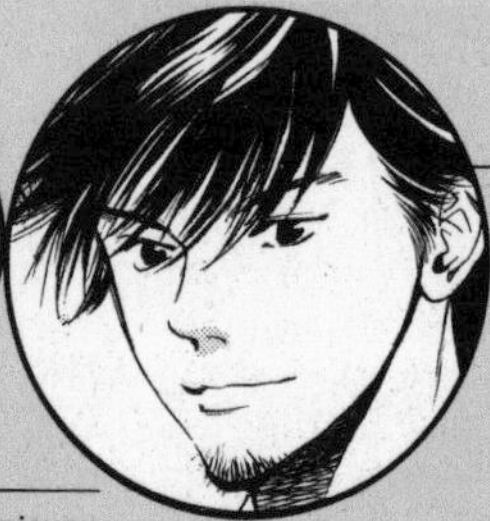

Teppei Iida

He is the manager of the recently opened pet shop Woofles. He is aware of Suguri's special ability and has hired her to work in his shop. He also lets Suguri and Kentaro crash with him.

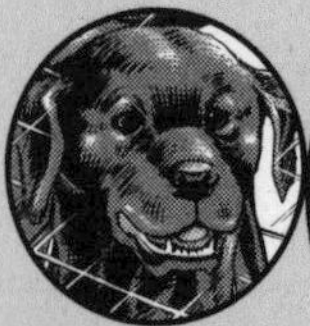

Noa

♀ Labrador retriever

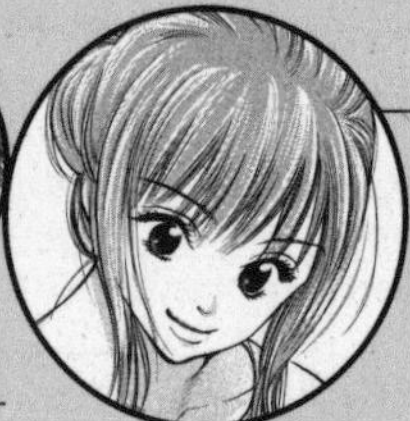

Momoko Takeuchi

Woofles Pet Shop (second location) pet groomer. At first she was a girl with many problems and she rarely smiled. But after meeting Suguri, she's changed, and the two are now best friends.

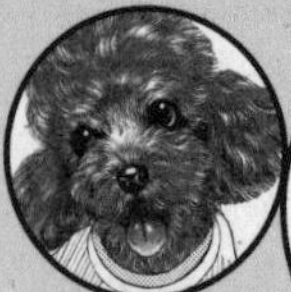

Mel

♀ Toy poodle

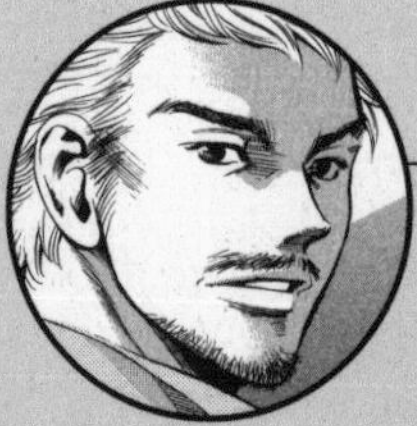

Show Kaneko

He is the manager of the main Woofles store and is Teppei's boss. He is very passionate about the business and makes TV appearances from time to time.

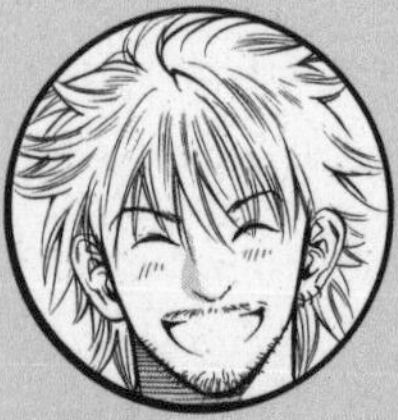

Kentaro Osada

A buddy of Teppei's from their high school days. He's on the staff at Woofles' second store.

Woofles

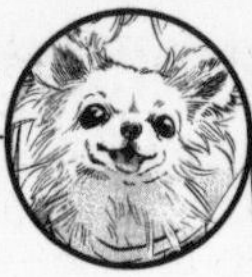

Melon

♂ Chihuahua

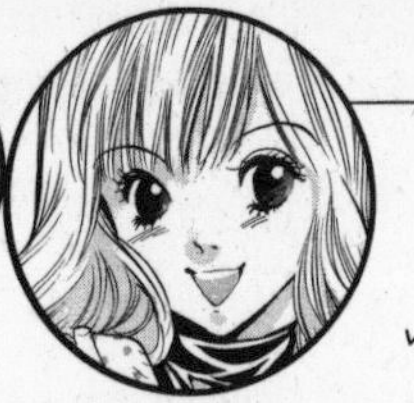

Chizuru Sawamura

She adopted a Chihuahua, Melon, after her long-time pet golden retriever Ricky alerted her that Melon was ill. She works at a hostess bar to repay Melon's medical fees.

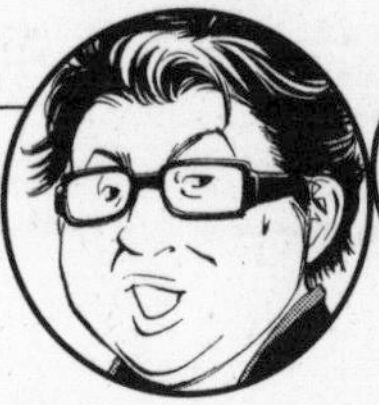

Hiroshi Akiba

Pop-idol otaku turned dog otaku. His dream is to publish a photo collection of his dog, Zidane. He is a government employee.

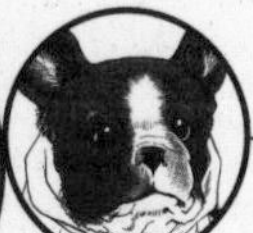

Zidane

♂ French bulldog

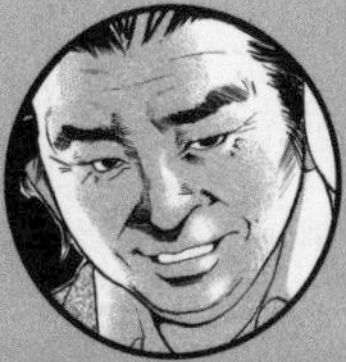

President of KAW KAW

The president of one of the largest online shopping sites, Kaw Kaw. He believes he can make a fortune in the pet business and invests a lot of money to achieve this goal by opening the Wan Kaw store.

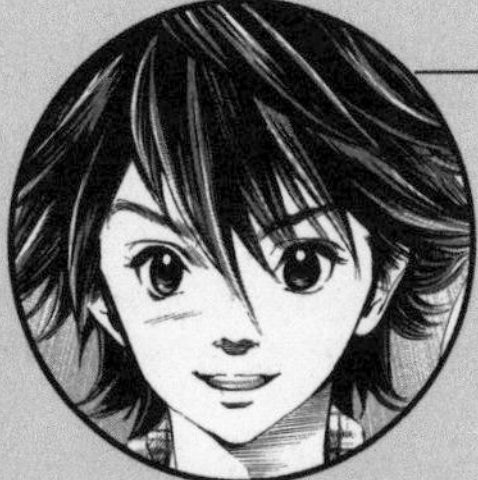

Ryusuke Mikage

A newcomer at Woofles who also works for Hibino. He went to Woofles as a spy for Wan Kaw. After gathering information from Woofles, his boss told him he was no longer needed...

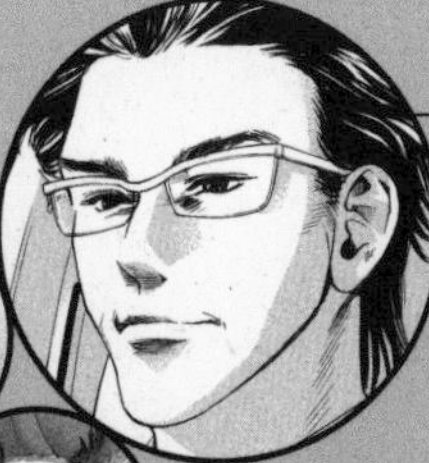

Motoshi Hibino

General manager of pet shop Wan Kaw, the rival store to Woofles. He noticed Suguri's talents and is plotting to recruit her for his store.

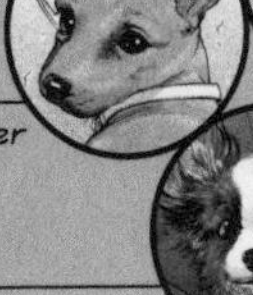

Sabrina

♀ Miniature pinscher

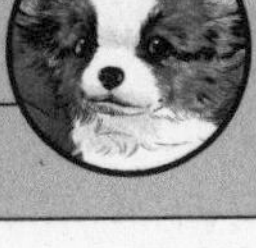

Anne

♀ Papillon

WAN KAW

INUBA*KA

CHAPTER 109: PARTING

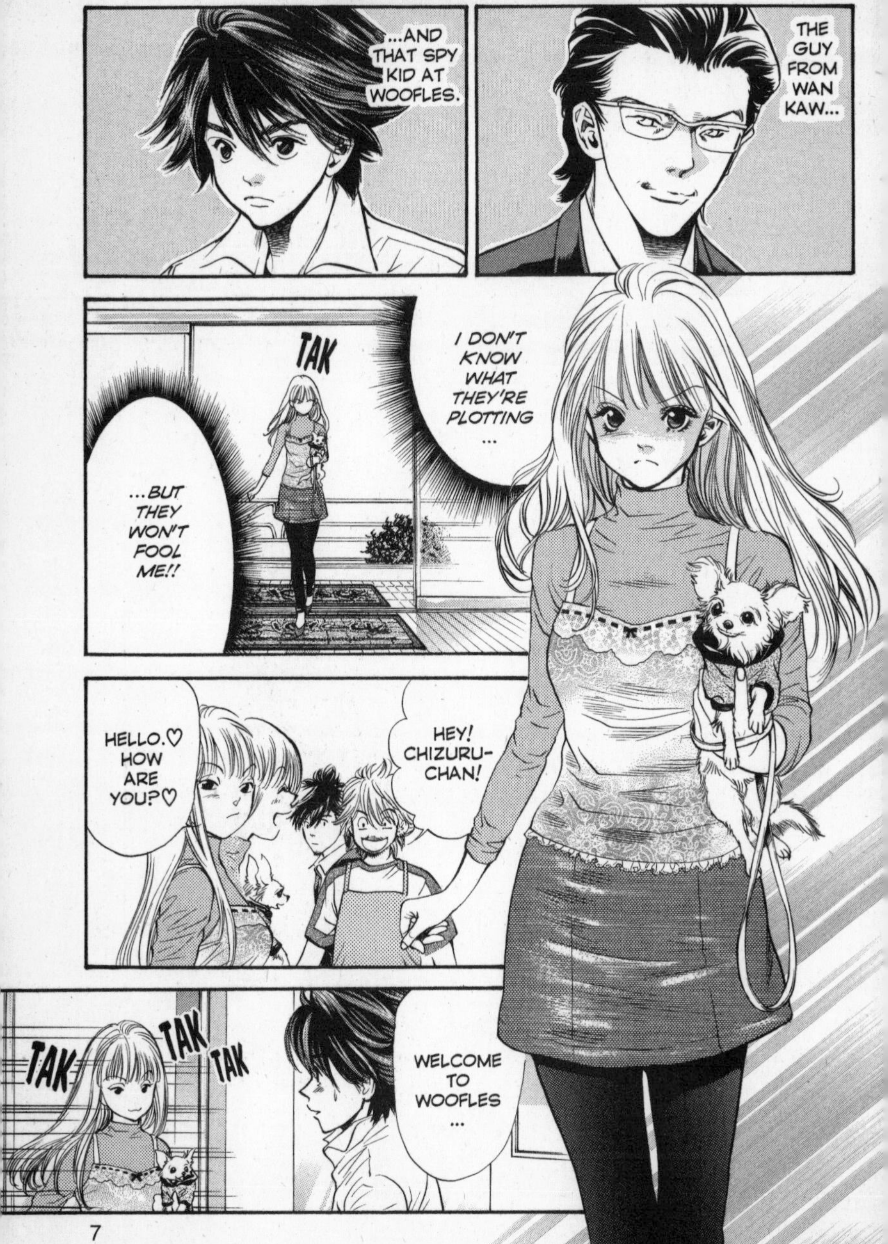

THE GUY FROM WAN KAW...
...AND THAT SPY KID AT WOOFLES.
TAK
I DON'T KNOW WHAT THEY'RE PLOTTING ...
...BUT THEY WON'T FOOL ME!!
HEY! CHIZURU-CHAN!
HELLO.♡ HOW ARE YOU?♡
WELCOME TO WOOFLES ...
TAK
TAK
TAK

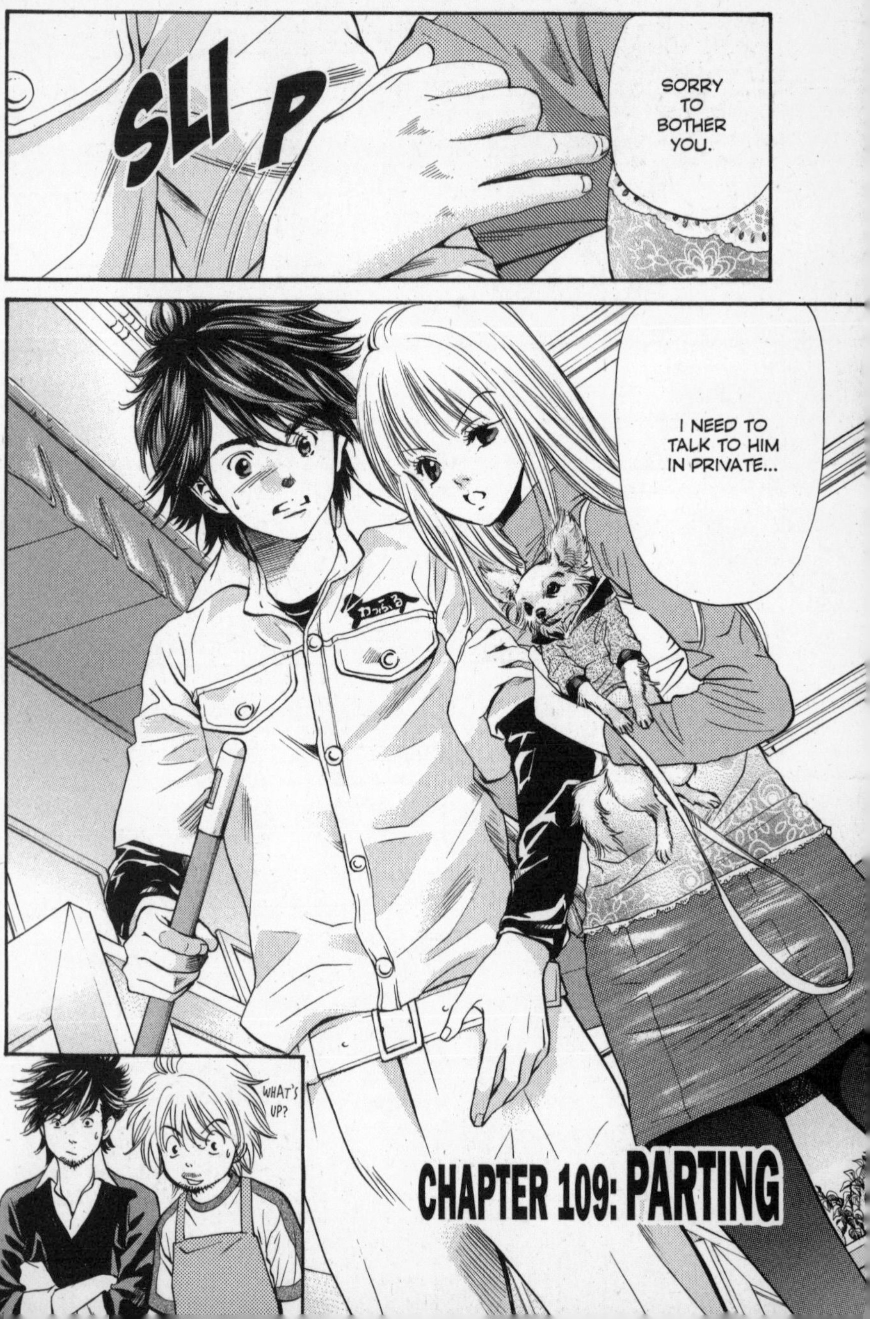
SLIP
SORRY TO BOTHER YOU.
I NEED TO TALK TO HIM IN PRIVATE...
WHAT'S UP?

CHAPTER 109: PARTING

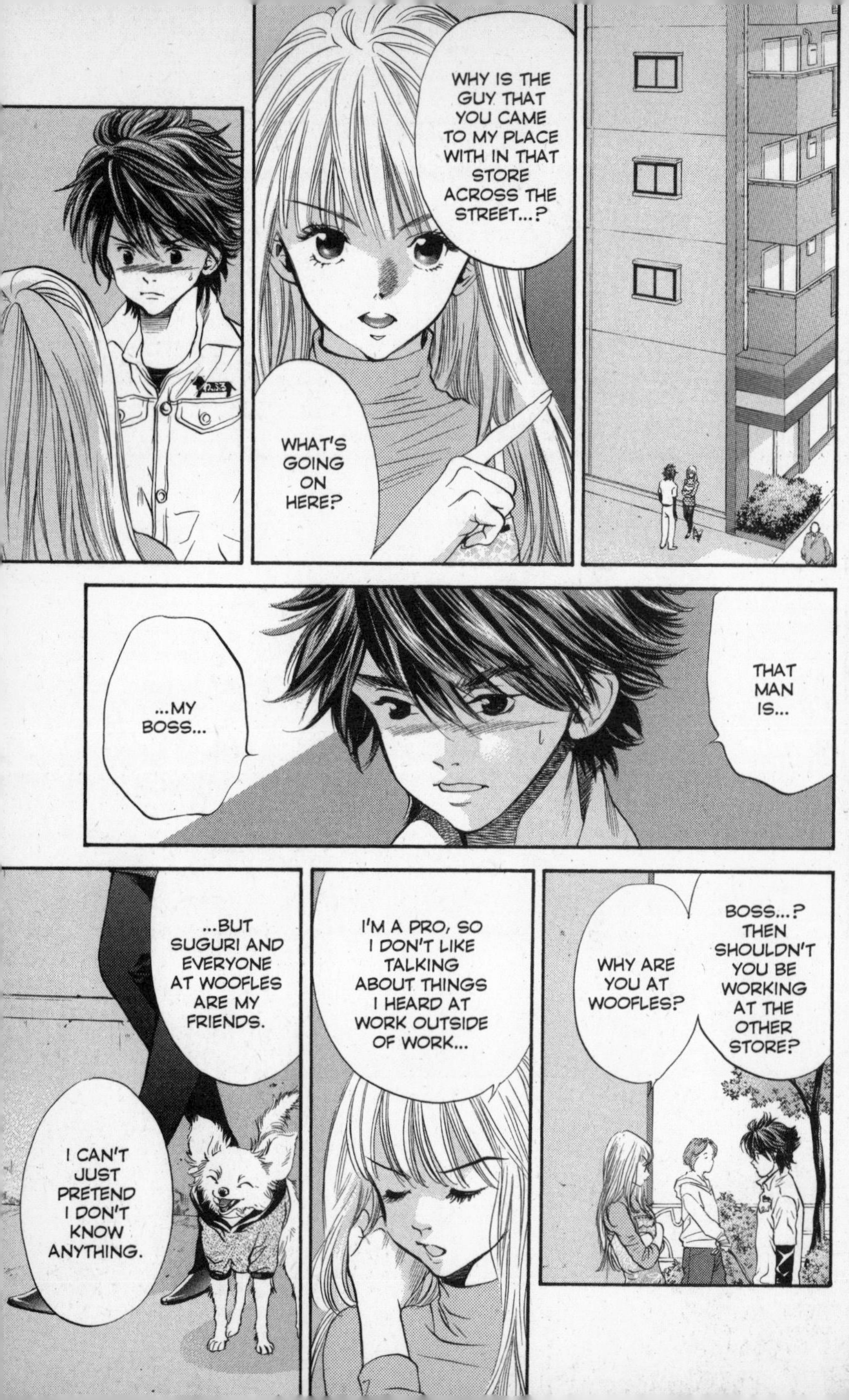
WHY IS THE GUY THAT YOU CAME TO MY PLACE WITH IN THAT STORE ACROSS THE STREET...?
WHAT'S GOING ON HERE?
THAT MAN IS...
...MY BOSS...
BOSS...? THEN SHOULDN'T YOU BE WORKING AT THE OTHER STORE?
WHY ARE YOU AT WOOFLES?
I'M A PRO, SO I DON'T LIKE TALKING ABOUT THINGS I HEARD AT WORK OUTSIDE OF WORK...
...BUT SUGURI AND EVERYONE AT WOOFLES ARE MY FRIENDS.
I CAN'T JUST PRETEND I DON'T KNOW ANYTHING.

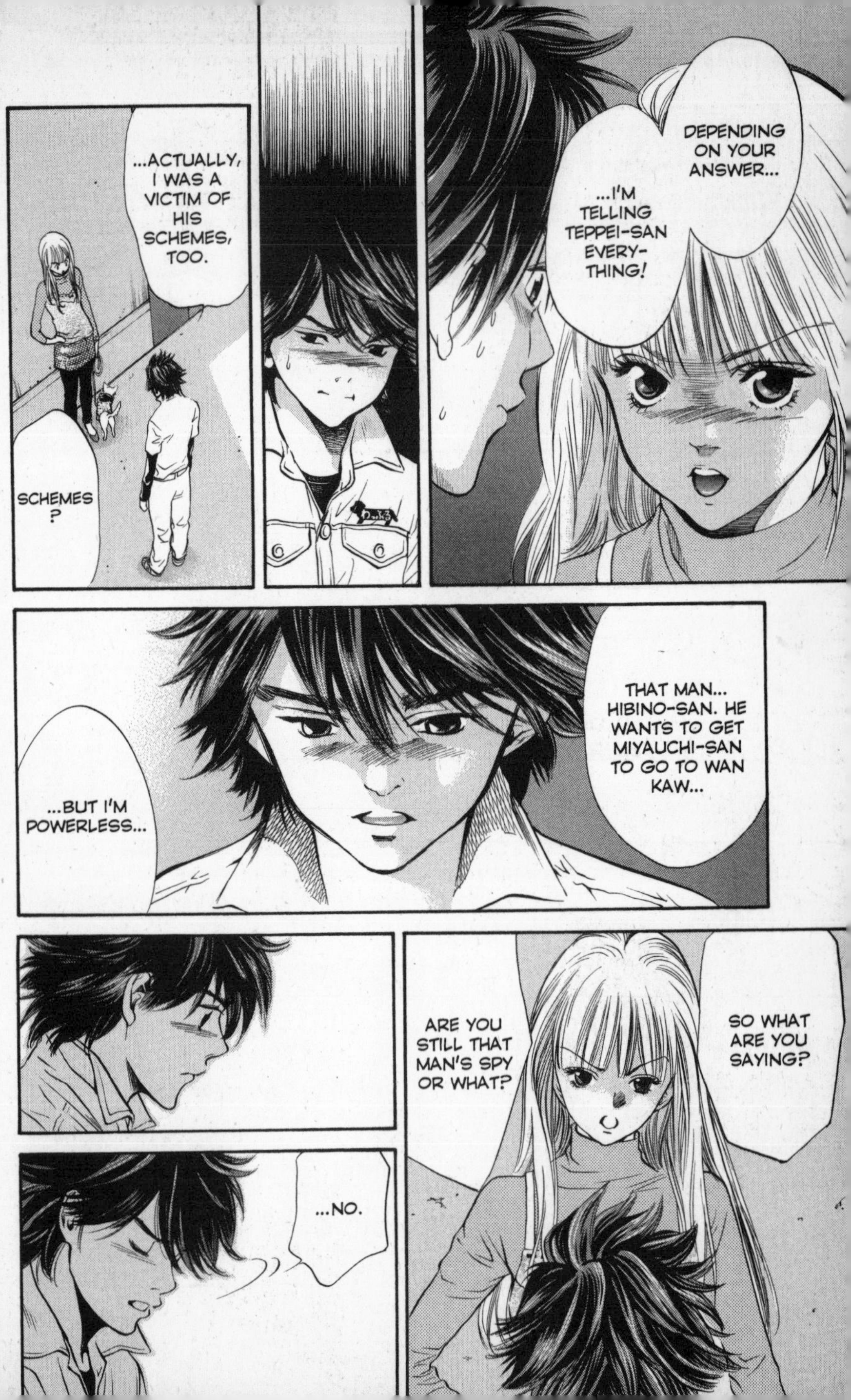
DEPENDING ON YOUR ANSWER...
...I'M TELLING TEPPEI-SAN EVERYTHING!
...ACTUALLY, I WAS A VICTIM OF HIS SCHEMES, TOO.
SCHEMES?
THAT MAN... HIBINO-SAN. HE WANTS TO GET MIYAUCHI-SAN TO GO TO WAN KAW...
...BUT I'M POWERLESS...
SO WHAT ARE YOU SAYING?
ARE YOU STILL THAT MAN'S SPY OR WHAT?
...NO.

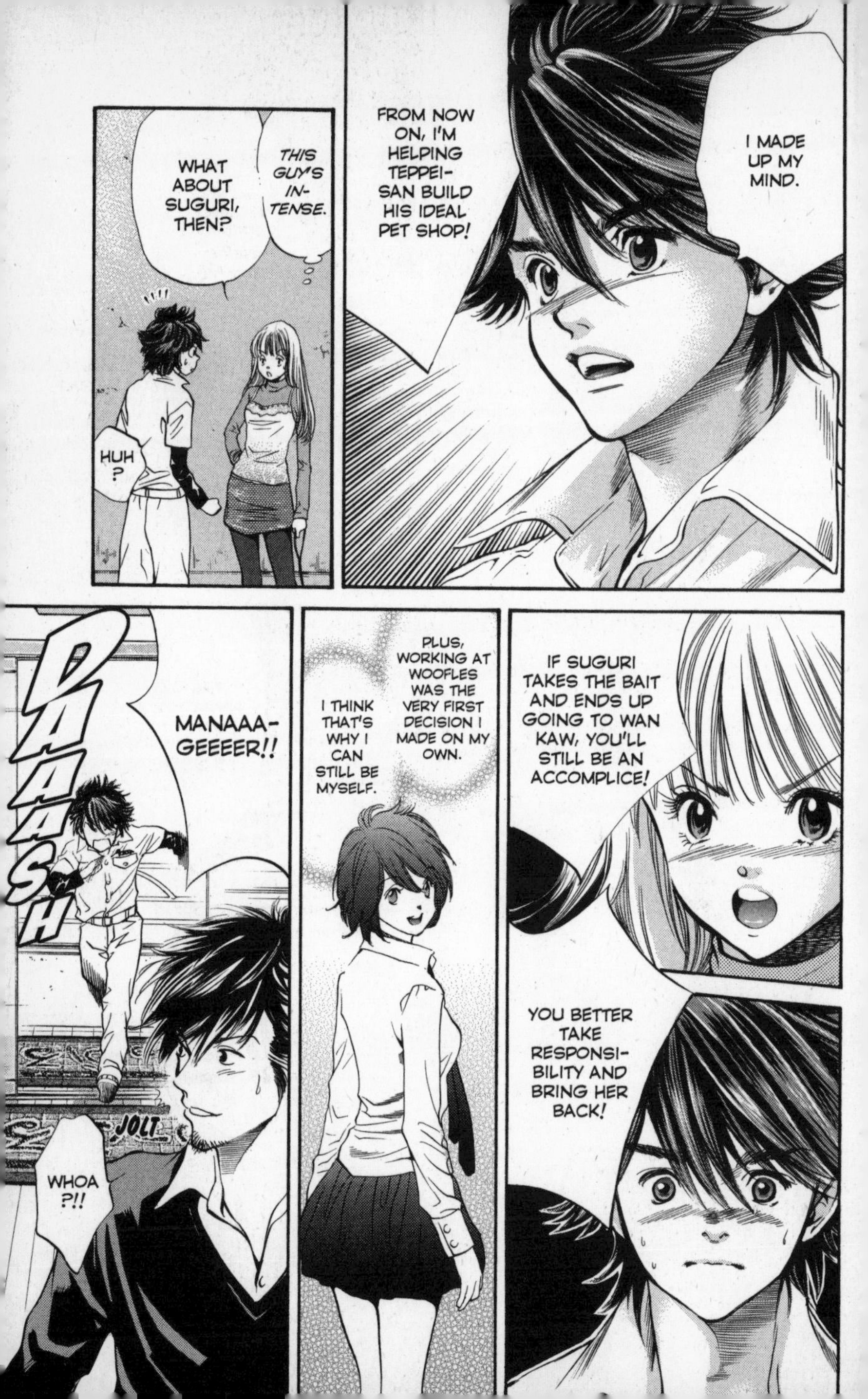
I MADE UP MY MIND.
FROM NOW ON, I'M HELPING TEPPEI-SAN BUILD HIS IDEAL PET SHOP!
THIS GUY'S IN-TENSE.
WHAT ABOUT SUGURI, THEN?
!!!
HUH?
IF SUGURI TAKES THE BAIT AND ENDS UP GOING TO WAN KAW, YOU'LL STILL BE AN ACCOMPLICE!
YOU BETTER TAKE RESPONSI-BILITY AND BRING HER BACK!
PLUS, WORKING AT WOOFLES WAS THE VERY FIRST DECISION I MADE ON MY OWN.
I THINK THAT'S WHY I CAN STILL BE MYSELF.
MANAAA-GEEEER!!
DAAAASH
JOLT
WHOA?!!

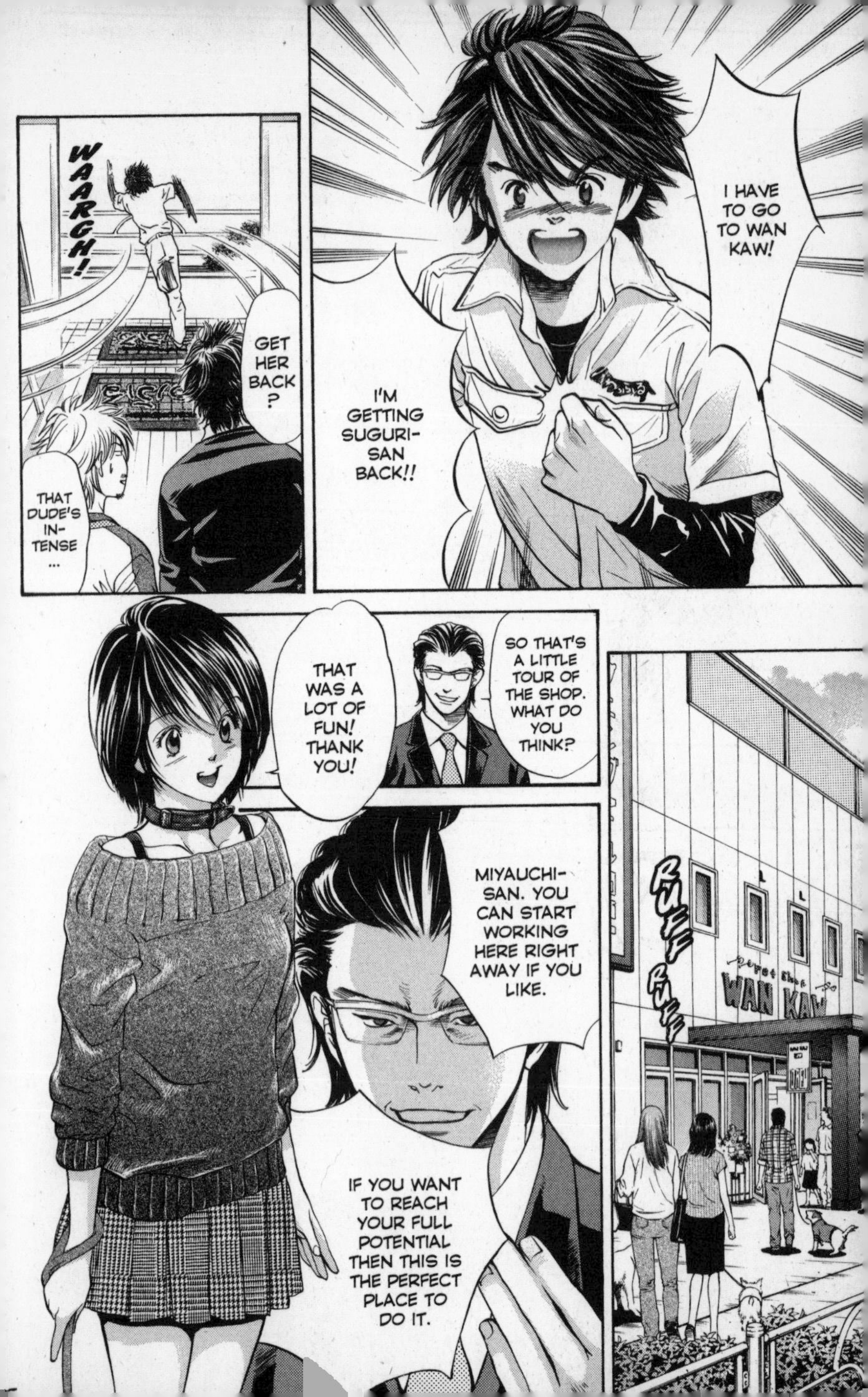
I HAVE TO GO TO WAN KAW!
I'M GETTING SUGURI-SAN BACK!!
WAARGH!
GET HER BACK?
THAT DUDE'S IN-TENSE...
RUFF RUFF
WAN KAW
SO THAT'S A LITTLE TOUR OF THE SHOP. WHAT DO YOU THINK?
THAT WAS A LOT OF FUN! THANK YOU!
MIYAUCHI-SAN. YOU CAN START WORKING HERE RIGHT AWAY IF YOU LIKE.
IF YOU WANT TO REACH YOUR FULL POTENTIAL THEN THIS IS THE PERFECT PLACE TO DO IT.

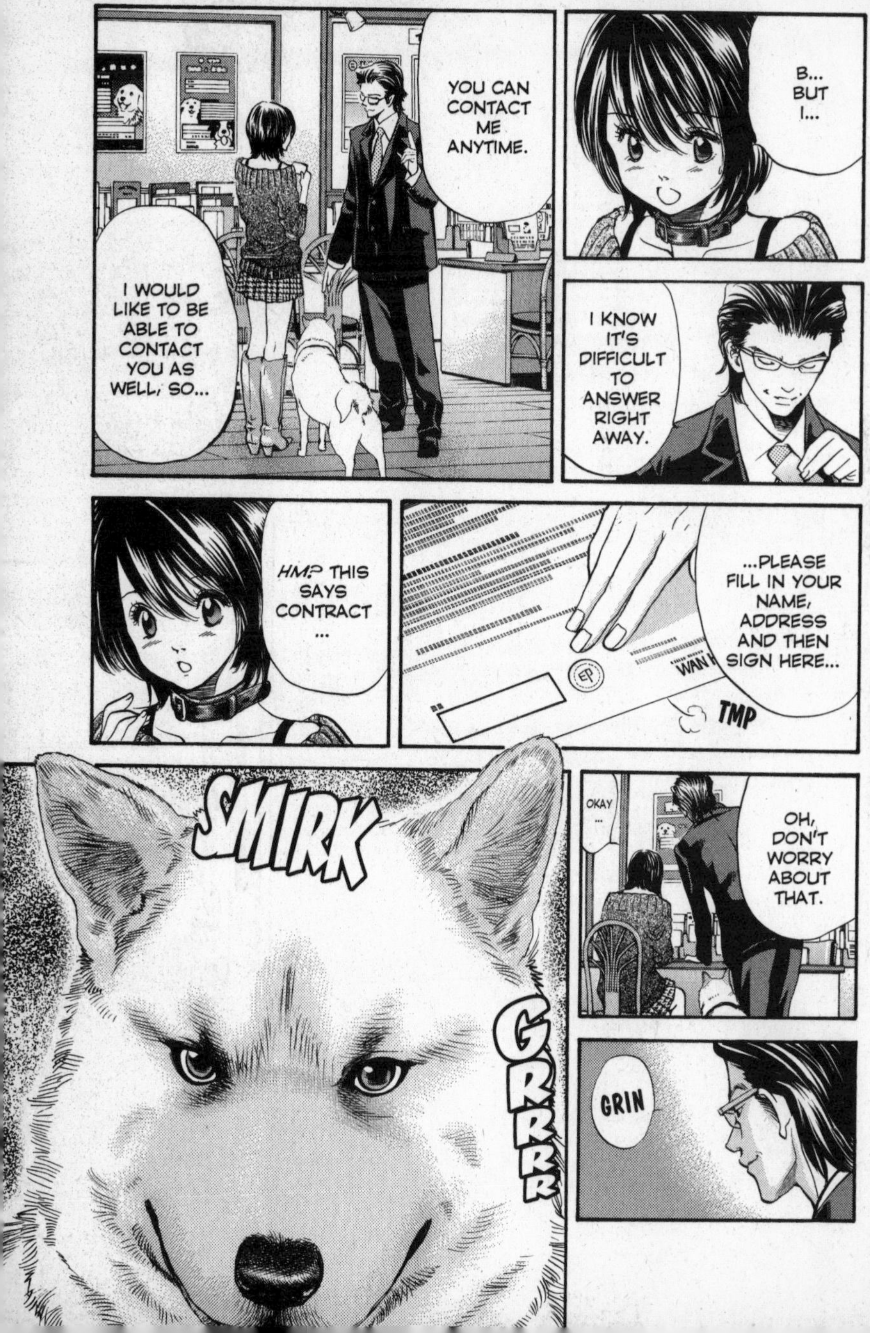
B... BUT I...
I KNOW IT'S DIFFICULT TO ANSWER RIGHT AWAY.
YOU CAN CONTACT ME ANYTIME.
I WOULD LIKE TO BE ABLE TO CONTACT YOU AS WELL, SO...
...PLEASE FILL IN YOUR NAME, ADDRESS AND THEN SIGN HERE...
EP
TMP
HM? THIS SAYS CONTRACT ...
OH, DON'T WORRY ABOUT THAT.
OKAY ...
GRIN
SMIRK
GRRRR

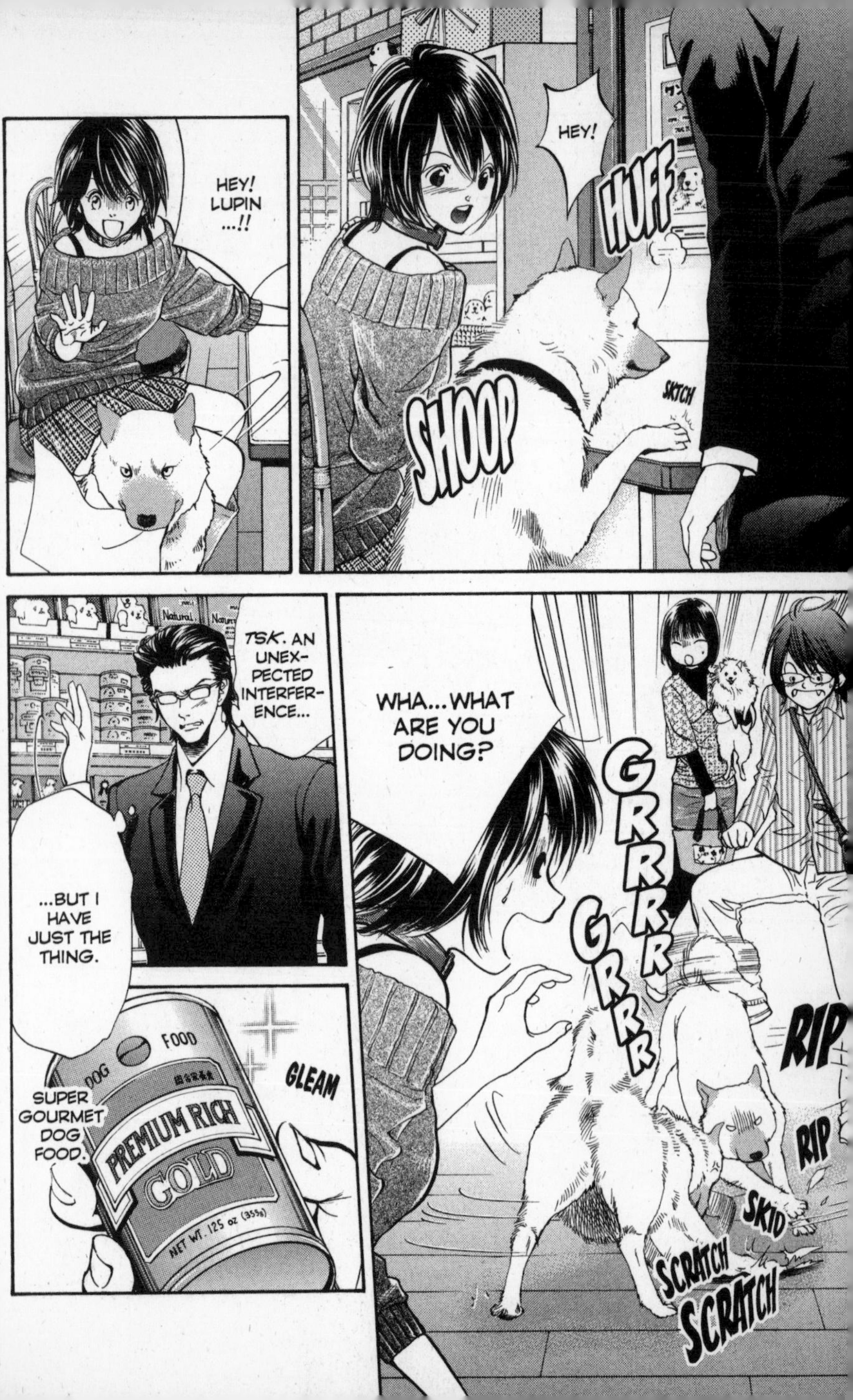
HEY!
HUFF
SHOOP
SKTCH
HEY! LUPIN ...!!
WHA...WHAT ARE YOU DOING?
GRRRR
GRRRR
RIP
RIP
SKID
SCRATCH
SCRATCH
TSK. AN UNEXPECTED INTERFERENCE...
...BUT I HAVE JUST THE THING.
GLEAM
SUPER GOURMET DOG FOOD.
DOG FOOD
PREMIUM RICH
GOLD

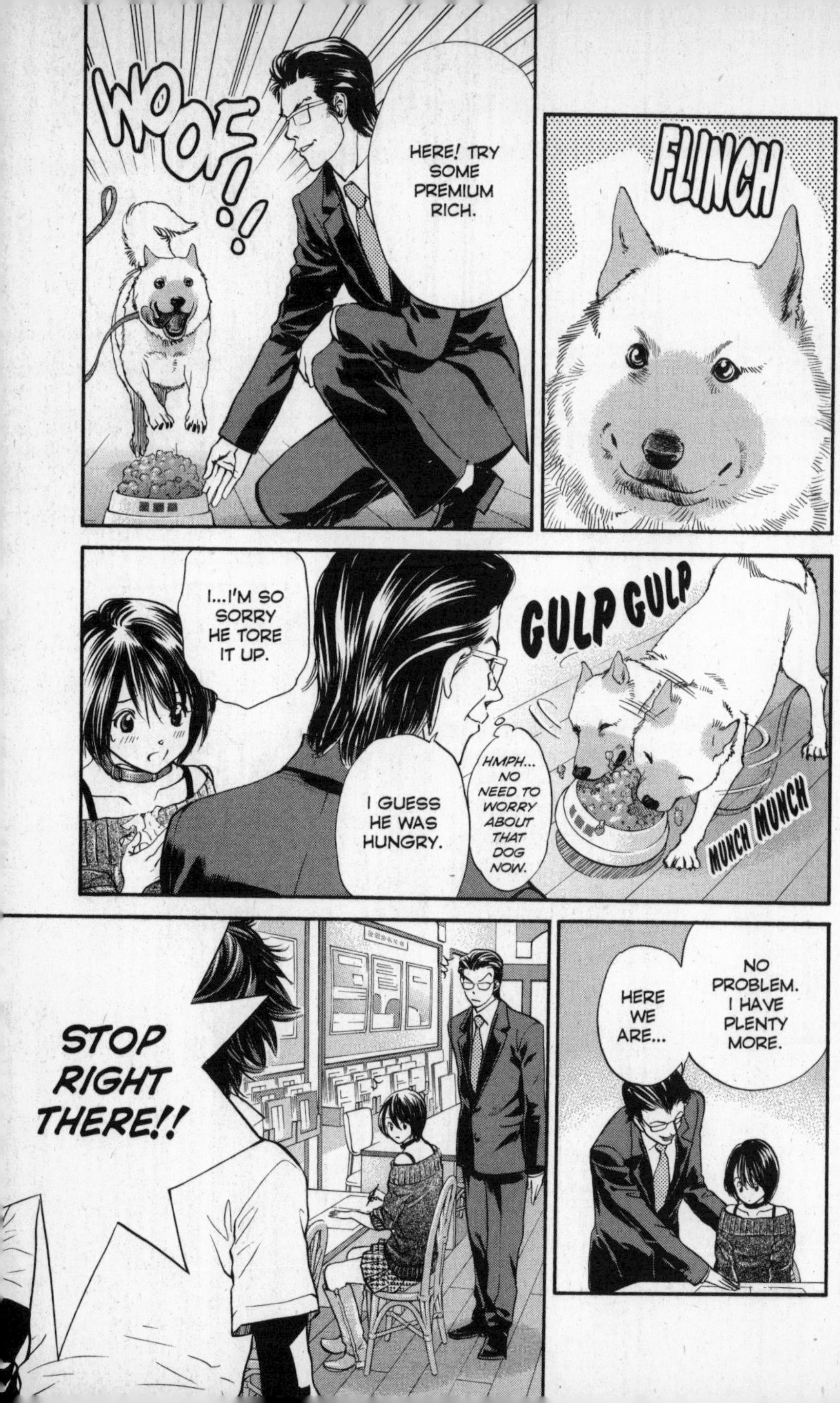
FLINCH
WOOF
HERE! TRY SOME PREMIUM RICH.
GULP GULP
I...I'M SO SORRY HE TORE IT UP.
HMPH... NO NEED TO WORRY ABOUT THAT DOG NOW.
I GUESS HE WAS HUNGRY.
MUNCH MUNCH
NO PROBLEM. I HAVE PLENTY MORE.
HERE WE ARE...
STOP RIGHT THERE!!

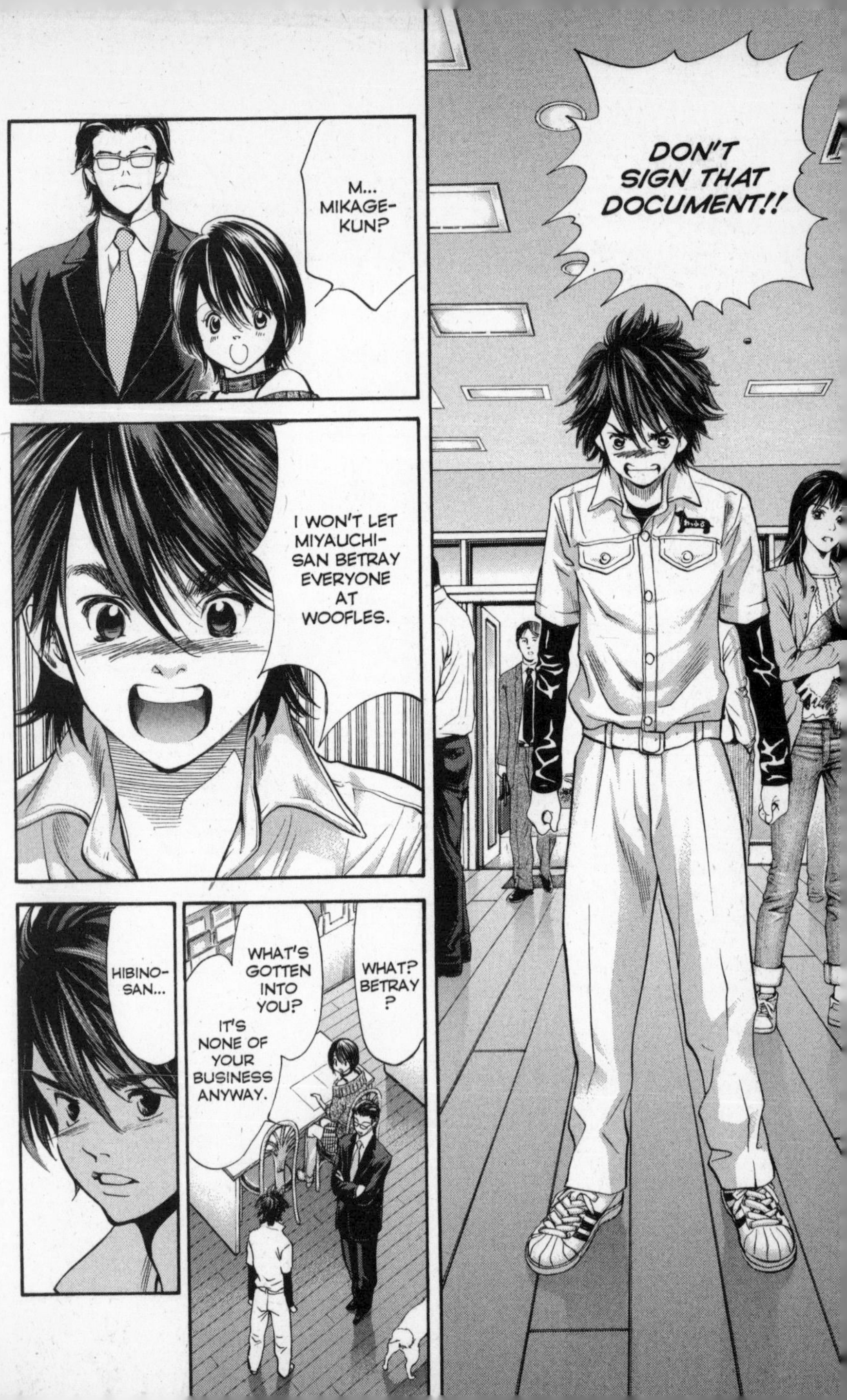
DON'T SIGN THAT DOCUMENT!!
M... MIKAGE-KUN?
I WON'T LET MIYAUCHI-SAN BETRAY EVERYONE AT WOOFLES.
WHAT? BETRAY?
WHAT'S GOTTEN INTO YOU?
IT'S NONE OF YOUR BUSINESS ANYWAY.
HIBINO-SAN...

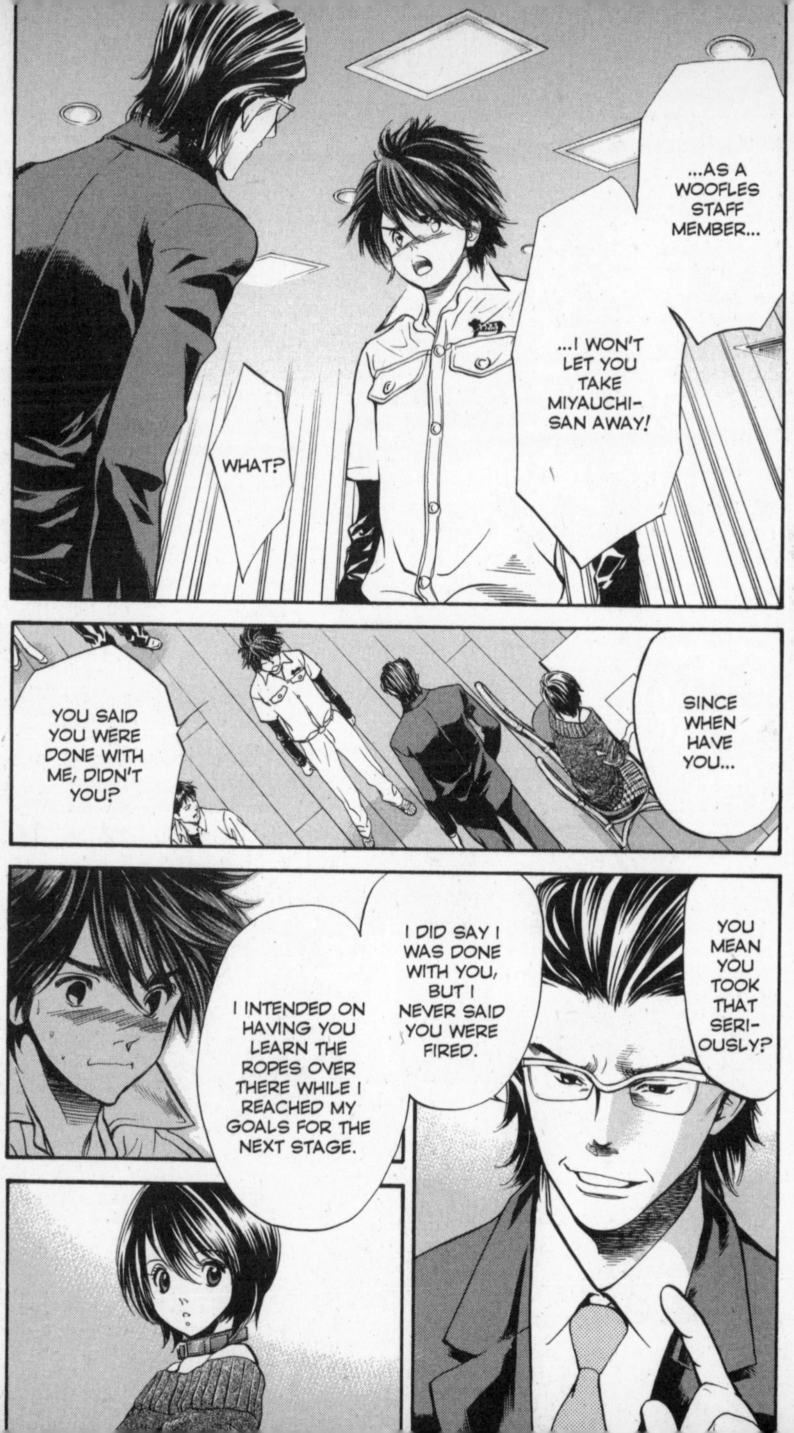
...AS A WOOFLES STAFF MEMBER...
...I WON'T LET YOU TAKE MIYAUCHI-SAN AWAY!
WHAT?
SINCE WHEN HAVE YOU...
YOU SAID YOU WERE DONE WITH ME, DIDN'T YOU?
YOU MEAN YOU TOOK THAT SERI-OUSLY?
I DID SAY I WAS DONE WITH YOU, BUT I NEVER SAID YOU WERE FIRED.
I INTENDED ON HAVING YOU LEARN THE ROPES OVER THERE WHILE I REACHED MY GOALS FOR THE NEXT STAGE.

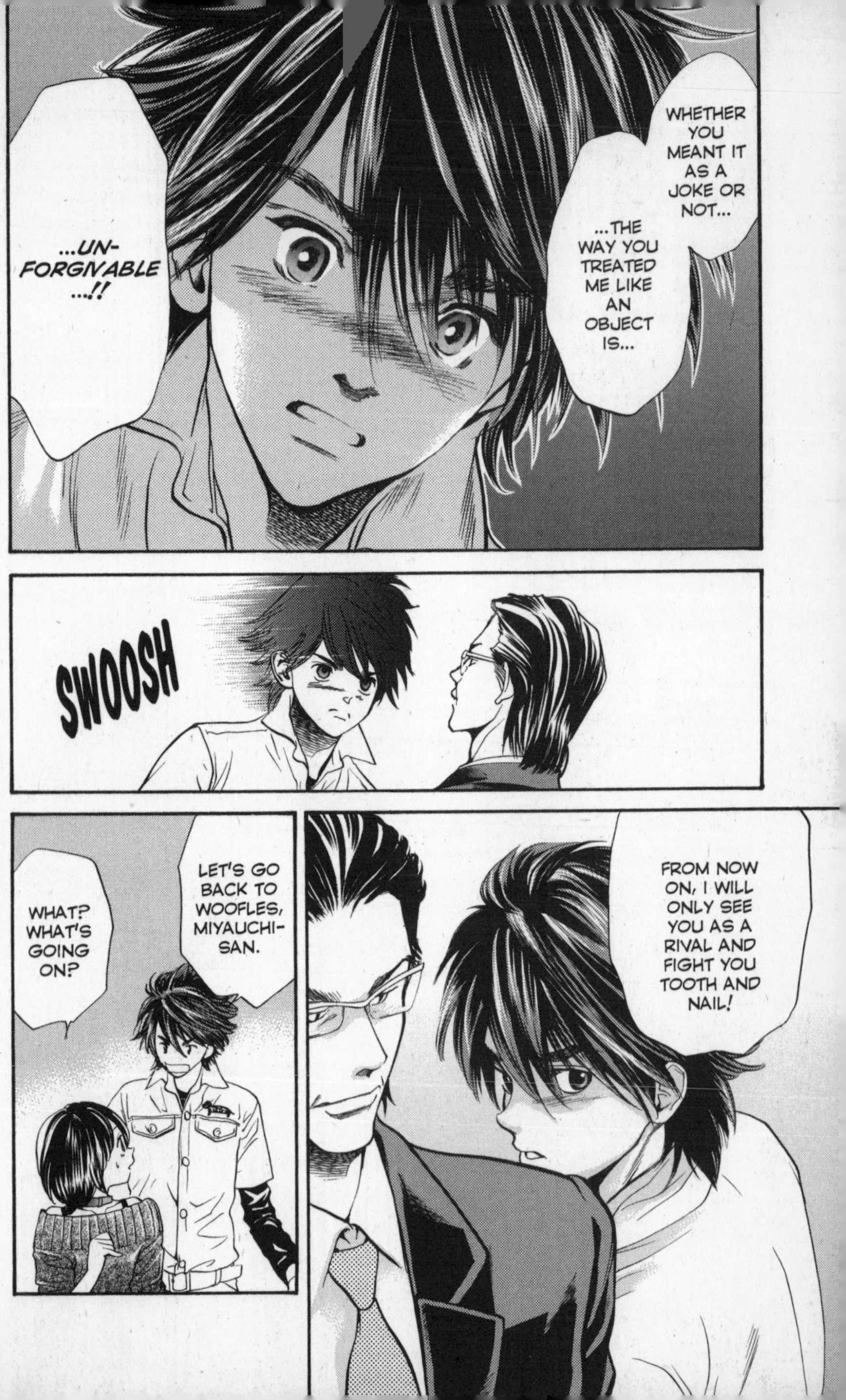
WHETHER YOU MEANT IT AS A JOKE OR NOT...
...THE WAY YOU TREATED ME LIKE AN OBJECT IS...
...UN-FORGIVABLE...!!
SWOOSH
FROM NOW ON, I WILL ONLY SEE YOU AS A RIVAL AND FIGHT YOU TOOTH AND NAIL!
LET'S GO BACK TO WOOFLES, MIYAUCHI-SAN.
WHAT? WHAT'S GOING ON?

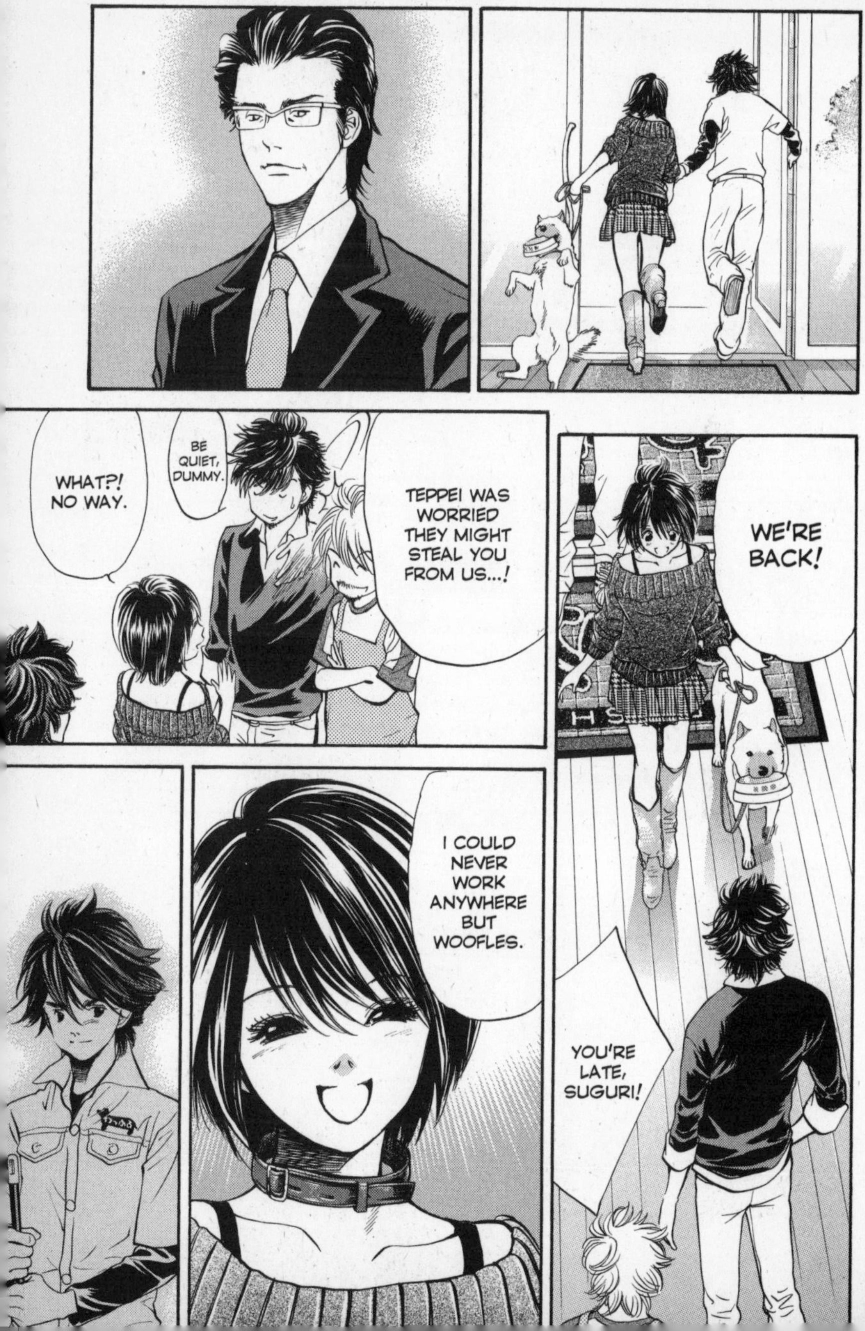
WE'RE BACK!
YOU'RE LATE, SUGURI!
TEPPEI WAS WORRIED THEY MIGHT STEAL YOU FROM US...!
BE QUIET, DUMMY.
WHAT?! NO WAY.
I COULD NEVER WORK ANYWHERE BUT WOOFLES.

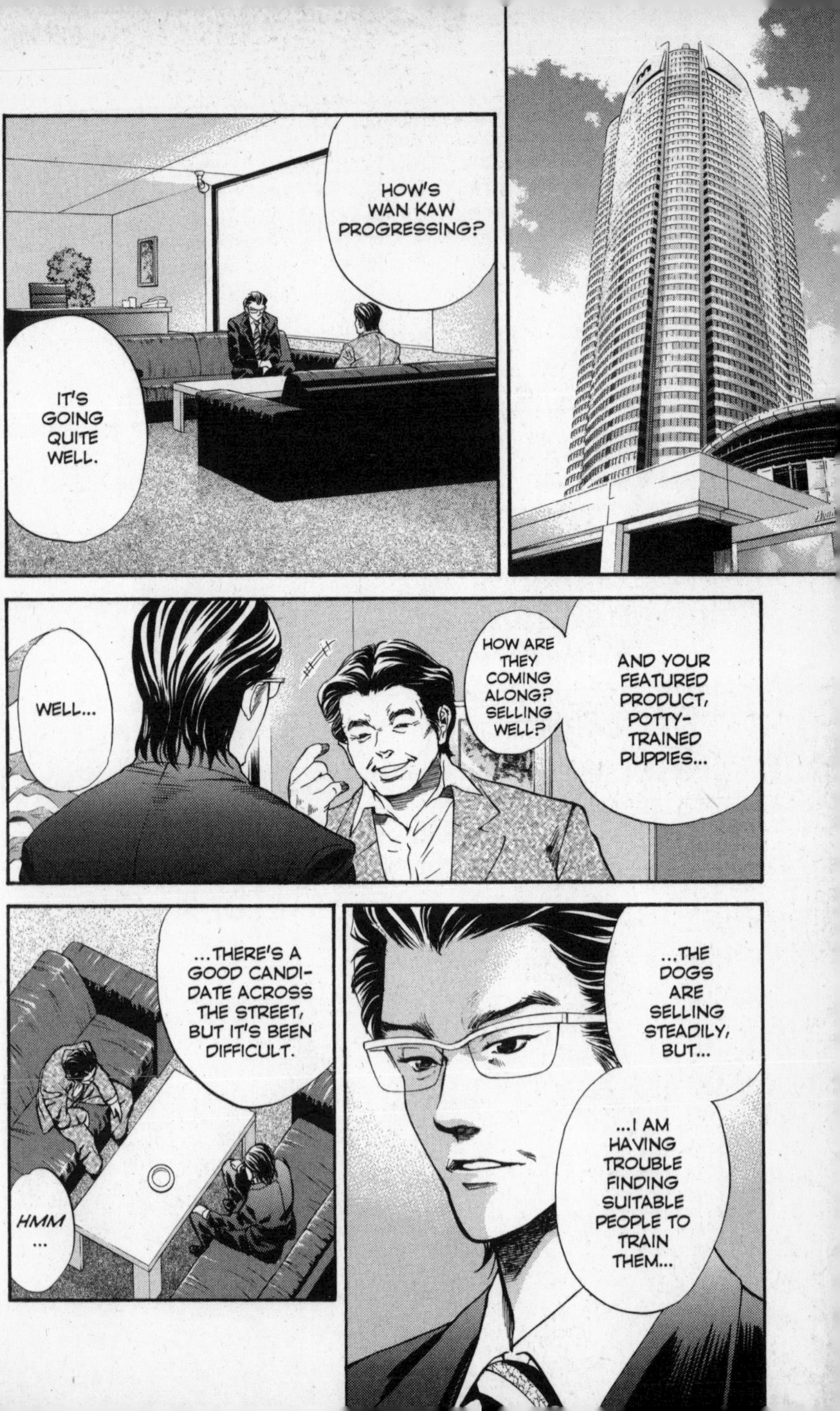
HOW'S WAN KAW PROGRESSING?
IT'S GOING QUITE WELL.
AND YOUR FEATURED PRODUCT, POTTY-TRAINED PUPPIES...
HOW ARE THEY COMING ALONG? SELLING WELL?
WELL...
...THE DOGS ARE SELLING STEADILY, BUT...
...I AM HAVING TROUBLE FINDING SUITABLE PEOPLE TO TRAIN THEM...
...THERE'S A GOOD CANDI-DATE ACROSS THE STREET, BUT IT'S BEEN DIFFICULT.
HMM ...

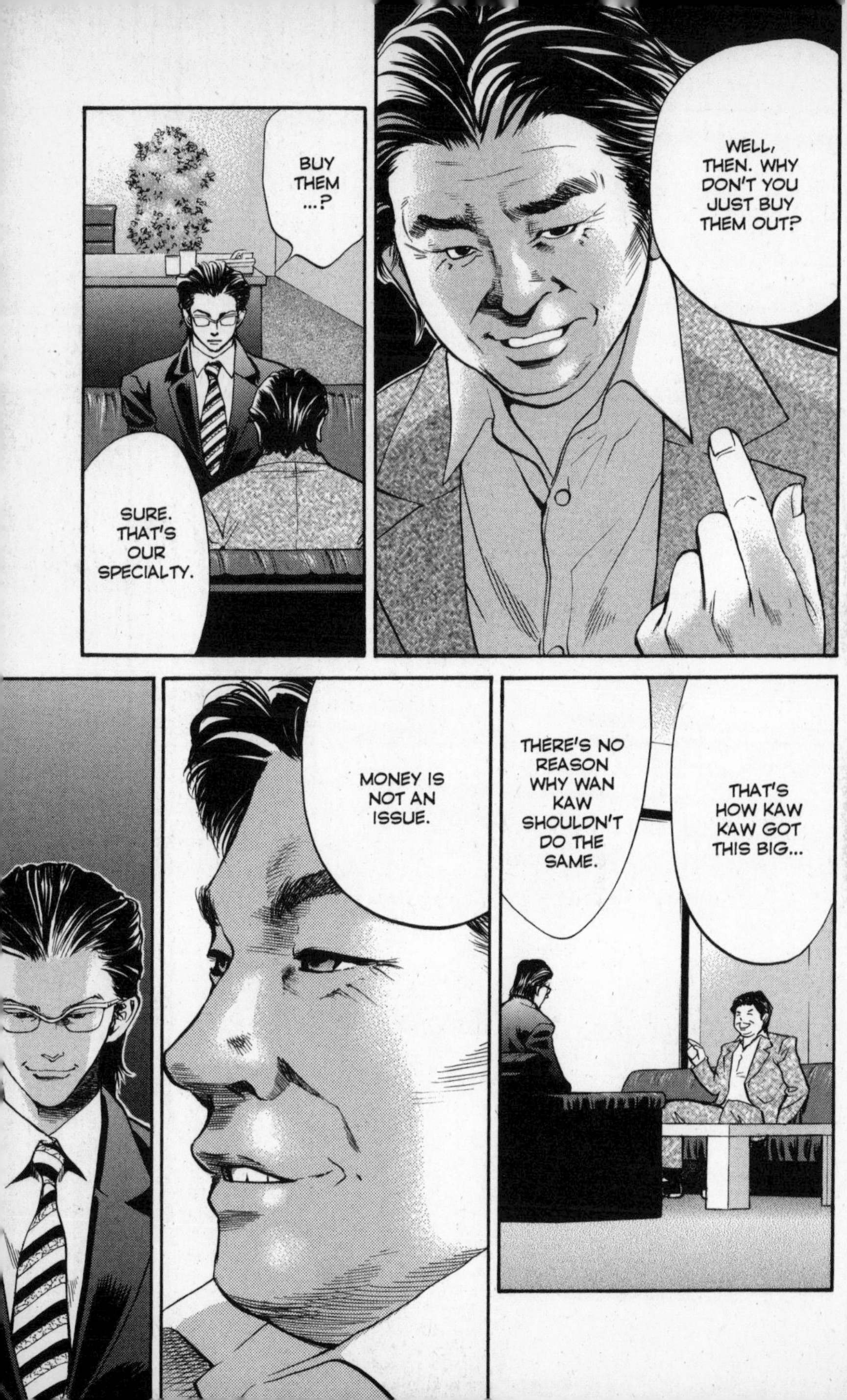
WELL, THEN. WHY DON'T YOU JUST BUY THEM OUT?
BUY THEM ...?
SURE. THAT'S OUR SPECIALTY.
THAT'S HOW KAW KAW GOT THIS BIG...
THERE'S NO REASON WHY WAN KAW SHOULDN'T DO THE SAME.
MONEY IS NOT AN ISSUE.

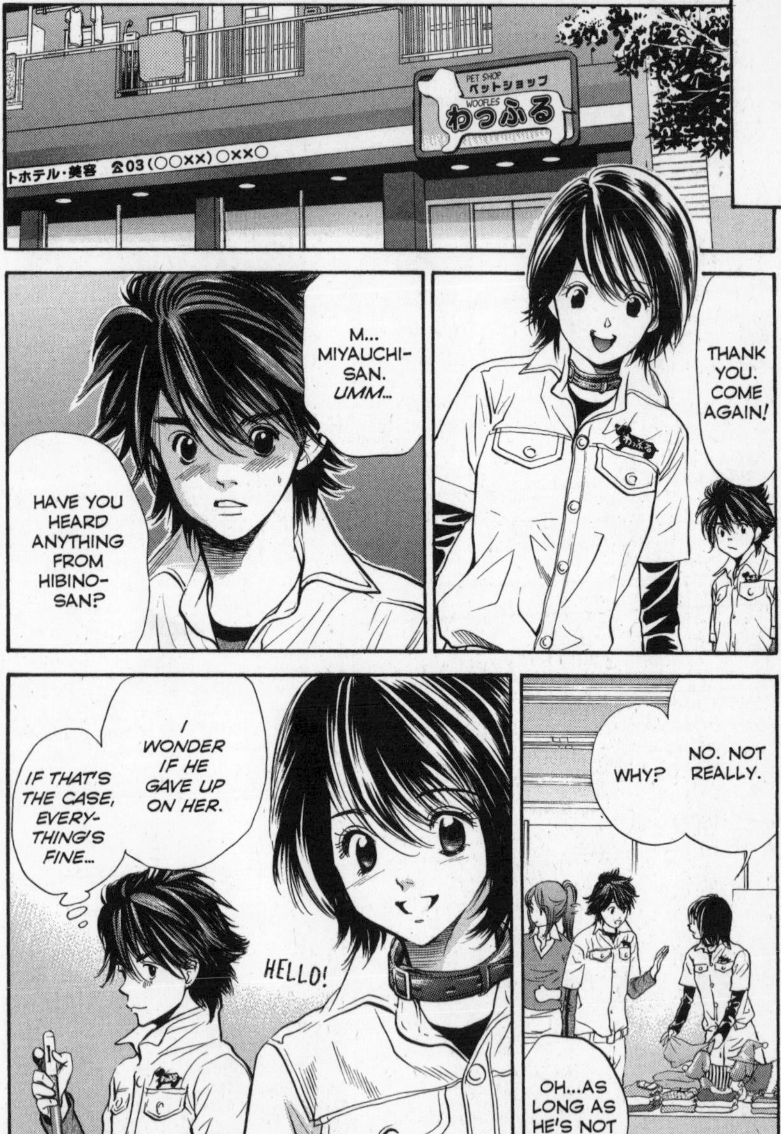
PET SHOP
ペットショップ
WOOFLES
わっふる
トホテル・美容 公03(○○××)○××○
THANK YOU. COME AGAIN!
M... MIYAUCHI-SAN. UMM...
HAVE YOU HEARD ANYTHING FROM HIBINO-SAN?
NO. NOT REALLY.
WHY?
OH...AS LONG AS HE'S NOT BOTHERING YOU.
I WONDER IF HE GAVE UP ON HER.
IF THAT'S THE CASE, EVERYTHING'S FINE...
HELLO!

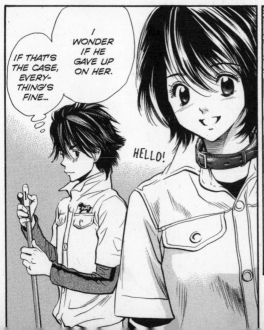

YELP

WHAP

WELCOME TO WOOFLES.

GRRR

OH, NO! I'M SORRY FOR STEPPING ON YOU. I DID IT AGAIN...!!

ARE YOU...

HEY!!

HMP? I FORGET WHAT THESE BLACK DOGS ARE...

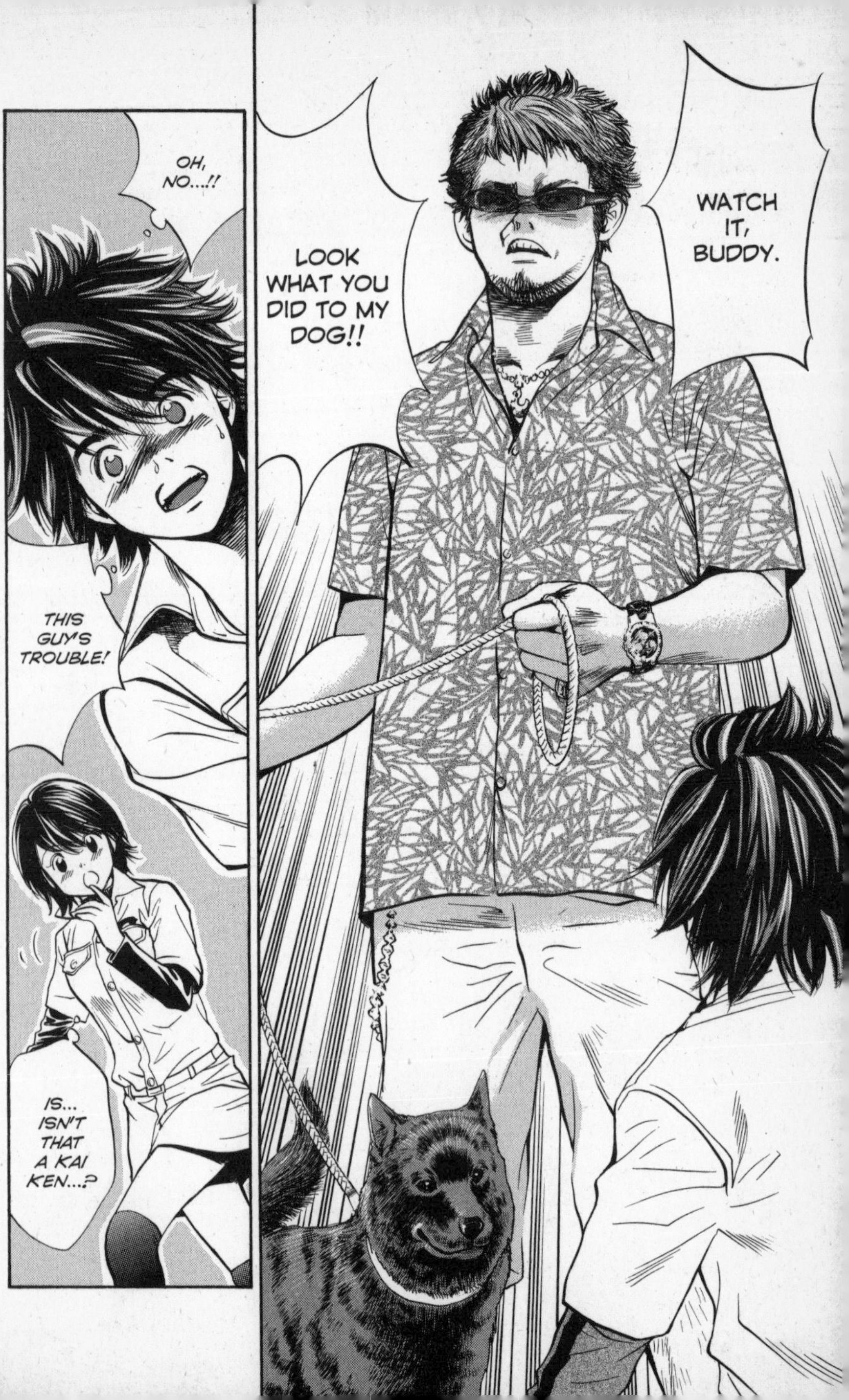
WATCH IT, BUDDY.
LOOK WHAT YOU DID TO MY DOG!!
OH, NO...!!
THIS GUY'S TROUBLE!
IS... ISN'T THAT A KAI KEN...?

INVESTIGATOR RICEBALL'S ADVENTURE!

TAKING A PEEK INTO THE SAKURA TEAM WORKSPACE!

HELLO! THIS IS INVESTIGATOR RICEBALL. I'VE DECIDED TO SNEAK INTO THE WORKSPACE OF THE SAKURA TEAM TODAY. IT'S ACTUALLY PRETTY ORGANIZED. (I'M IMPRESSED.) IT LOOKS LIKE EVERYONE IS WORKING HAPPILY TOGETHER. THE ATMOSPHERE SEEMS NOT ONLY TO CALL FOR PEOPLE WITH ARTISTIC SKILLS, BUT ALSO FOR PEOPLE WITH A GREAT SENSE OF HUMOR...NOTE THAT THE SENSEI IS BEING LAUGHED AT AGAIN FOR MISHEARING THINGS. (LOL) THE STAFF HERE WORKS ABOUT FOUR DAYS A WEEK FROM 10 A.M. TO 10 P.M. ONLY GIRLS ARE ALLOWED TO SPEND THE NIGHT IN THE OFFICE. I'D LOVE TO JOIN THE SLEEPOVER ONE OF THESE DAYS (^_^)...!!

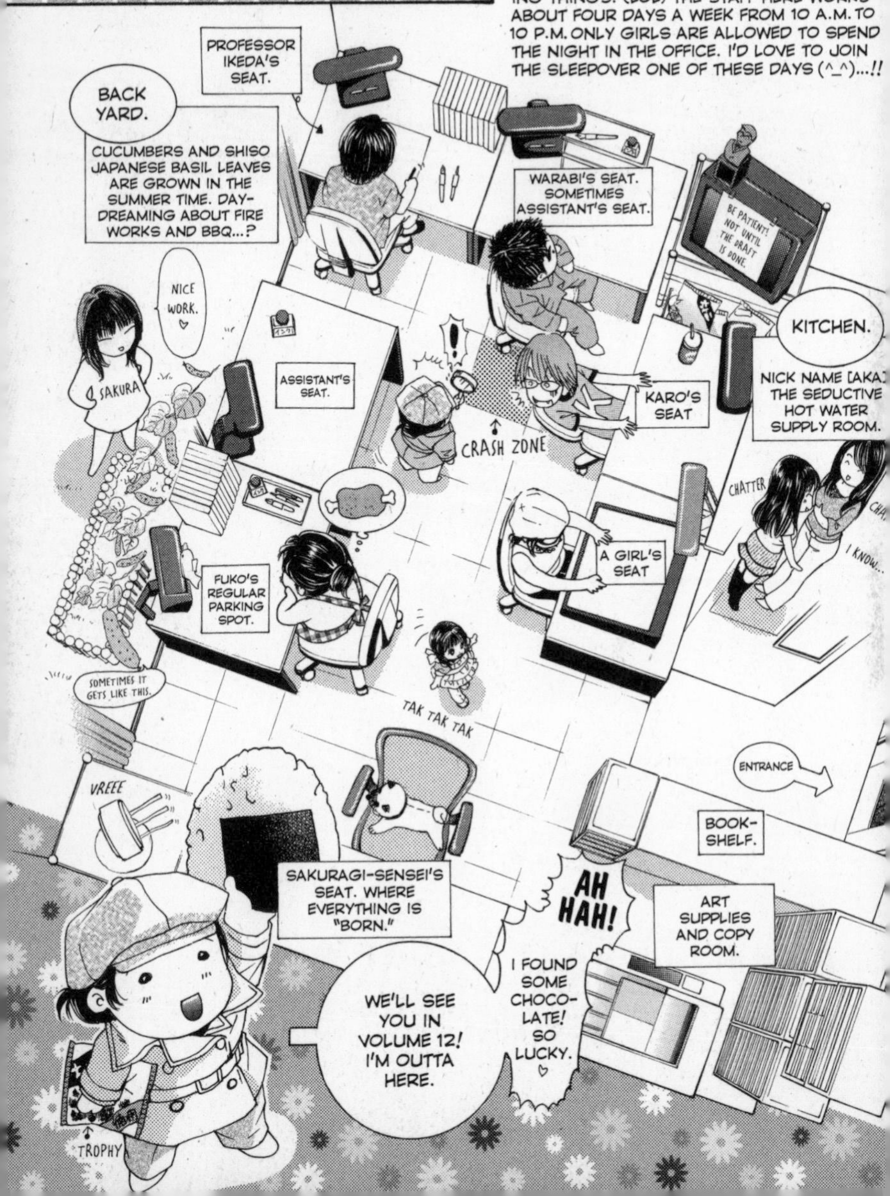
PROFESSOR IKEDA'S SEAT.
BACK YARD.
CUCUMBERS AND SHISO JAPANESE BASIL LEAVES ARE GROWN IN THE SUMMER TIME. DAY-DREAMING ABOUT FIRE WORKS AND BBQ...?
WARABI'S SEAT. SOMETIMES ASSISTANT'S SEAT.
BE PATIENT! NOT UNTIL THE DRAFT IS DONE.
KITCHEN.
NICK NAME [AKA] THE SEDUCTIVE HOT WATER SUPPLY ROOM.
KARO'S SEAT
ASSISTANT'S SEAT.
CRASH ZONE
NICE WORK.
SAKURA
CHATTER
I KNOW...
A GIRL'S SEAT
FUKO'S REGULAR PARKING SPOT.
SOMETIMES IT GETS LIKE THIS.
TAK TAK TAK
ENTRANCE
VREEE
BOOK-SHELF.
SAKURAGI-SENSEI'S SEAT. WHERE EVERYTHING IS "BORN."
AH HAH!
ART SUPPLIES AND COPY ROOM.
I FOUND SOME CHOCO-LATE! SO LUCKY.
WE'LL SEE YOU IN VOLUME 12! I'M OUTTA HERE.
TROPHY

CHAPTER 110: A RUDE CUSTOMER

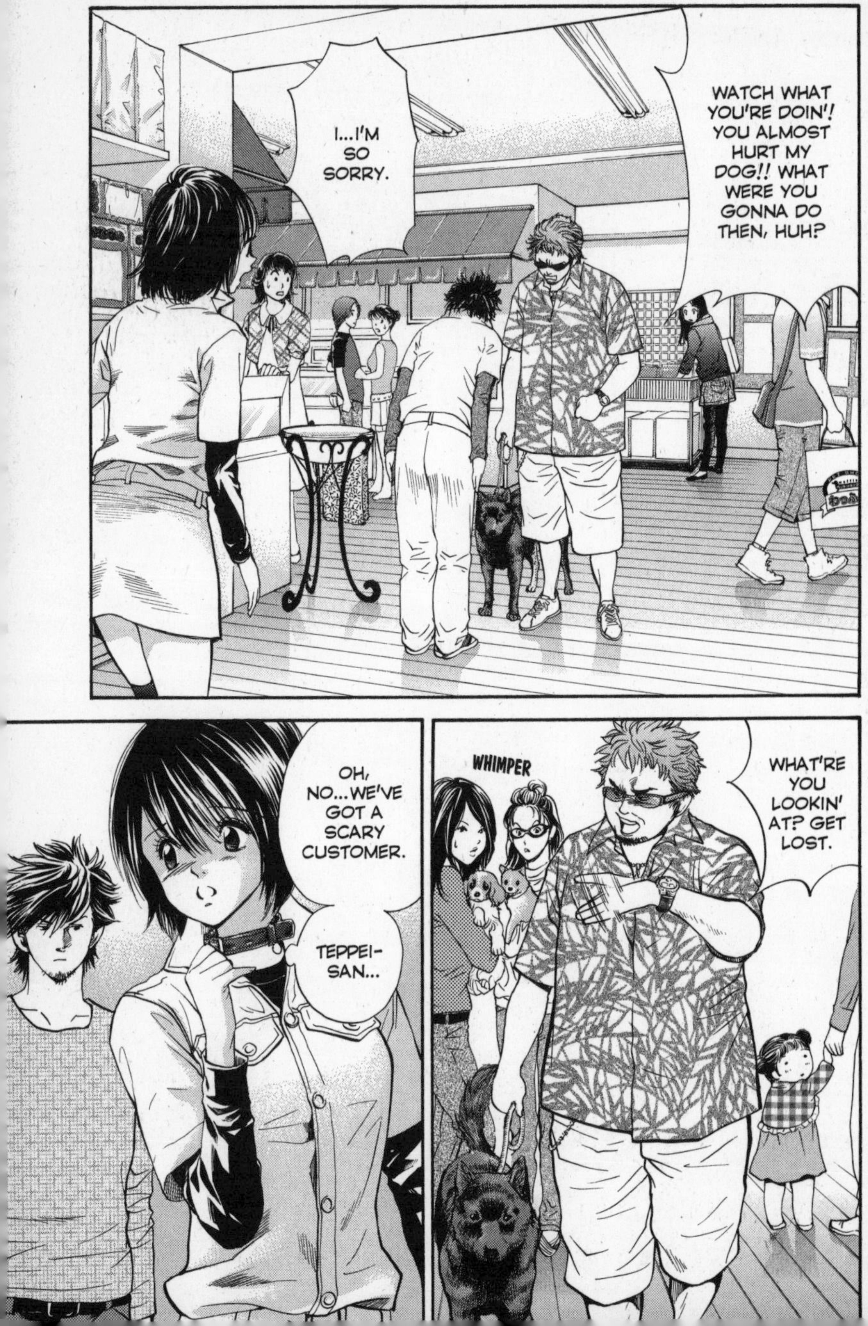
WATCH WHAT YOU'RE DOIN'! YOU ALMOST HURT MY DOG!! WHAT WERE YOU GONNA DO THEN, HUH?
I...I'M SO SORRY.
WHAT'RE YOU LOOKIN' AT? GET LOST.
WHIMPER
OH, NO...WE'VE GOT A SCARY CUSTOMER.
TEPPEI-SAN...

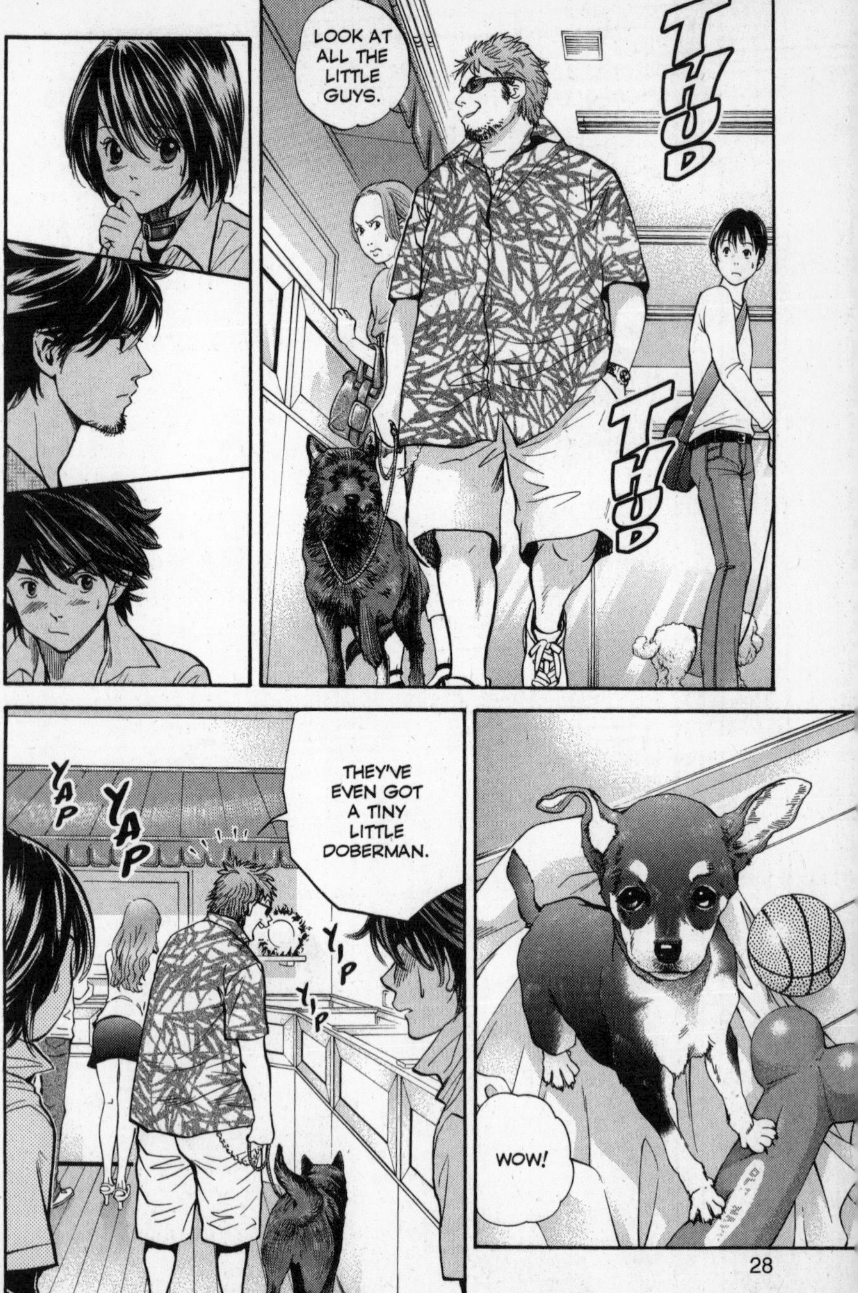
THUD
LOOK AT ALL THE LITTLE GUYS.
THUD
WOW!
THEY'VE EVEN GOT A TINY LITTLE DOBERMAN.
YAP YAP
YIP
YIP

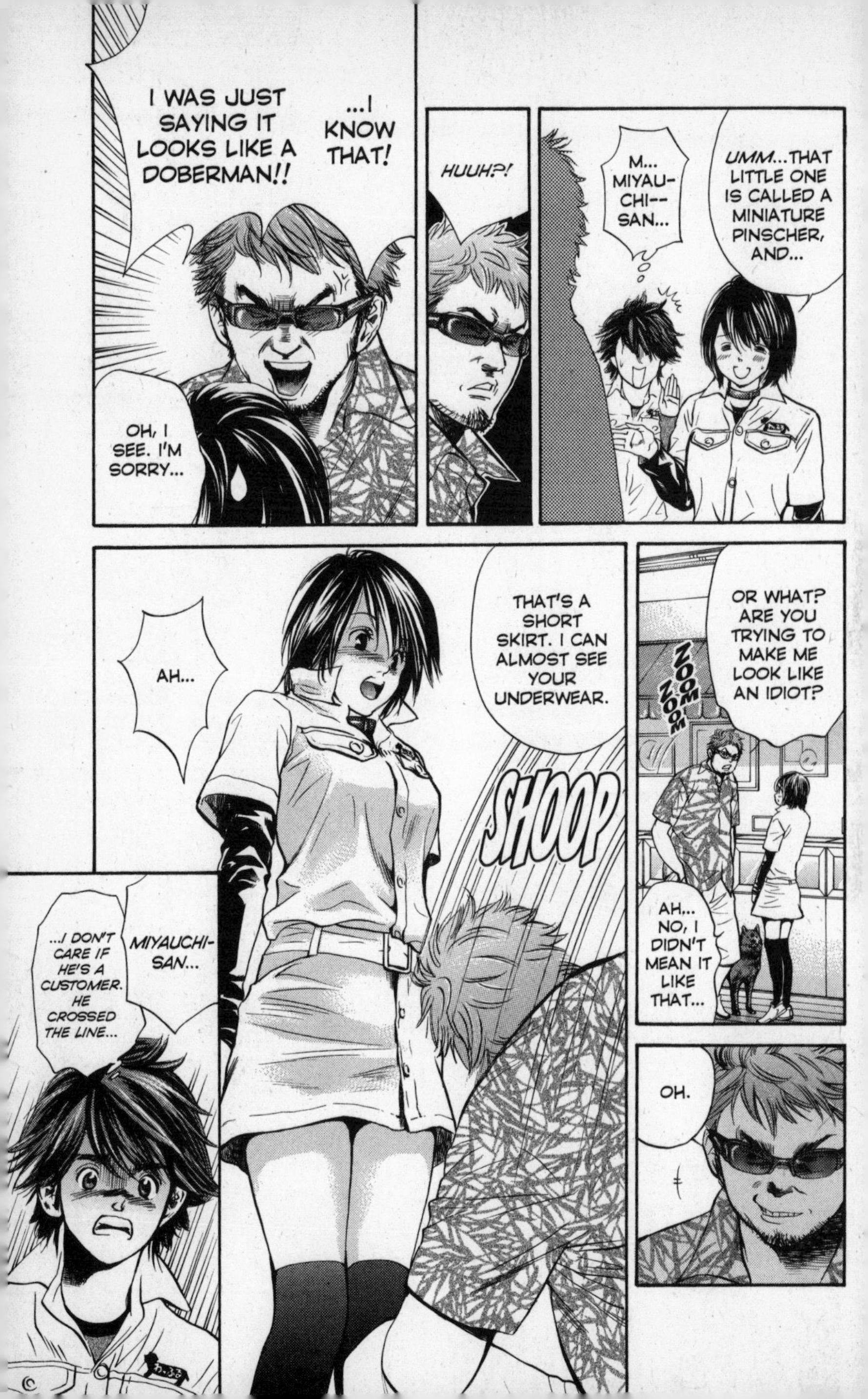
UMM...THAT LITTLE ONE IS CALLED A MINIATURE PINSCHER, AND...
M... MIYAU-CHI--SAN...
HUUH?!
...I KNOW THAT!
I WAS JUST SAYING IT LOOKS LIKE A DOBERMAN!!
OH, I SEE. I'M SORRY...
OR WHAT? ARE YOU TRYING TO MAKE ME LOOK LIKE AN IDIOT?
ZOOM ZOOM
AH... NO, I DIDN'T MEAN IT LIKE THAT...
OH.
THAT'S A SHORT SKIRT. I CAN ALMOST SEE YOUR UNDERWEAR.
SHOOP
AH...
MIYAUCHI-SAN...
...I DON'T CARE IF HE'S A CUSTOMER. HE CROSSED THE LINE...

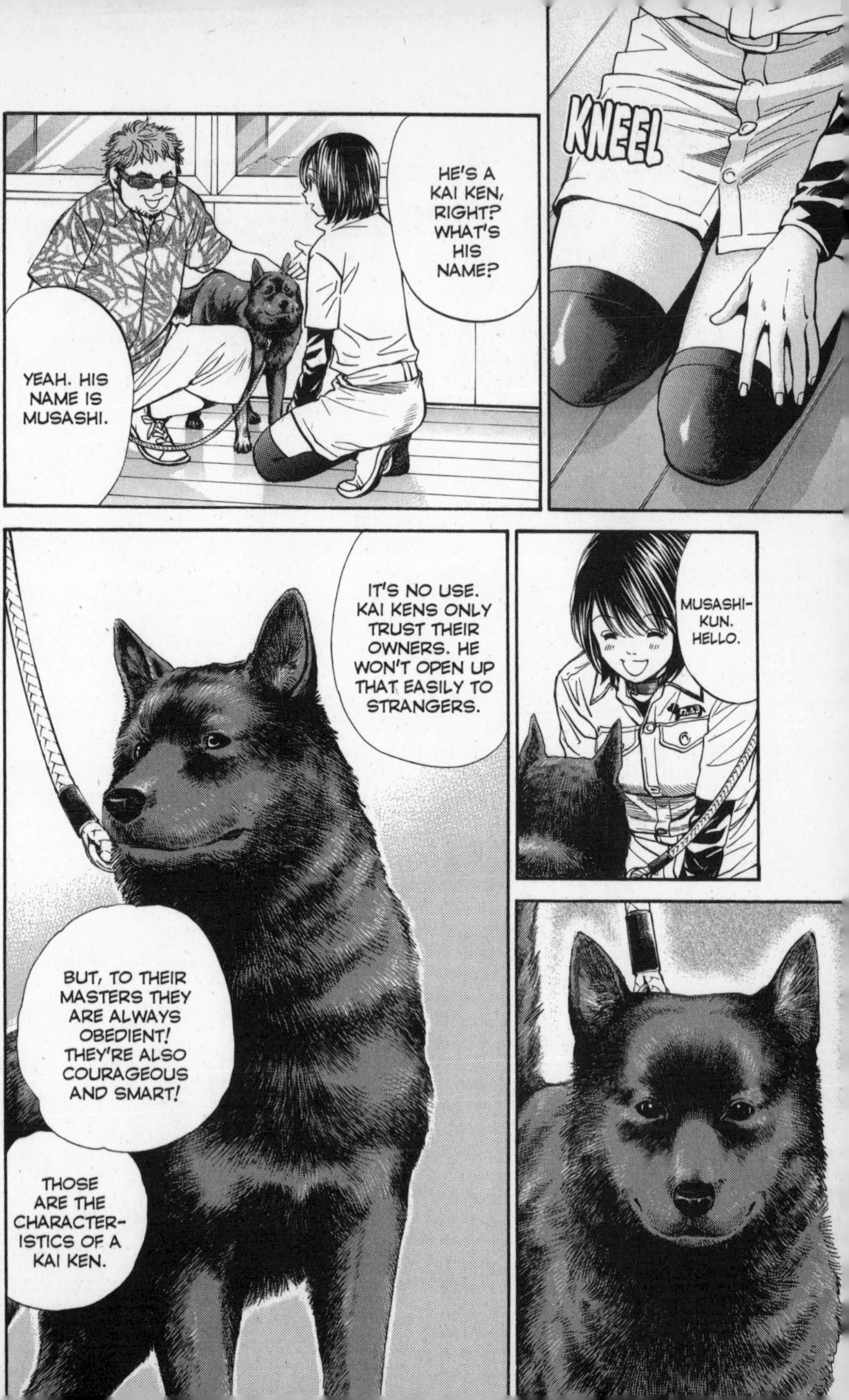
KNEEL
HE'S A KAI KEN, RIGHT? WHAT'S HIS NAME?
YEAH. HIS NAME IS MUSASHI.
MUSASHI-KUN. HELLO.
IT'S NO USE. KAI KENS ONLY TRUST THEIR OWNERS. HE WON'T OPEN UP THAT EASILY TO STRANGERS.
BUT, TO THEIR MASTERS THEY ARE ALWAYS OBEDIENT! THEY'RE ALSO COURAGEOUS AND SMART!
THOSE ARE THE CHARACTER-ISTICS OF A KAI KEN.

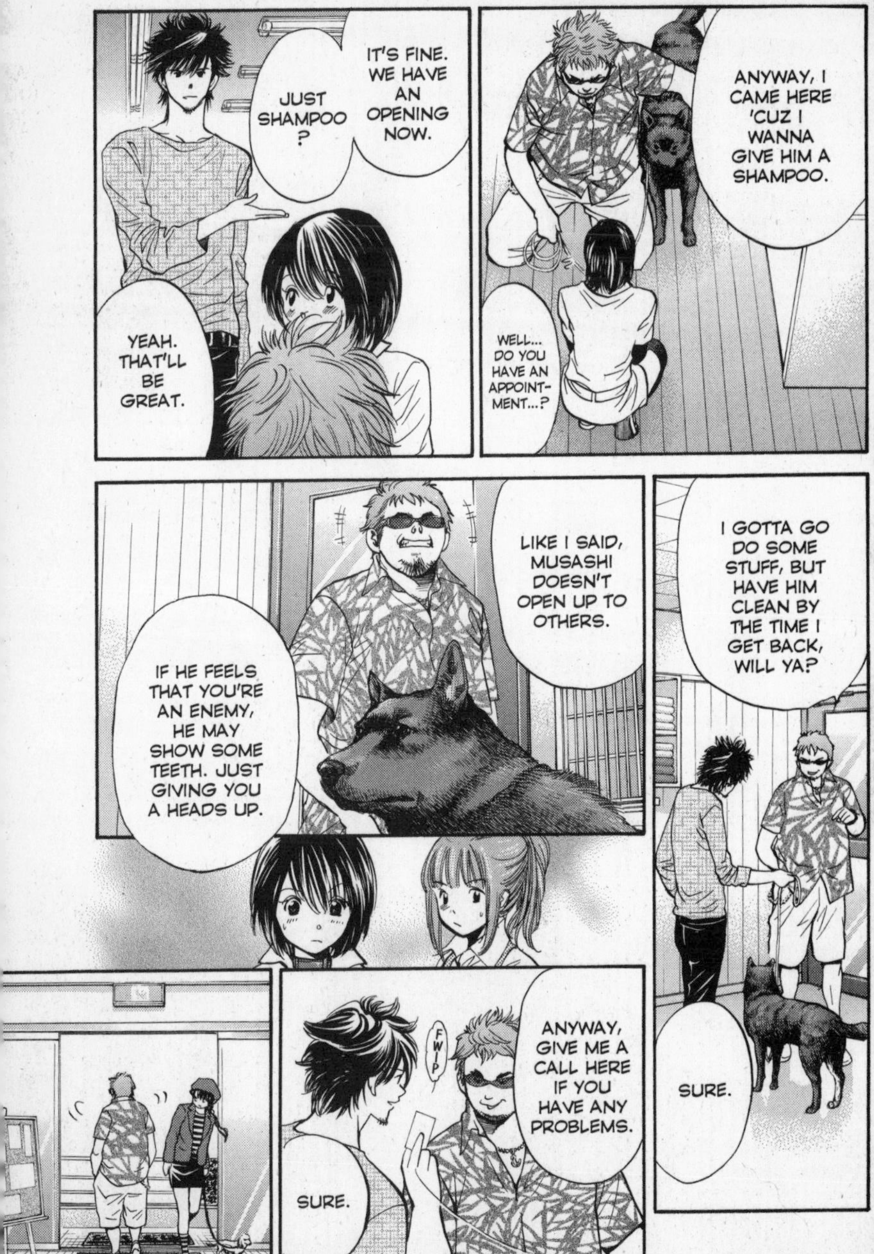
ANYWAY, I CAME HERE 'CUZ I WANNA GIVE HIM A SHAMPOO.
WELL... DO YOU HAVE AN APPOINTMENT...?
IT'S FINE. WE HAVE AN OPENING NOW.
JUST SHAMPOO?
YEAH. THAT'LL BE GREAT.
I GOTTA GO DO SOME STUFF, BUT HAVE HIM CLEAN BY THE TIME I GET BACK, WILL YA?
SURE.
LIKE I SAID, MUSASHI DOESN'T OPEN UP TO OTHERS.
IF HE FEELS THAT YOU'RE AN ENEMY, HE MAY SHOW SOME TEETH. JUST GIVING YOU A HEADS UP.
ANYWAY, GIVE ME A CALL HERE IF YOU HAVE ANY PROBLEMS.
FWIP
SURE.

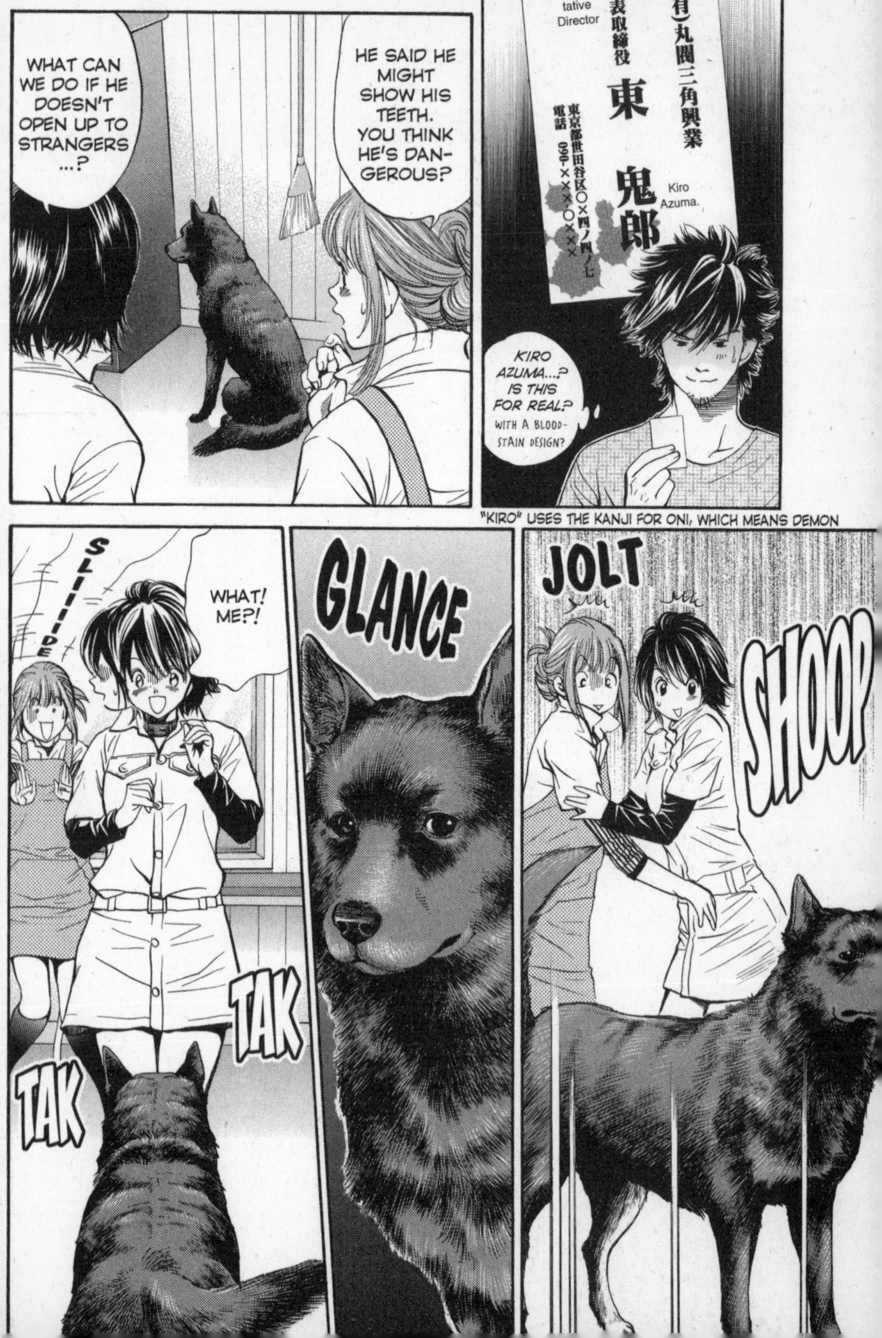
CircleExTriangle Promotions Ltd.
(有)丸閥三角興業
Represen-tative Director
代表取締役
東 鬼郎
Kiro Azuma.
東京都世田谷区○×四ノ四ノ七
電話 090-××××-○×××
KIRO AZUMA...? IS THIS FOR REAL? WITH A BLOOD-STAIN DESIGN?
HE SAID HE MIGHT SHOW HIS TEETH. YOU THINK HE'S DAN-GEROUS?
WHAT CAN WE DO IF HE DOESN'T OPEN UP TO STRANGERS ...?
"KIRO" USES THE KANJI FOR ONI, WHICH MEANS DEMON
JOLT
SHOOP
GLANCE
SLIIIIDE
WHAT! ME?!
TAK
TAK

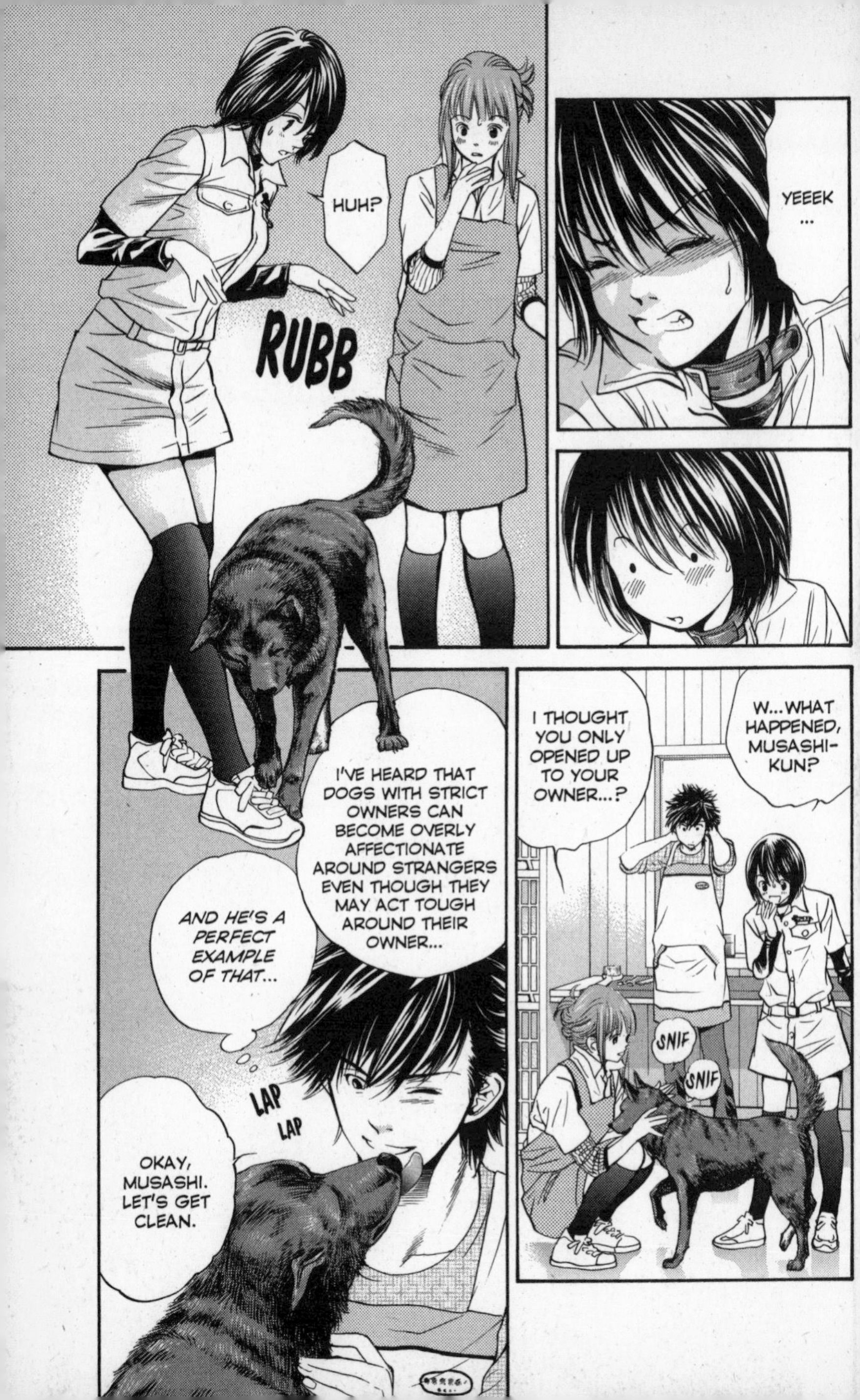
YEEEK ...
HUH?
RUBB
W...WHAT HAPPENED, MUSASHI-KUN?
I THOUGHT YOU ONLY OPENED UP TO YOUR OWNER...?
SNIF
SNIF
I'VE HEARD THAT DOGS WITH STRICT OWNERS CAN BECOME OVERLY AFFECTIONATE AROUND STRANGERS EVEN THOUGH THEY MAY ACT TOUGH AROUND THEIR OWNER...
AND HE'S A PERFECT EXAMPLE OF THAT...
LAP
LAP
OKAY, MUSASHI. LET'S GET CLEAN.

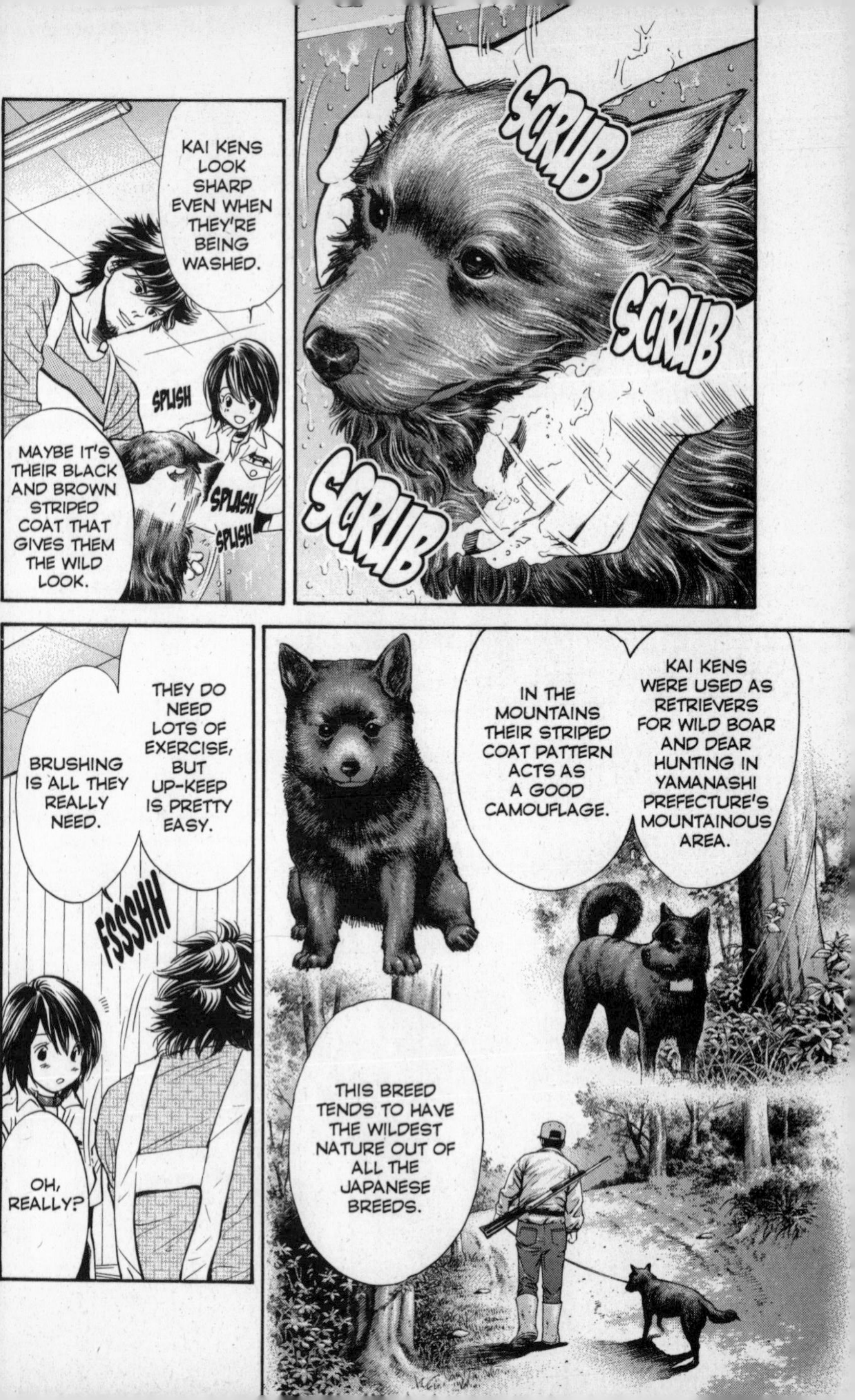
SCRUB
SCRUB
SCRUB
KAI KENS LOOK SHARP EVEN WHEN THEY'RE BEING WASHED.
SPLISH
SPLASH
SPLISH
MAYBE IT'S THEIR BLACK AND BROWN STRIPED COAT THAT GIVES THEM THE WILD LOOK.
KAI KENS WERE USED AS RETRIEVERS FOR WILD BOAR AND DEAR HUNTING IN YAMANASHI PREFECTURE'S MOUNTAINOUS AREA.
IN THE MOUNTAINS THEIR STRIPED COAT PATTERN ACTS AS A GOOD CAMOUFLAGE.
THIS BREED TENDS TO HAVE THE WILDEST NATURE OUT OF ALL THE JAPANESE BREEDS.
THEY DO NEED LOTS OF EXERCISE, BUT UP-KEEP IS PRETTY EASY.
BRUSHING IS ALL THEY REALLY NEED.
FSSSHH
OH, REALLY?

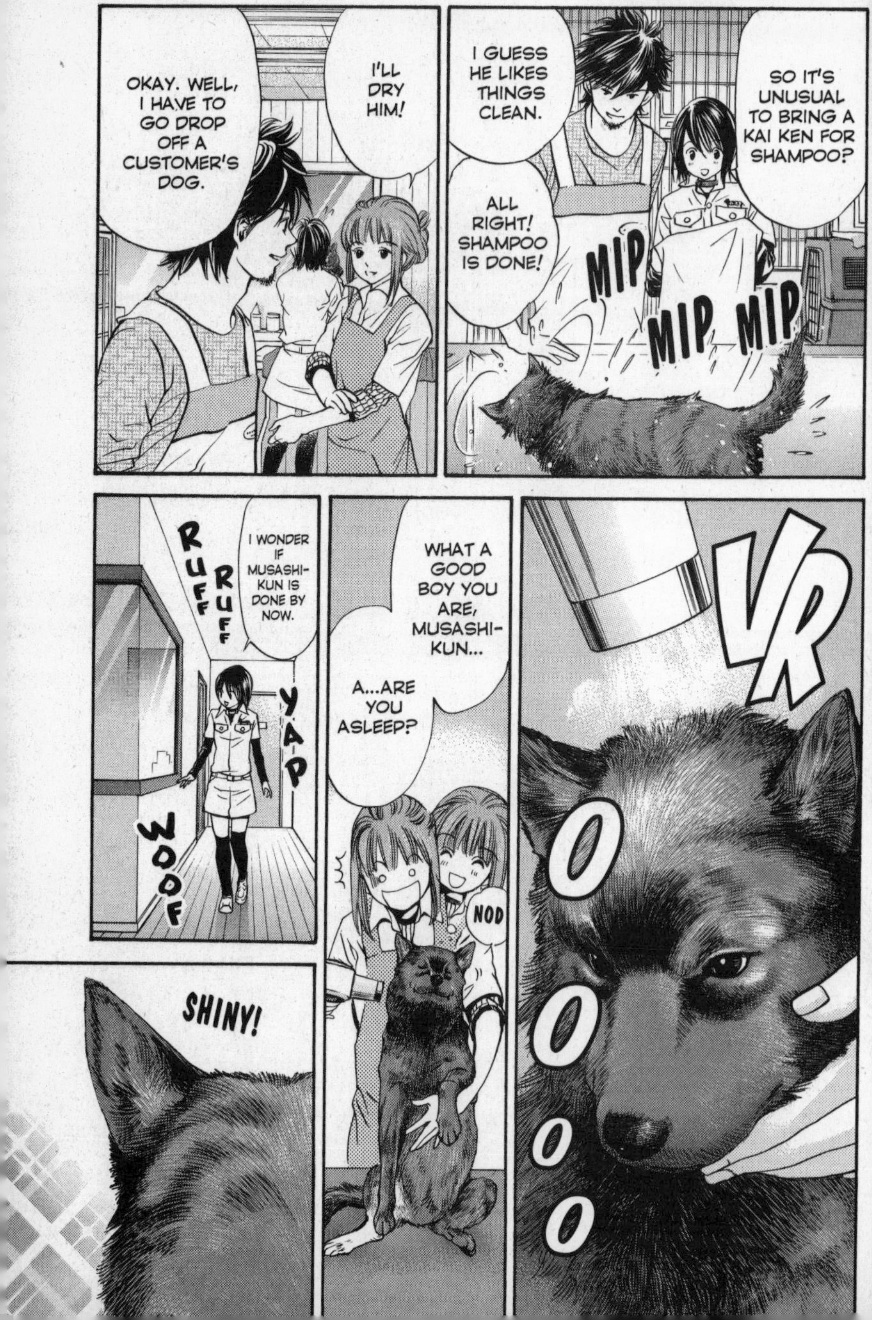
SO IT'S UNUSUAL TO BRING A KAI KEN FOR SHAMPOO?
I GUESS HE LIKES THINGS CLEAN.
ALL RIGHT! SHAMPOO IS DONE!
MIP
MIP MIP
I'LL DRY HIM!
OKAY. WELL, I HAVE TO GO DROP OFF A CUSTOMER'S DOG.
VR
OOOOO
WHAT A GOOD BOY YOU ARE, MUSASHI-KUN...
A...ARE YOU ASLEEP?
NOD
I WONDER IF MUSASHI-KUN IS DONE BY NOW.
RUFF
RUFF
YAP
WOOF
SHINY!

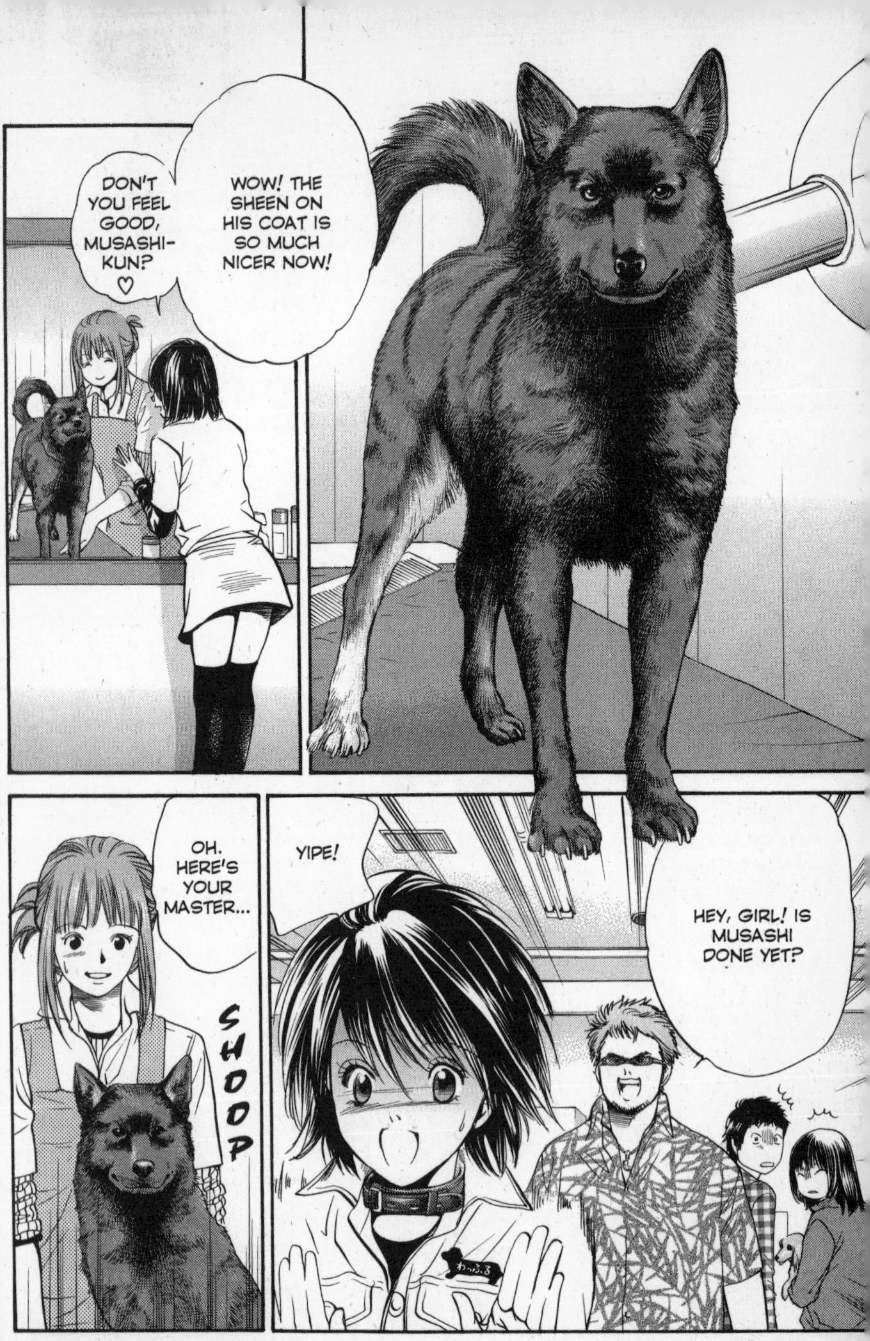
WOW! THE SHEEN ON HIS COAT IS SO MUCH NICER NOW!
DON'T YOU FEEL GOOD, MUSASHI-KUN? ♡
HEY, GIRL! IS MUSASHI DONE YET?
YIPE!
OH. HERE'S YOUR MASTER...
SHOODP

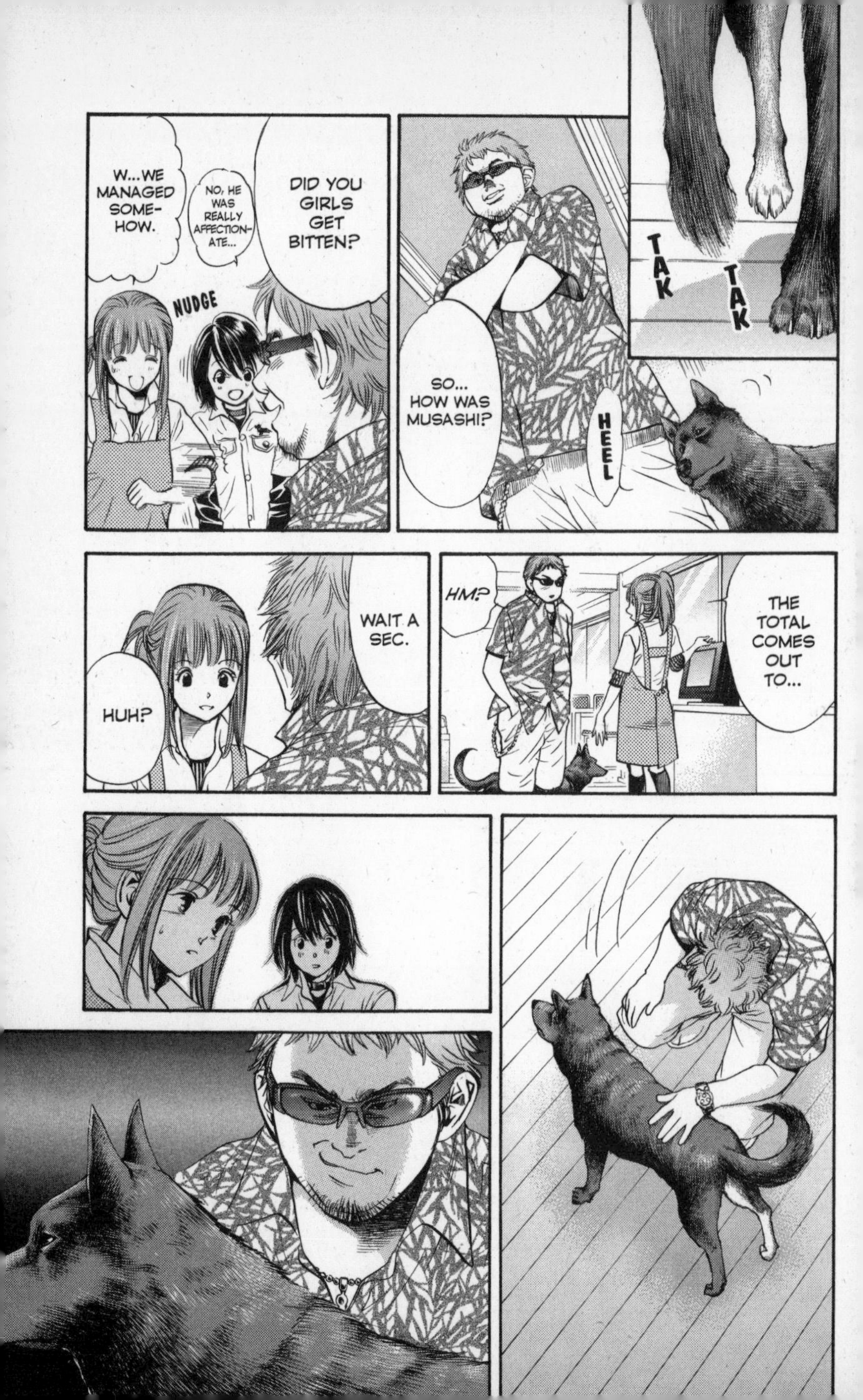
TAK
TAK
HEEL
SO... HOW WAS MUSASHI?
DID YOU GIRLS GET BITTEN?
NO, HE WAS REALLY AFFECTIONATE...
W...WE MANAGED SOMEHOW.
NUDGE
THE TOTAL COMES OUT TO...
HM?
WAIT A SEC.
HUH?

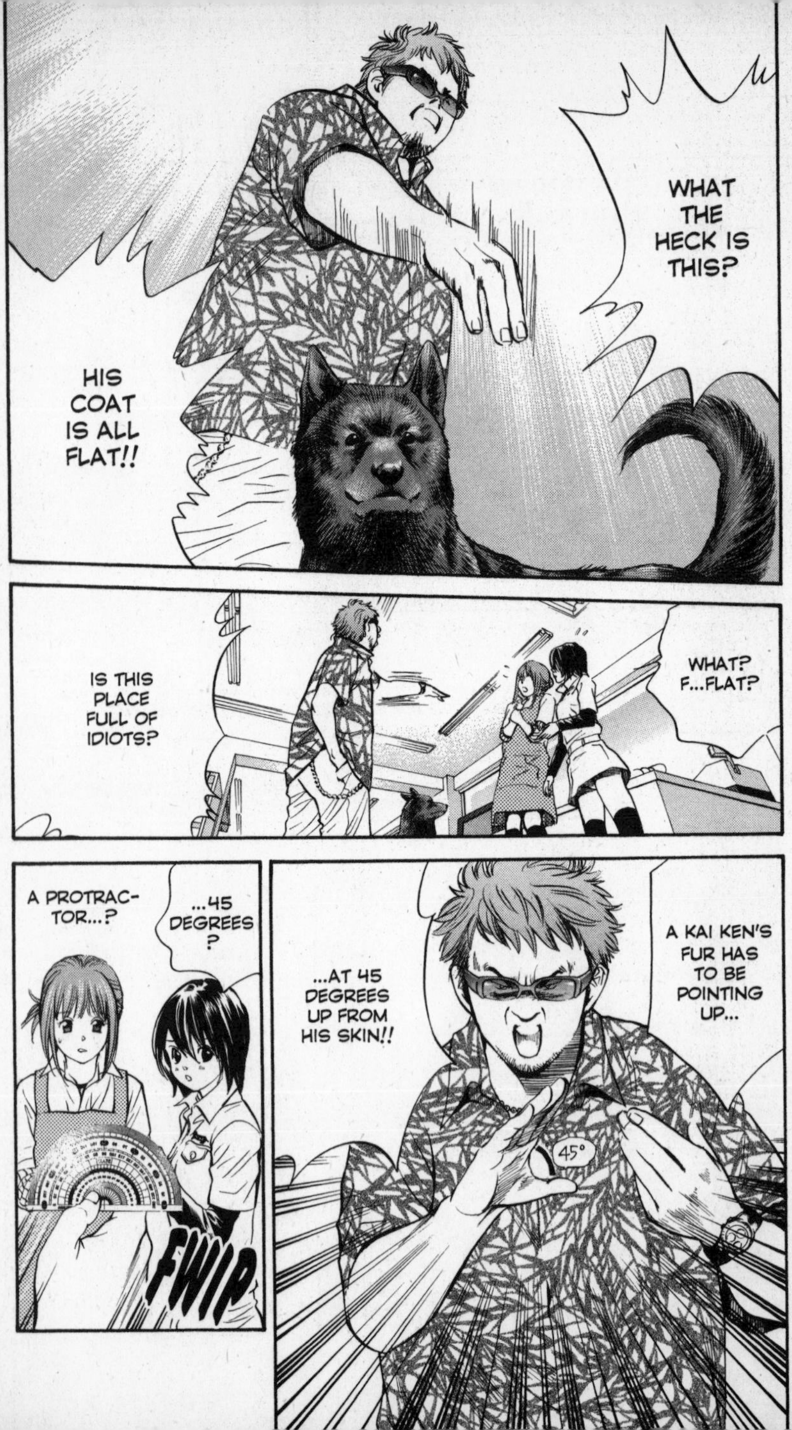
WHAT THE HECK IS THIS?
HIS COAT IS ALL FLAT!!
WHAT? F...FLAT?
IS THIS PLACE FULL OF IDIOTS?
A KAI KEN'S FUR HAS TO BE POINTING UP...
...AT 45 DEGREES UP FROM HIS SKIN!!
45°
...45 DEGREES ?
A PROTRAC-TOR...?
FWIP

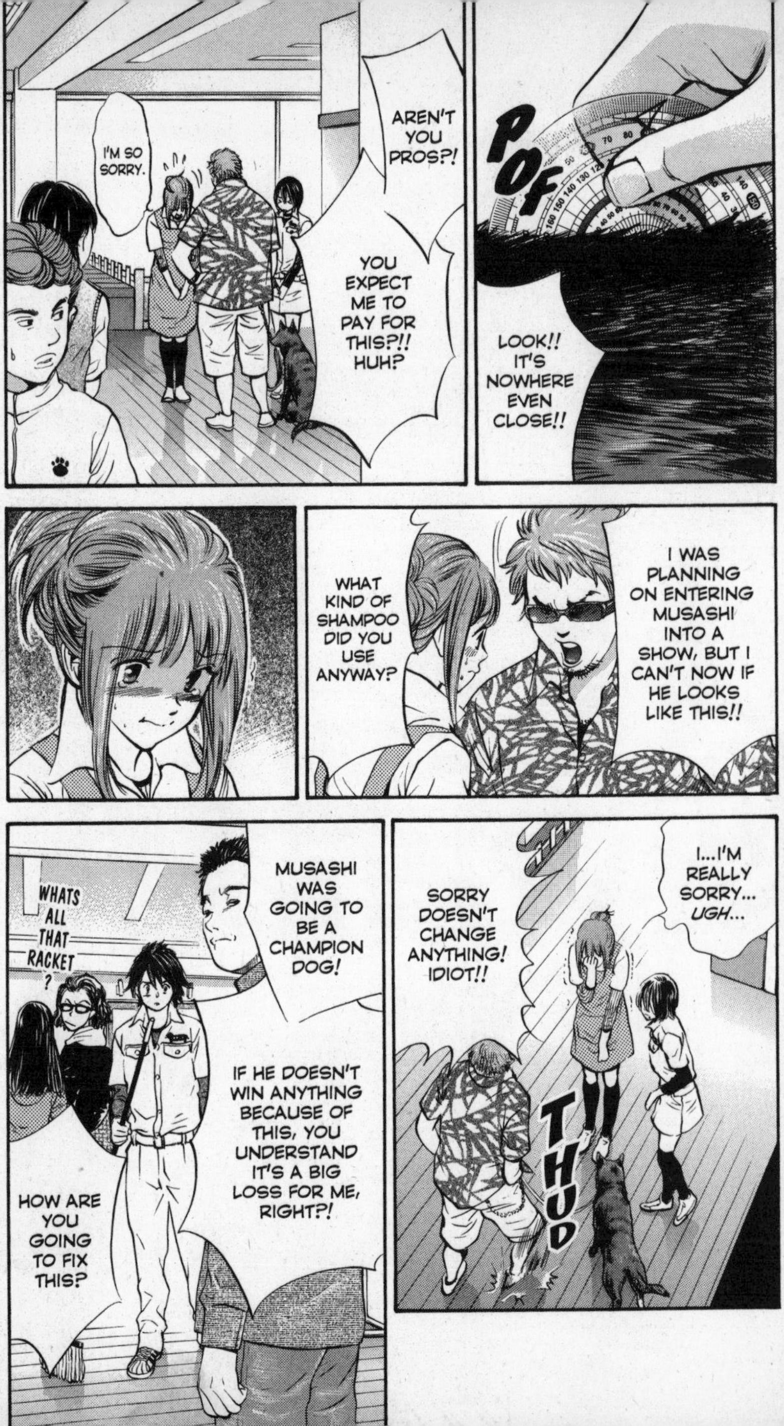
POF
LOOK!! IT'S NOWHERE EVEN CLOSE!!
AREN'T YOU PROS?!
YOU EXPECT ME TO PAY FOR THIS?!! HUH?
I'M SO SORRY.
I WAS PLANNING ON ENTERING MUSASHI INTO A SHOW, BUT I CAN'T NOW IF HE LOOKS LIKE THIS!!
WHAT KIND OF SHAMPOO DID YOU USE ANYWAY?
I...I'M REALLY SORRY... *UGH*...
SORRY DOESN'T CHANGE ANYTHING! IDIOT!!
THUD
MUSASHI WAS GOING TO BE A CHAMPION DOG!
IF HE DOESN'T WIN ANYTHING BECAUSE OF THIS, YOU UNDERSTAND IT'S A BIG LOSS FOR ME, RIGHT?!
HOW ARE YOU GOING TO FIX THIS?
WHATS ALL THAT RACKET?

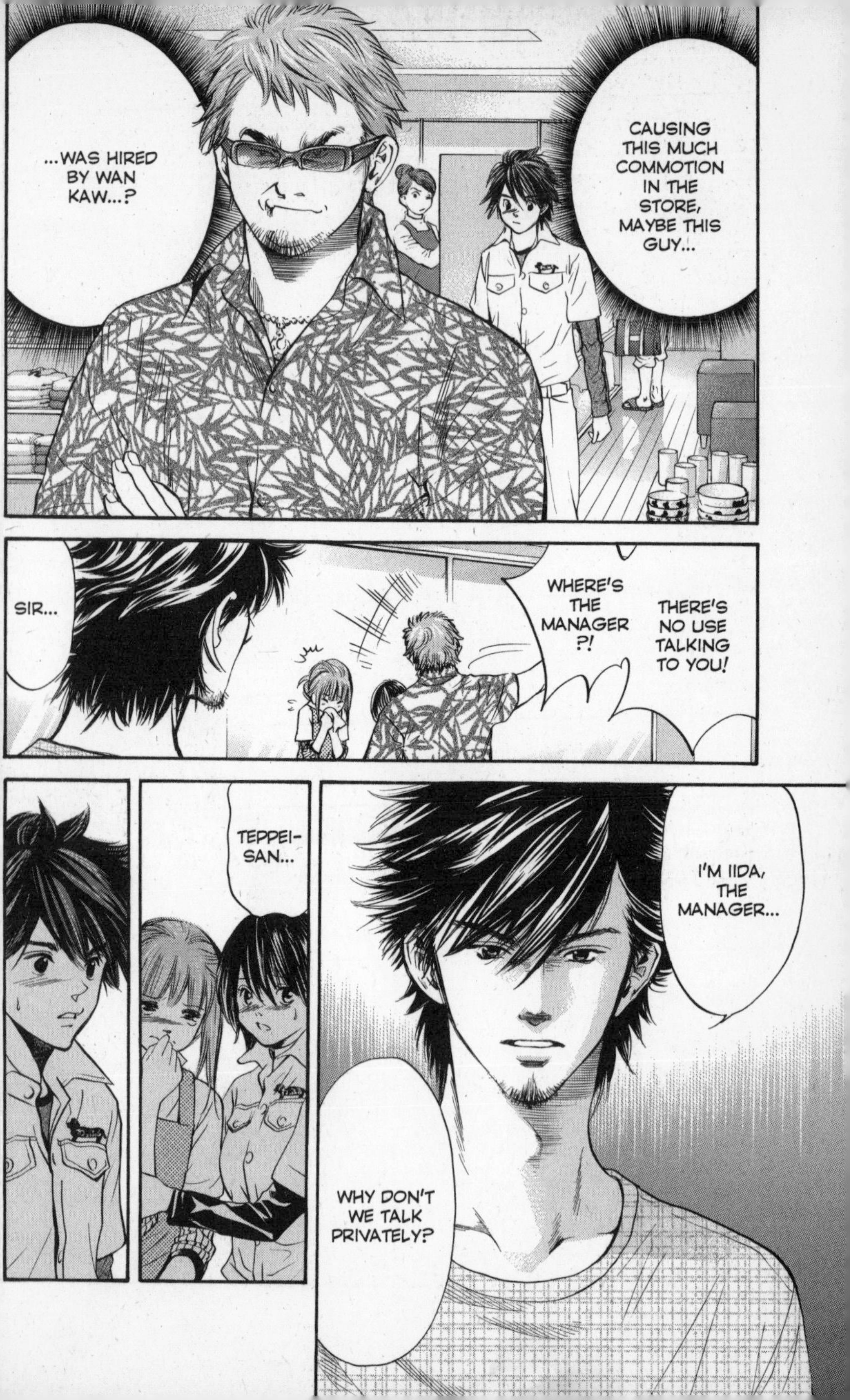
CAUSING THIS MUCH COMMOTION IN THE STORE, MAYBE THIS GUY...
...WAS HIRED BY WAN KAW...?
THERE'S NO USE TALKING TO YOU!
WHERE'S THE MANAGER?!
SIR...
I'M IIDA, THE MANAGER...
WHY DON'T WE TALK PRIVATELY?
TEPPEI-SAN...

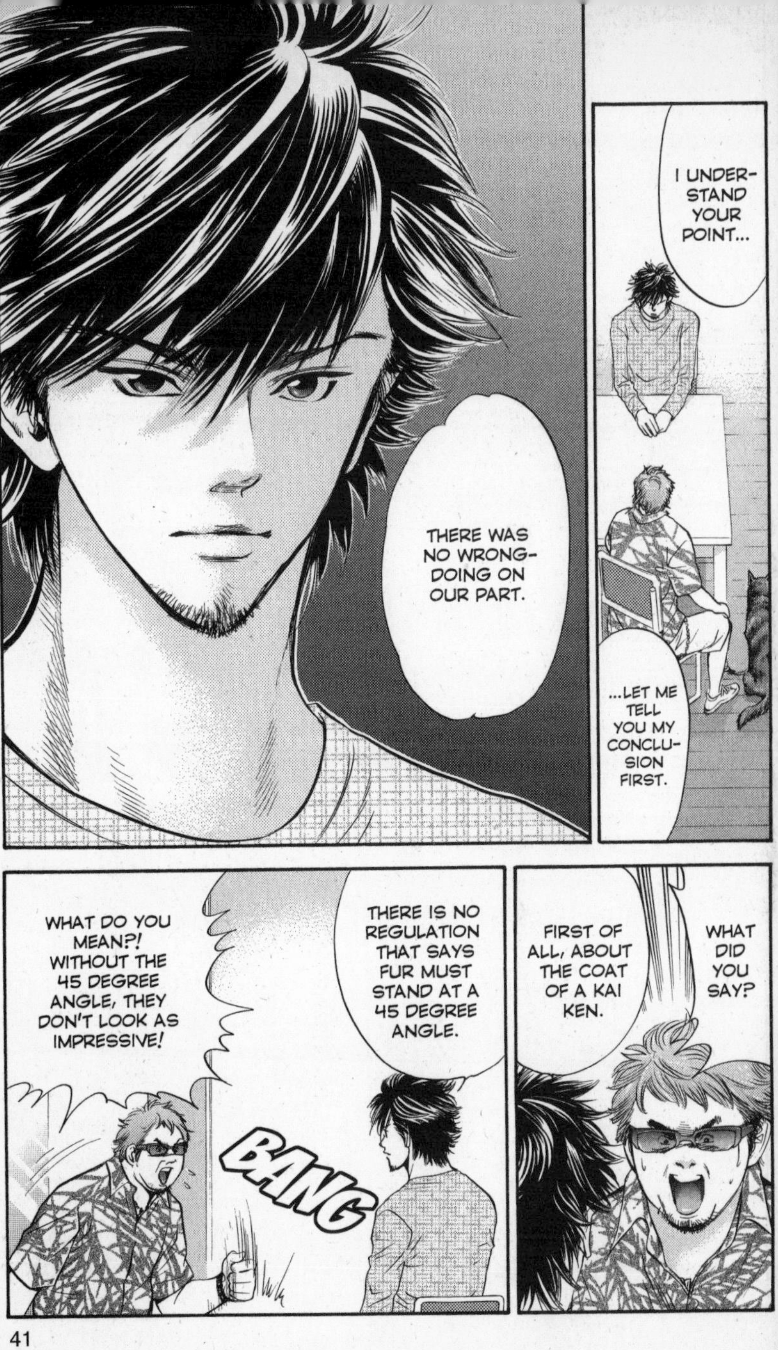
I UNDERSTAND YOUR POINT...
...LET ME TELL YOU MY CONCLUSION FIRST.
THERE WAS NO WRONGDOING ON OUR PART.
WHAT DID YOU SAY?
FIRST OF ALL, ABOUT THE COAT OF A KAI KEN.
THERE IS NO REGULATION THAT SAYS FUR MUST STAND AT A 45 DEGREE ANGLE.
WHAT DO YOU MEAN?! WITHOUT THE 45 DEGREE ANGLE, THEY DON'T LOOK AS IMPRESSIVE!
BANG

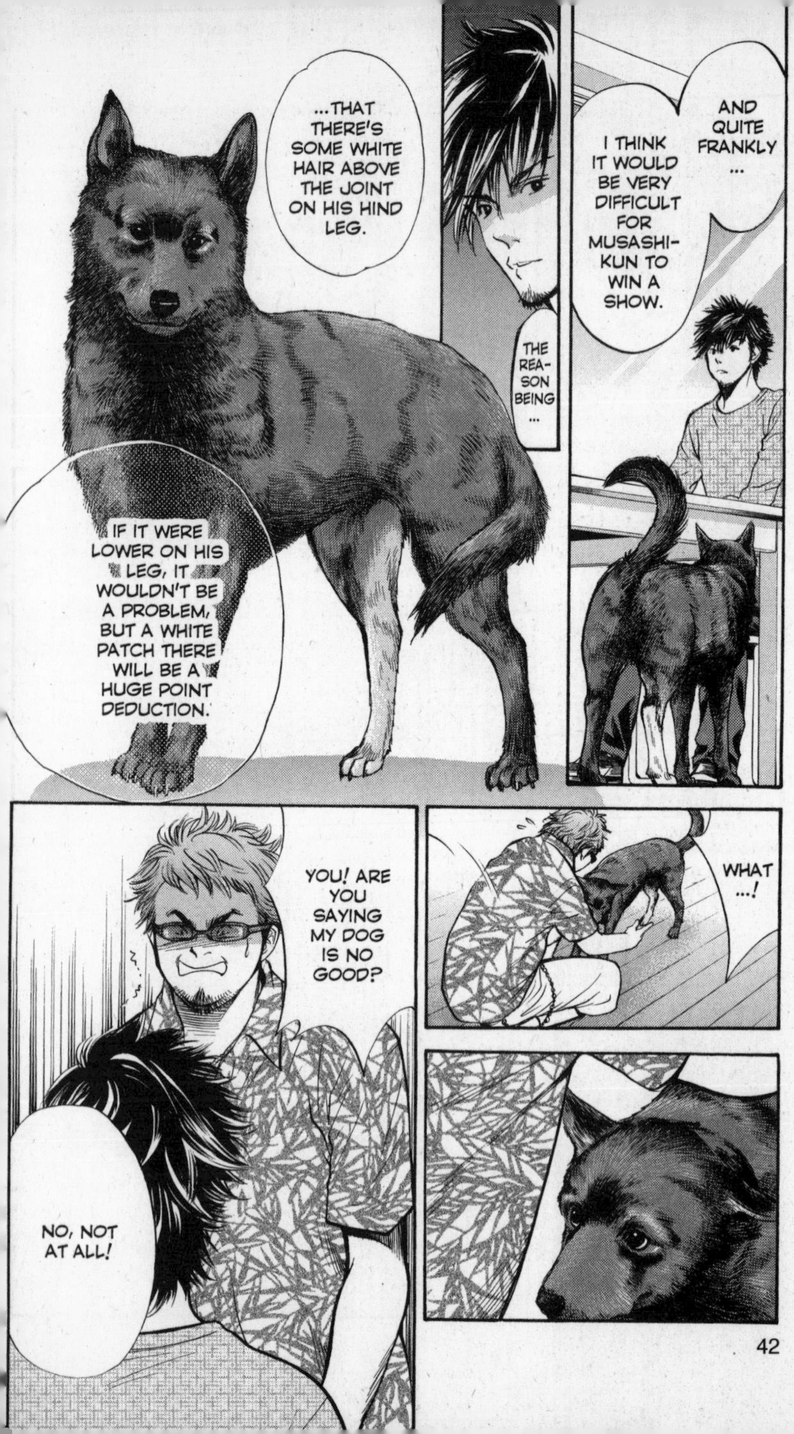
AND QUITE FRANKLY ...
I THINK IT WOULD BE VERY DIFFICULT FOR MUSASHI-KUN TO WIN A SHOW.
THE REA-SON BEING ...
...THAT THERE'S SOME WHITE HAIR ABOVE THE JOINT ON HIS HIND LEG.
IF IT WERE LOWER ON HIS LEG, IT WOULDN'T BE A PROBLEM, BUT A WHITE PATCH THERE WILL BE A HUGE POINT DEDUCTION.
WHAT ...!
YOU! ARE YOU SAYING MY DOG IS NO GOOD?
NO, NOT AT ALL!

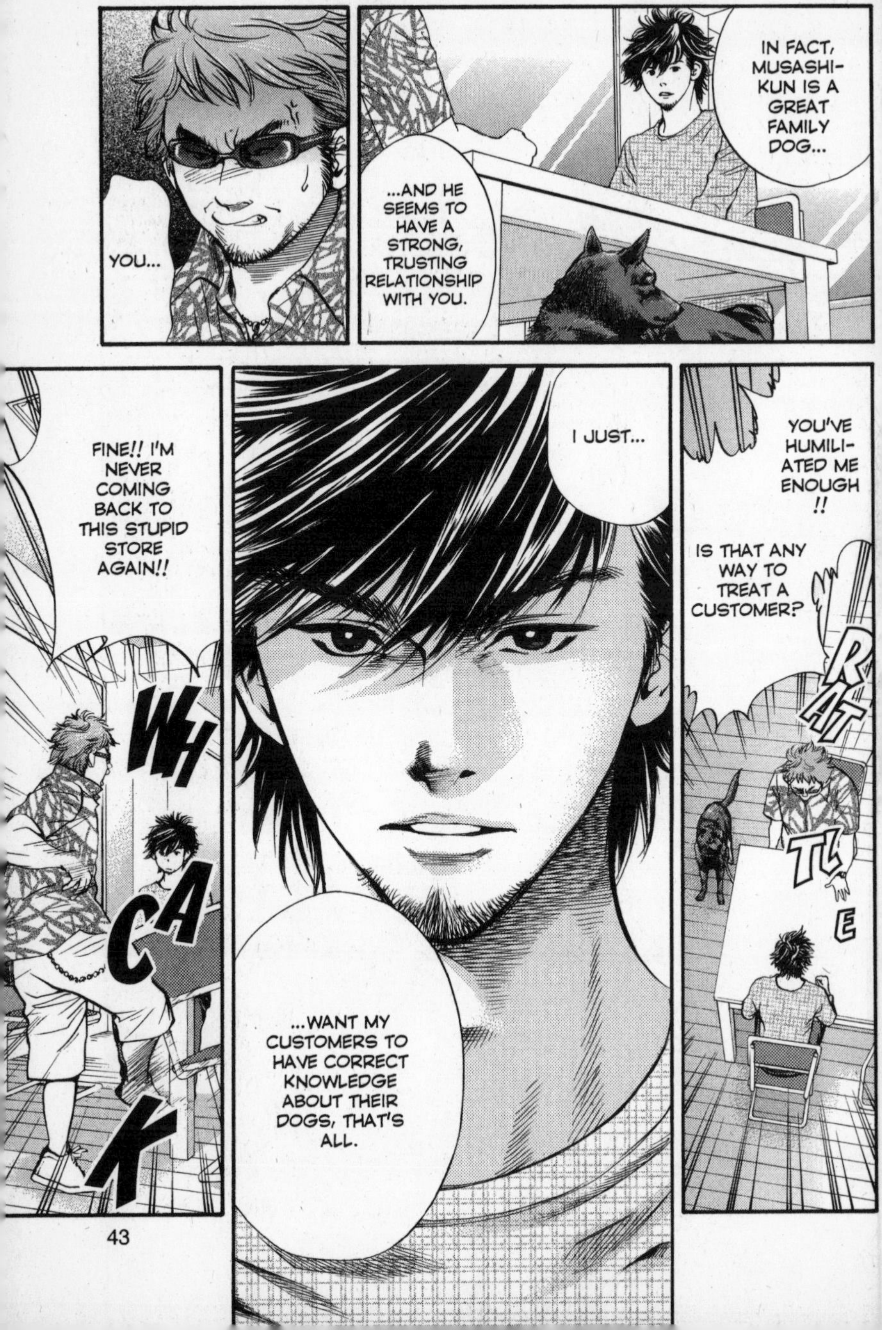
IN FACT, MUSASHI-KUN IS A GREAT FAMILY DOG...
...AND HE SEEMS TO HAVE A STRONG, TRUSTING RELATIONSHIP WITH YOU.
YOU...
YOU'VE HUMILIATED ME ENOUGH!!
IS THAT ANY WAY TO TREAT A CUSTOMER?
RATTLE
I JUST...
...WANT MY CUSTOMERS TO HAVE CORRECT KNOWLEDGE ABOUT THEIR DOGS, THAT'S ALL.
FINE!! I'M NEVER COMING BACK TO THIS STUPID STORE AGAIN!!
WHACK

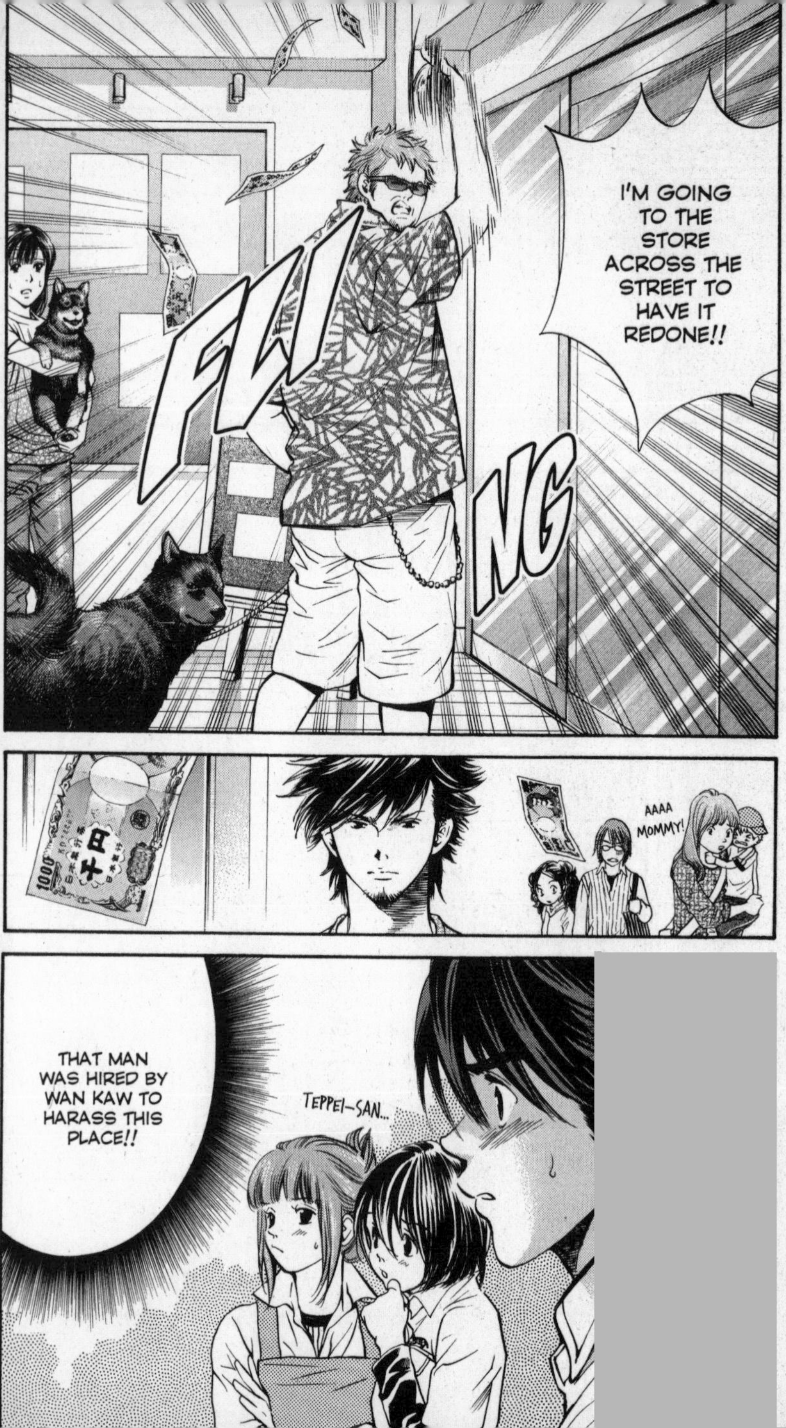
I'M GOING TO THE STORE ACROSS THE STREET TO HAVE IT REDONE!!
FLING
AAAA MOMMY!
THAT MAN WAS HIRED BY WAN KAW TO HARASS THIS PLACE!!
TEPPEI-SAN...

CHAPTER 111: MERGER NEGOTIATION...?

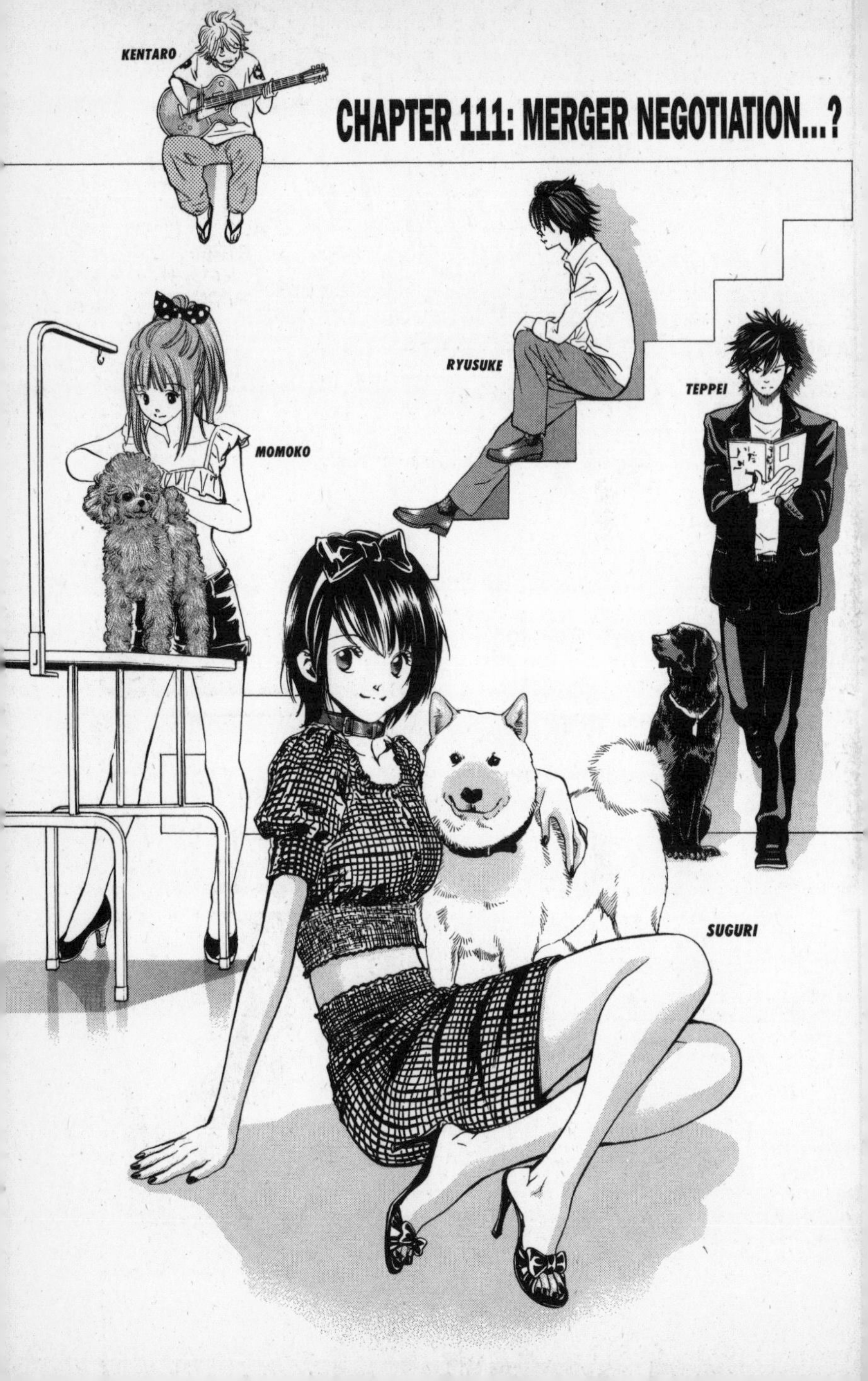
KENTARO
RYUSUKE
TEPPEI
MOMOKO
SUGURI

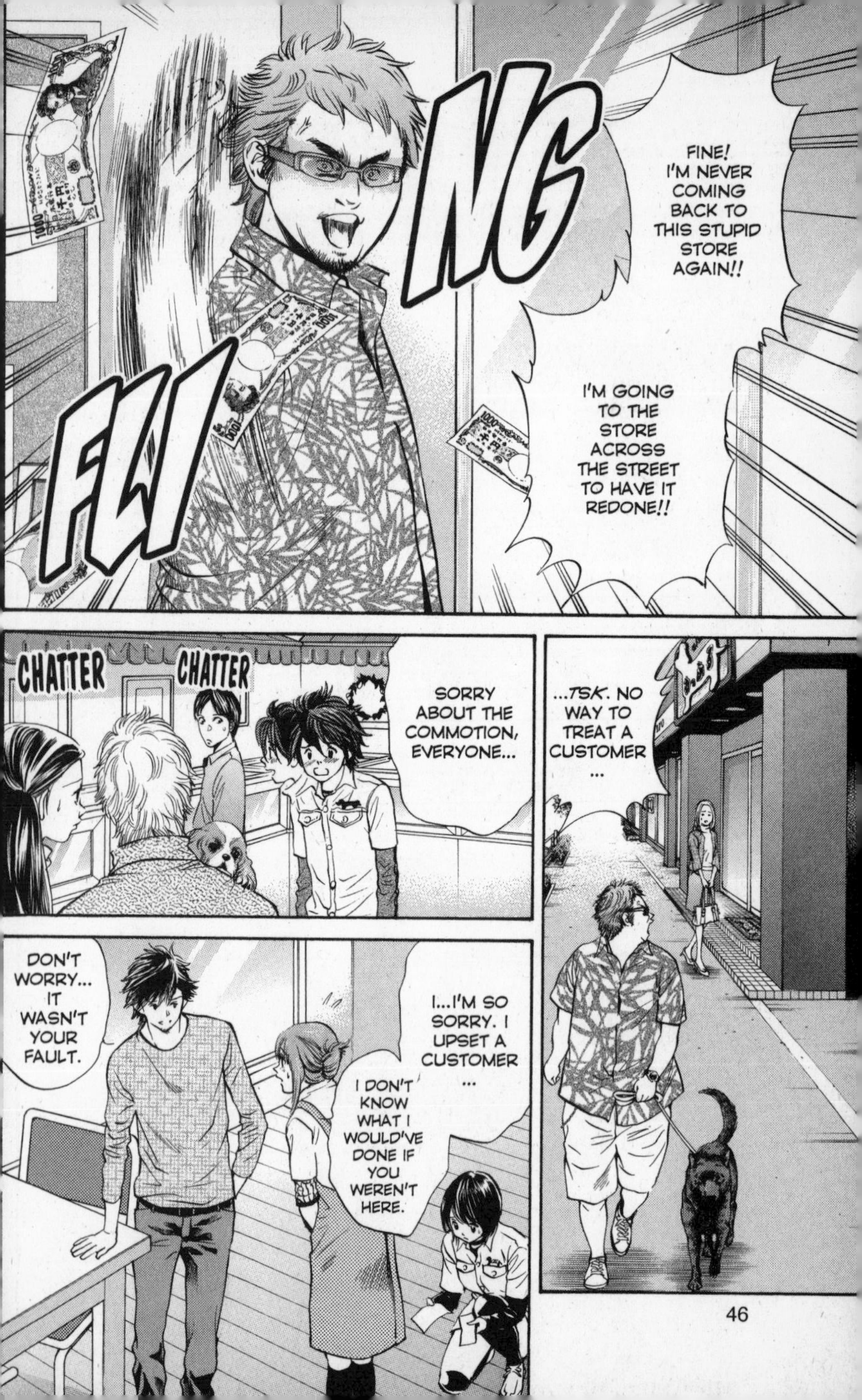
FINE! I'M NEVER COMING BACK TO THIS STUPID STORE AGAIN!!
I'M GOING TO THE STORE ACROSS THE STREET TO HAVE IT REDONE!!
FLI
NG
...TSK. NO WAY TO TREAT A CUSTOMER ...
SORRY ABOUT THE COMMOTION, EVERYONE...
CHATTER
CHATTER
I...I'M SO SORRY. I UPSET A CUSTOMER ...
I DON'T KNOW WHAT I WOULD'VE DONE IF YOU WEREN'T HERE.
DON'T WORRY... IT WASN'T YOUR FAULT.

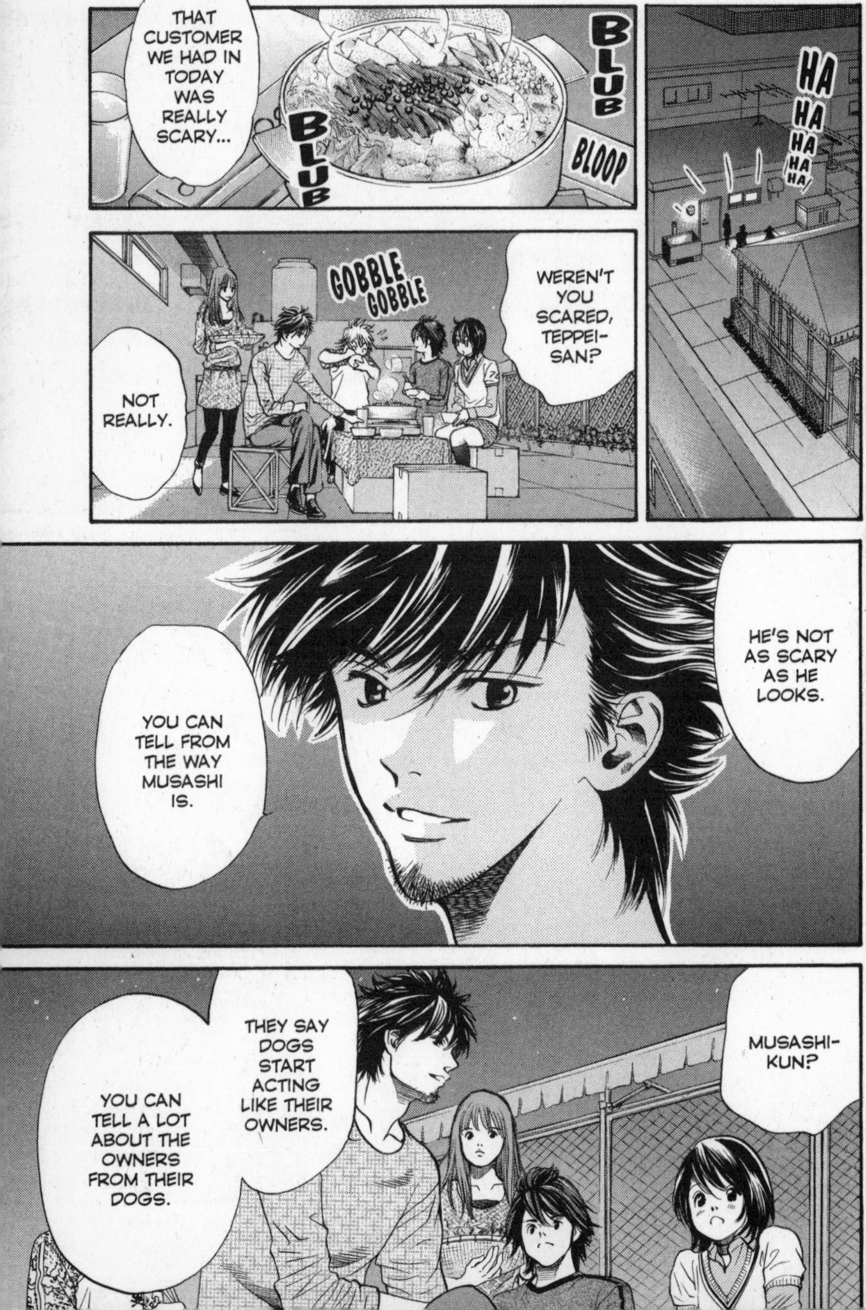
HA HA HA HA HA
THAT CUSTOMER WE HAD IN TODAY WAS REALLY SCARY...
BLUB
BLUB
BLOOP
WEREN'T YOU SCARED, TEPPEI-SAN?
GOBBLE GOBBLE
NOT REALLY.
HE'S NOT AS SCARY AS HE LOOKS.
YOU CAN TELL FROM THE WAY MUSASHI IS.
MUSASHI-KUN?
THEY SAY DOGS START ACTING LIKE THEIR OWNERS.
YOU CAN TELL A LOT ABOUT THE OWNERS FROM THEIR DOGS.

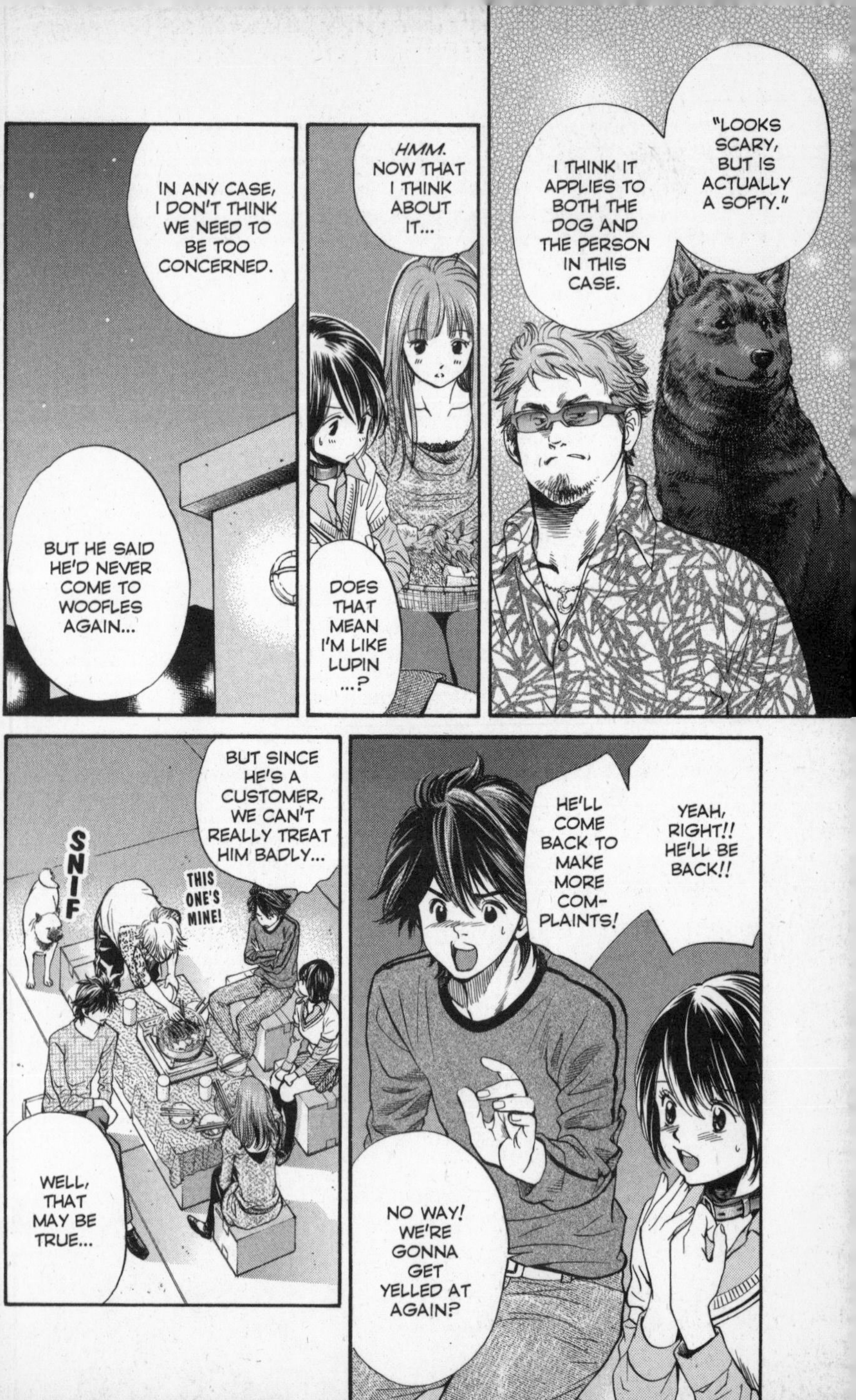
"LOOKS SCARY, BUT IS ACTUALLY A SOFTY."
I THINK IT APPLIES TO BOTH THE DOG AND THE PERSON IN THIS CASE.
HMM. NOW THAT I THINK ABOUT IT...
DOES THAT MEAN I'M LIKE LUPIN ...?
IN ANY CASE, I DON'T THINK WE NEED TO BE TOO CONCERNED.
BUT HE SAID HE'D NEVER COME TO WOOFLES AGAIN...
YEAH, RIGHT!! HE'LL BE BACK!!
HE'LL COME BACK TO MAKE MORE COM-PLAINTS!
NO WAY! WE'RE GONNA GET YELLED AT AGAIN?
BUT SINCE HE'S A CUSTOMER, WE CAN'T REALLY TREAT HIM BADLY...
SNIF
THIS ONE'S MINE!
WELL, THAT MAY BE TRUE...

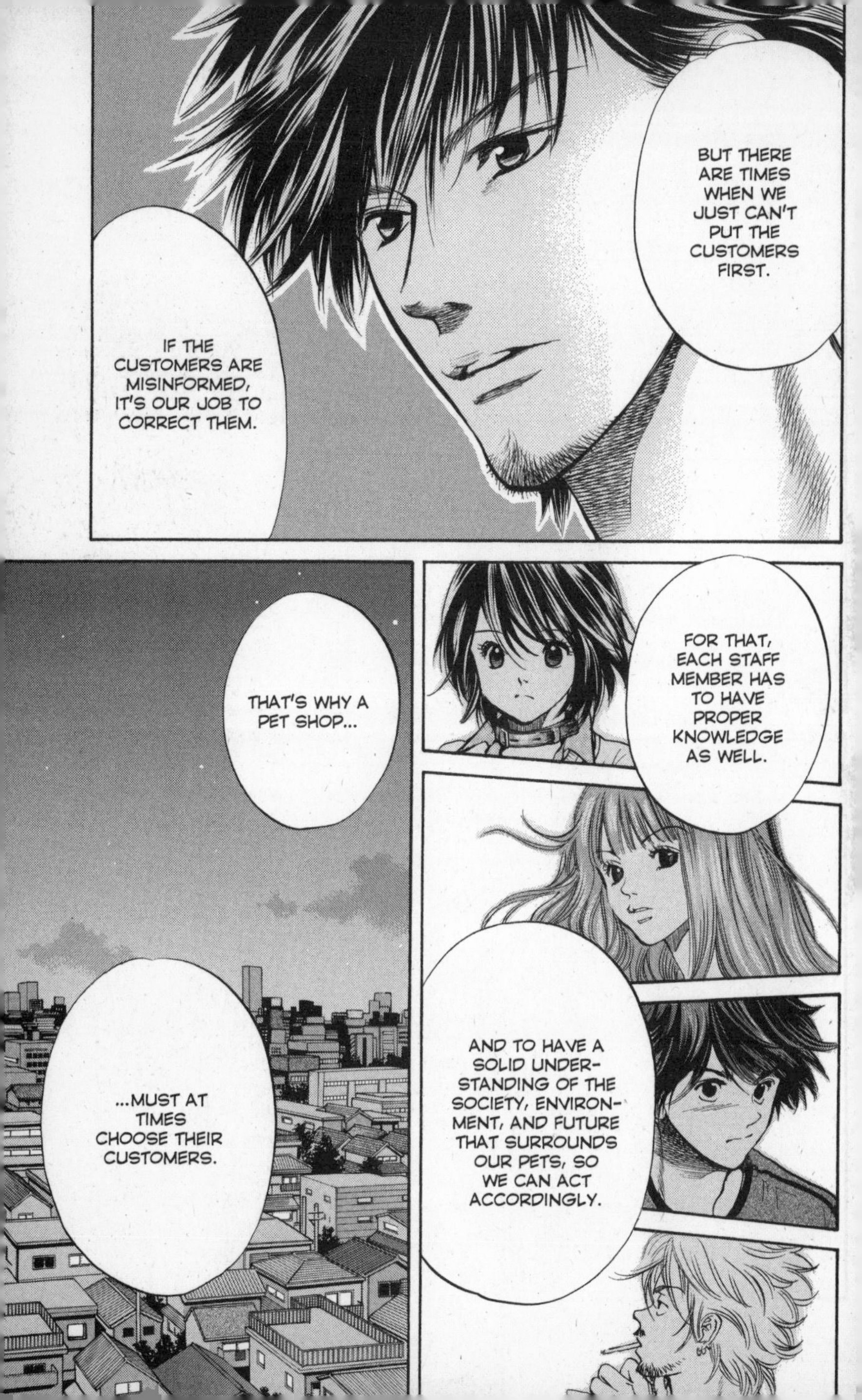
BUT THERE ARE TIMES WHEN WE JUST CAN'T PUT THE CUSTOMERS FIRST.
IF THE CUSTOMERS ARE MISINFORMED, IT'S OUR JOB TO CORRECT THEM.
FOR THAT, EACH STAFF MEMBER HAS TO HAVE PROPER KNOWLEDGE AS WELL.
AND TO HAVE A SOLID UNDER-STANDING OF THE SOCIETY, ENVIRON-MENT, AND FUTURE THAT SURROUNDS OUR PETS, SO WE CAN ACT ACCORDINGLY.
THAT'S WHY A PET SHOP...
...MUST AT TIMES CHOOSE THEIR CUSTOMERS.

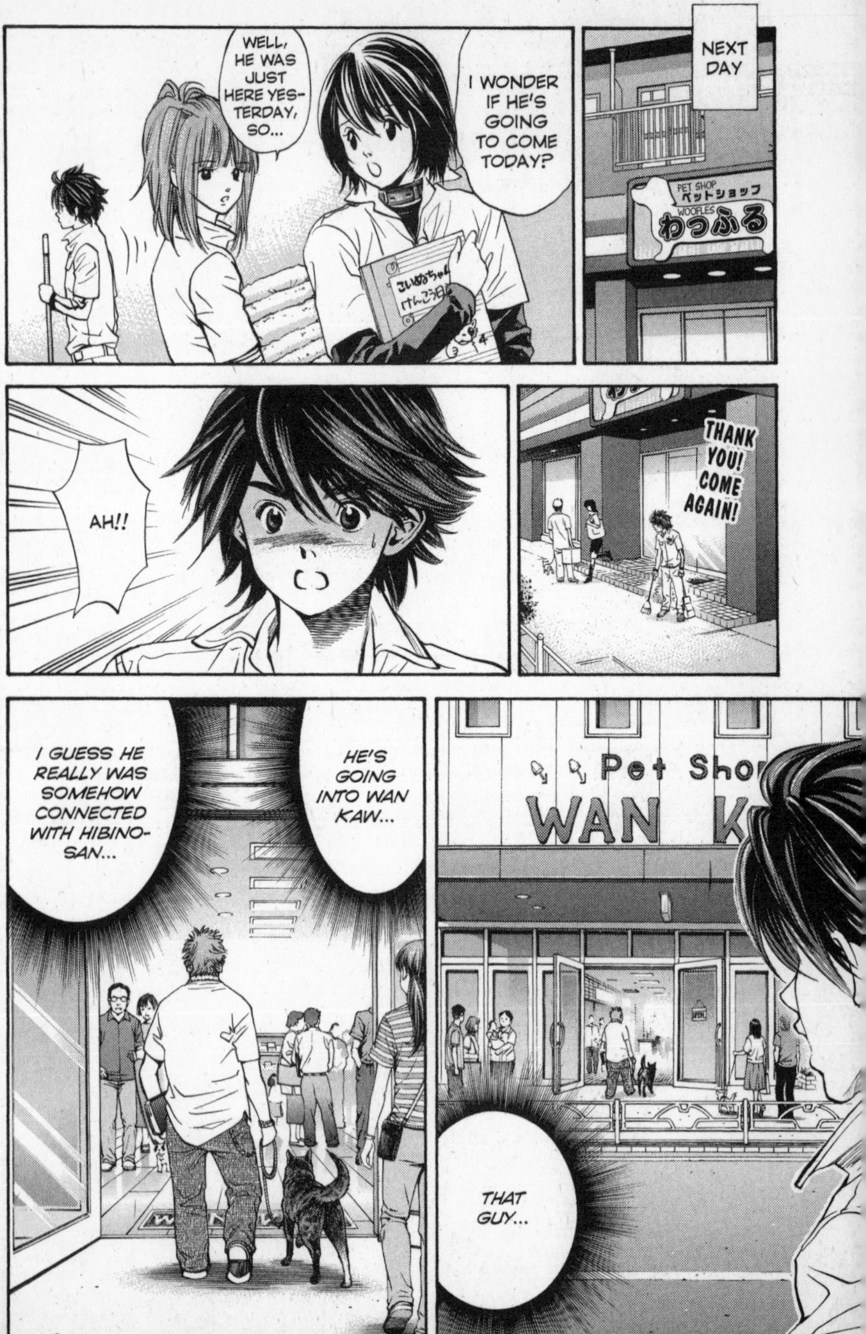
NEXT DAY
PET SHOP ペットショップ
WOOFLES わっふる
I WONDER IF HE'S GOING TO COME TODAY?
WELL, HE WAS JUST HERE YESTERDAY, SO...
THANK YOU! COME AGAIN!
AH!!
Pet Sho
WAN K
THAT GUY...
HE'S GOING INTO WAN KAW...
I GUESS HE REALLY WAS SOMEHOW CONNECTED WITH HIBINO-SAN...

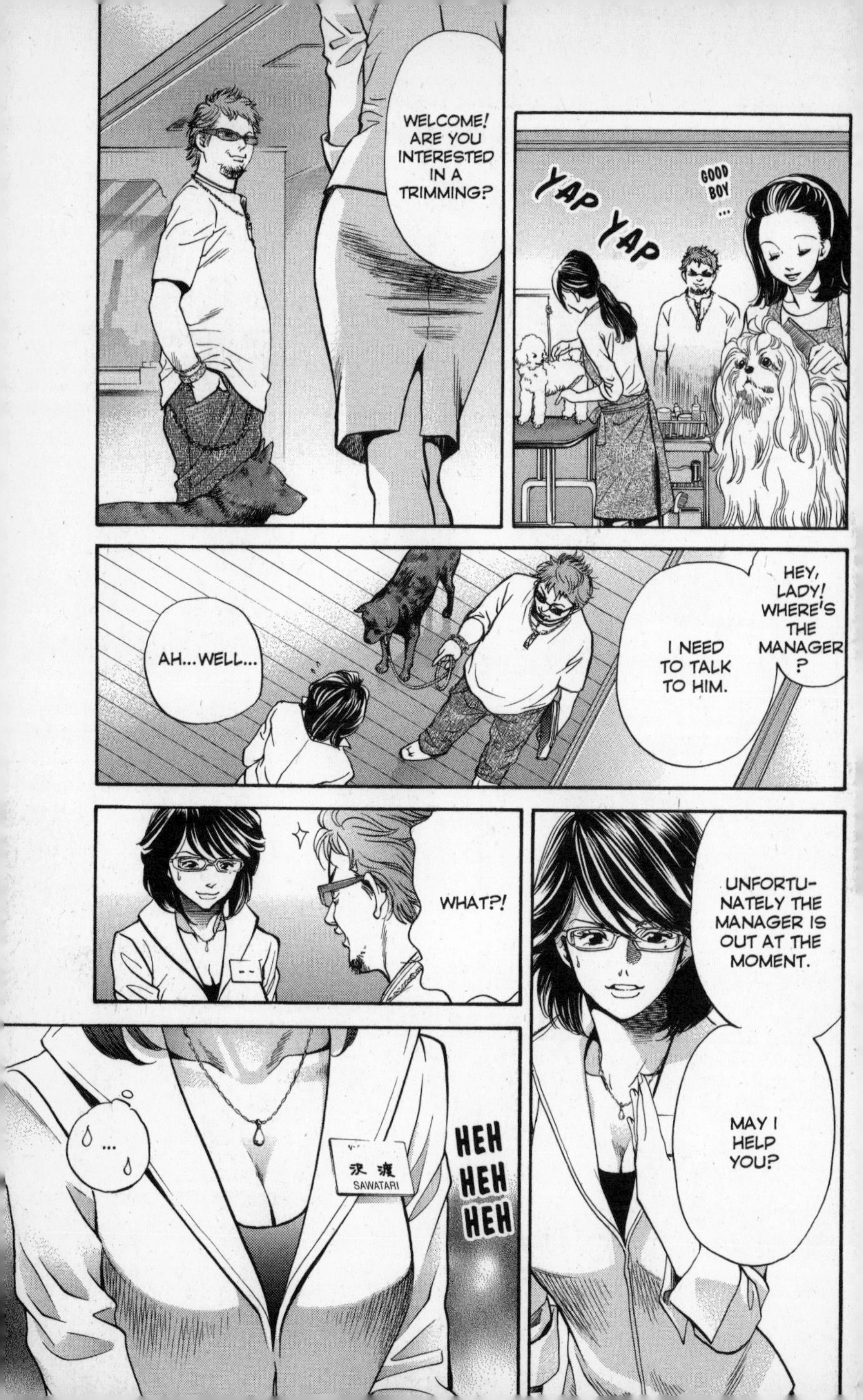
YAP YAP
GOOD BOY ...
WELCOME! ARE YOU INTERESTED IN A TRIMMING?
HEY, LADY! WHERE'S THE MANAGER?
I NEED TO TALK TO HIM.
AH...WELL...
UNFORTU-NATELY THE MANAGER IS OUT AT THE MOMENT.
MAY I HELP YOU?
WHAT?!
HEH HEH HEH
沢渡
SAWATARI
...

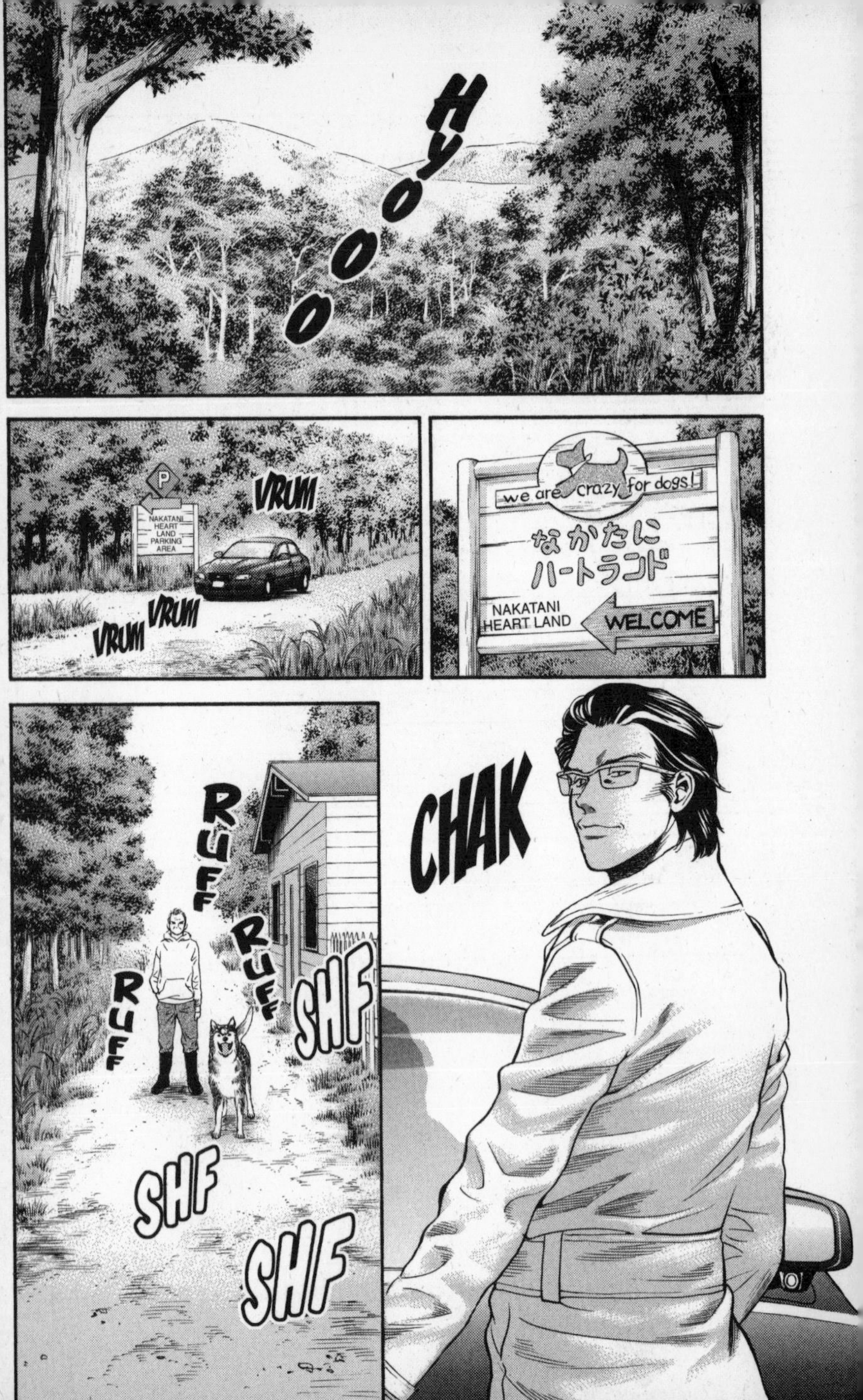
HYOOOO
we are crazy for dogs!
なかたに
ハートランド
NAKATANI HEART LAND
WELCOME
NAKATANI HEART LAND PARKING AREA
VRUM
VRUM
VRUM
CHAK
RUFF
RUFF
RUFF
SHF
SHF
SHF

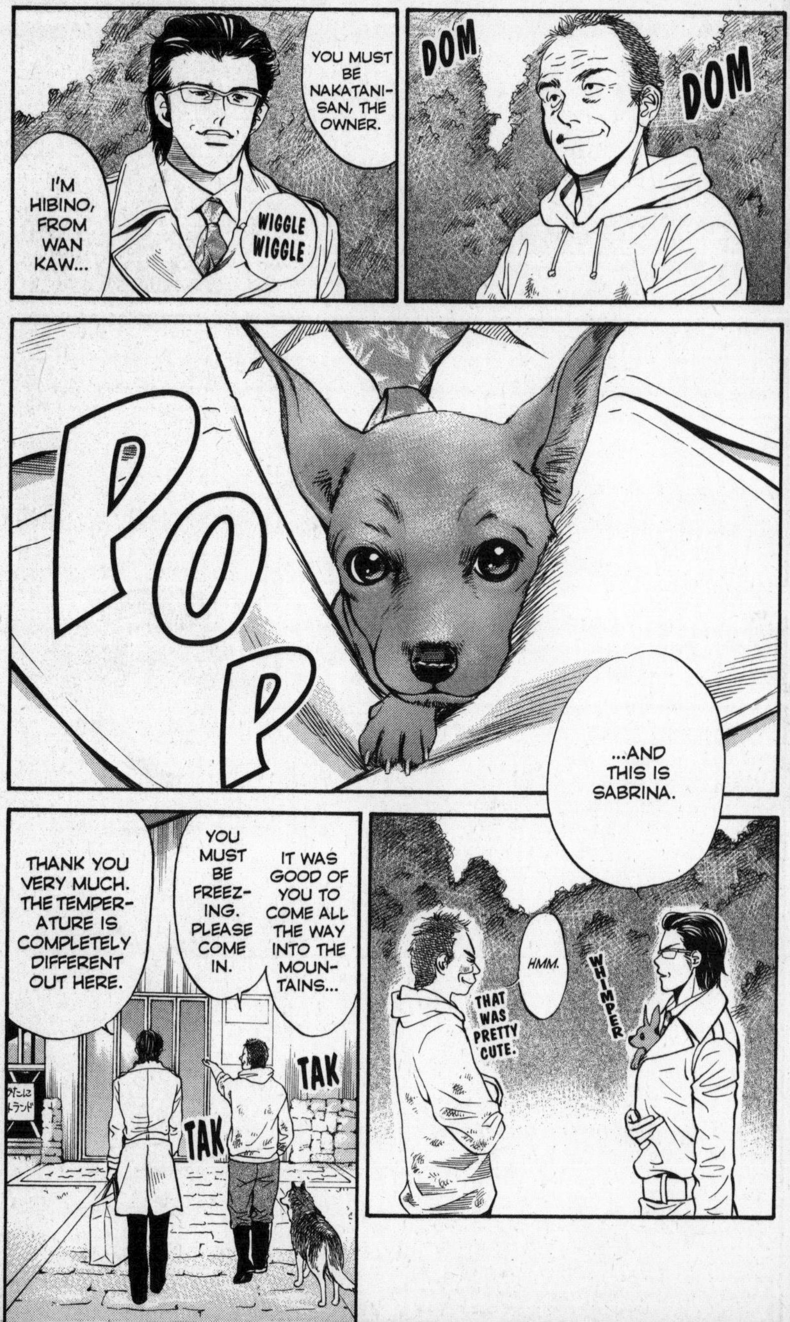
DOM
DOM
YOU MUST BE NAKATANI-SAN, THE OWNER.
I'M HIBINO, FROM WAN KAW...
WIGGLE WIGGLE
POP
...AND THIS IS SABRINA.
WHIMPER
HMM.
THAT WAS PRETTY CUTE.
IT WAS GOOD OF YOU TO COME ALL THE WAY INTO THE MOUNTAINS...
YOU MUST BE FREEZING. PLEASE COME IN.
THANK YOU VERY MUCH. THE TEMPERATURE IS COMPLETELY DIFFERENT OUT HERE.
TAK
TAK

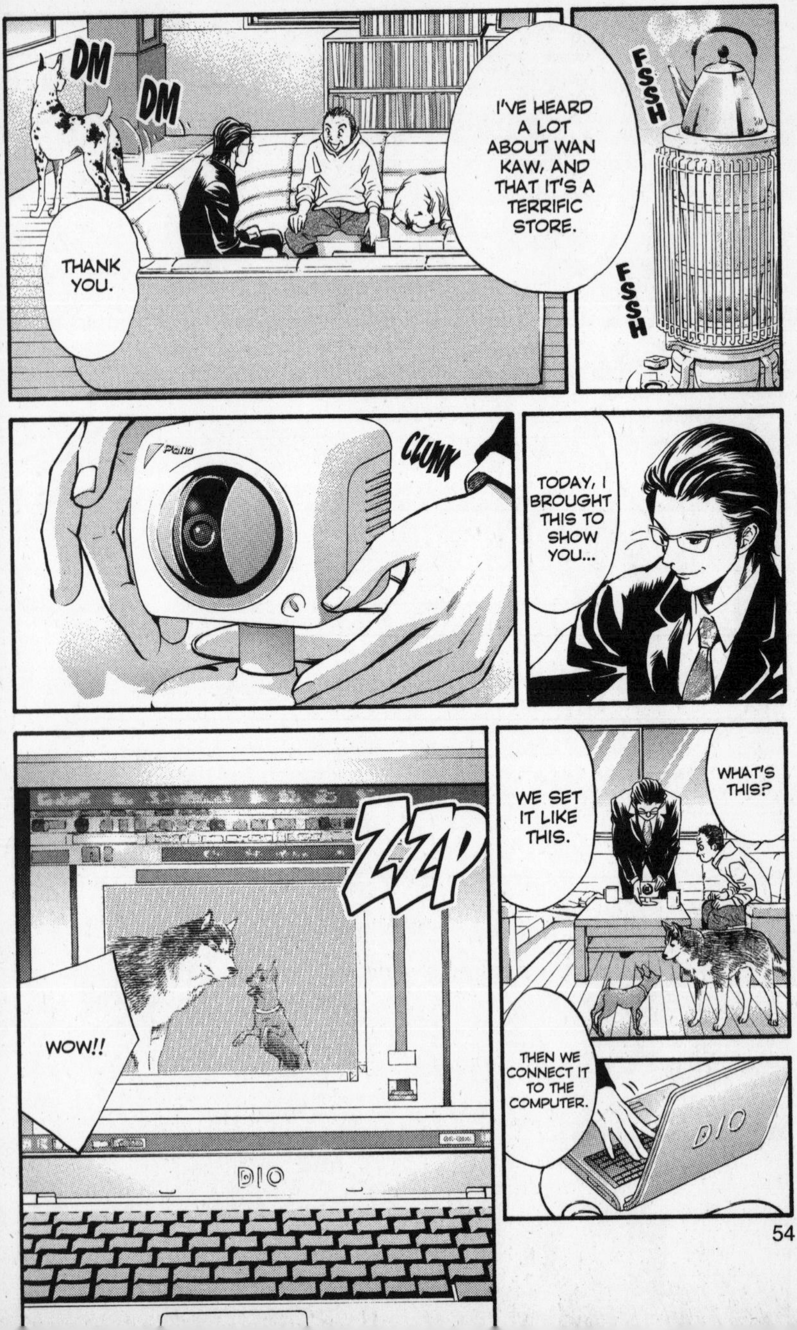
FSSH
FSSH
I'VE HEARD A LOT ABOUT WAN KAW, AND THAT IT'S A TERRIFIC STORE.
DM DM
THANK YOU.
TODAY, I BROUGHT THIS TO SHOW YOU...
CLUNK
WHAT'S THIS?
WE SET IT LIKE THIS.
THEN WE CONNECT IT TO THE COMPUTER.
DIO
ZZP
WOW!!
DIO

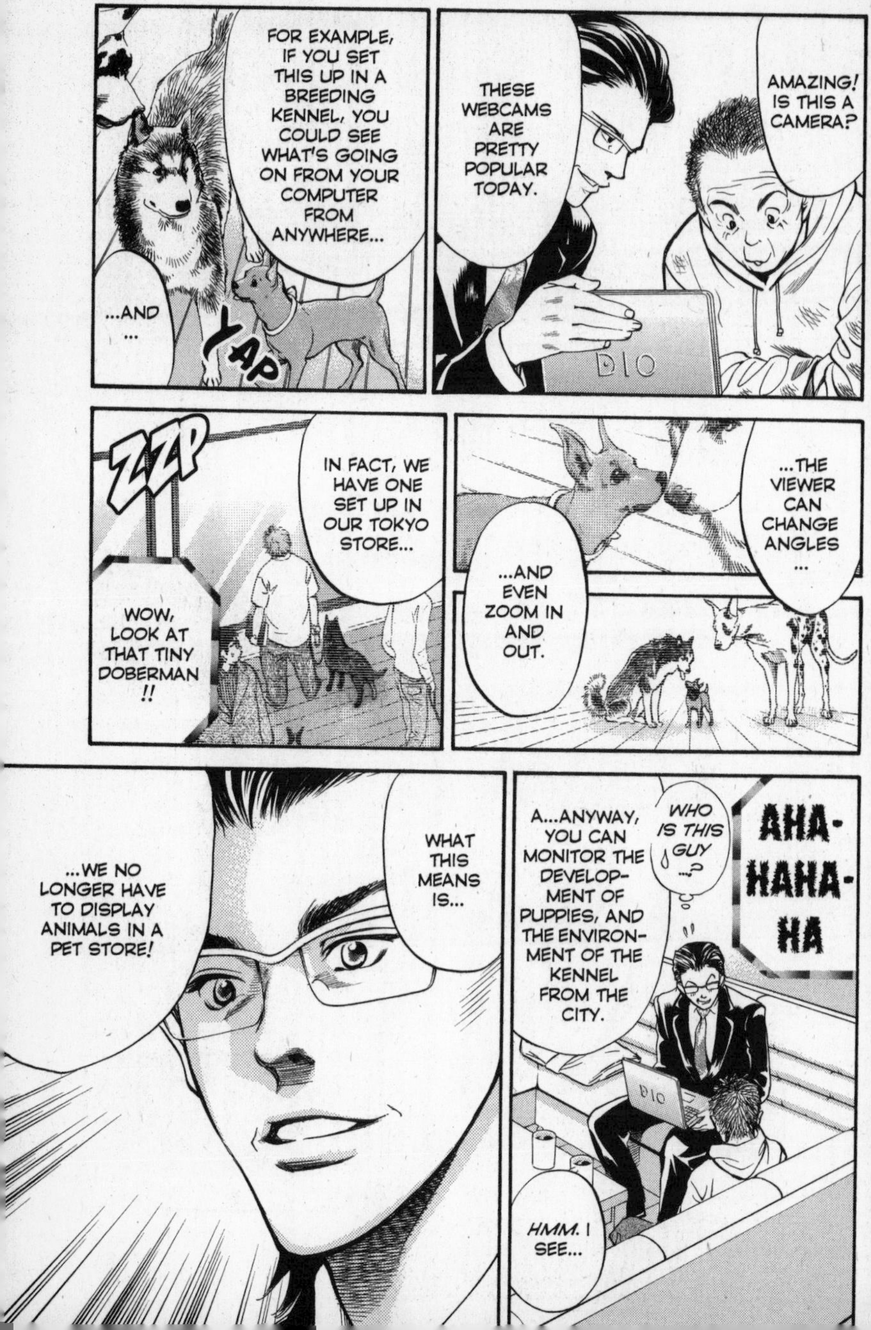
AMAZING! IS THIS A CAMERA?
THESE WEBCAMS ARE PRETTY POPULAR TODAY.
DIO
FOR EXAMPLE, IF YOU SET THIS UP IN A BREEDING KENNEL, YOU COULD SEE WHAT'S GOING ON FROM YOUR COMPUTER FROM ANYWHERE...
...AND ...
YAP
...THE VIEWER CAN CHANGE ANGLES ...
...AND EVEN ZOOM IN AND OUT.
ZZP
IN FACT, WE HAVE ONE SET UP IN OUR TOKYO STORE...
WOW, LOOK AT THAT TINY DOBERMAN !!
AHA-HAHA-HA
WHO IS THIS GUY ...?
A...ANYWAY, YOU CAN MONITOR THE DEVELOP-MENT OF PUPPIES, AND THE ENVIRON-MENT OF THE KENNEL FROM THE CITY.
DIO
HMM. I SEE...
WHAT THIS MEANS IS...
...WE NO LONGER HAVE TO DISPLAY ANIMALS IN A PET STORE!

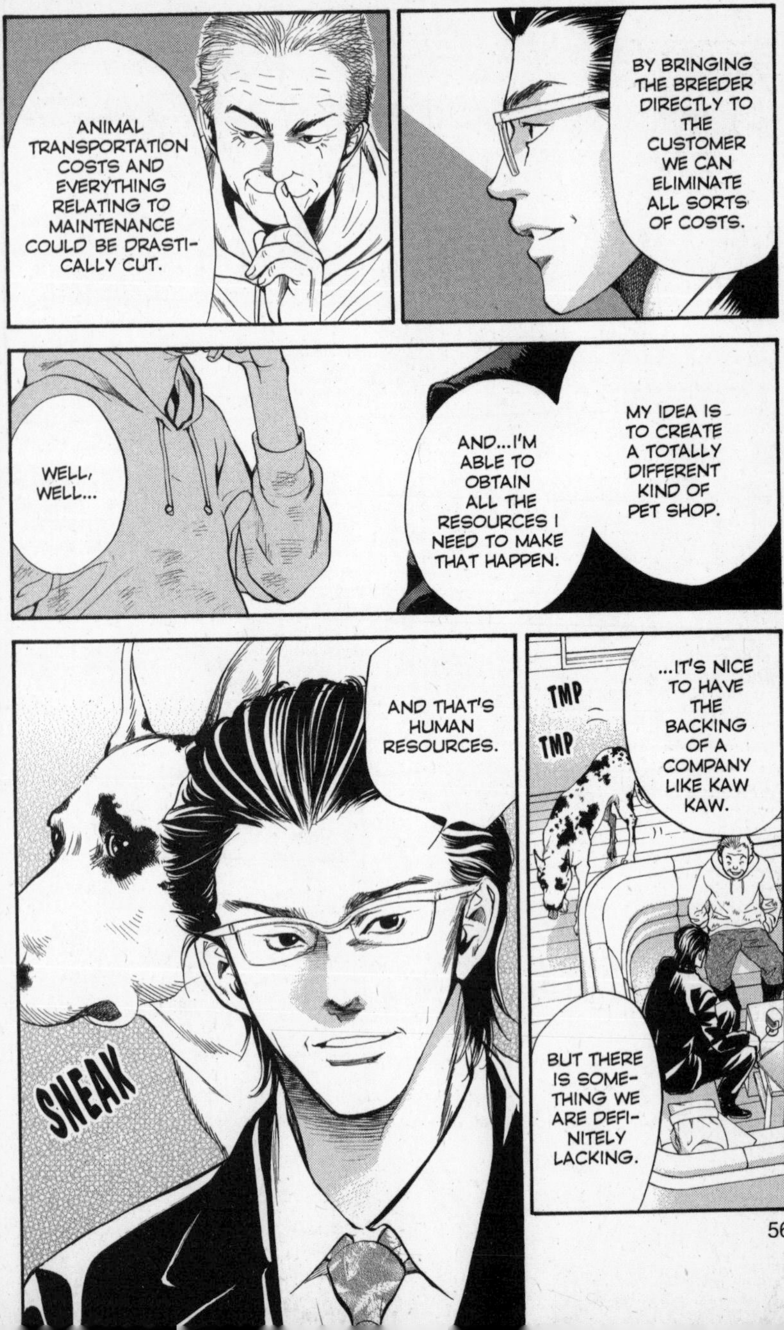
BY BRINGING THE BREEDER DIRECTLY TO THE CUSTOMER WE CAN ELIMINATE ALL SORTS OF COSTS.
ANIMAL TRANSPORTATION COSTS AND EVERYTHING RELATING TO MAINTENANCE COULD BE DRASTI-CALLY CUT.
MY IDEA IS TO CREATE A TOTALLY DIFFERENT KIND OF PET SHOP.
AND...I'M ABLE TO OBTAIN ALL THE RESOURCES I NEED TO MAKE THAT HAPPEN.
WELL, WELL...
...IT'S NICE TO HAVE THE BACKING OF A COMPANY LIKE KAW KAW.
TMP
TMP
BUT THERE IS SOME-THING WE ARE DEFI-NITELY LACKING.
AND THAT'S HUMAN RESOURCES.
SNEAK

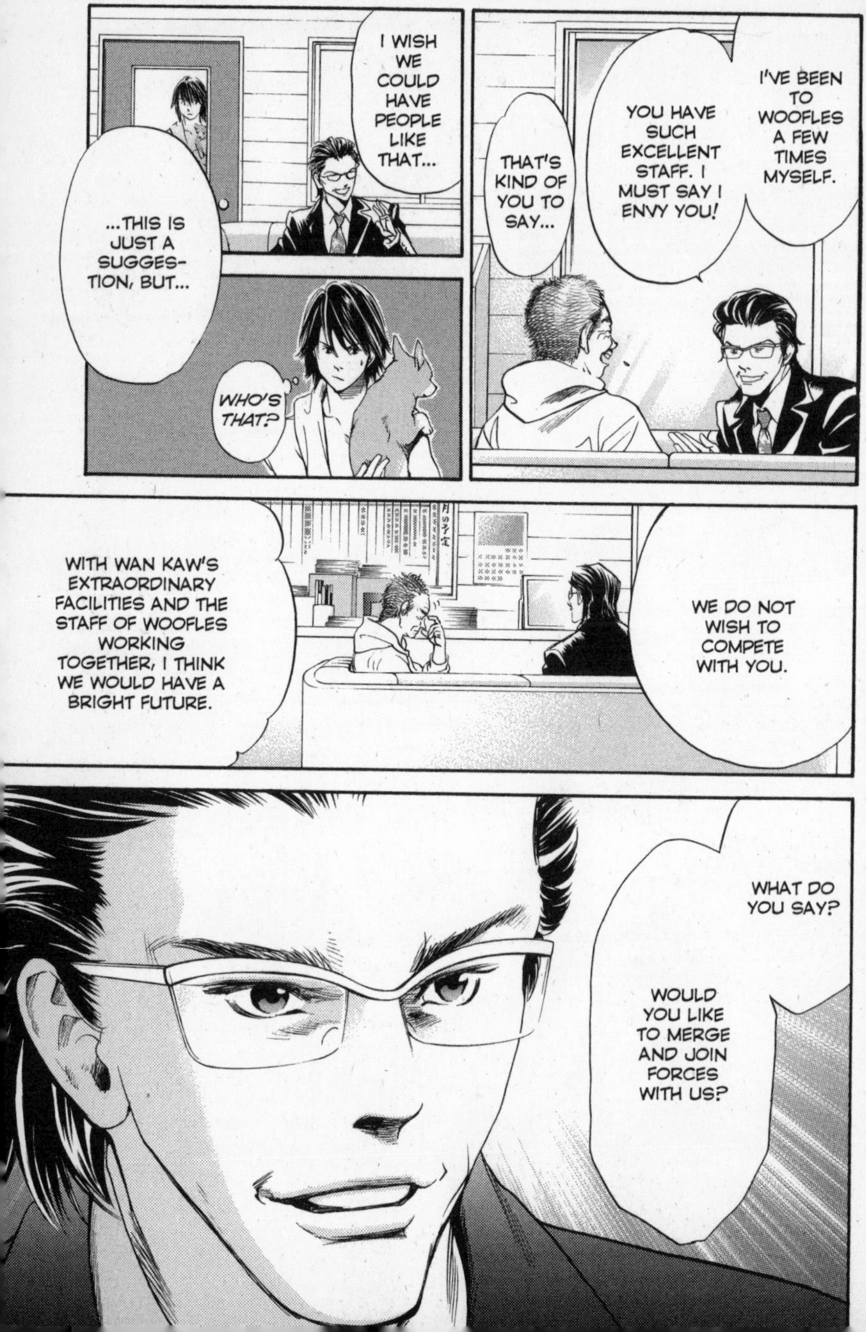
I'VE BEEN TO WOOFLES A FEW TIMES MYSELF.
YOU HAVE SUCH EXCELLENT STAFF. I MUST SAY I ENVY YOU!
THAT'S KIND OF YOU TO SAY...
I WISH WE COULD HAVE PEOPLE LIKE THAT...
...THIS IS JUST A SUGGESTION, BUT...
WHO'S THAT?
WE DO NOT WISH TO COMPETE WITH YOU.
WITH WAN KAW'S EXTRAORDINARY FACILITIES AND THE STAFF OF WOOFLES WORKING TOGETHER, I THINK WE WOULD HAVE A BRIGHT FUTURE.
WHAT DO YOU SAY?
WOULD YOU LIKE TO MERGE AND JOIN FORCES WITH US?

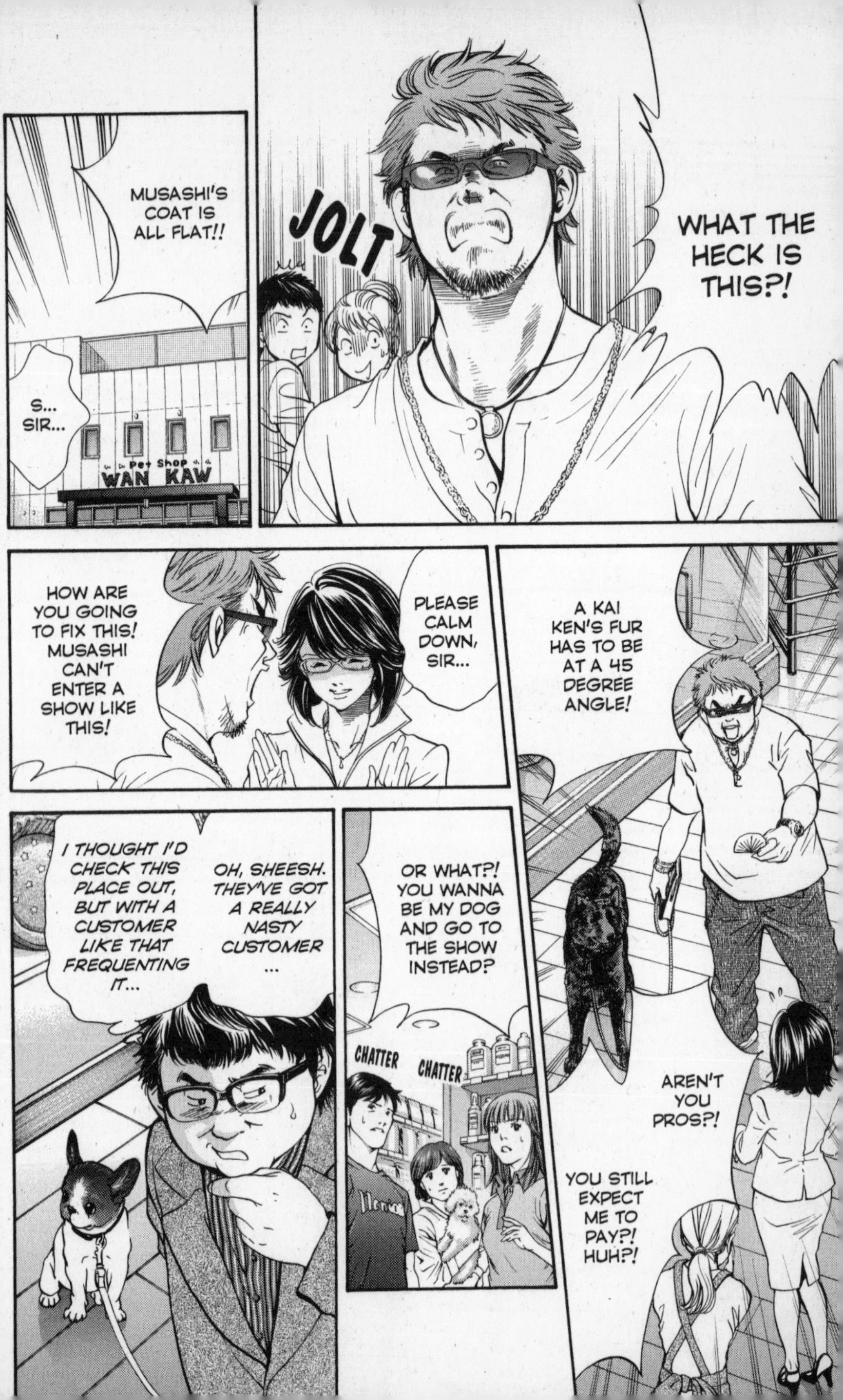
WHAT THE HECK IS THIS?!
JOLT
MUSASHI'S COAT IS ALL FLAT!!
S... SIR...
Pet Shop
WAN KAW
A KAI KEN'S FUR HAS TO BE AT A 45 DEGREE ANGLE!
AREN'T YOU PROS?!
YOU STILL EXPECT ME TO PAY?! HUH?!
PLEASE CALM DOWN, SIR...
HOW ARE YOU GOING TO FIX THIS! MUSASHI CAN'T ENTER A SHOW LIKE THIS!
OR WHAT?! YOU WANNA BE MY DOG AND GO TO THE SHOW INSTEAD?
CHATTER
CHATTER
OH, SHEESH. THEY'VE GOT A REALLY NASTY CUSTOMER ...
I THOUGHT I'D CHECK THIS PLACE OUT, BUT WITH A CUSTOMER LIKE THAT FREQUENTING IT...

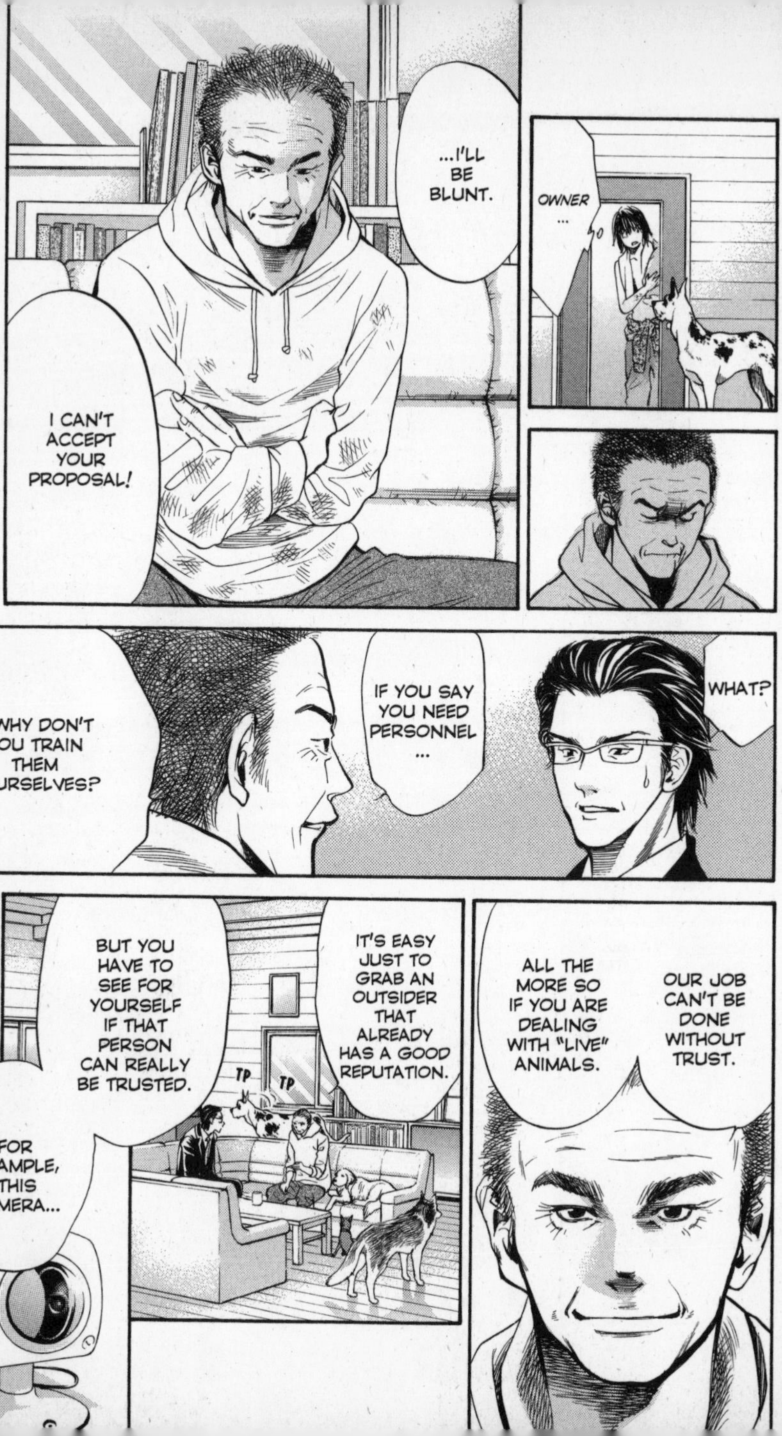
OWNER ...
...I'LL BE BLUNT.
I CAN'T ACCEPT YOUR PROPOSAL!
WHAT?
IF YOU SAY YOU NEED PERSONNEL ...
...WHY DON'T YOU TRAIN THEM YOURSELVES?
OUR JOB CAN'T BE DONE WITHOUT TRUST.
ALL THE MORE SO IF YOU ARE DEALING WITH "LIVE" ANIMALS.
IT'S EASY JUST TO GRAB AN OUTSIDER THAT ALREADY HAS A GOOD REPUTATION.
BUT YOU HAVE TO SEE FOR YOURSELF IF THAT PERSON CAN REALLY BE TRUSTED.
TP TP
FOR EXAMPLE, THIS CAMERA...

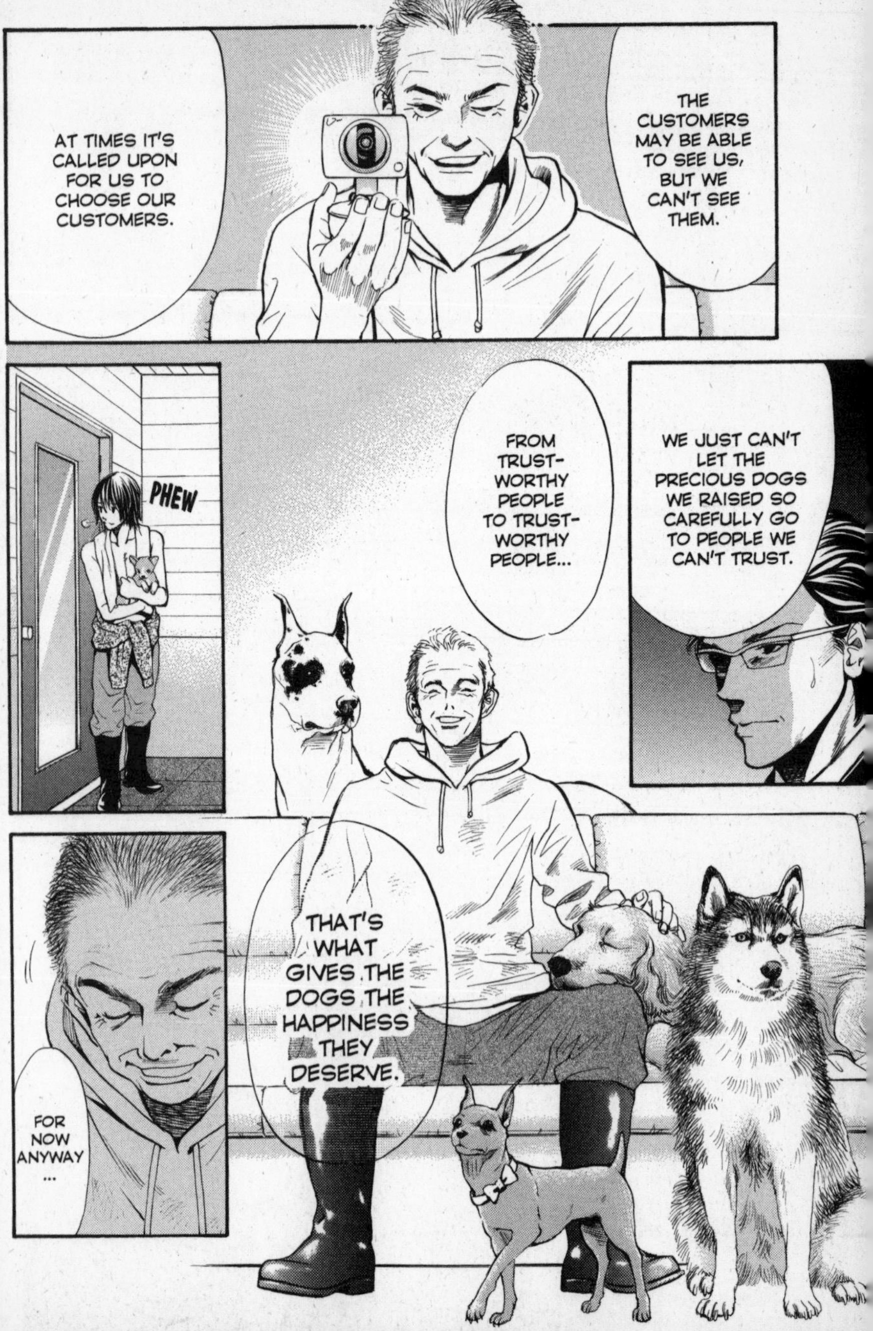
THE CUSTOMERS MAY BE ABLE TO SEE US, BUT WE CAN'T SEE THEM.
AT TIMES IT'S CALLED UPON FOR US TO CHOOSE OUR CUSTOMERS.
WE JUST CAN'T LET THE PRECIOUS DOGS WE RAISED SO CAREFULLY GO TO PEOPLE WE CAN'T TRUST.
FROM TRUST-WORTHY PEOPLE TO TRUST-WORTHY PEOPLE...
THAT'S WHAT GIVES THE DOGS THE HAPPINESS THEY DESERVE.
PHEW
FOR NOW ANYWAY ...

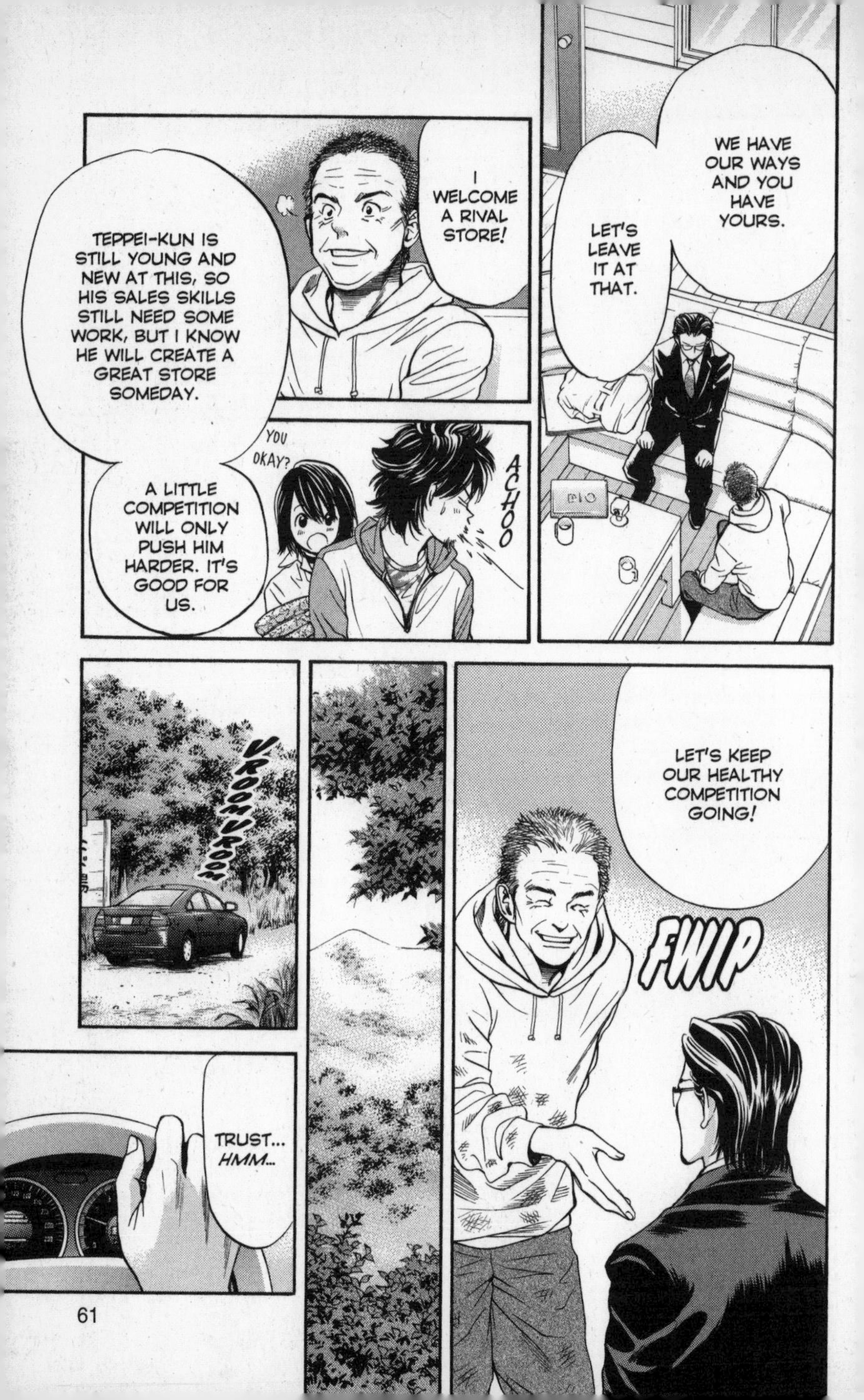
WE HAVE OUR WAYS AND YOU HAVE YOURS.
LET'S LEAVE IT AT THAT.
I WELCOME A RIVAL STORE!
TEPPEI-KUN IS STILL YOUNG AND NEW AT THIS, SO HIS SALES SKILLS STILL NEED SOME WORK, BUT I KNOW HE WILL CREATE A GREAT STORE SOMEDAY.
A LITTLE COMPETITION WILL ONLY PUSH HIM HARDER. IT'S GOOD FOR US.
ACHOO
YOU OKAY?
LET'S KEEP OUR HEALTHY COMPETITION GOING!
FWIP
VROOM VROOM
TRUST... HMM...

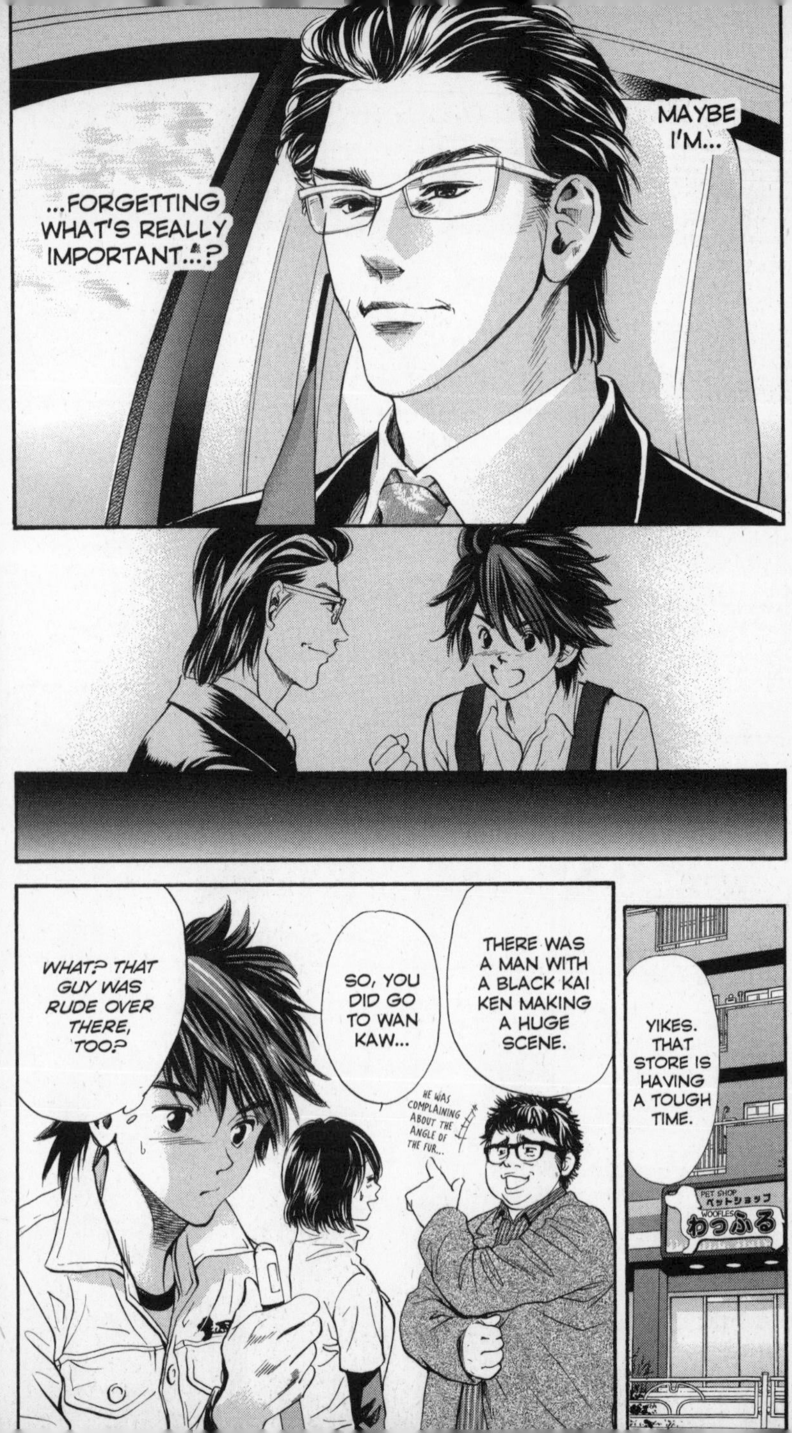
MAYBE I'M...
...FORGETTING WHAT'S REALLY IMPORTANT...?
YIKES. THAT STORE IS HAVING A TOUGH TIME.
PET SHOP ペットショップ WOOFLES わっふる
THERE WAS A MAN WITH A BLACK KAI KEN MAKING A HUGE SCENE.
HE WAS COMPLAINING ABOUT THE ANGLE OF THE FUR...
SO, YOU DID GO TO WAN KAW...
WHAT? THAT GUY WAS RUDE OVER THERE, TOO?

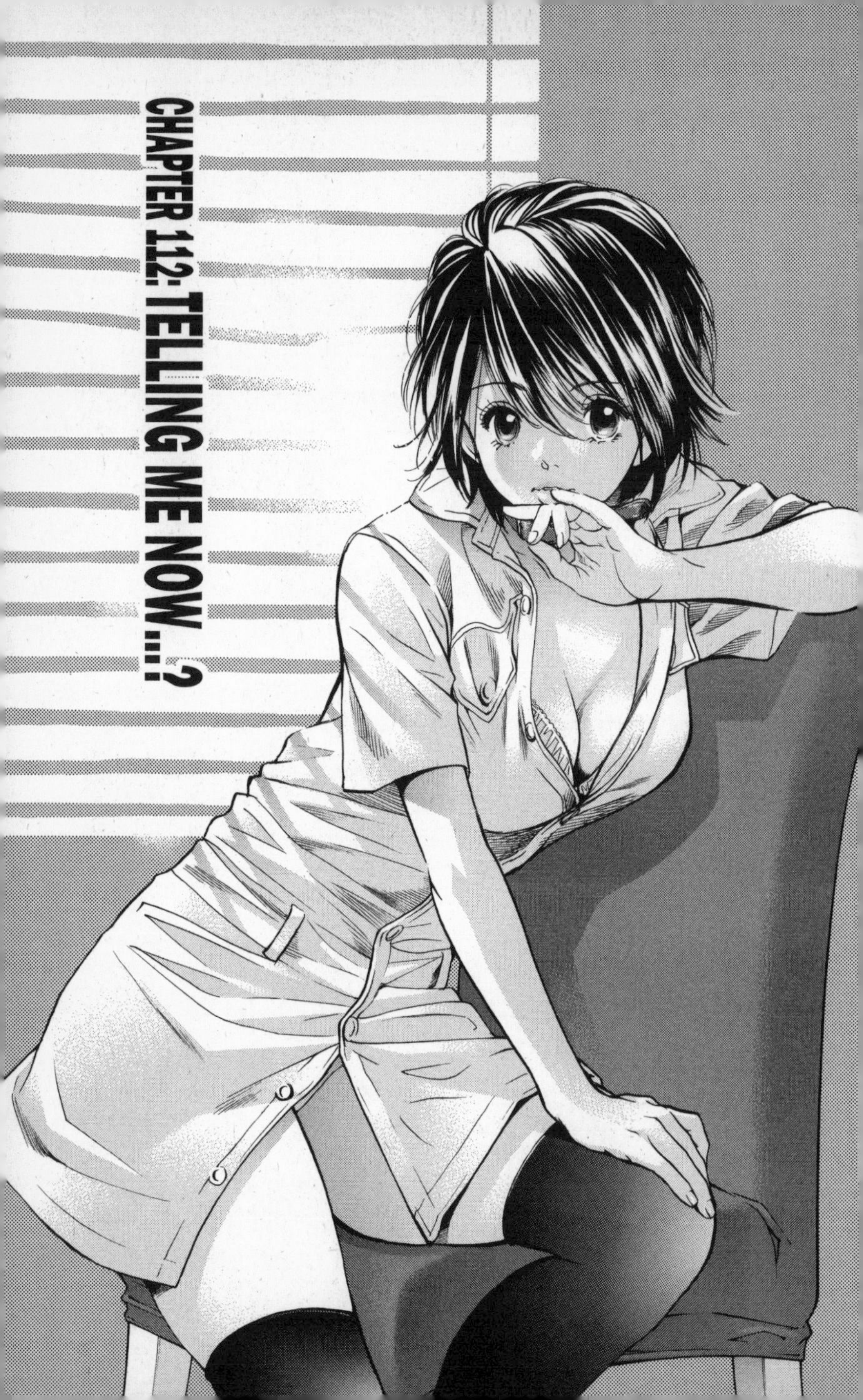
CHAPTER 112: TELLING ME NOW...!?

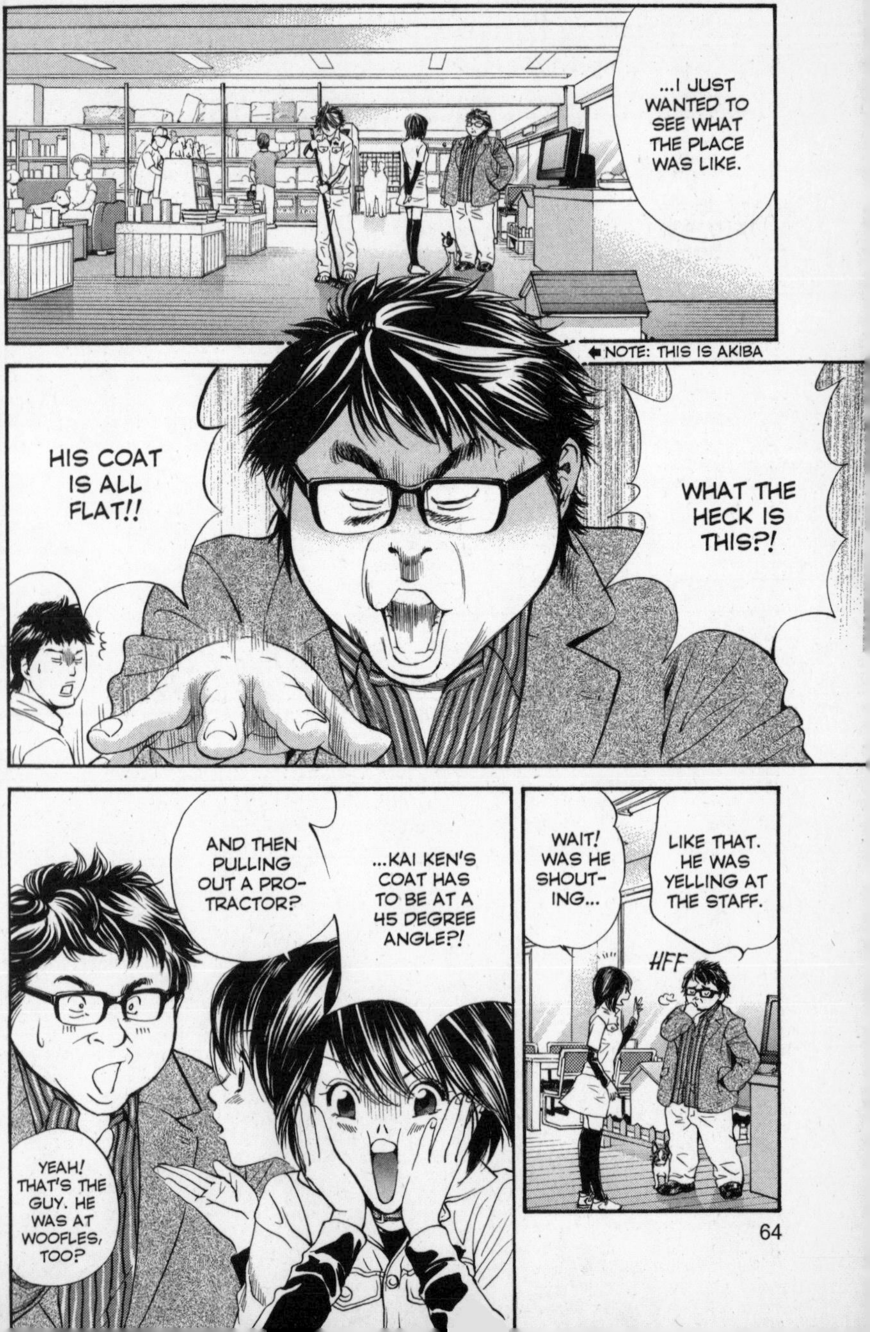
...I JUST WANTED TO SEE WHAT THE PLACE WAS LIKE.
NOTE: THIS IS AKIBA
WHAT THE HECK IS THIS?!
HIS COAT IS ALL FLAT!!
LIKE THAT. HE WAS YELLING AT THE STAFF.
WAIT! WAS HE SHOUTING...
HFF
...KAI KEN'S COAT HAS TO BE AT A 45 DEGREE ANGLE?!
AND THEN PULLING OUT A PRO-TRACTOR?
YEAH! THAT'S THE GUY. HE WAS AT WOOFLES, TOO?

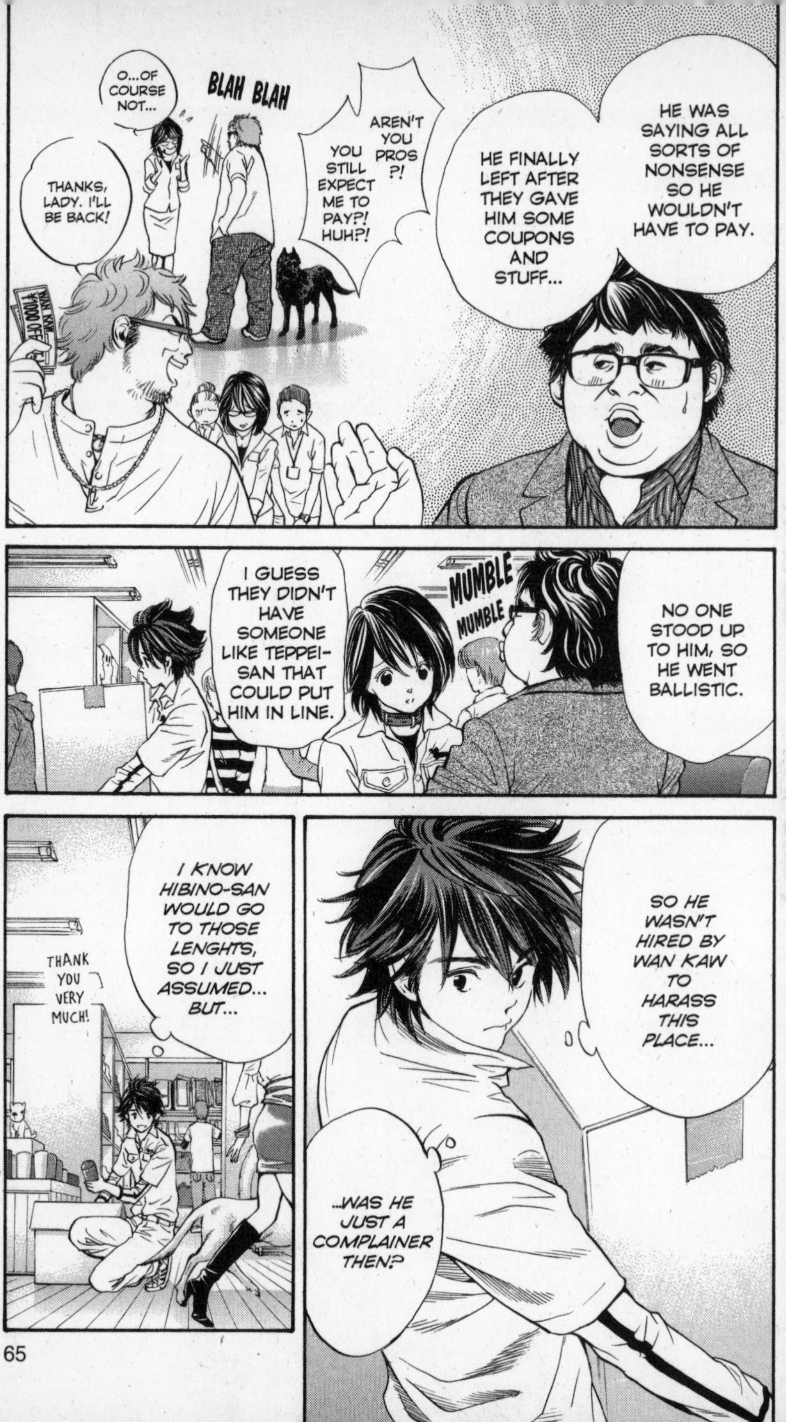
HE WAS SAYING ALL SORTS OF NONSENSE SO HE WOULDN'T HAVE TO PAY.
HE FINALLY LEFT AFTER THEY GAVE HIM SOME COUPONS AND STUFF...
AREN'T YOU PROS?!
YOU STILL EXPECT ME TO PAY?! HUH?!
BLAH BLAH
O...OF COURSE NOT...
THANKS, LADY. I'LL BE BACK!
NO ONE STOOD UP TO HIM, SO HE WENT BALLISTIC.
MUMBLE
MUMBLE
I GUESS THEY DIDN'T HAVE SOMEONE LIKE TEPPEI-SAN THAT COULD PUT HIM IN LINE.
SO HE WASN'T HIRED BY WAN KAW TO HARASS THIS PLACE...
...WAS HE JUST A COMPLAINER THEN?
I KNOW HIBINO-SAN WOULD GO TO THOSE LENGHTS, SO I JUST ASSUMED... BUT...
THANK YOU VERY MUCH!

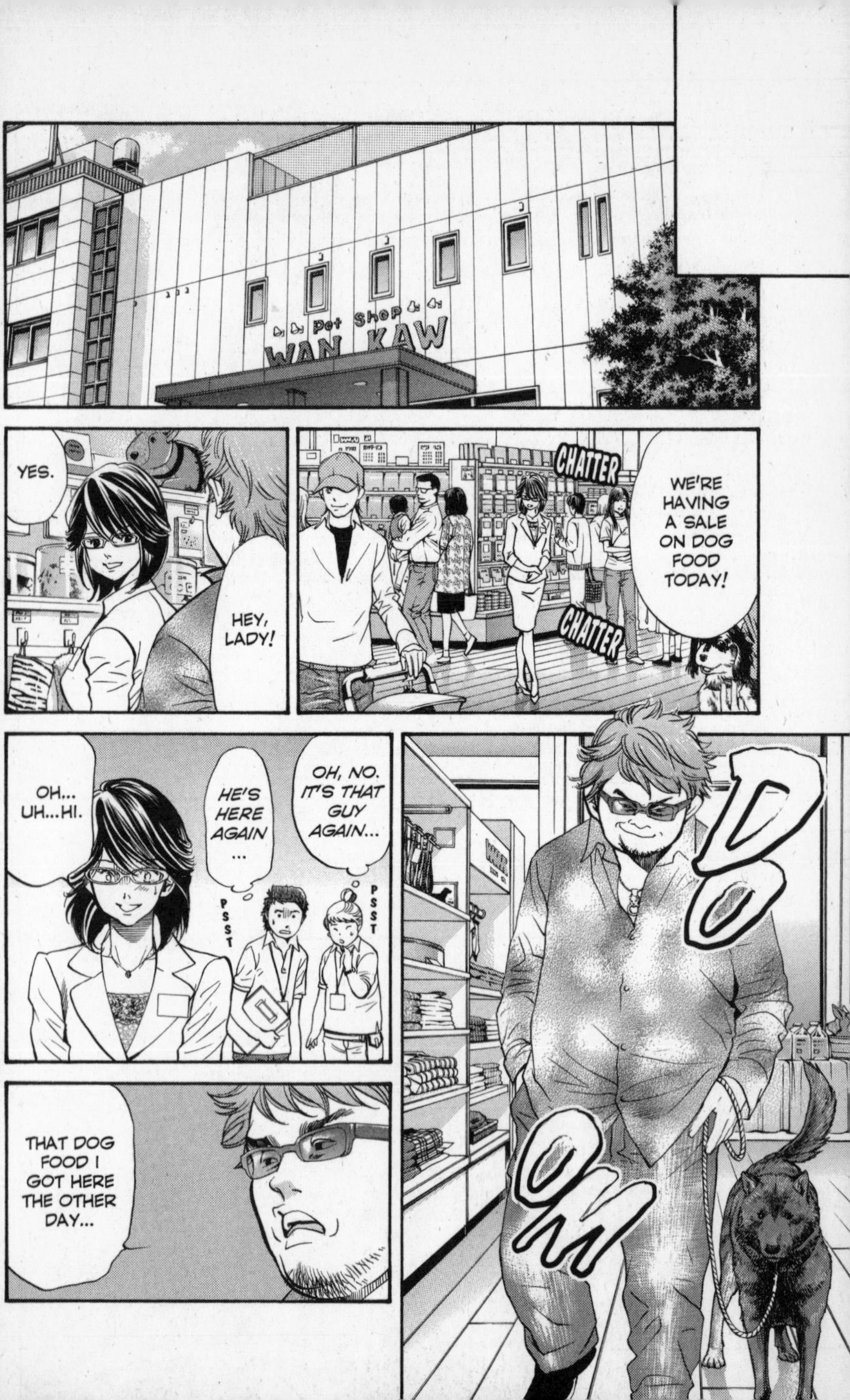
Pet Shop
WAN KAW
CHATTER
WE'RE HAVING A SALE ON DOG FOOD TODAY!
CHATTER
HEY, LADY!
YES.
DO
OM
OH, NO. IT'S THAT GUY AGAIN...
PSST
HE'S HERE AGAIN ...
PSST
OH... UH...HI.
THAT DOG FOOD I GOT HERE THE OTHER DAY...

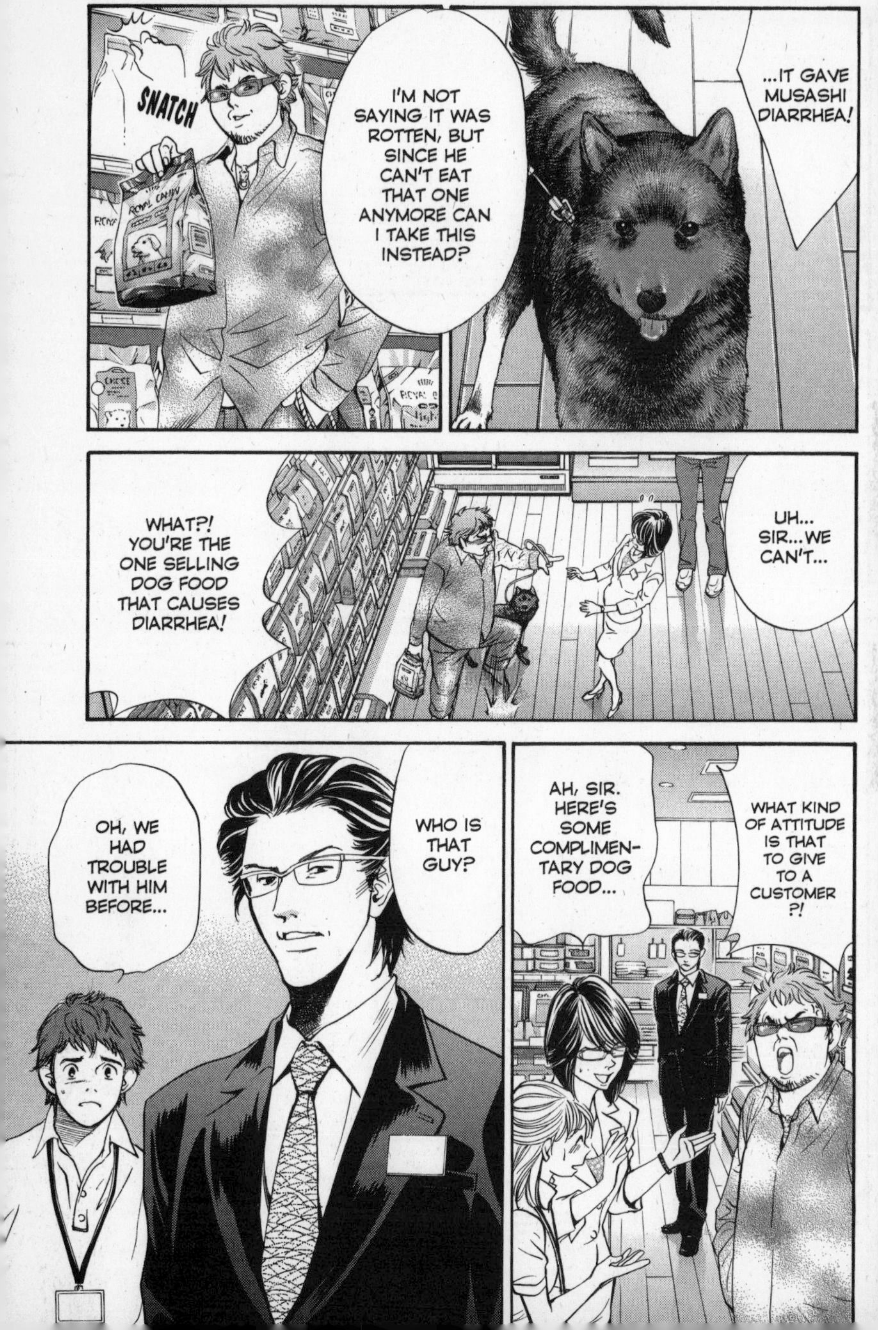
...IT GAVE MUSASHI DIARRHEA!
I'M NOT SAYING IT WAS ROTTEN, BUT SINCE HE CAN'T EAT THAT ONE ANYMORE CAN I TAKE THIS INSTEAD?
SNATCH
UH... SIR...WE CAN'T...
WHAT?! YOU'RE THE ONE SELLING DOG FOOD THAT CAUSES DIARRHEA!
WHAT KIND OF ATTITUDE IS THAT TO GIVE TO A CUSTOMER ?!
AH, SIR. HERE'S SOME COMPLIMENTARY DOG FOOD...
WHO IS THAT GUY?
OH, WE HAD TROUBLE WITH HIM BEFORE...

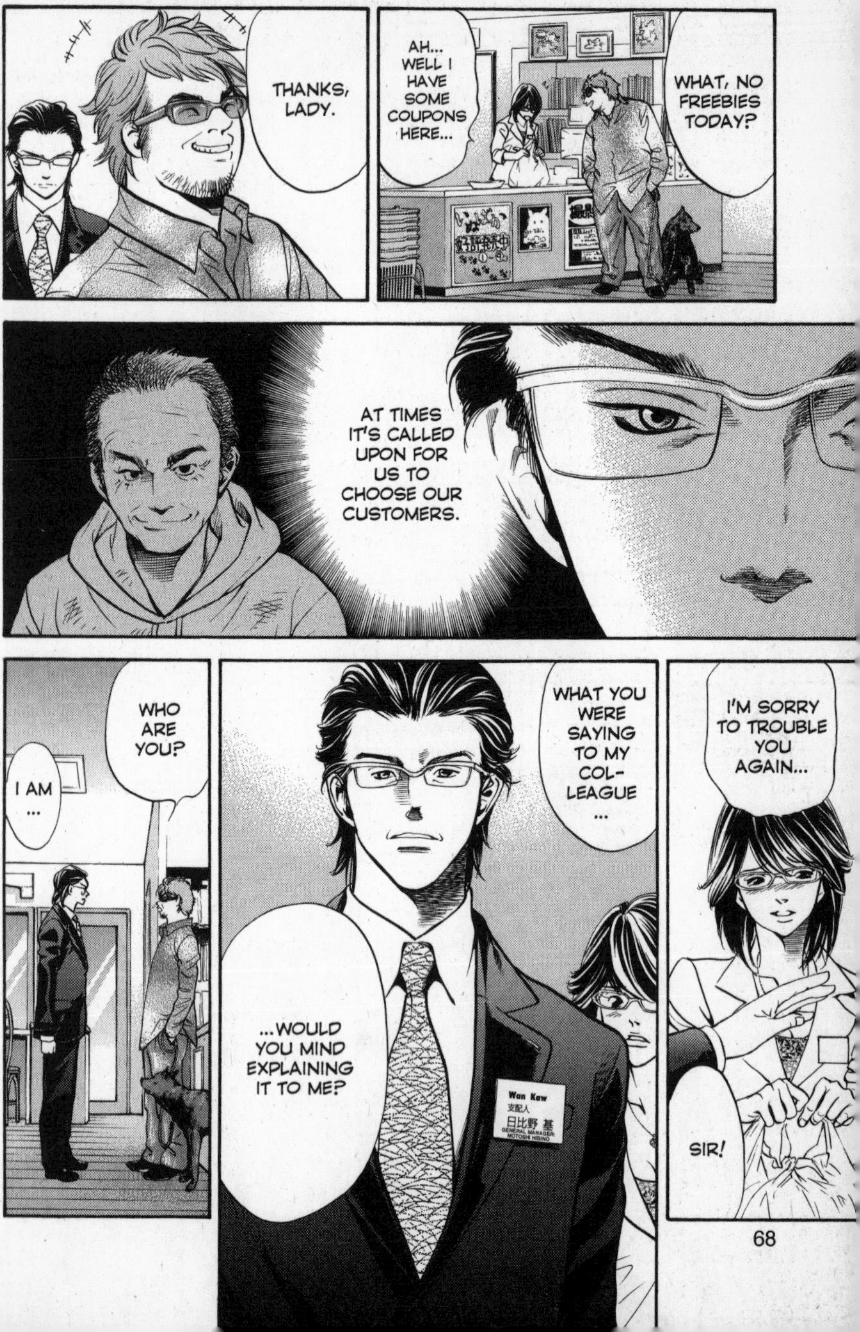
WHAT, NO FREEBIES TODAY?
AH... WELL I HAVE SOME COUPONS HERE...
THANKS, LADY.
AT TIMES IT'S CALLED UPON FOR US TO CHOOSE OUR CUSTOMERS.
I'M SORRY TO TROUBLE YOU AGAIN...
SIR!
WHAT YOU WERE SAYING TO MY COL-LEAGUE ...
...WOULD YOU MIND EXPLAINING IT TO ME?
Wan Kaw
支配人
日比野 基
GENERAL MANAGER: MOTOSHI HIBINO
WHO ARE YOU?
I AM ...

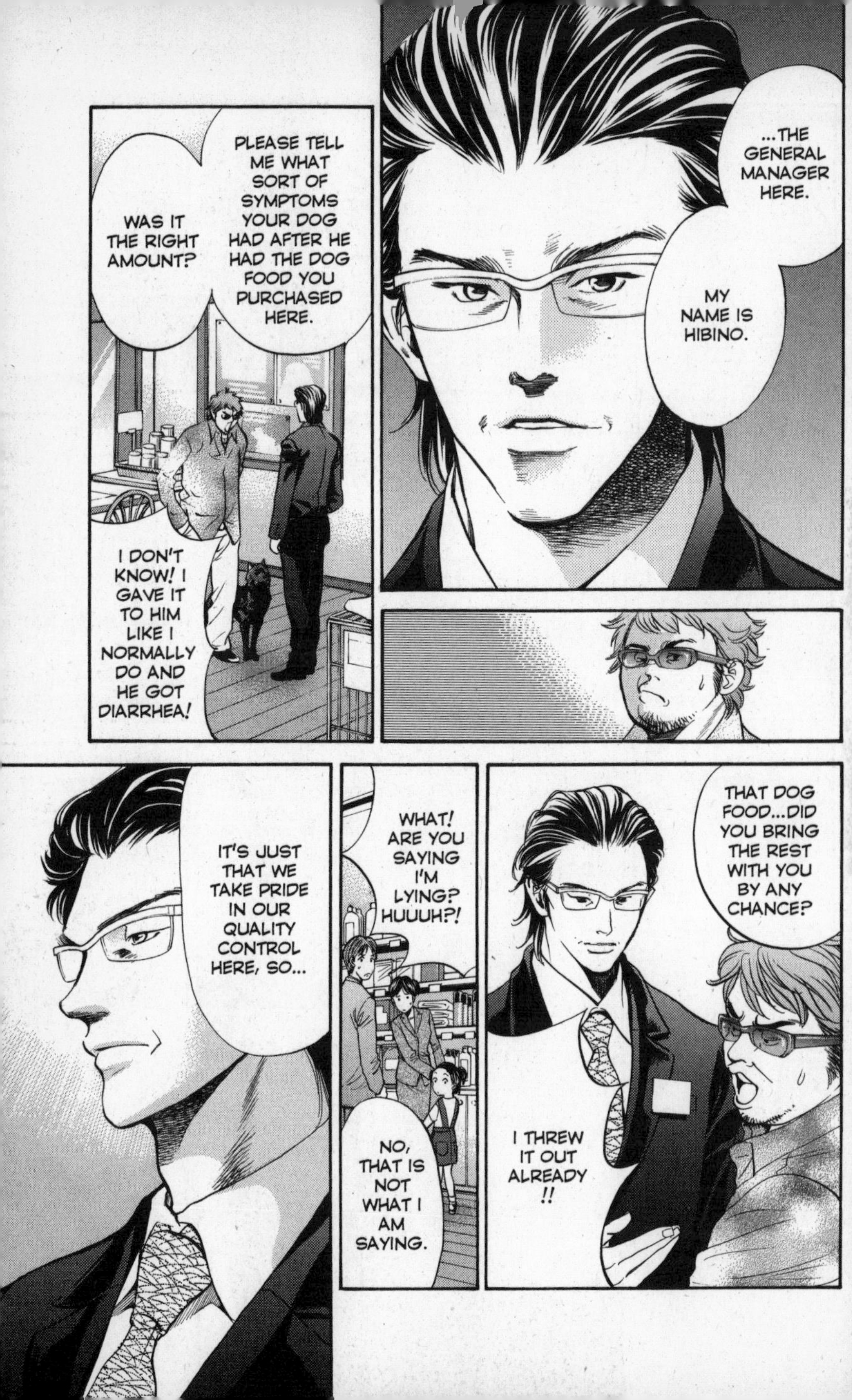
...THE GENERAL MANAGER HERE.
MY NAME IS HIBINO.
PLEASE TELL ME WHAT SORT OF SYMPTOMS YOUR DOG HAD AFTER HE HAD THE DOG FOOD YOU PURCHASED HERE.
WAS IT THE RIGHT AMOUNT?
I DON'T KNOW! I GAVE IT TO HIM LIKE I NORMALLY DO AND HE GOT DIARRHEA!
THAT DOG FOOD...DID YOU BRING THE REST WITH YOU BY ANY CHANCE?
I THREW IT OUT ALREADY!!
WHAT! ARE YOU SAYING I'M LYING? HUUUH?!
NO, THAT IS NOT WHAT I AM SAYING.
IT'S JUST THAT WE TAKE PRIDE IN OUR QUALITY CONTROL HERE, SO...

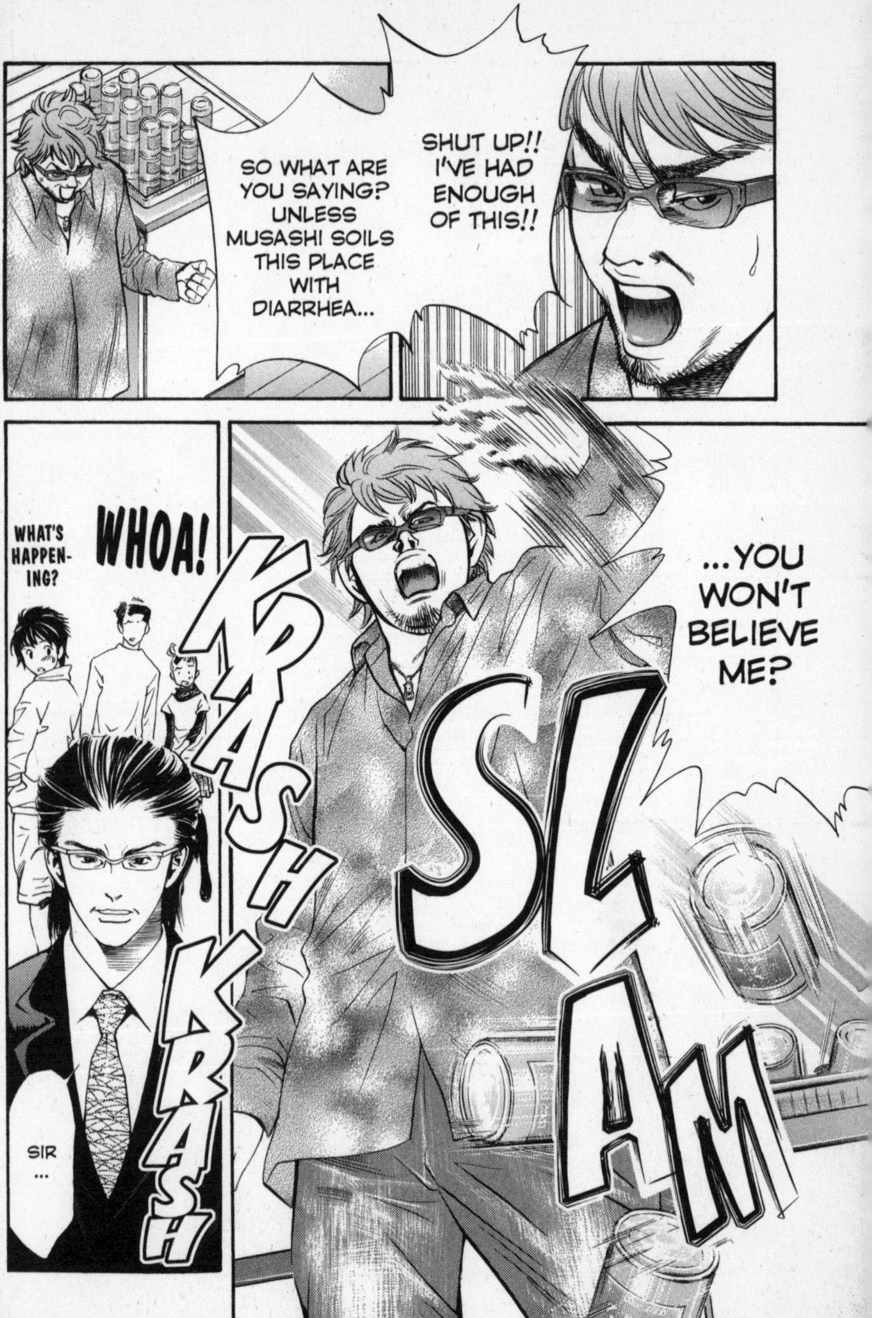
SHUT UP!! I'VE HAD ENOUGH OF THIS!!
SO WHAT ARE YOU SAYING? UNLESS MUSASHI SOILS THIS PLACE WITH DIARRHEA...
...YOU WON'T BELIEVE ME?
SLAM
KRASH
KRASH
WHOA!
WHAT'S HAPPEN-ING?
SIR ...

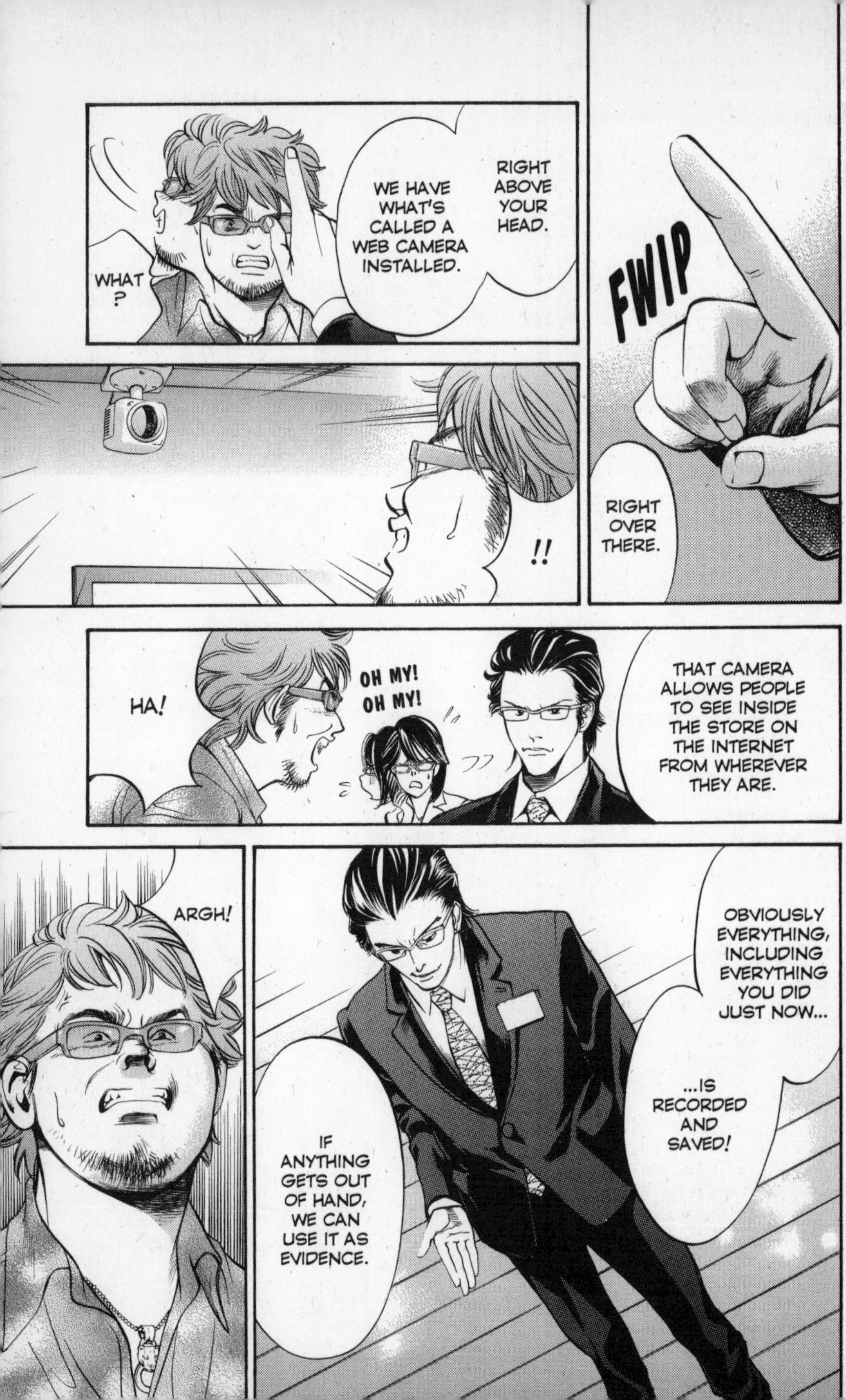
FWIP
RIGHT OVER THERE.
WE HAVE WHAT'S CALLED A WEB CAMERA INSTALLED. RIGHT ABOVE YOUR HEAD.
WHAT ?
!!
THAT CAMERA ALLOWS PEOPLE TO SEE INSIDE THE STORE ON THE INTERNET FROM WHEREVER THEY ARE.
OH MY! OH MY!
HA!
OBVIOUSLY EVERYTHING, INCLUDING EVERYTHING YOU DID JUST NOW...
...IS RECORDED AND SAVED!
IF ANYTHING GETS OUT OF HAND, WE CAN USE IT AS EVIDENCE.
ARGH!

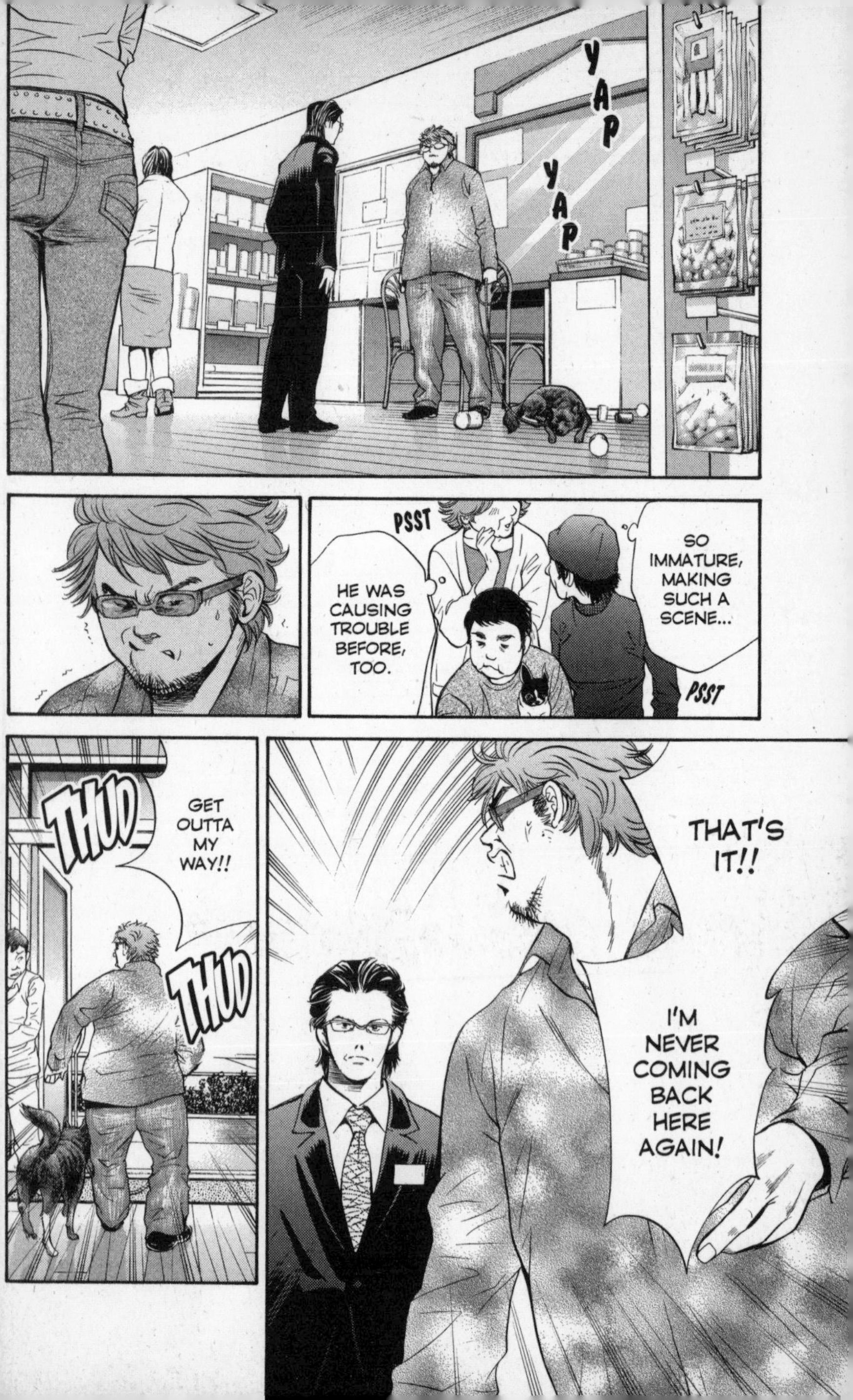
YAP YAP
YAP YAP
SO IMMATURE, MAKING SUCH A SCENE...
PSST
HE WAS CAUSING TROUBLE BEFORE, TOO.
PSST
THAT'S IT!!
I'M NEVER COMING BACK HERE AGAIN!
THUD
GET OUTTA MY WAY!!
THUD

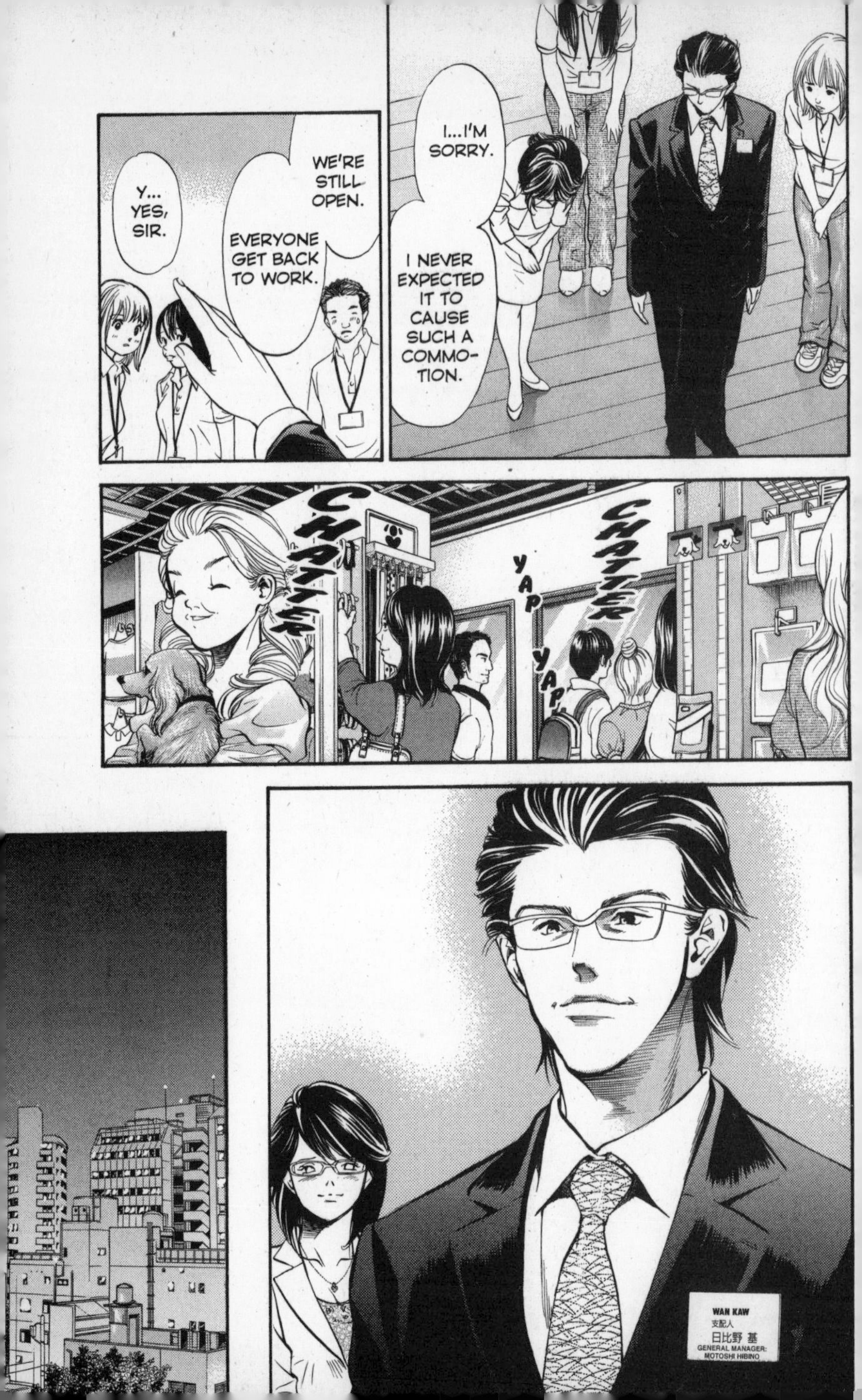
I...I'M SORRY.
I NEVER EXPECTED IT TO CAUSE SUCH A COMMOTION.
WE'RE STILL OPEN.
EVERYONE GET BACK TO WORK.
Y... YES, SIR.
CHATTER
YAP YAP
CHATTER
WAN KAW
支配人
日比野 基
GENERAL MANAGER: MOTOSHI HIBINO

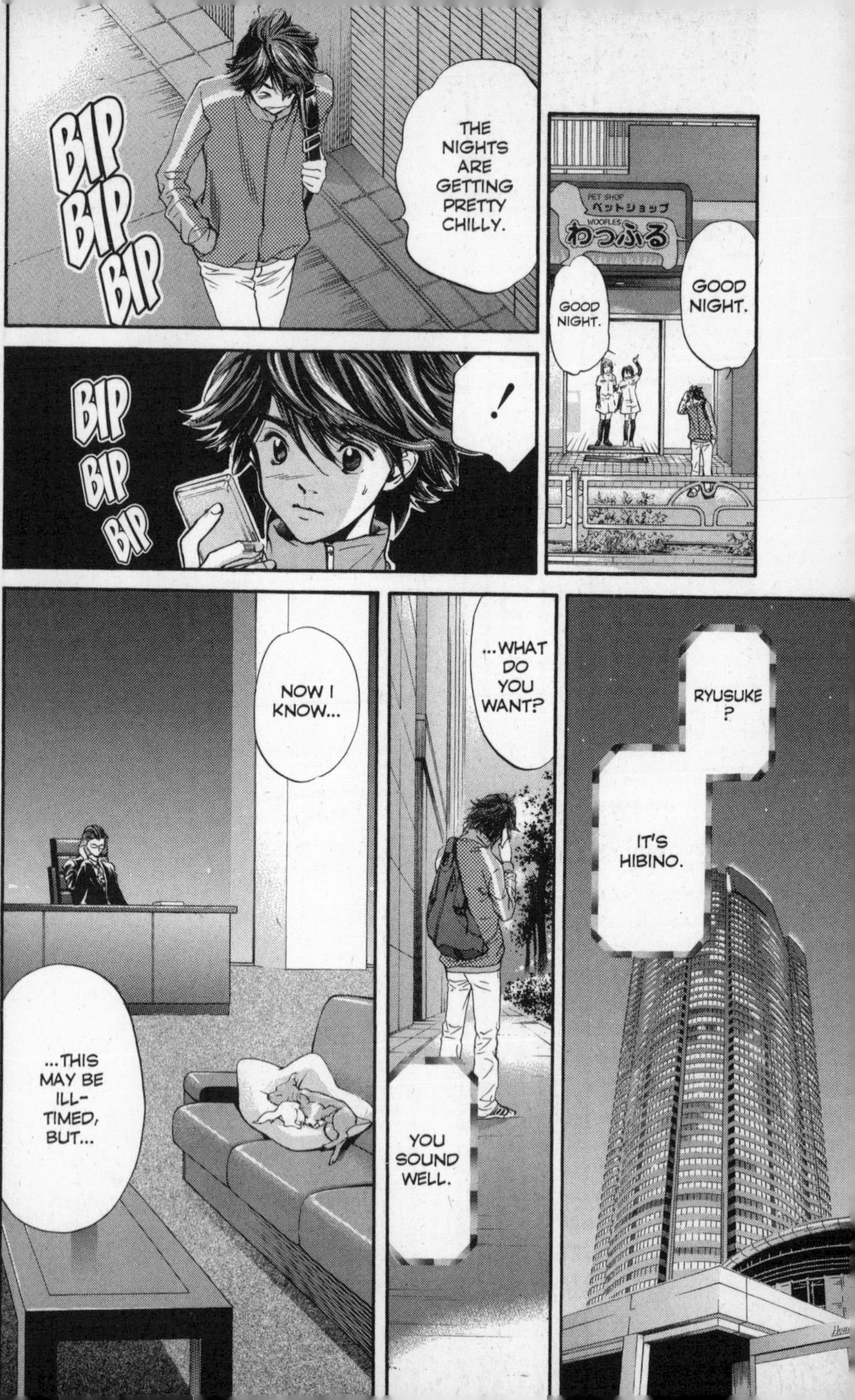
PET SHOP
ペットショップ
WOOFLES
わつふる
GOOD NIGHT.
GOOD NIGHT.
BIP BIP BIP
THE NIGHTS ARE GETTING PRETTY CHILLY.
BIP BIP BIP
!
RYUSUKE?
IT'S HIBINO.
...WHAT DO YOU WANT?
YOU SOUND WELL.
NOW I KNOW...
...THIS MAY BE ILL-TIMED, BUT...

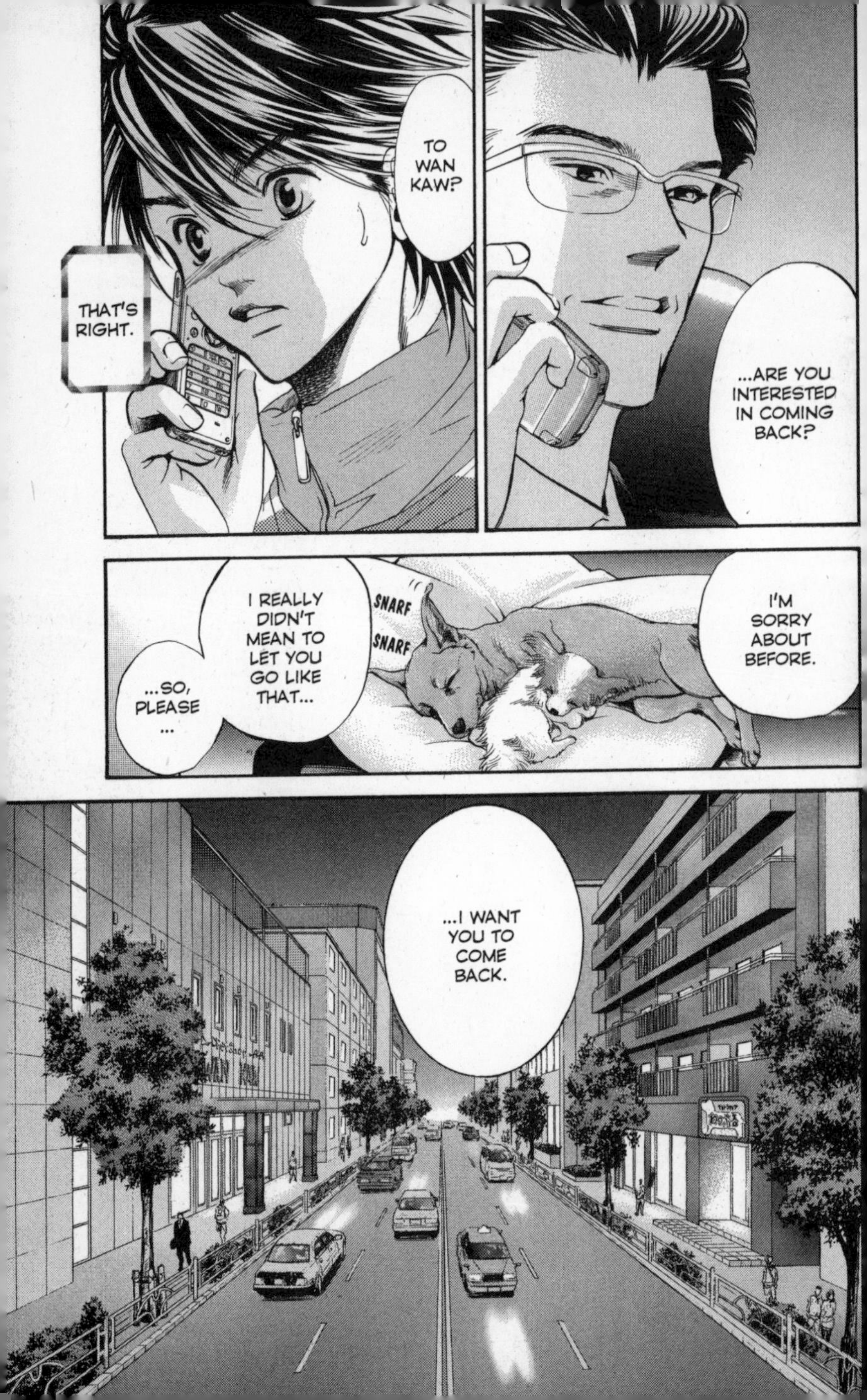
...ARE YOU INTERESTED IN COMING BACK?
TO WAN KAW?
THAT'S RIGHT.
I'M SORRY ABOUT BEFORE.
SNARF
SNARF
I REALLY DIDN'T MEAN TO LET YOU GO LIKE THAT...
...SO, PLEASE ...
...I WANT YOU TO COME BACK.

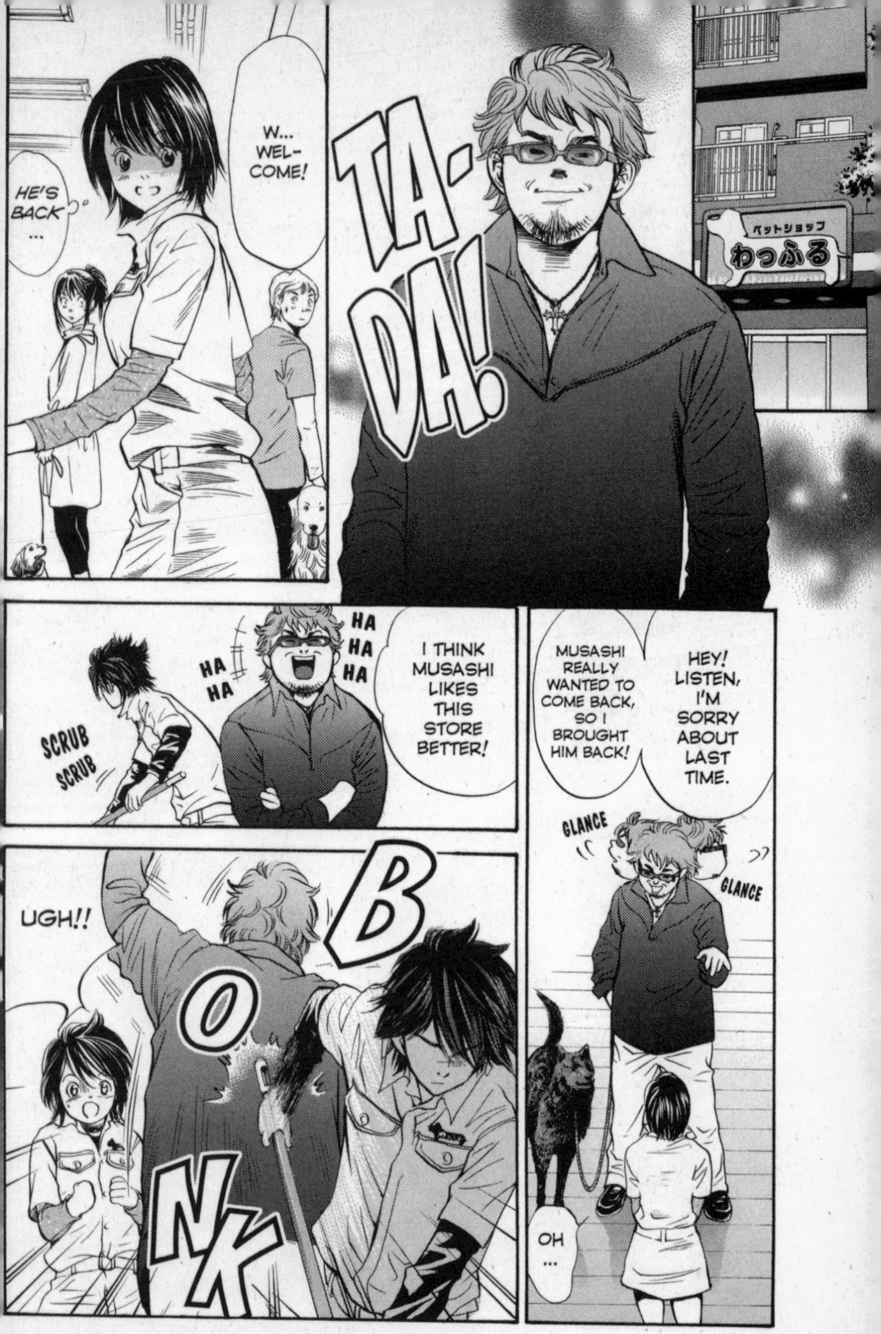
ペットショップ
わっふる
TA-DA!
W... WEL-COME!
HE'S BACK ...
HEY! LISTEN, I'M SORRY ABOUT LAST TIME.
MUSASHI REALLY WANTED TO COME BACK, SO I BROUGHT HIM BACK!
GLANCE
GLANCE
OH ...
I THINK MUSASHI LIKES THIS STORE BETTER!
HA HA HA
HA HA
SCRUB SCRUB
BONK
UGH!!

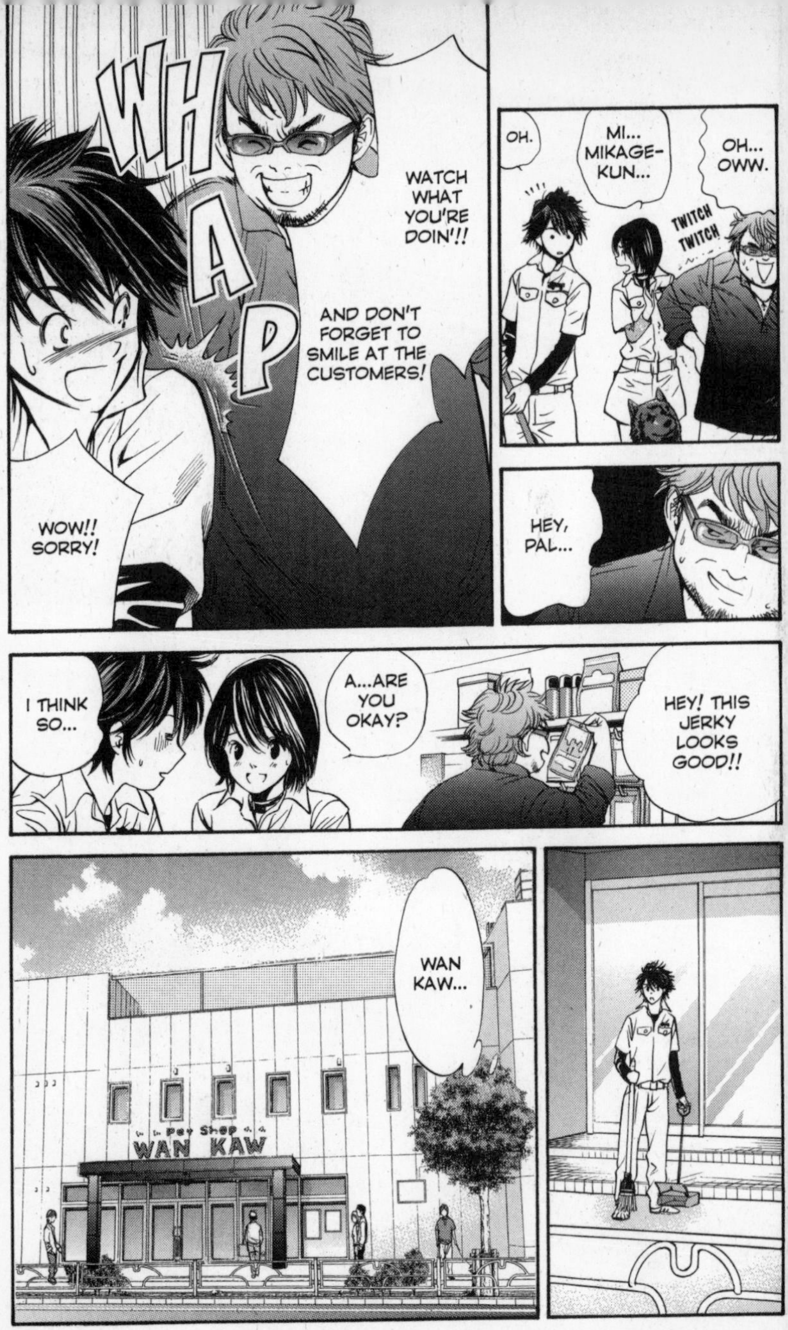
OH... OWW.
MI... MIKAGE-KUN...
OH.
TWITCH TWITCH
HEY, PAL...
WHAP
WATCH WHAT YOU'RE DOIN'!!
AND DON'T FORGET TO SMILE AT THE CUSTOMERS!
WOW!! SORRY!
HEY! THIS JERKY LOOKS GOOD!!
A...ARE YOU OKAY?
I THINK SO...
WAN KAW...
Pet Shop
WAN KAW

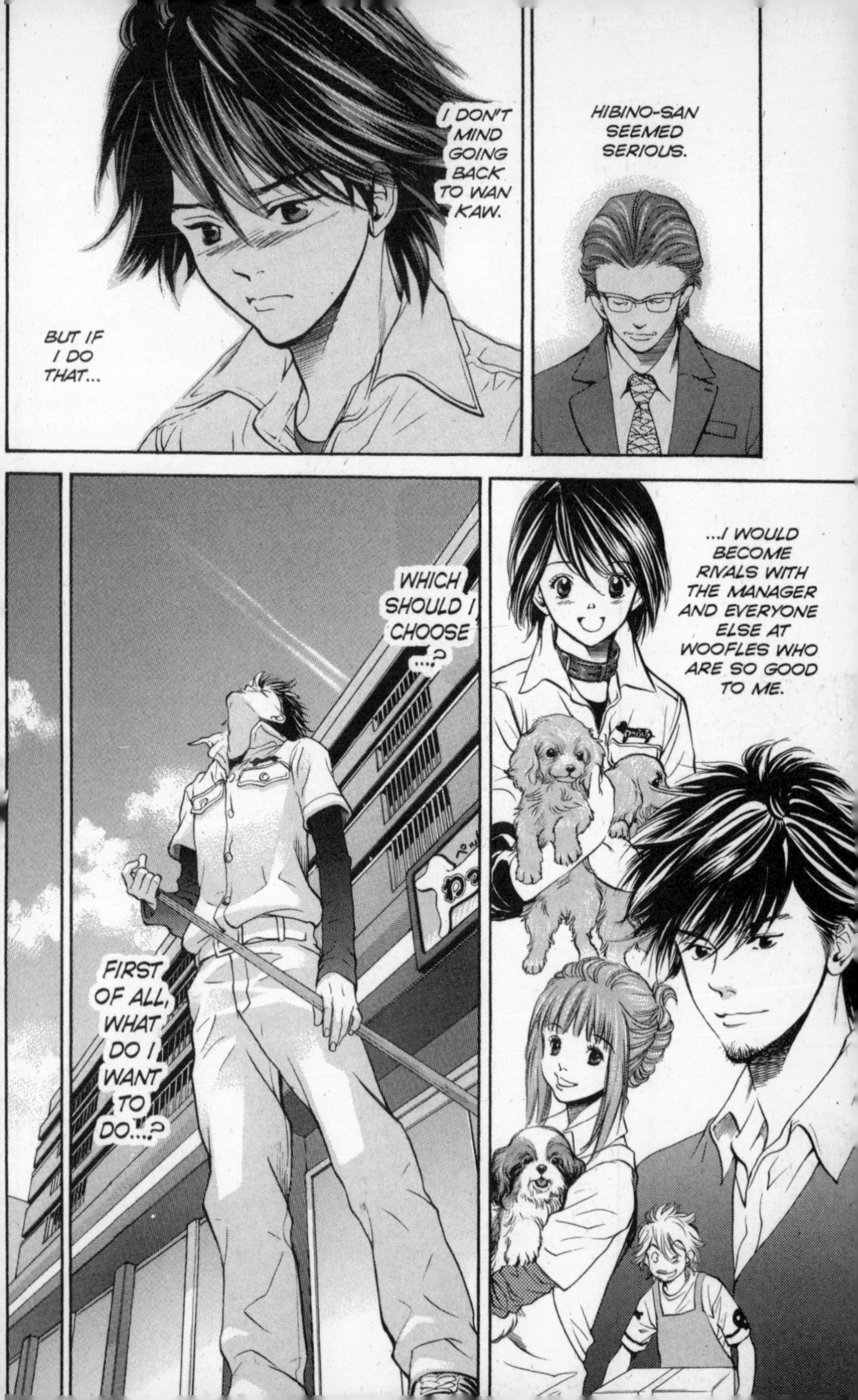
HIBINO-SAN SEEMED SERIOUS.
I DON'T MIND GOING BACK TO WAN KAW.
BUT IF I DO THAT...
...I WOULD BECOME RIVALS WITH THE MANAGER AND EVERYONE ELSE AT WOOFLES WHO ARE SO GOOD TO ME.
WHICH SHOULD I CHOOSE ...?
FIRST OF ALL, WHAT DO I WANT TO DO...?

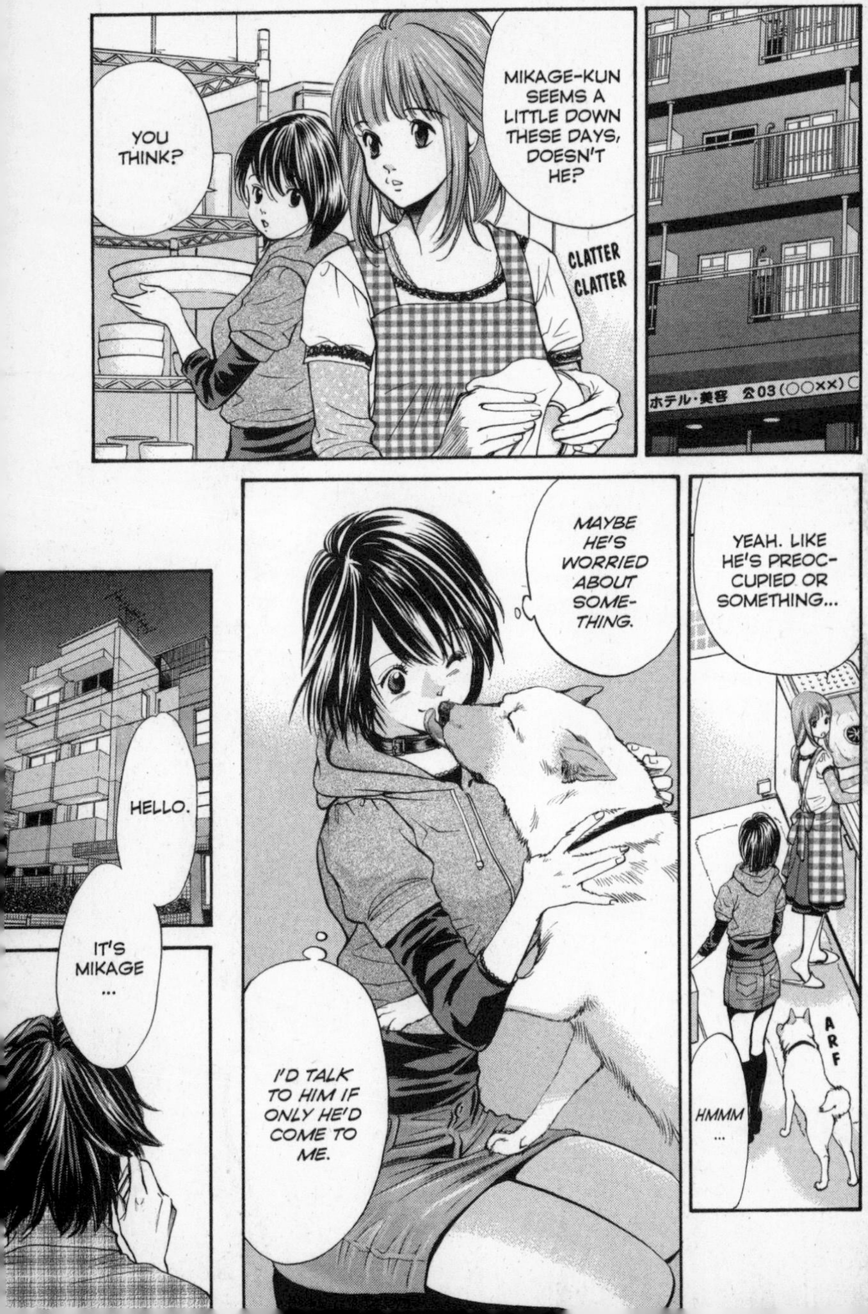

ホテル・美容
MIKAGE-KUN SEEMS A LITTLE DOWN THESE DAYS, DOESN'T HE?
YOU THINK?
CLATTER CLATTER
YEAH. LIKE HE'S PREOCCUPIED OR SOMETHING...
HMMM ...
ARF
MAYBE HE'S WORRIED ABOUT SOMETHING.
I'D TALK TO HIM IF ONLY HE'D COME TO ME.
HELLO.
IT'S MIKAGE ...

I THINK...

...I'M QUITTING WOOFLES SOON.

I'VE DECIDED.

NO.

I SEE. THEN...

WHA...

I'M SORRY BUT...

...I'M NOT GOING BACK TO WAN KAW EITHER!

CHAPTER 113: THE GUY STUCK IN BETWEEN

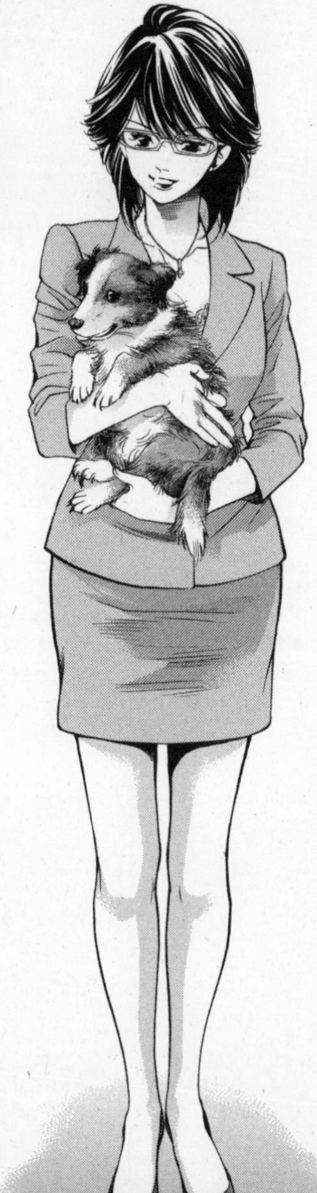

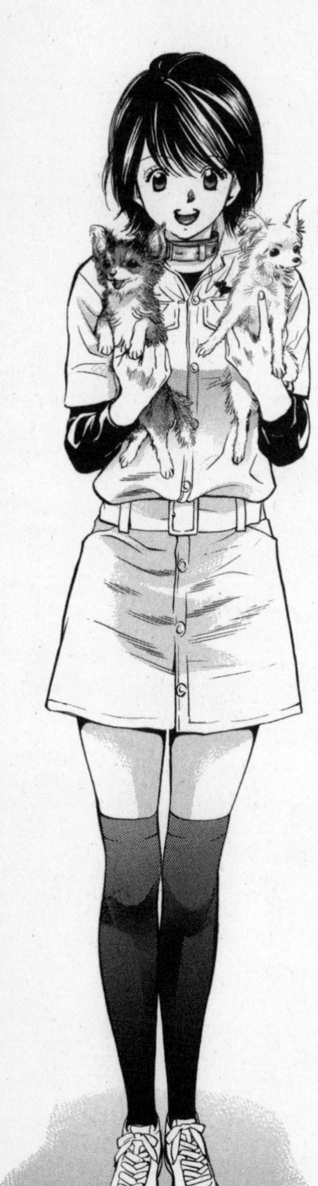

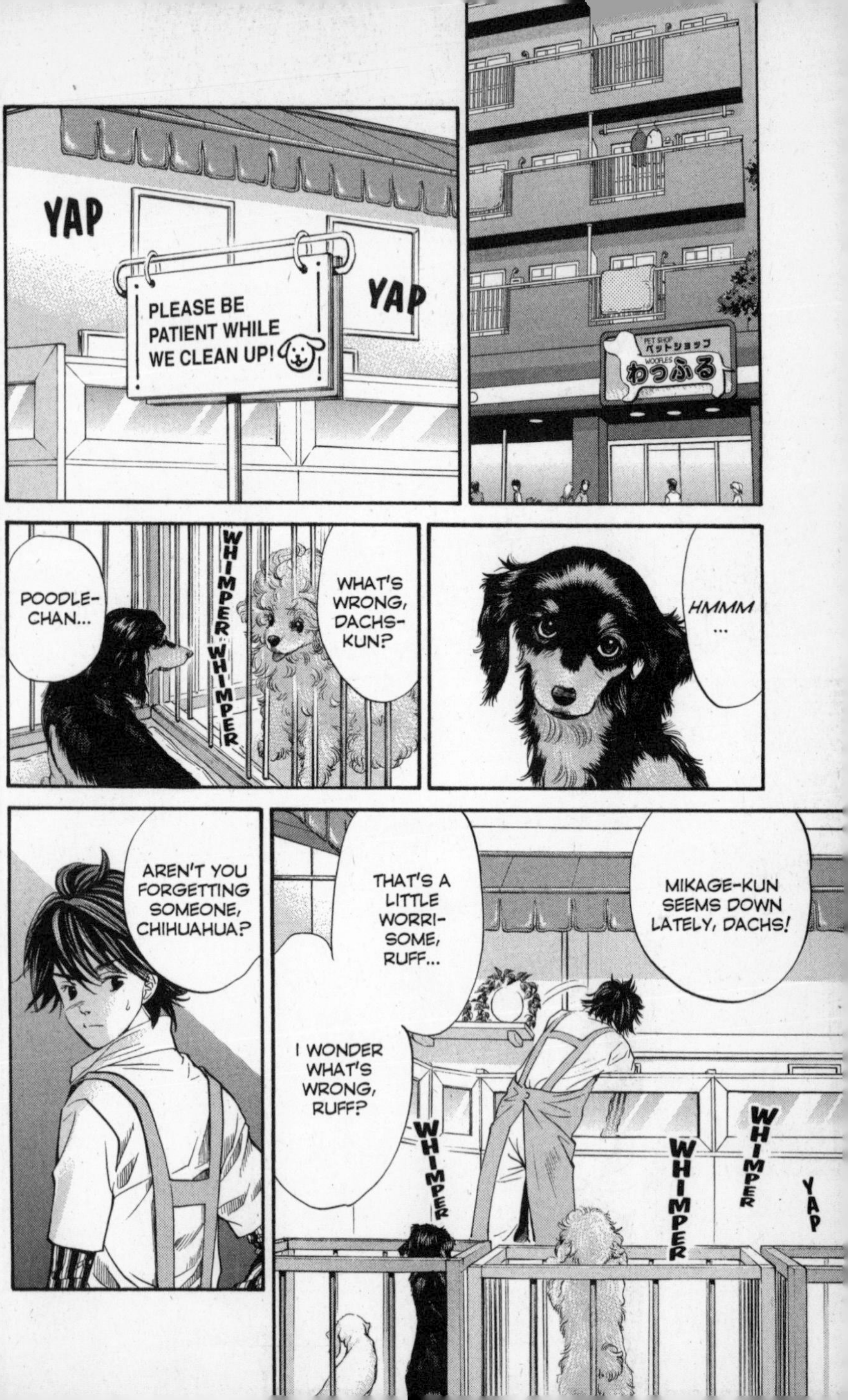
PET SHOP
ペットショップ
WOOFLES
わっふる
YAP
YAP
PLEASE BE PATIENT WHILE WE CLEAN UP!
HMMM ...
WHAT'S WRONG, DACHS-KUN?
WHIMPER WHIMPER
POODLE-CHAN...
MIKAGE-KUN SEEMS DOWN LATELY, DACHS!
THAT'S A LITTLE WORRI-SOME, RUFF...
I WONDER WHAT'S WRONG, RUFF?
YAP
WHIMPER
WHIMPER
WHIMPER
AREN'T YOU FORGETTING SOMEONE, CHIHUAHUA?

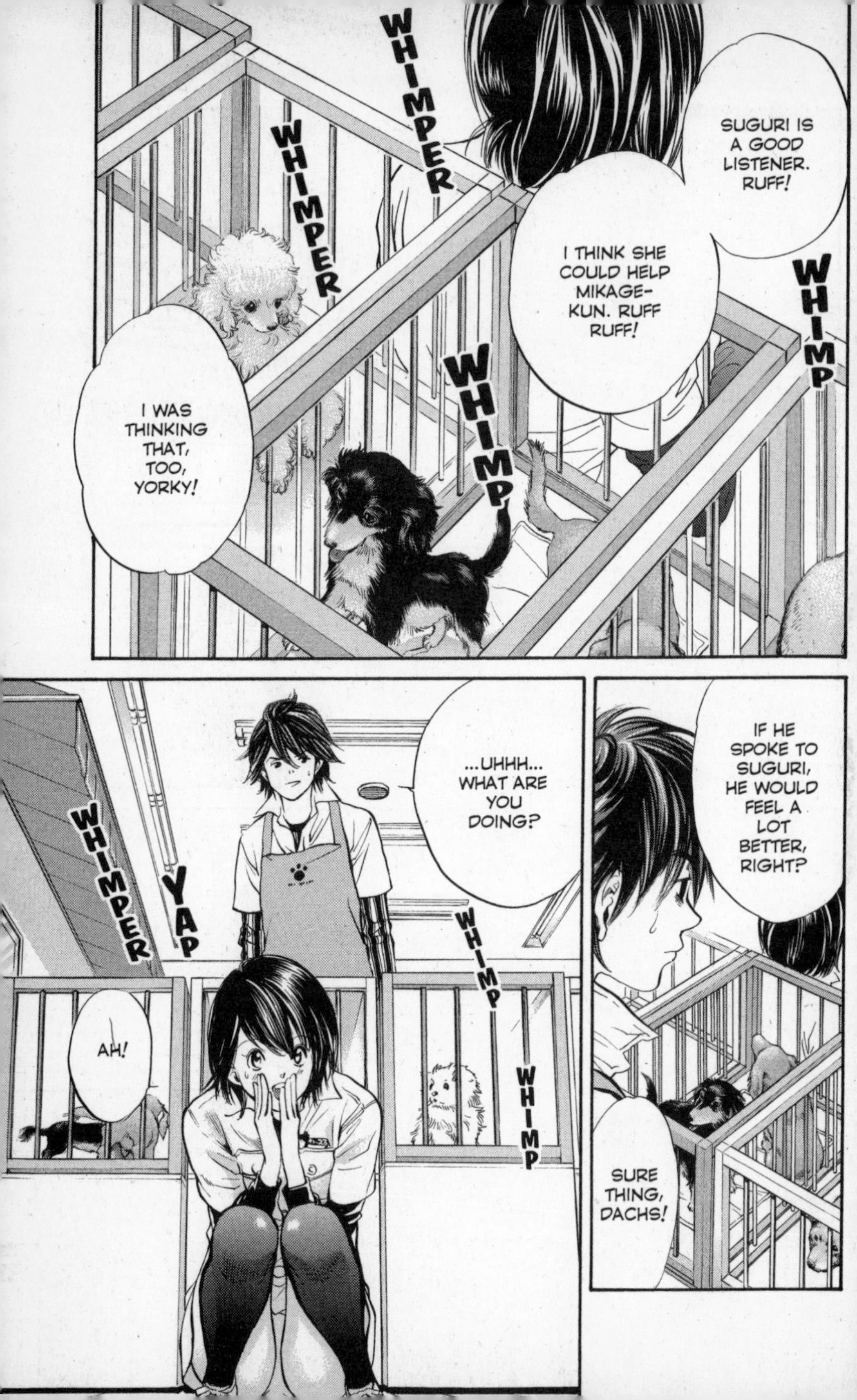
SUGURI IS A GOOD LISTENER. RUFF!
WHIMPER
WHIMPER
I THINK SHE COULD HELP MIKAGE-KUN. RUFF RUFF!
WHIMP
WHIMP
I WAS THINKING THAT, TOO, YORKY!
IF HE SPOKE TO SUGURI, HE WOULD FEEL A LOT BETTER, RIGHT?
SURE THING, DACHS!
...UHHH... WHAT ARE YOU DOING?
WHIMP
YAP
WHIMPER
WHIMP
AH!

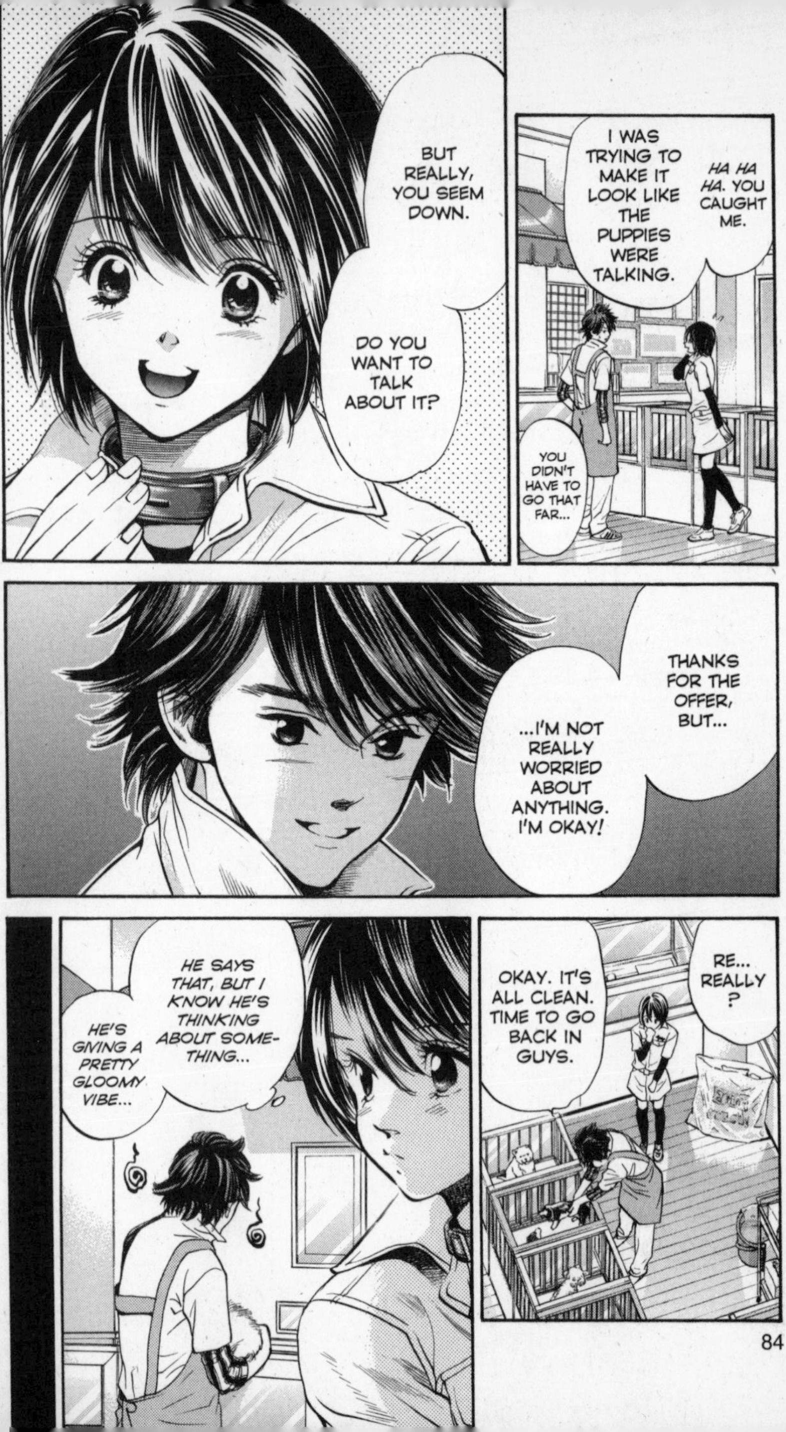
HA HA HA. YOU CAUGHT ME.
I WAS TRYING TO MAKE IT LOOK LIKE THE PUPPIES WERE TALKING.
YOU DIDN'T HAVE TO GO THAT FAR...
BUT REALLY, YOU SEEM DOWN.
DO YOU WANT TO TALK ABOUT IT?
THANKS FOR THE OFFER, BUT...
...I'M NOT REALLY WORRIED ABOUT ANYTHING. I'M OKAY!
RE... REALLY?
OKAY. IT'S ALL CLEAN. TIME TO GO BACK IN GUYS.
HE SAYS THAT, BUT I KNOW HE'S THINKING ABOUT SOME-THING...
HE'S GIVING A PRETTY GLOOMY VIBE...

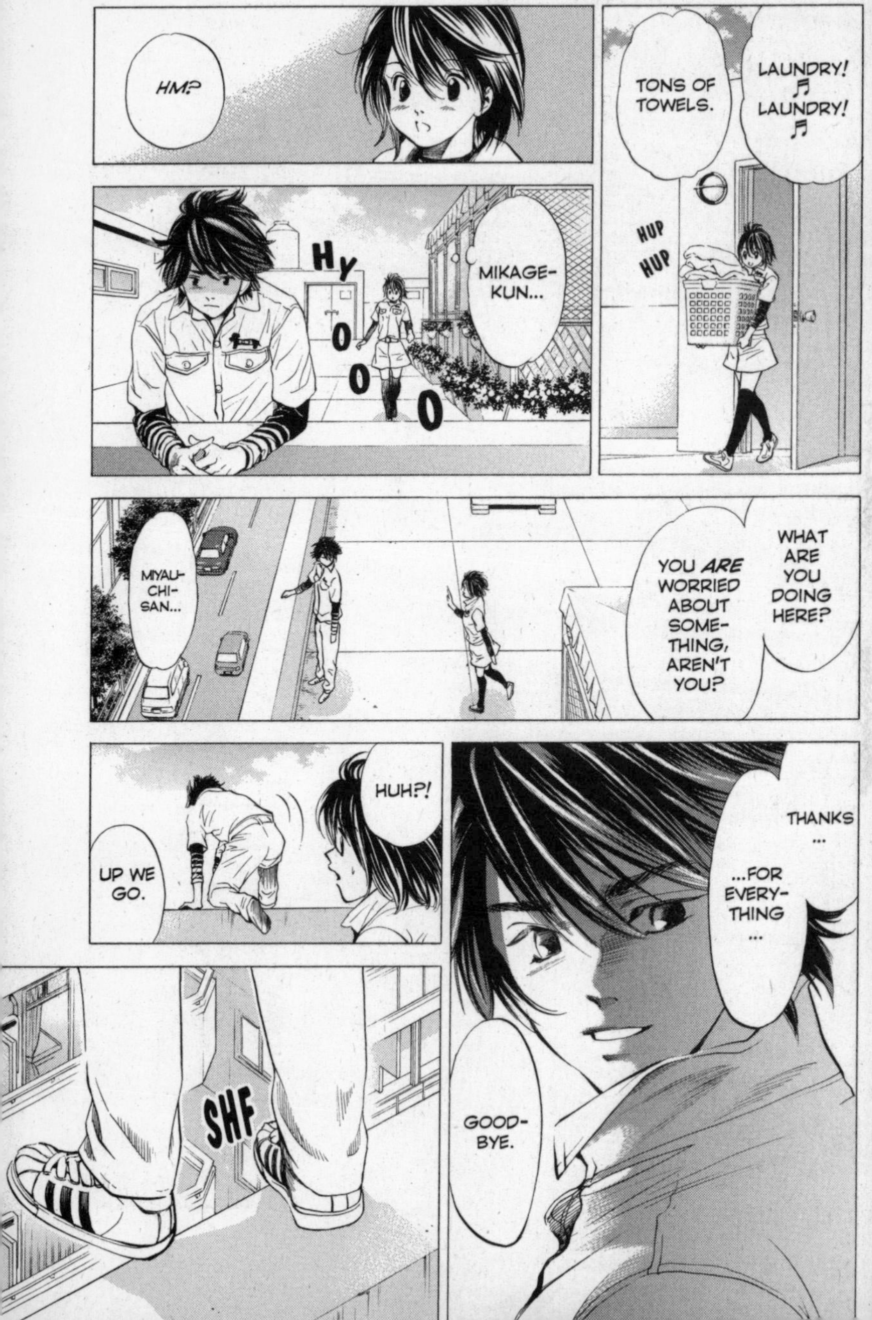

LAUNDRY! ♬ LAUNDRY! ♬
TONS OF TOWELS.
HUP HUP
HM?
MIKAGE-KUN...
HYOOO
WHAT ARE YOU DOING HERE?
YOU *ARE* WORRIED ABOUT SOMETHING, AREN'T YOU?
MIYAUCHI-SAN...
THANKS...
...FOR EVERYTHING...
GOODBYE.
HUH?!
UP WE GO.
SHF

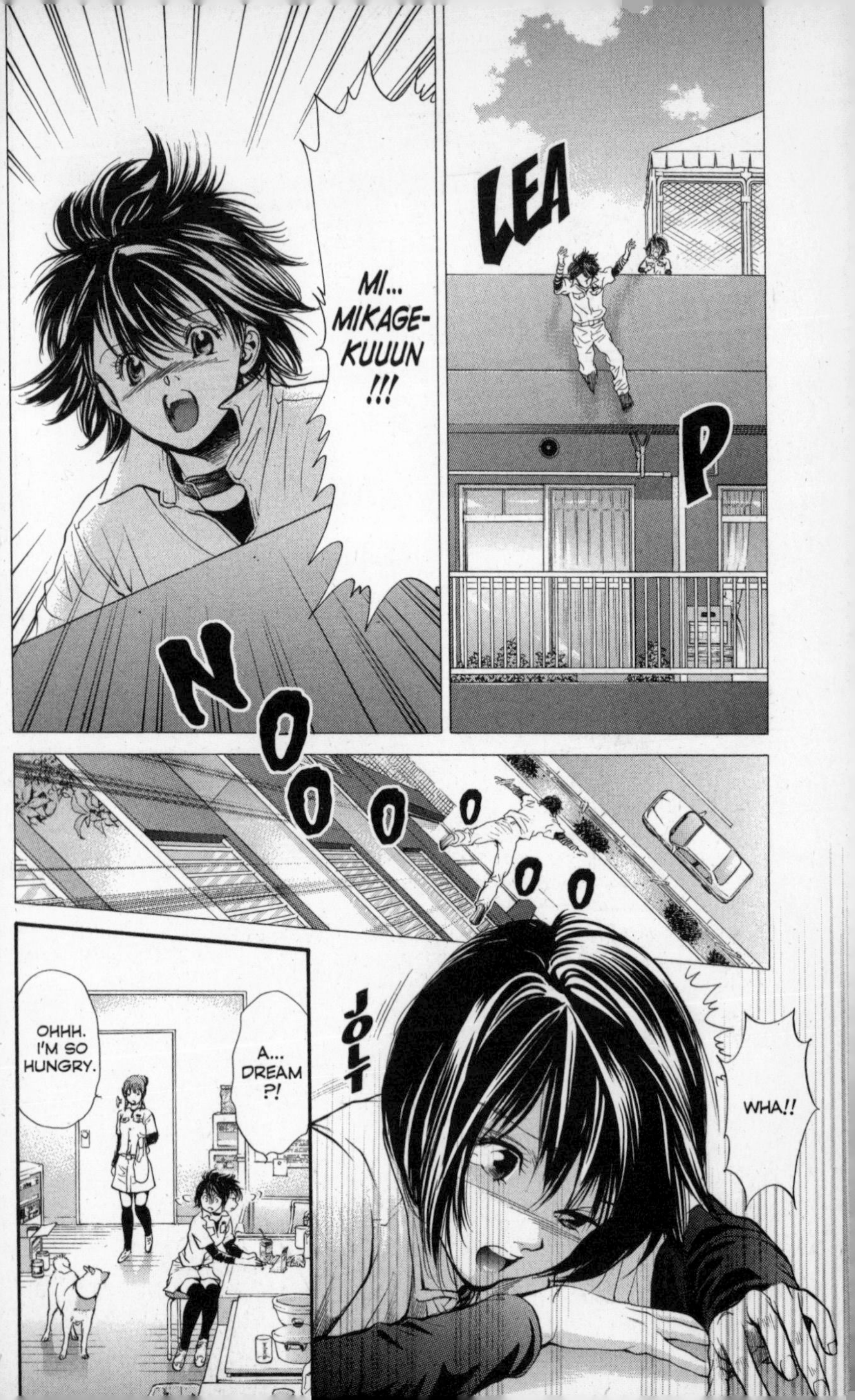
LEAP
MI... MIKAGE-KUUUN!!!
NOOOOOO
JOLT
WHA!!
A... DREAM?!
OHHH. I'M SO HUNGRY.

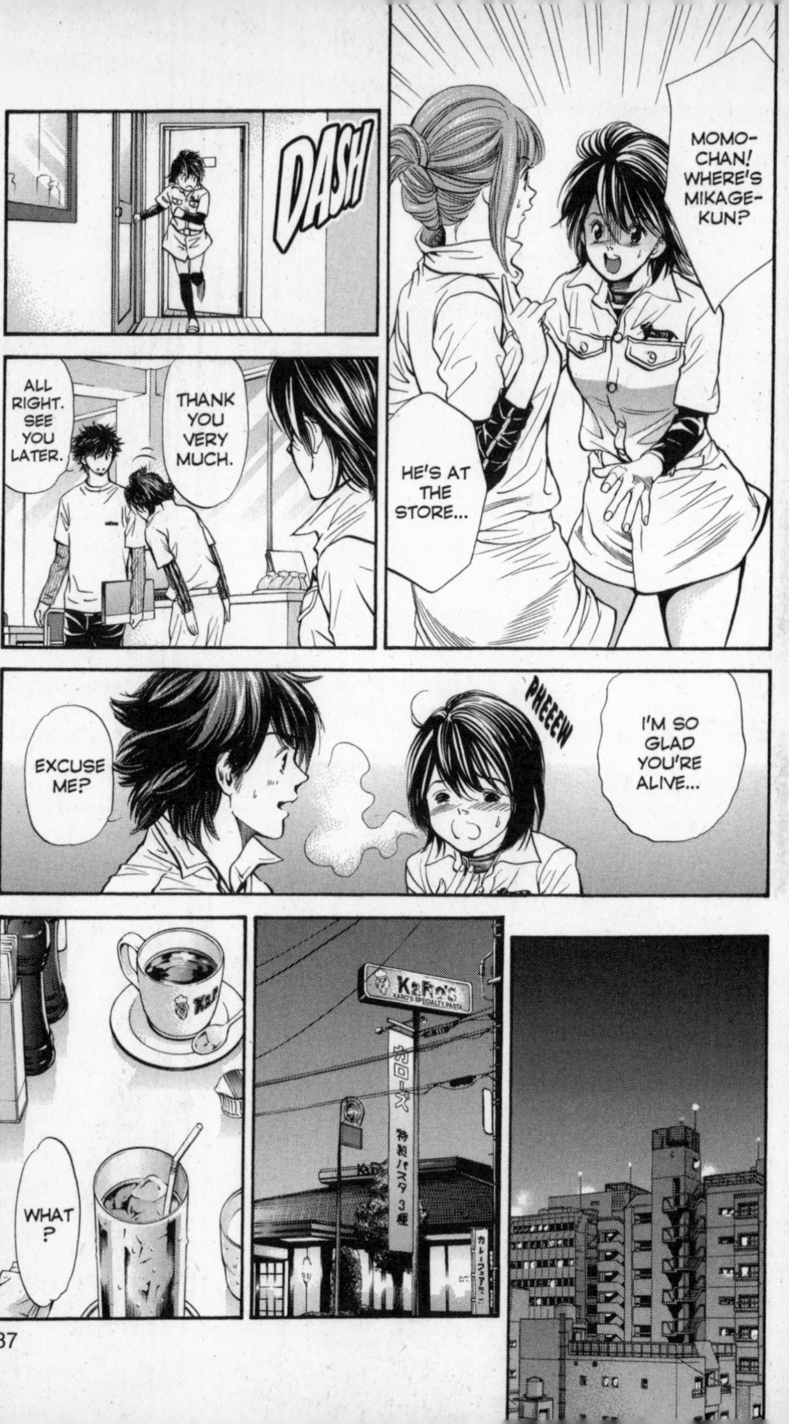
MOMO-CHAN! WHERE'S MIKAGE-KUN?
HE'S AT THE STORE...
DASH
THANK YOU VERY MUCH.
ALL RIGHT. SEE YOU LATER.
I'M SO GLAD YOU'RE ALIVE...
PHEEEW
EXCUSE ME?
KaRo's
KARO'S SPECIALTY PASTA
カローズ
特製パスタ 3種
WHAT?

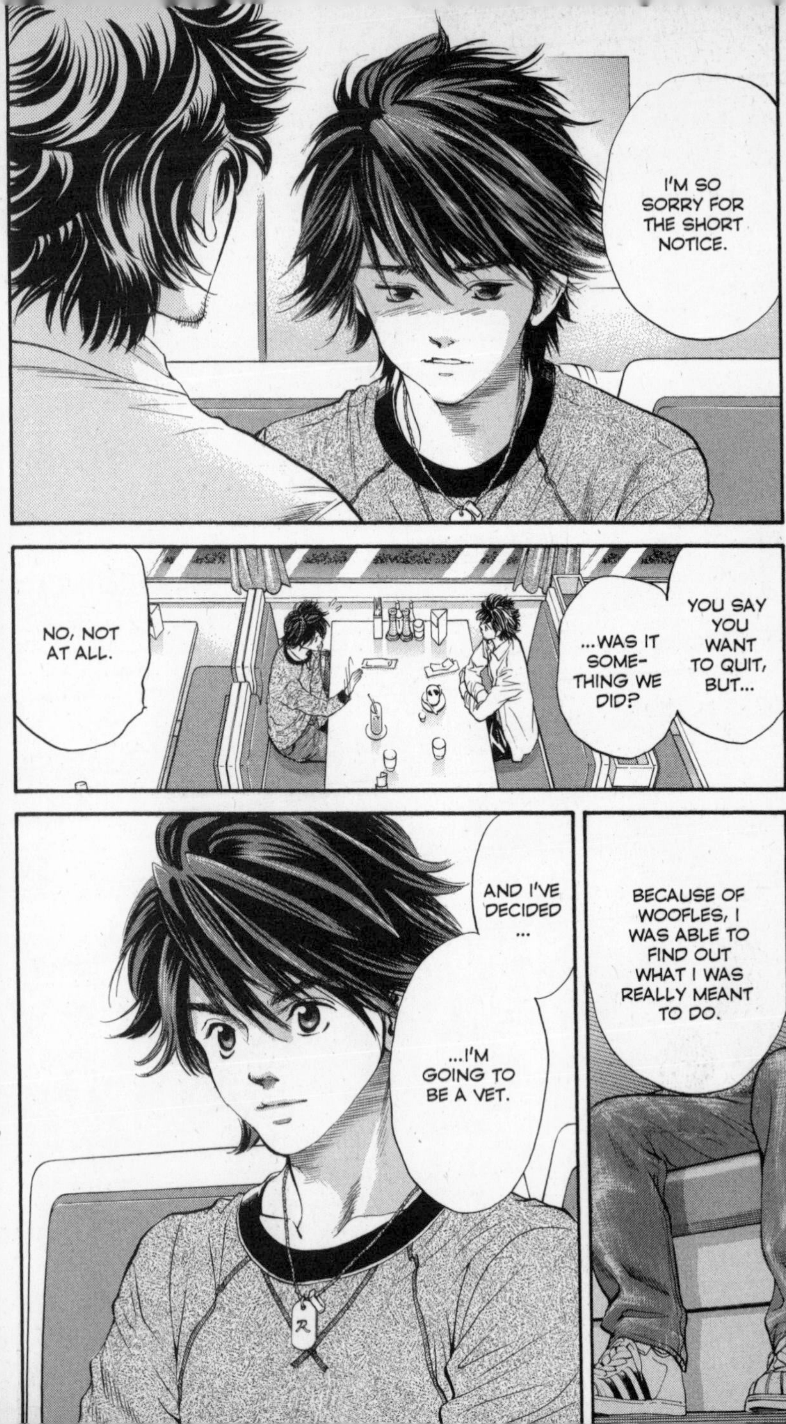
I'M SO SORRY FOR THE SHORT NOTICE.
YOU SAY YOU WANT TO QUIT, BUT...
...WAS IT SOMETHING WE DID?
NO, NOT AT ALL.
BECAUSE OF WOOFLES, I WAS ABLE TO FIND OUT WHAT I WAS REALLY MEANT TO DO.
AND I'VE DECIDED ...
...I'M GOING TO BE A VET.

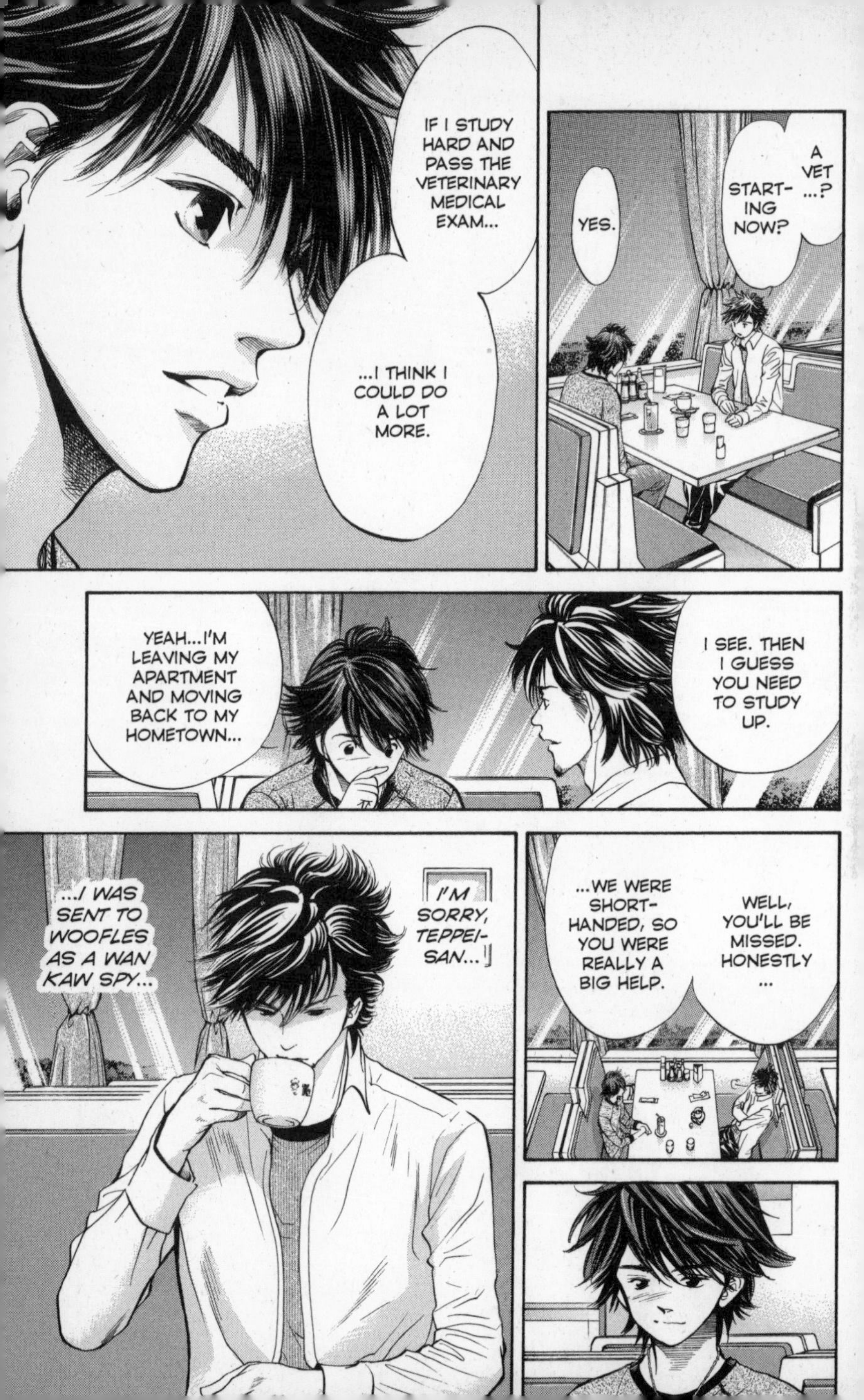
A VET ...?
STARTING NOW?
YES.
IF I STUDY HARD AND PASS THE VETERINARY MEDICAL EXAM...
...I THINK I COULD DO A LOT MORE.
I SEE. THEN I GUESS YOU NEED TO STUDY UP.
YEAH...I'M LEAVING MY APARTMENT AND MOVING BACK TO MY HOMETOWN...
WELL, YOU'LL BE MISSED. HONESTLY ...
...WE WERE SHORT-HANDED, SO YOU WERE REALLY A BIG HELP.
I'M SORRY, TEPPEI-SAN...
...I WAS SENT TO WOOFLES AS A WAN KAW SPY...

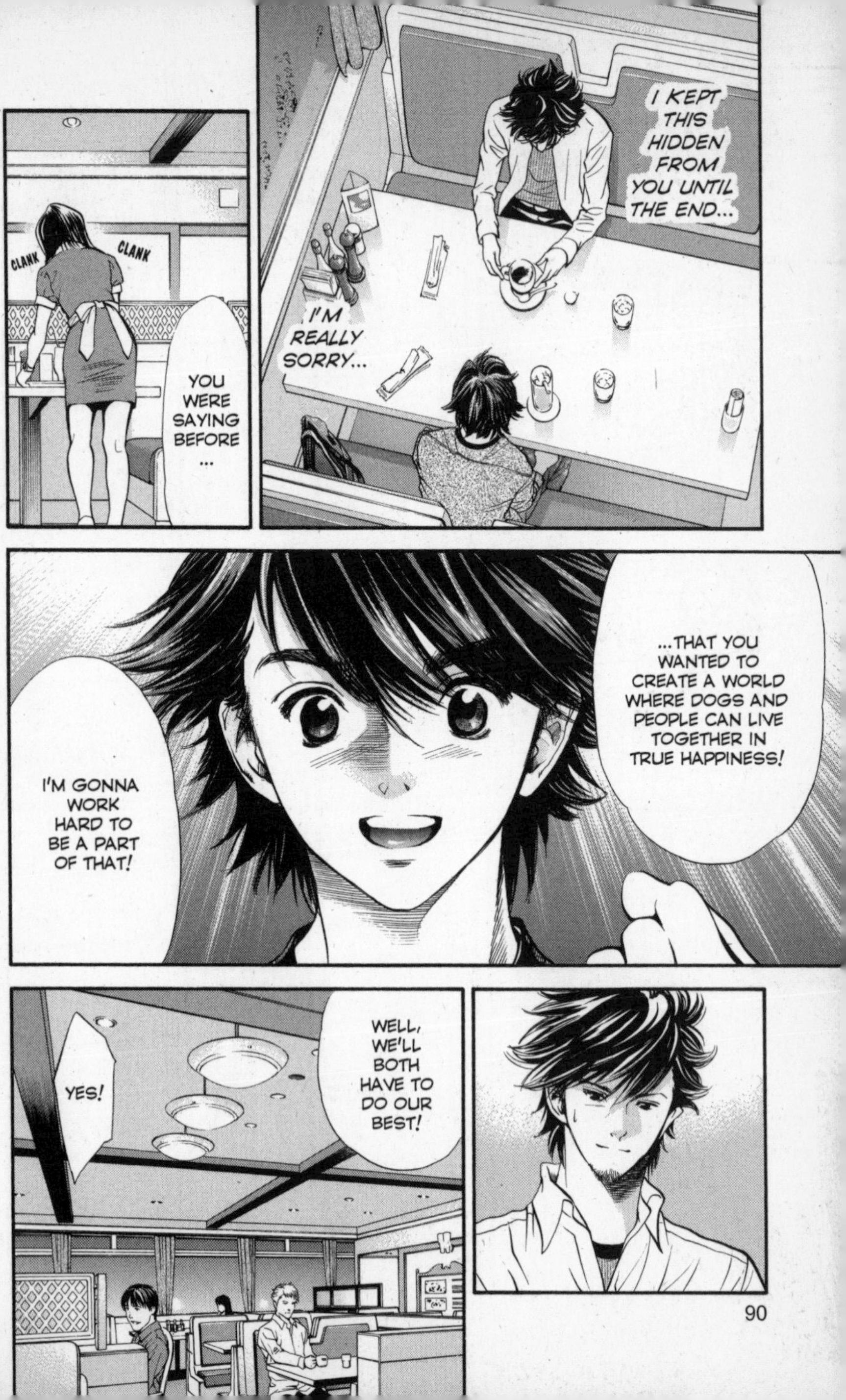
I KEPT THIS HIDDEN FROM YOU UNTIL THE END...
I'M REALLY SORRY...
CLANK
CLANK
YOU WERE SAYING BEFORE ...
...THAT YOU WANTED TO CREATE A WORLD WHERE DOGS AND PEOPLE CAN LIVE TOGETHER IN TRUE HAPPINESS!
I'M GONNA WORK HARD TO BE A PART OF THAT!
WELL, WE'LL BOTH HAVE TO DO OUR BEST!
YES!

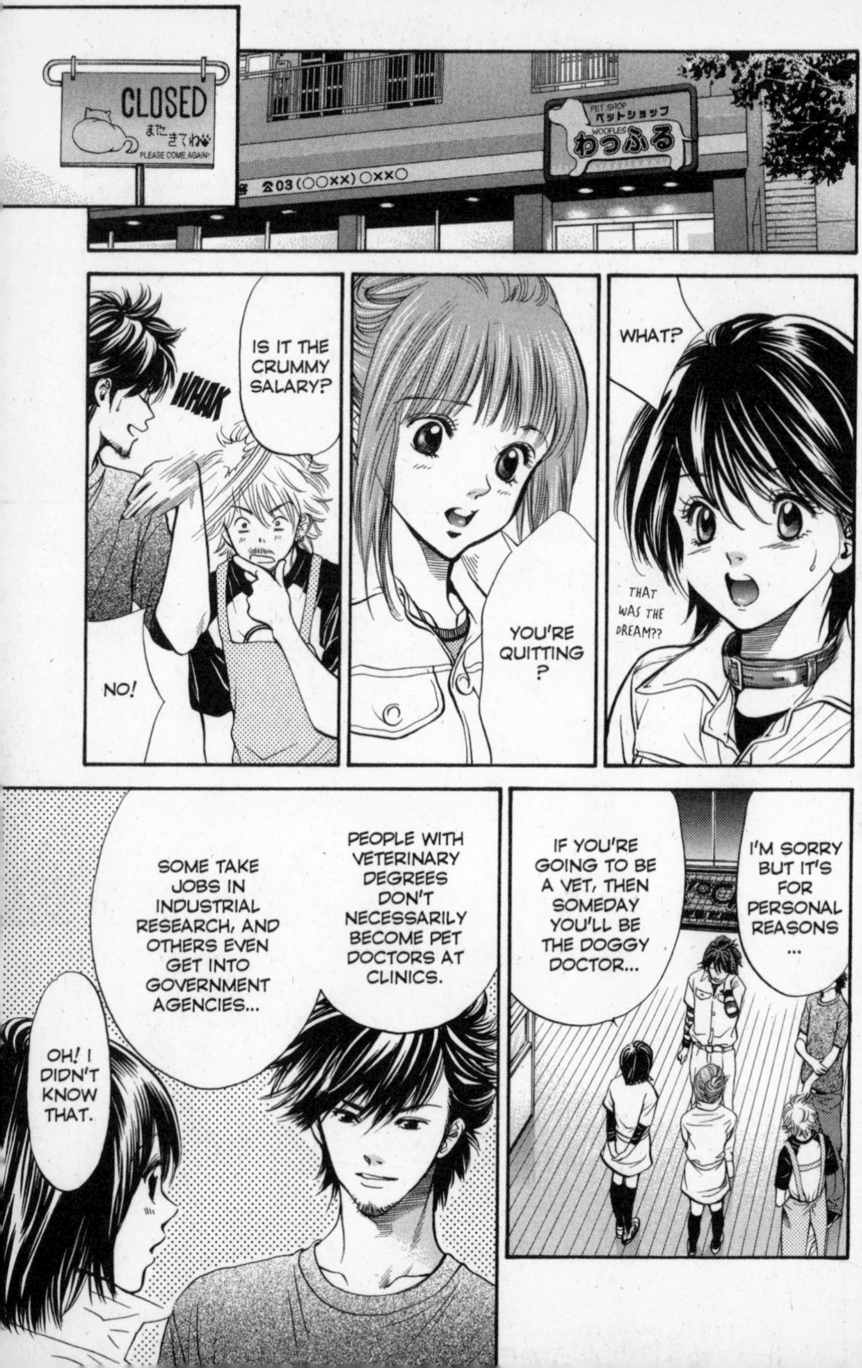
CLOSED
またきてね
PLEASE COME AGAIN!
PET SHOP ペットショップ
WOOFLES わつふる
☎03(○○XX)○XX○
WHAT?
THAT WAS THE DREAM??
YOU'RE QUITTING?
IS IT THE CRUMMY SALARY?
WHAK
NO!
I'M SORRY BUT IT'S FOR PERSONAL REASONS...
IF YOU'RE GOING TO BE A VET, THEN SOMEDAY YOU'LL BE THE DOGGY DOCTOR...
PEOPLE WITH VETERINARY DEGREES DON'T NECESSARILY BECOME PET DOCTORS AT CLINICS.
SOME TAKE JOBS IN INDUSTRIAL RESEARCH, AND OTHERS EVEN GET INTO GOVERNMENT AGENCIES...
OH! I DIDN'T KNOW THAT.

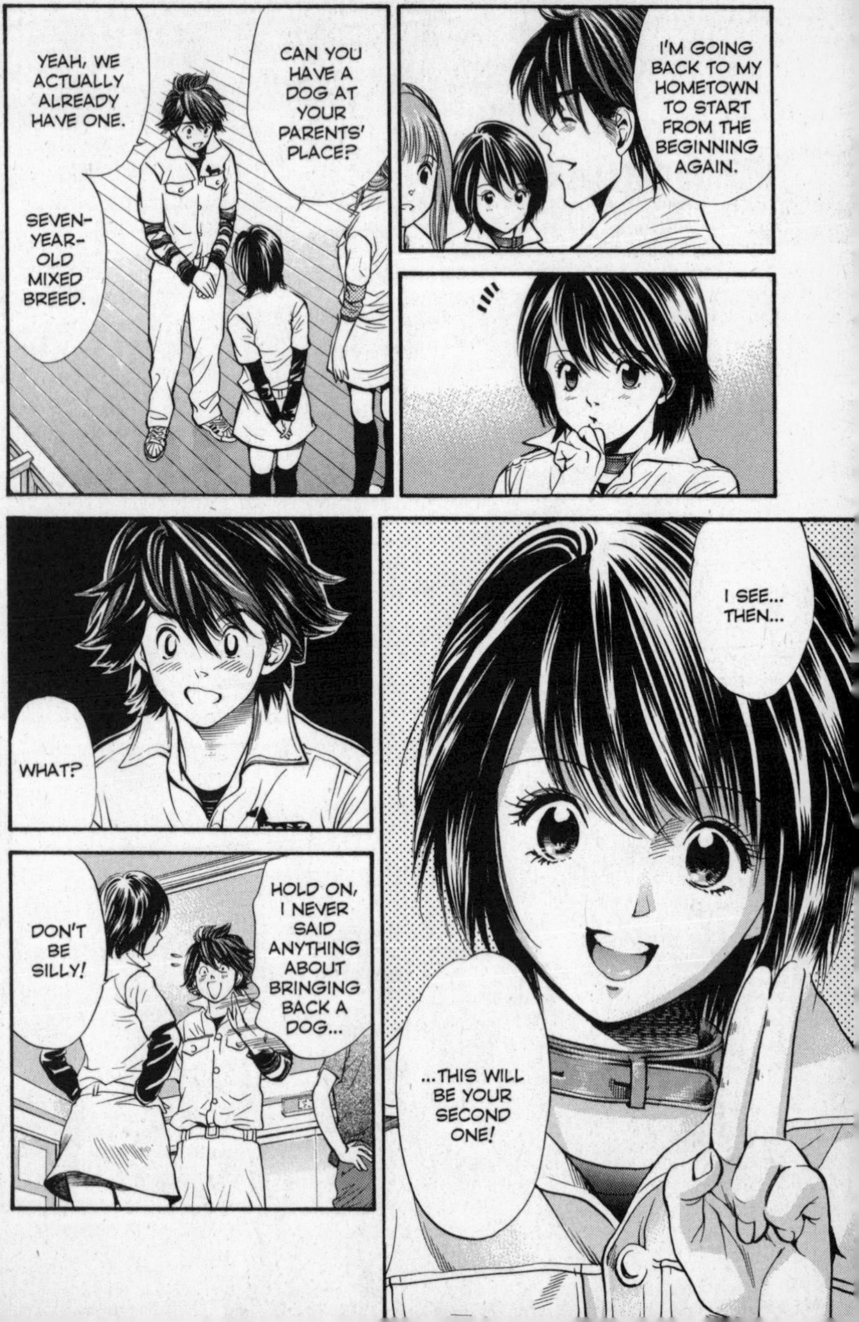
I'M GOING BACK TO MY HOMETOWN TO START FROM THE BEGINNING AGAIN.
CAN YOU HAVE A DOG AT YOUR PARENTS' PLACE?
YEAH, WE ACTUALLY ALREADY HAVE ONE.
SEVEN-YEAR-OLD MIXED BREED.
I SEE... THEN...
...THIS WILL BE YOUR SECOND ONE!
WHAT?
HOLD ON, I NEVER SAID ANYTHING ABOUT BRINGING BACK A DOG...
DON'T BE SILLY!

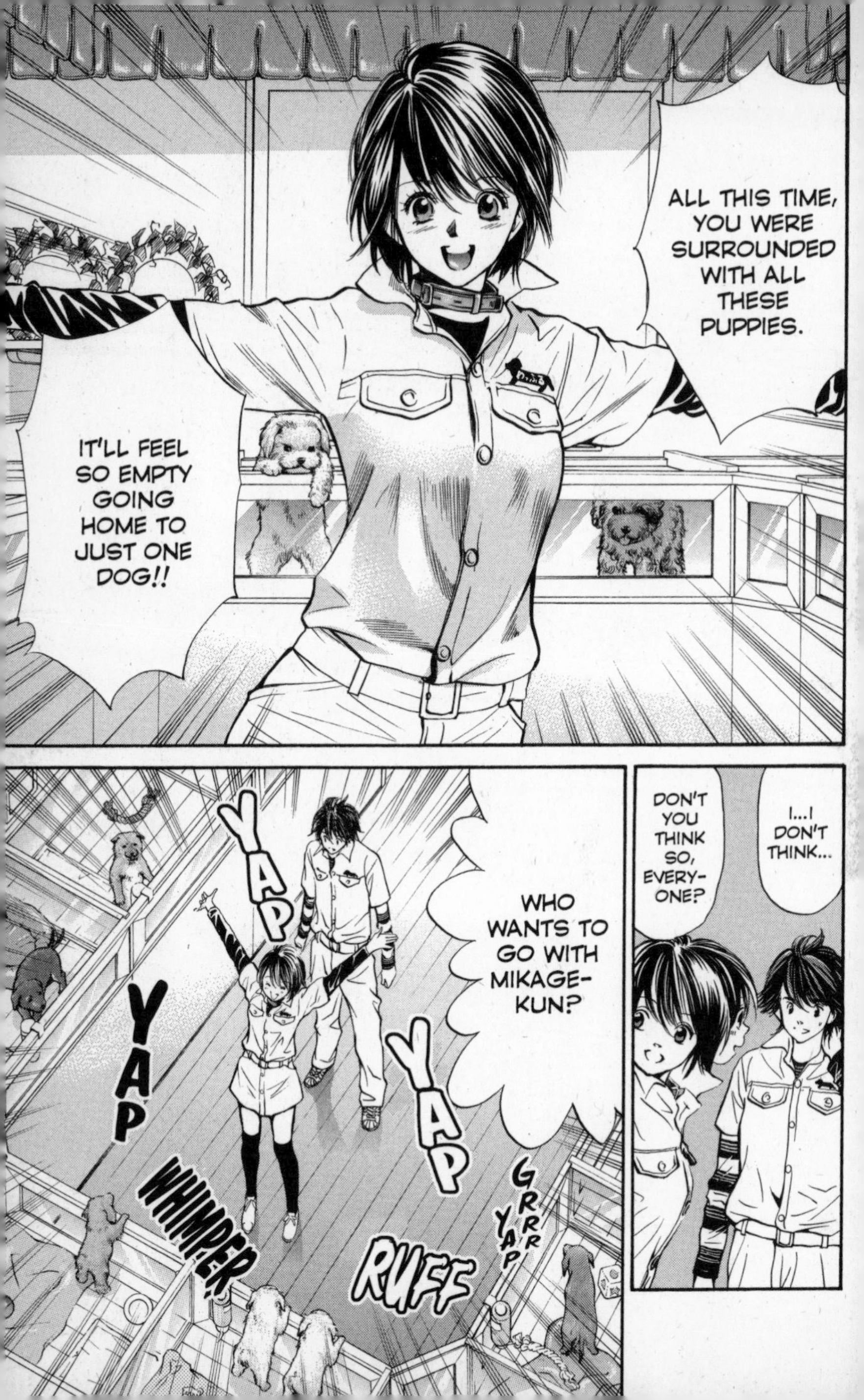
ALL THIS TIME, YOU WERE SURROUNDED WITH ALL THESE PUPPIES.
IT'LL FEEL SO EMPTY GOING HOME TO JUST ONE DOG!!
I...I DON'T THINK...
DON'T YOU THINK SO, EVERYONE?
WHO WANTS TO GO WITH MIKAGE-KUN?
YAP
YAP
YAP
GRRR
YAP
RUFF
WHIMPER

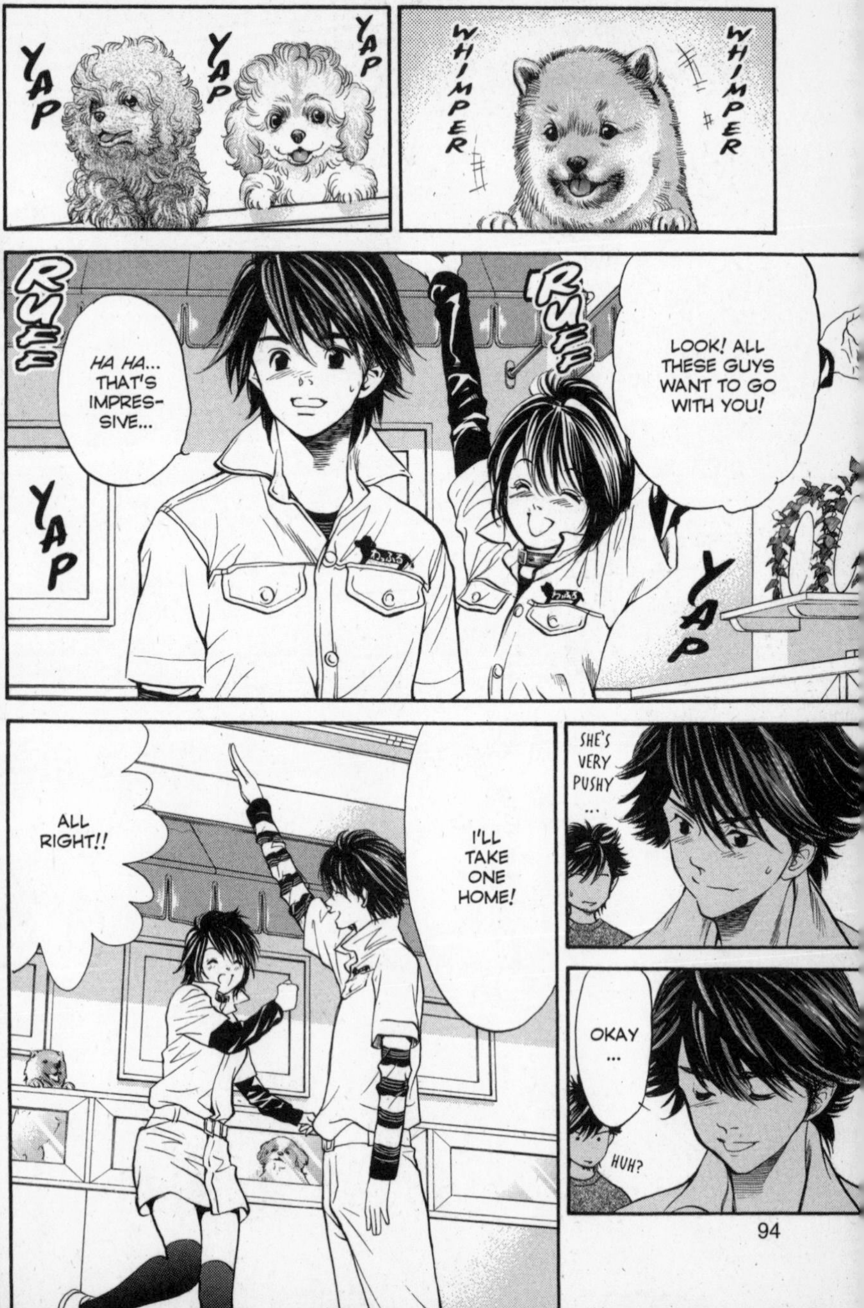
WHIMPER
WHIMPER
YAP YAP
YAP
YAP
RUFF
LOOK! ALL THESE GUYS WANT TO GO WITH YOU!
RUFF
HA HA... THAT'S IMPRES-SIVE...
YAP YAP
YAP YAP
SHE'S VERY PUSHY ...
OKAY ...
HUH?
I'LL TAKE ONE HOME!
ALL RIGHT!!

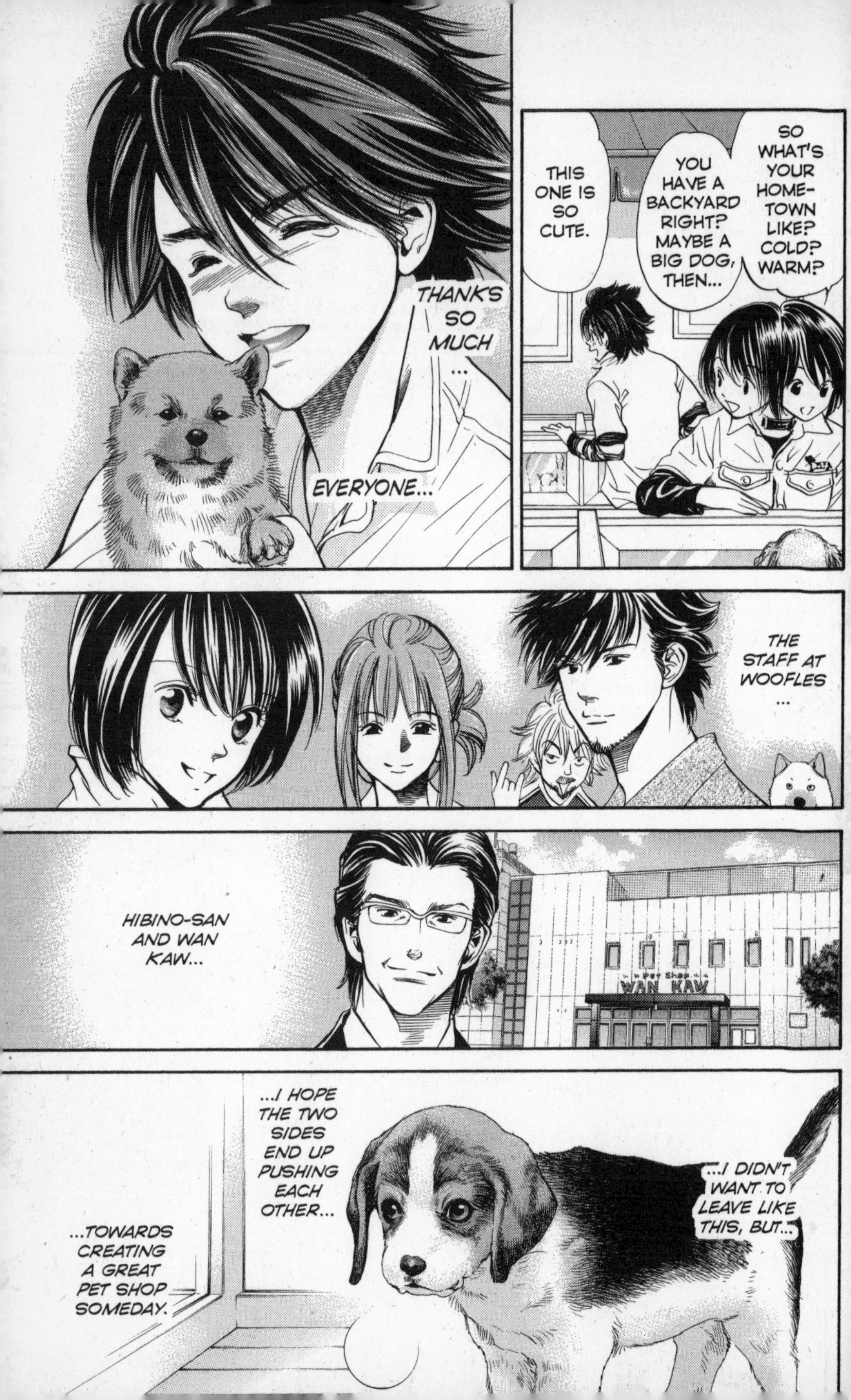
SO WHAT'S YOUR HOME-TOWN LIKE? COLD? WARM?
YOU HAVE A BACKYARD RIGHT? MAYBE A BIG DOG, THEN...
THIS ONE IS SO CUTE.
THANKS SO MUCH ...
EVERYONE...
THE STAFF AT WOOFLES ...
Pet Shop WAN KAW
HIBINO-SAN AND WAN KAW...
...I DIDN'T WANT TO LEAVE LIKE THIS, BUT...
...I HOPE THE TWO SIDES END UP PUSHING EACH OTHER...
...TOWARDS CREATING A GREAT PET SHOP SOMEDAY.

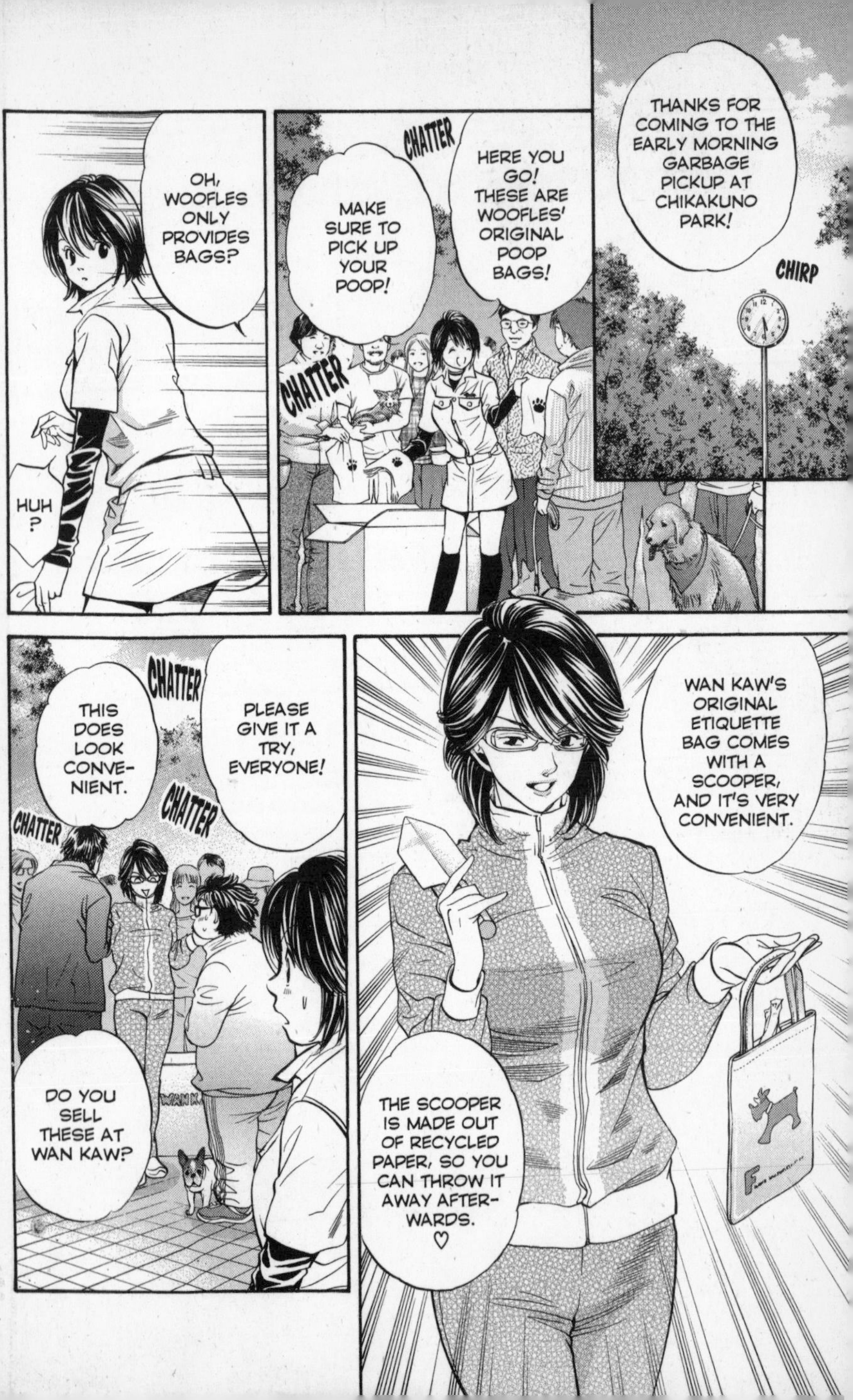
THANKS FOR COMING TO THE EARLY MORNING GARBAGE PICKUP AT CHIKAKUNO PARK!
CHIRP
HERE YOU GO! THESE ARE WOOFLES' ORIGINAL POOP BAGS!
CHATTER
MAKE SURE TO PICK UP YOUR POOP!
CHATTER
OH, WOOFLES ONLY PROVIDES BAGS?
HUH?
WAN KAW'S ORIGINAL ETIQUETTE BAG COMES WITH A SCOOPER, AND IT'S VERY CONVENIENT.
THE SCOOPER IS MADE OUT OF RECYCLED PAPER, SO YOU CAN THROW IT AWAY AFTER-WARDS. ♡
PLEASE GIVE IT A TRY, EVERYONE!
CHATTER
THIS DOES LOOK CONVE-NIENT.
CHATTER
CHATTER
DO YOU SELL THESE AT WAN KAW?

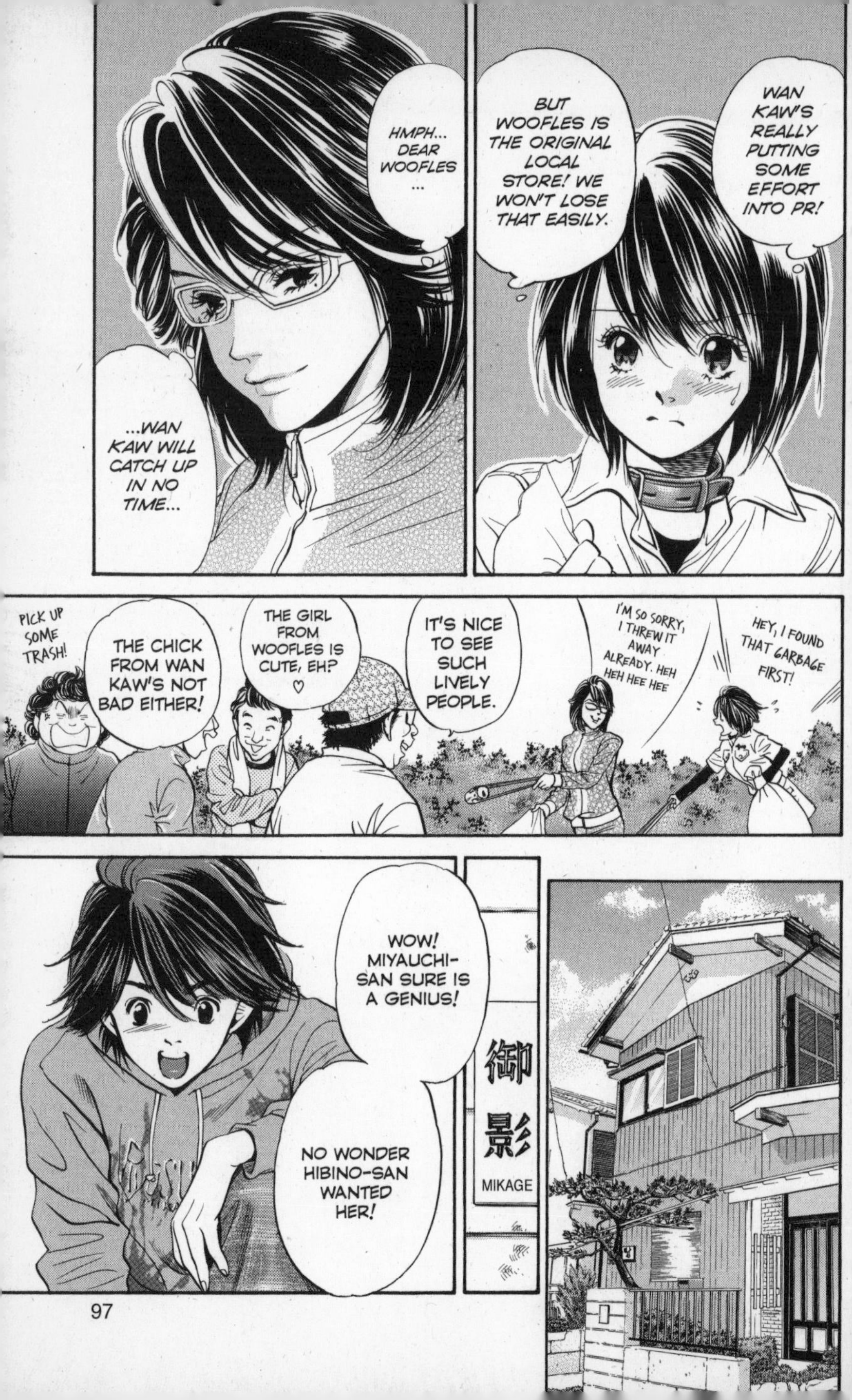
WAN KAW'S REALLY PUTTING SOME EFFORT INTO PR!
BUT WOOFLES IS THE ORIGINAL LOCAL STORE! WE WON'T LOSE THAT EASILY.
HMPH... DEAR WOOFLES ...
...WAN KAW WILL CATCH UP IN NO TIME...
HEY, I FOUND THAT GARBAGE FIRST!
I'M SO SORRY, I THREW IT AWAY ALREADY. HEH HEH HEE HEE
IT'S NICE TO SEE SUCH LIVELY PEOPLE.
THE GIRL FROM WOOFLES IS CUTE, EH? ♡
THE CHICK FROM WAN KAW'S NOT BAD EITHER!
PICK UP SOME TRASH!
御影
MIKAGE
WOW! MIYAUCHI-SAN SURE IS A GENIUS!
NO WONDER HIBINO-SAN WANTED HER!

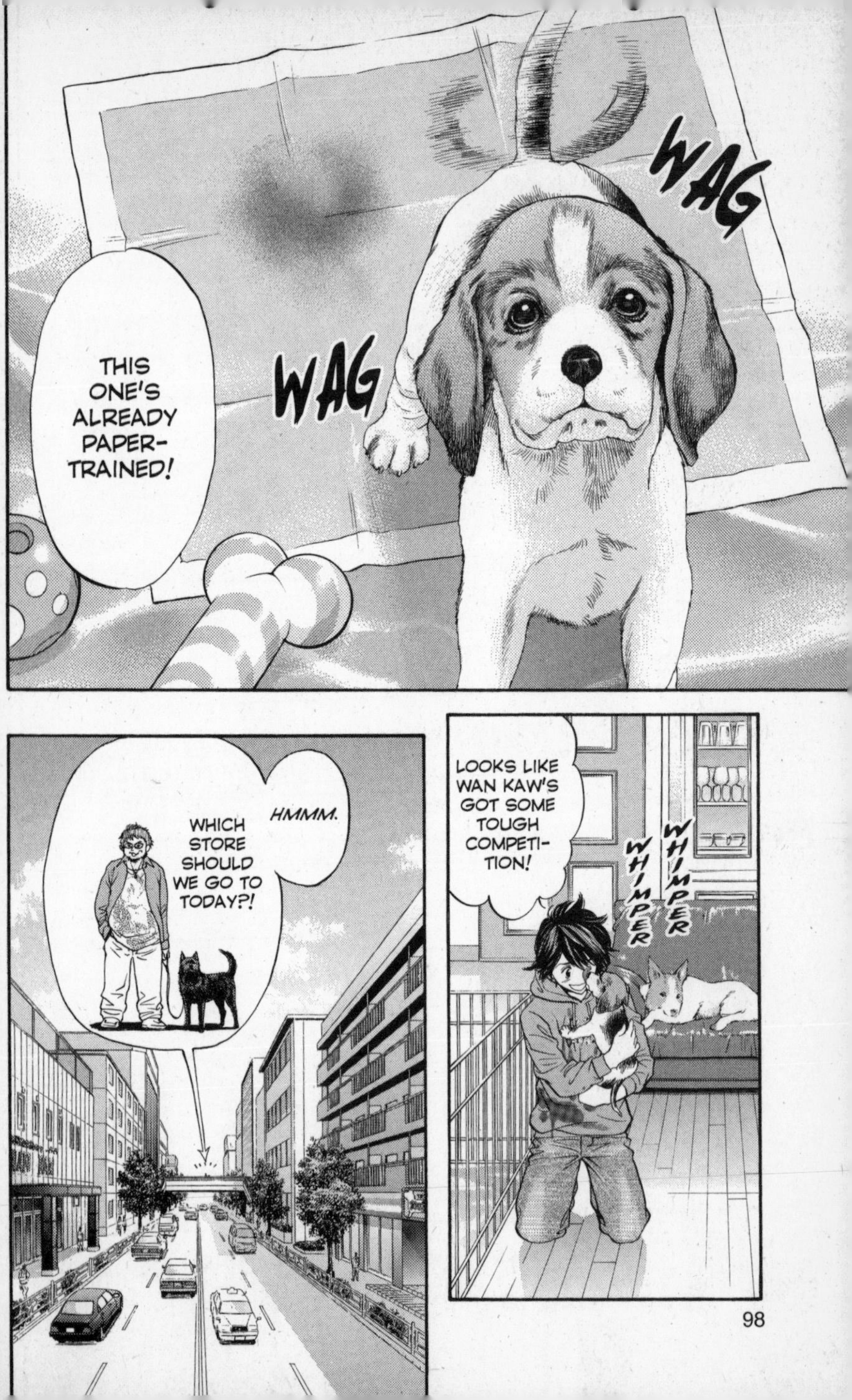
WAG
THIS ONE'S ALREADY PAPER-TRAINED!
WAG
LOOKS LIKE WAN KAW'S GOT SOME TOUGH COMPETITION!
WHIMPER
WHIMPER
HMMM.
WHICH STORE SHOULD WE GO TO TODAY?!

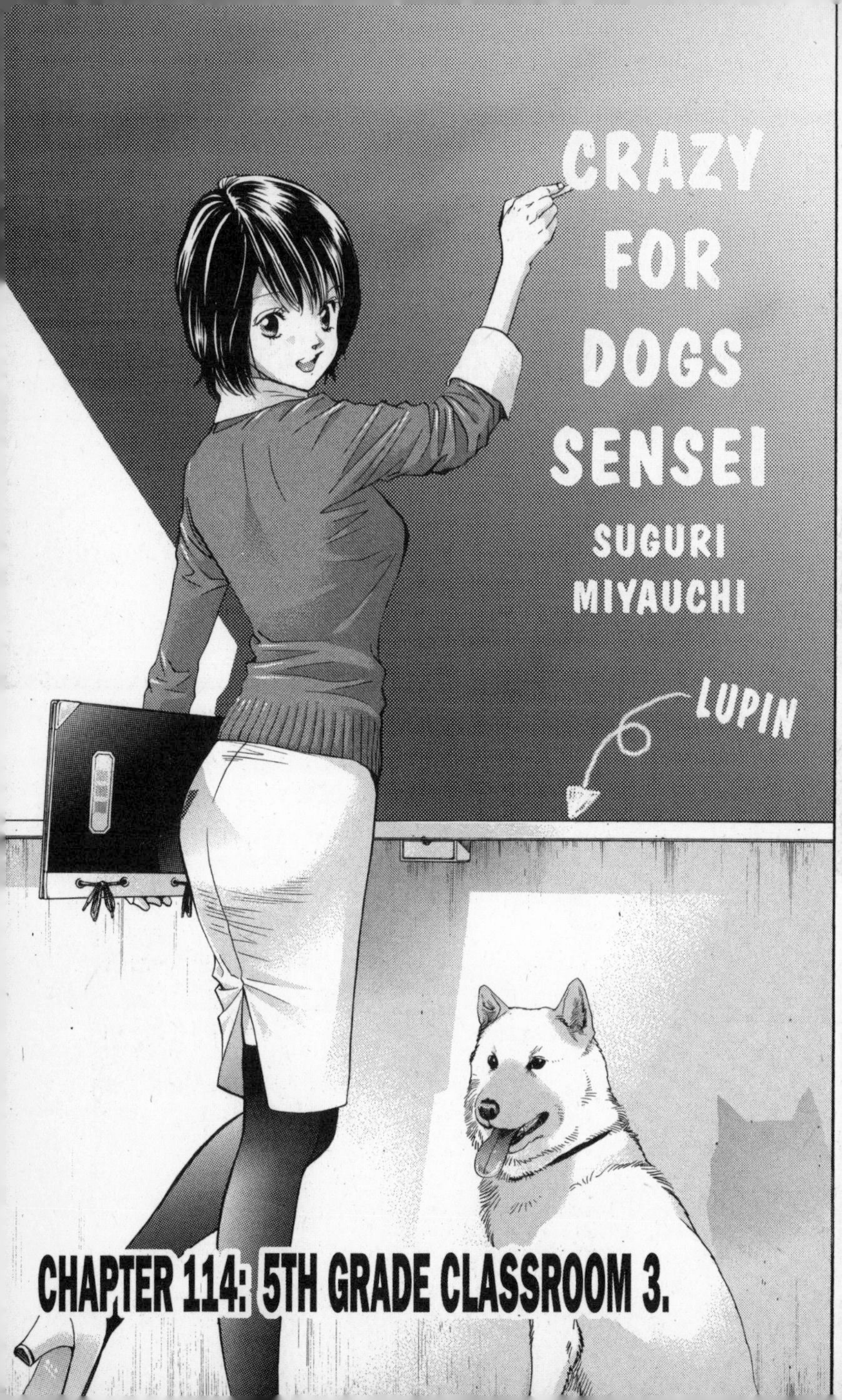
CRAZY FOR DOGS SENSEI
SUGURI MIYAUCHI
LUPIN
CHAPTER 114: 5TH GRADE CLASSROOM 3.

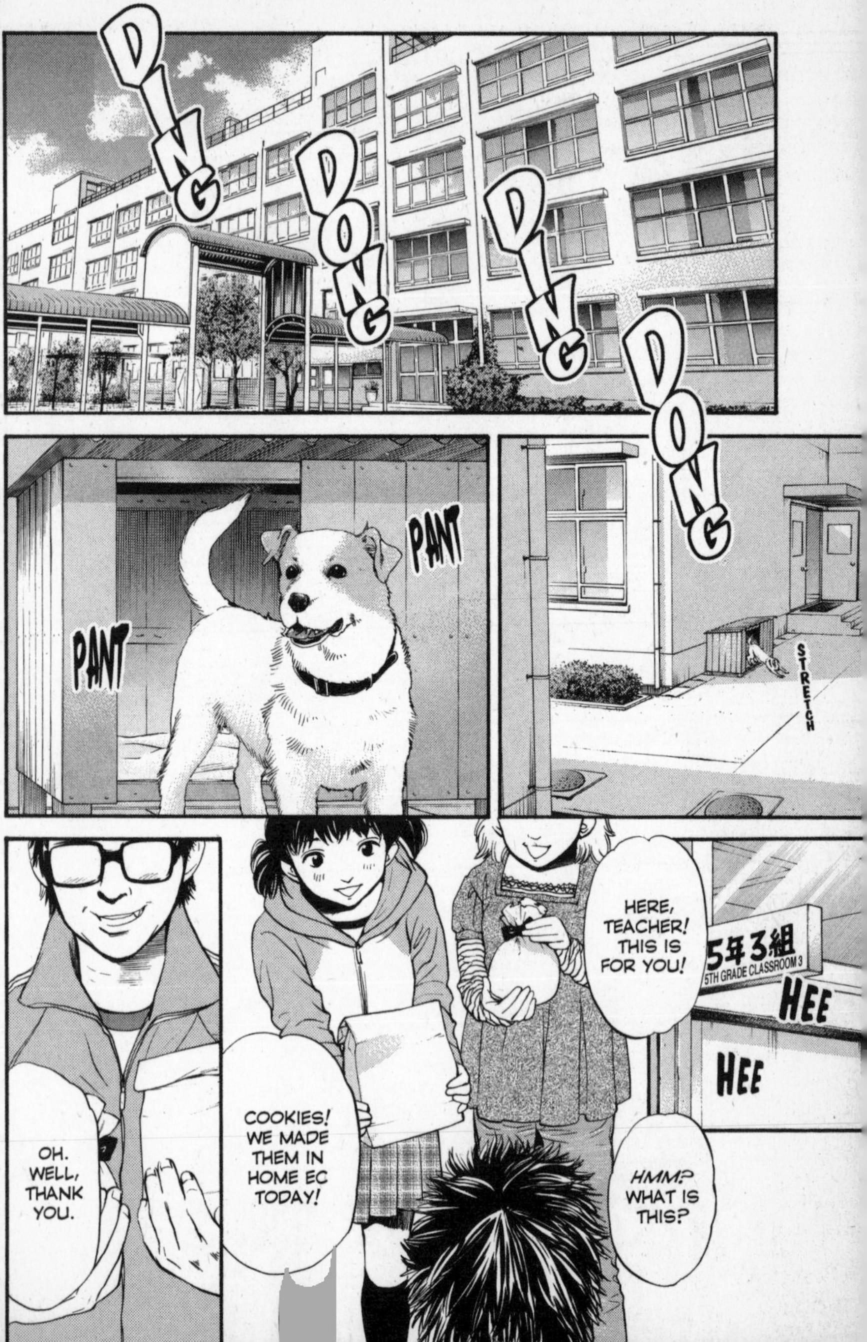
DING
DONG
DING
DONG
STRETCH
PANT
PANT
5年3組
5TH GRADE CLASSROOM 3
HEE
HEE
HERE, TEACHER! THIS IS FOR YOU!
HMM? WHAT IS THIS?
COOKIES! WE MADE THEM IN HOME EC TODAY!
OH. WELL, THANK YOU.

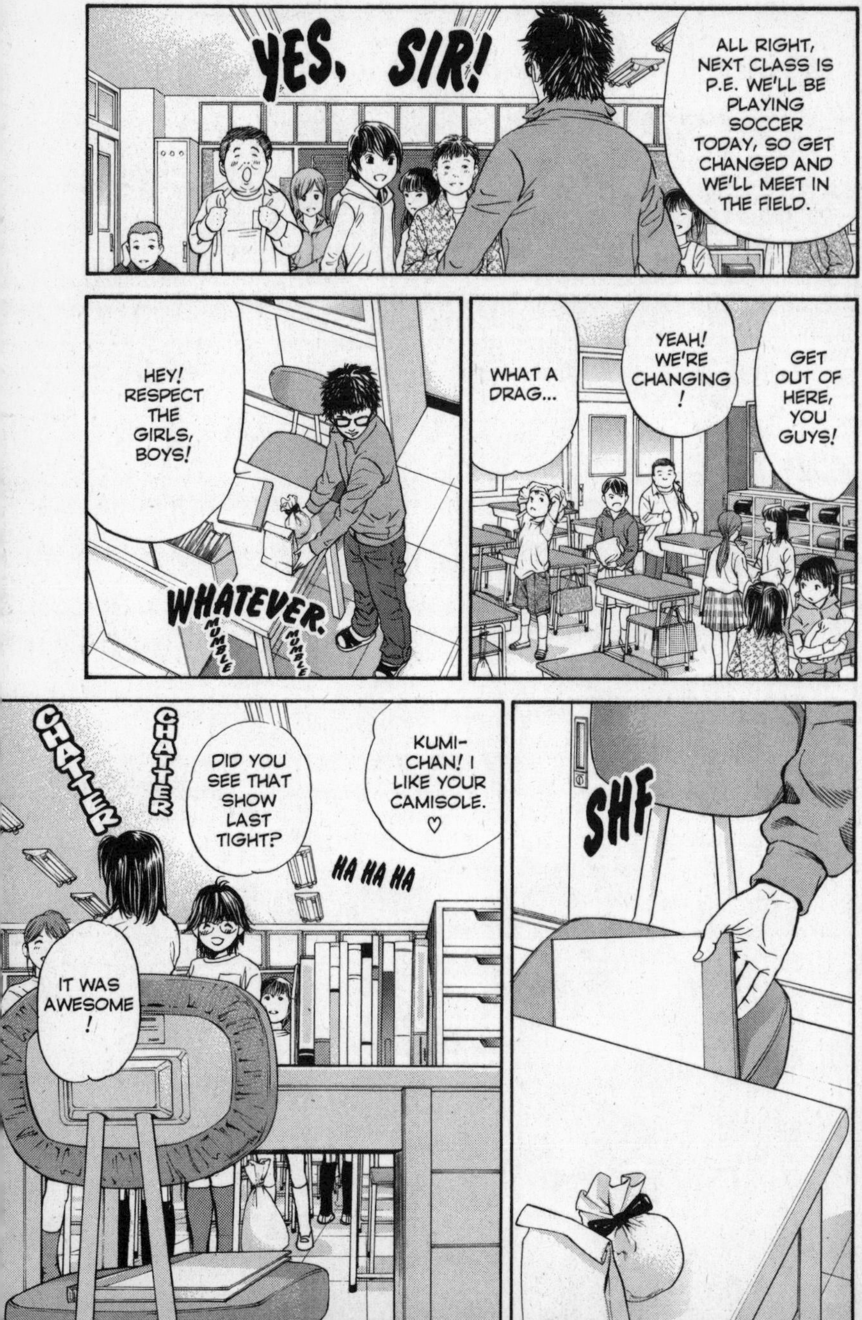
ALL RIGHT, NEXT CLASS IS P.E. WE'LL BE PLAYING SOCCER TODAY, SO GET CHANGED AND WE'LL MEET IN THE FIELD.
YES, SIR!
GET OUT OF HERE, YOU GUYS!
YEAH! WE'RE CHANGING!
WHAT A DRAG...
HEY! RESPECT THE GIRLS, BOYS!
WHATEVER.
MUMBLE
MUMBLE
SHF
KUMI-CHAN! I LIKE YOUR CAMISOLE. ♡
CHATTER
DID YOU SEE THAT SHOW LAST TIGHT?
CHATTER
HA HA HA
IT WAS AWESOME!

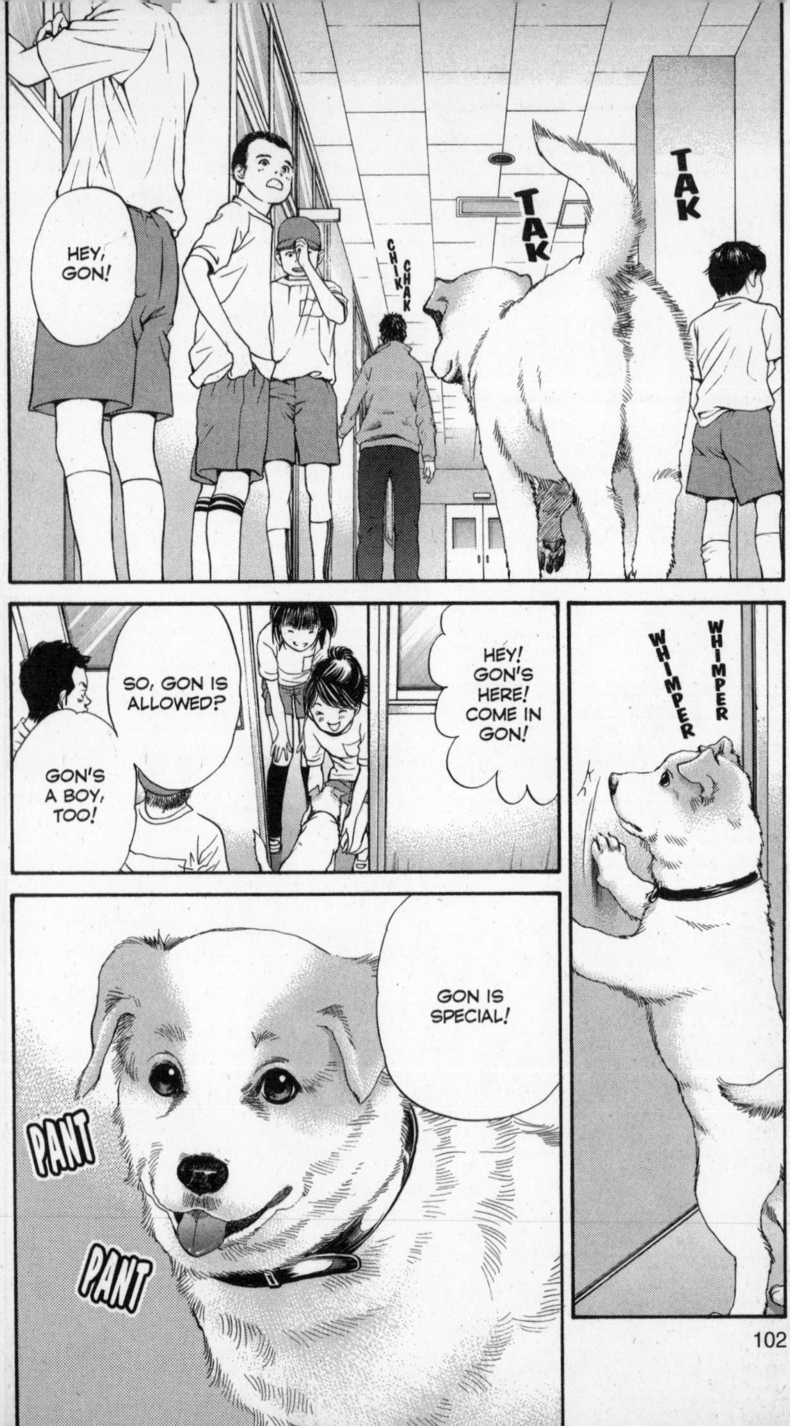
TAK
TAK
CHIK CHAK
HEY, GON!
WHIMPER
WHIMPER
HEY! GON'S HERE! COME IN GON!
SO, GON IS ALLOWED?
GON'S A BOY, TOO!
GON IS SPECIAL!
PANT
PANT

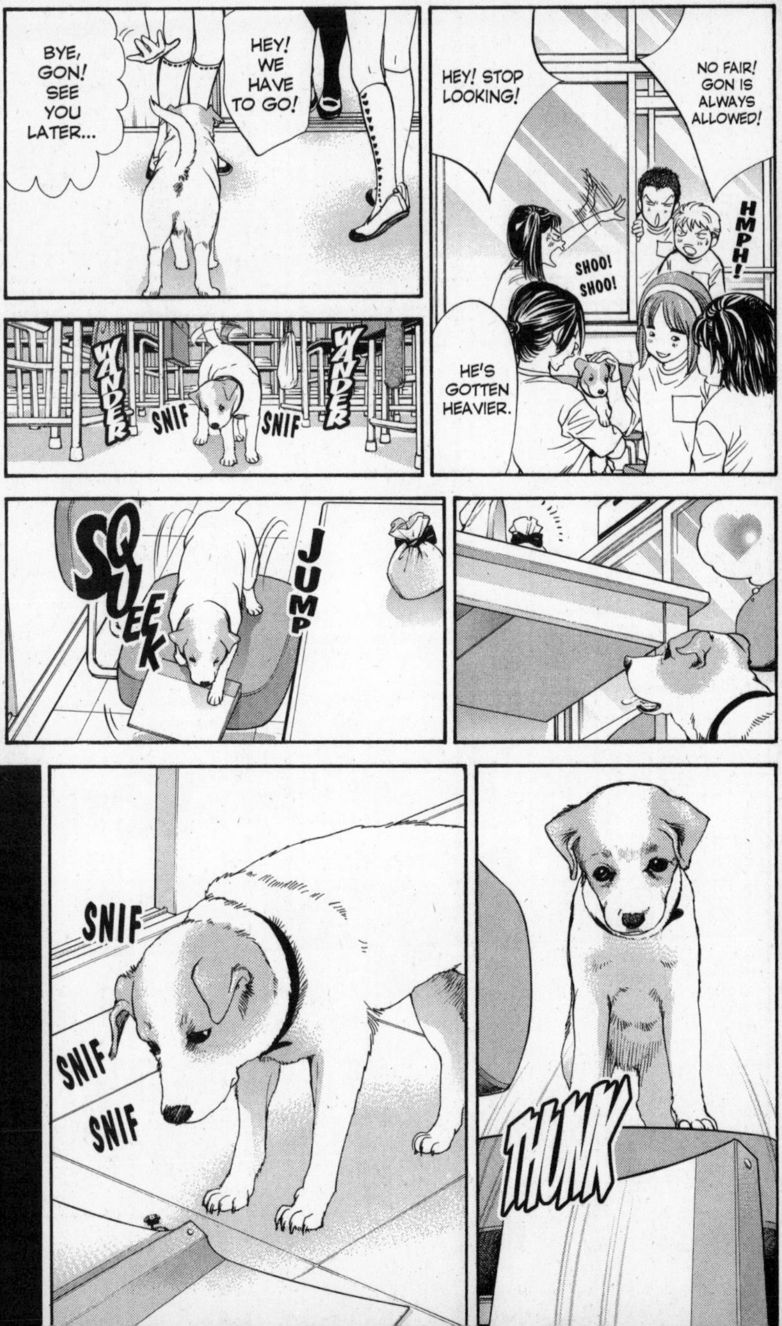
NO FAIR! GON IS ALWAYS ALLOWED!
HEY! STOP LOOKING!
HMPH!
SHOO! SHOO!
HE'S GOTTEN HEAVIER.
HEY! WE HAVE TO GO!
BYE, GON! SEE YOU LATER...
WANDER
SNIF
SNIF
WANDER
JUMP
SQUEEK
THUNK
SNIF
SNIF
SNIF

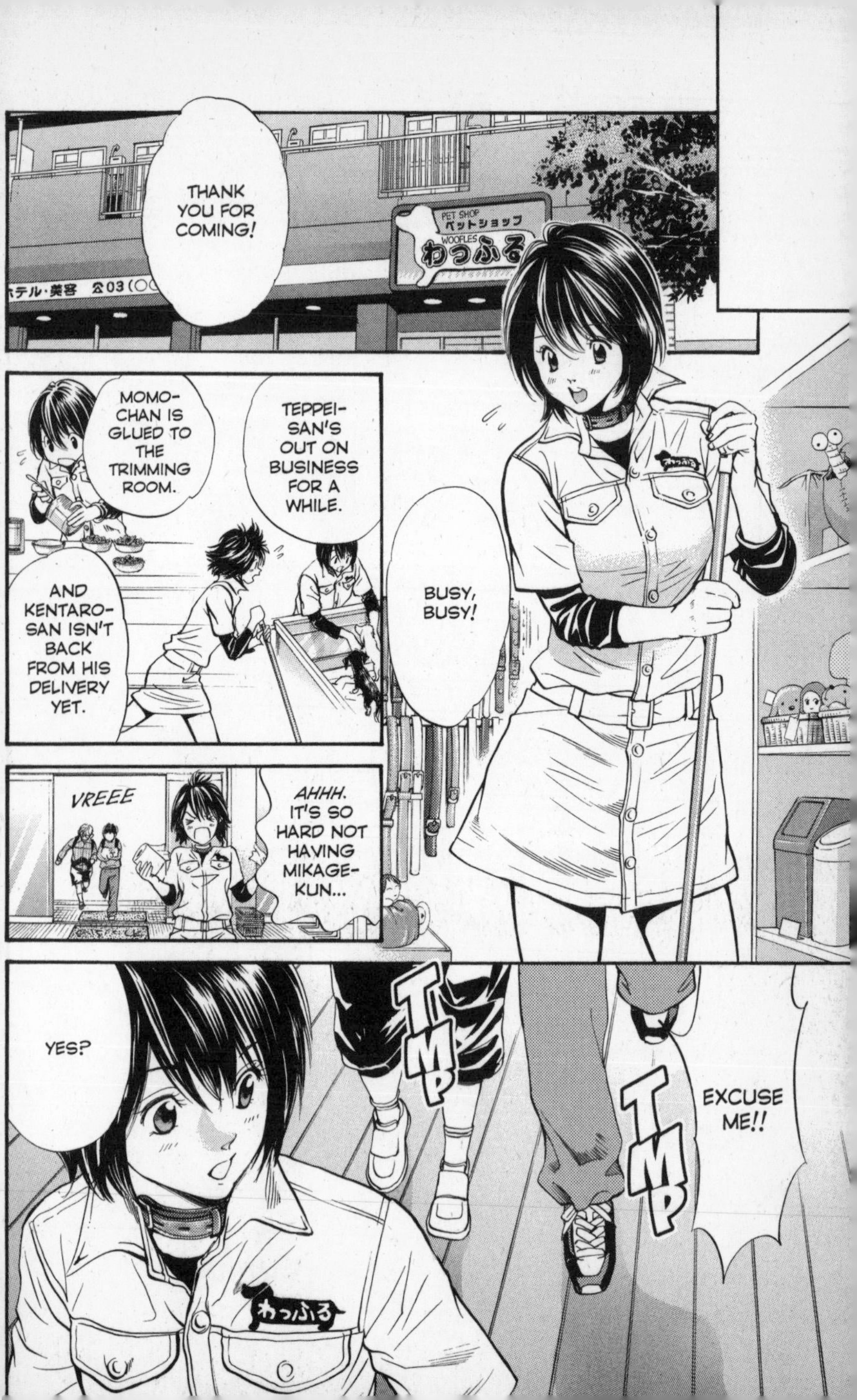
PET SHOP
ペットショップ
WOOFLES
わっふる
THANK YOU FOR COMING!
BUSY, BUSY!
TEPPEI-SAN'S OUT ON BUSINESS FOR A WHILE.
MOMO-CHAN IS GLUED TO THE TRIMMING ROOM.
AND KENTARO-SAN ISN'T BACK FROM HIS DELIVERY YET.
AHHH. IT'S SO HARD NOT HAVING MIKAGE-KUN...
VREEE
EXCUSE ME!!
TMP
TMP
YES?

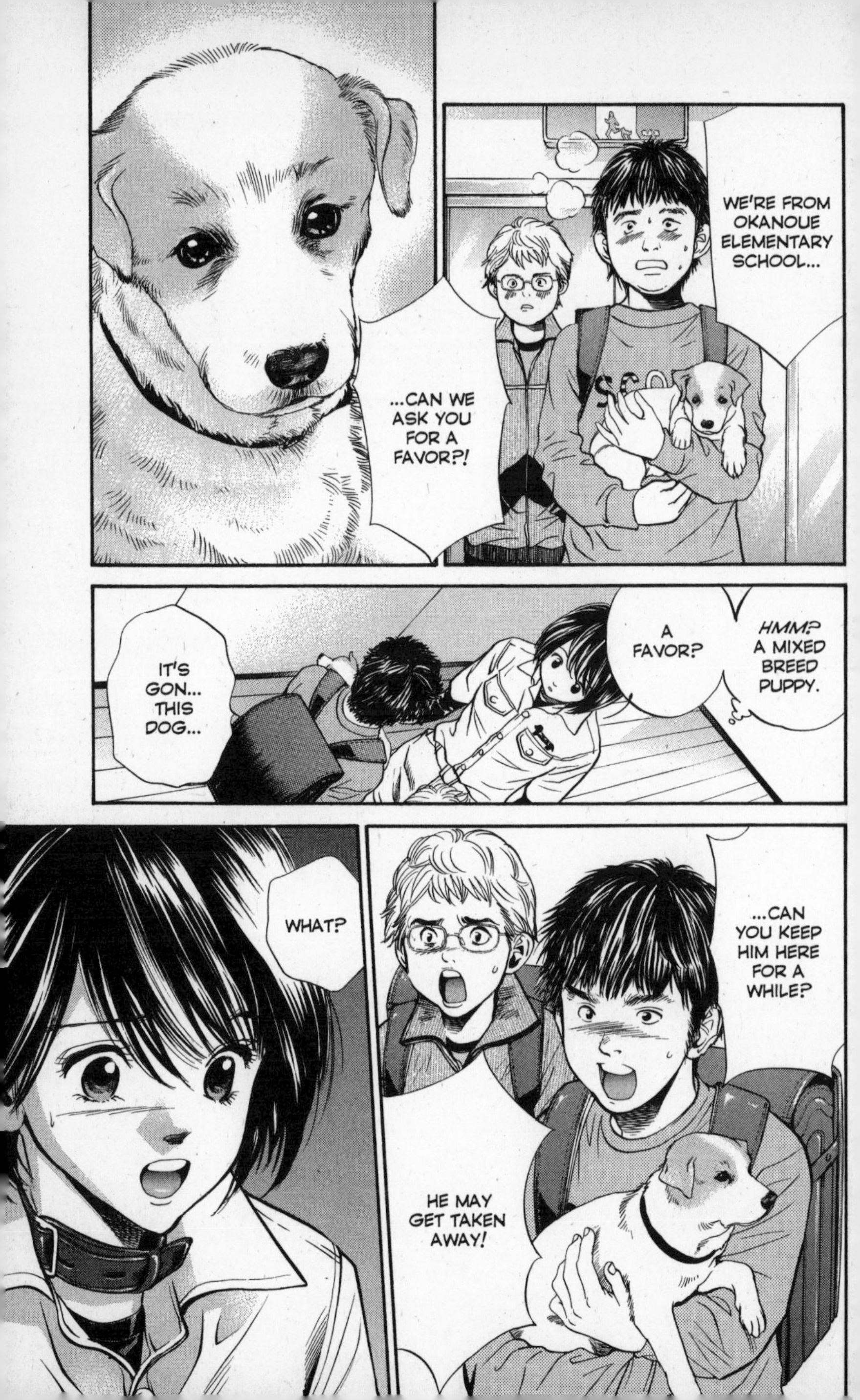
WE'RE FROM OKANOUE ELEMENTARY SCHOOL...
...CAN WE ASK YOU FOR A FAVOR?!
HMM? A MIXED BREED PUPPY.
A FAVOR?
IT'S GON... THIS DOG...
...CAN YOU KEEP HIM HERE FOR A WHILE?
HE MAY GET TAKEN AWAY!
WHAT?

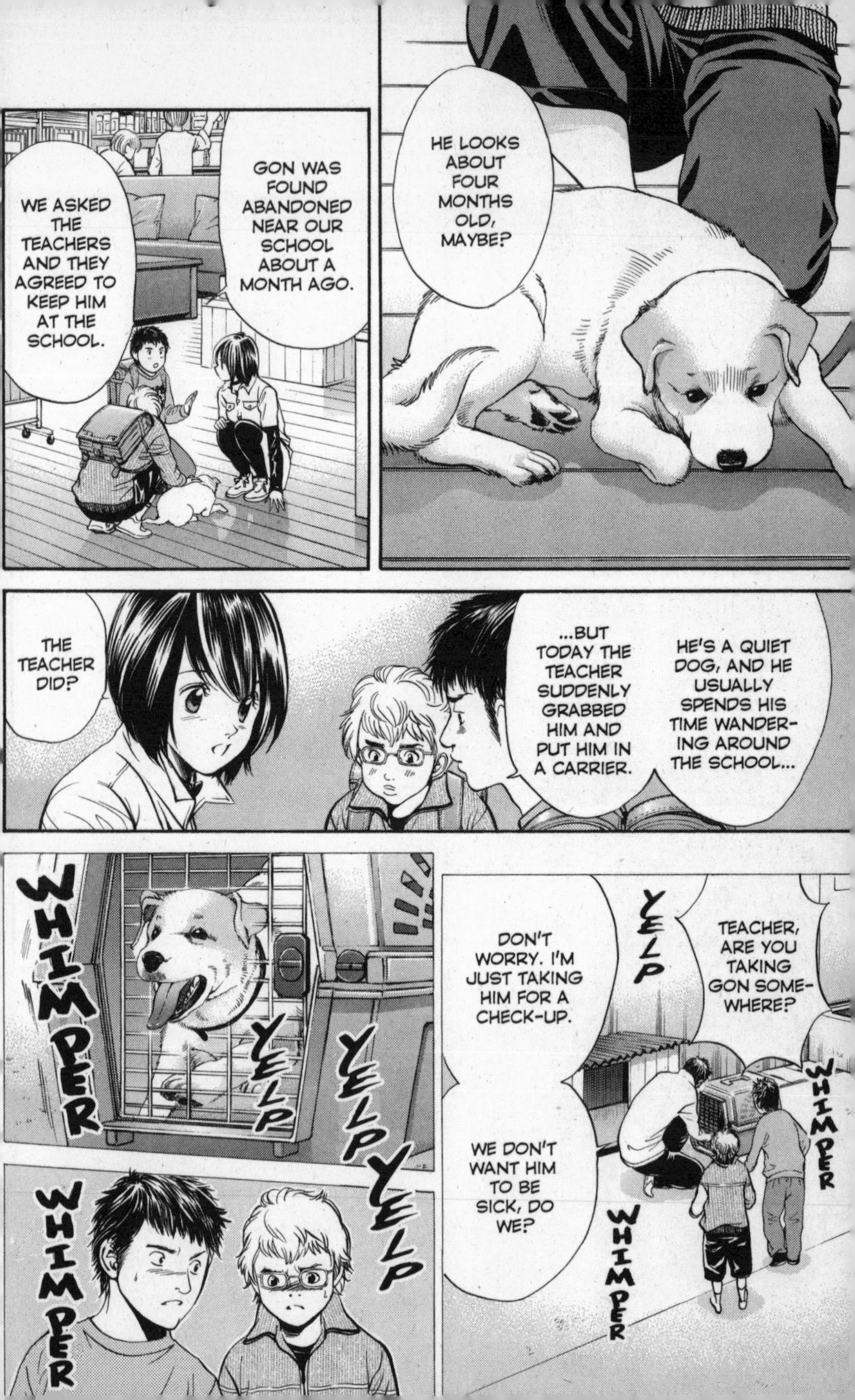
HE LOOKS ABOUT FOUR MONTHS OLD, MAYBE?
GON WAS FOUND ABANDONED NEAR OUR SCHOOL ABOUT A MONTH AGO.
WE ASKED THE TEACHERS AND THEY AGREED TO KEEP HIM AT THE SCHOOL.
HE'S A QUIET DOG, AND HE USUALLY SPENDS HIS TIME WANDERING AROUND THE SCHOOL...
...BUT TODAY THE TEACHER SUDDENLY GRABBED HIM AND PUT HIM IN A CARRIER.
THE TEACHER DID?
TEACHER, ARE YOU TAKING GON SOMEWHERE?
YELP
DON'T WORRY. I'M JUST TAKING HIM FOR A CHECK-UP.
WE DON'T WANT HIM TO BE SICK, DO WE?
WHIMPER
WHIMPER
YELP
YELP
WHIMPER
YELP
WHIMPER

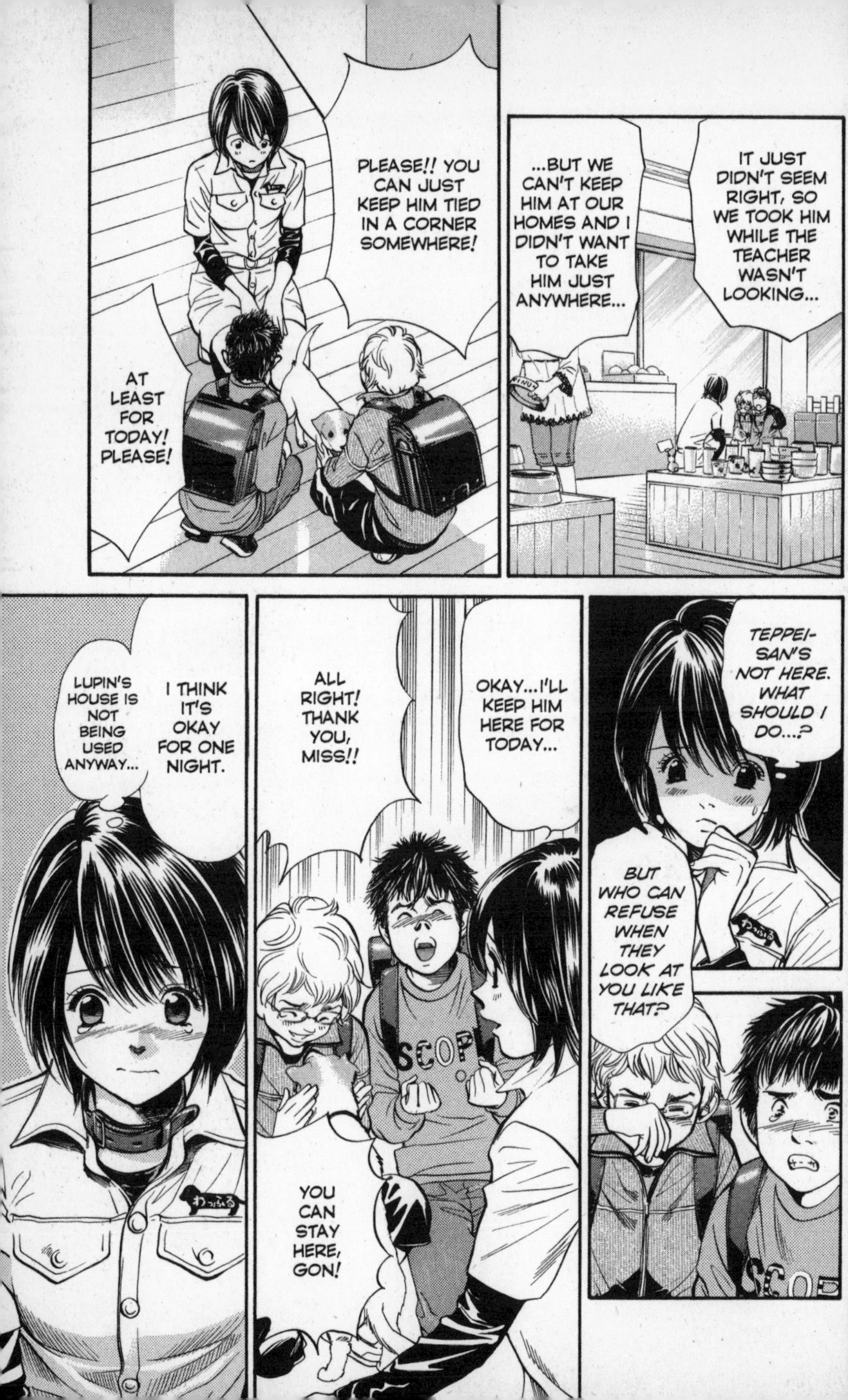
IT JUST DIDN'T SEEM RIGHT, SO WE TOOK HIM WHILE THE TEACHER WASN'T LOOKING...
...BUT WE CAN'T KEEP HIM AT OUR HOMES AND I DIDN'T WANT TO TAKE HIM JUST ANYWHERE...
PLEASE!! YOU CAN JUST KEEP HIM TIED IN A CORNER SOMEWHERE!
AT LEAST FOR TODAY! PLEASE!
TEPPEI-SAN'S NOT HERE. WHAT SHOULD I DO...?
BUT WHO CAN REFUSE WHEN THEY LOOK AT YOU LIKE THAT?
OKAY...I'LL KEEP HIM HERE FOR TODAY...
ALL RIGHT! THANK YOU, MISS!!
YOU CAN STAY HERE, GON!
I THINK IT'S OKAY FOR ONE NIGHT.
LUPIN'S HOUSE IS NOT BEING USED ANYWAY...

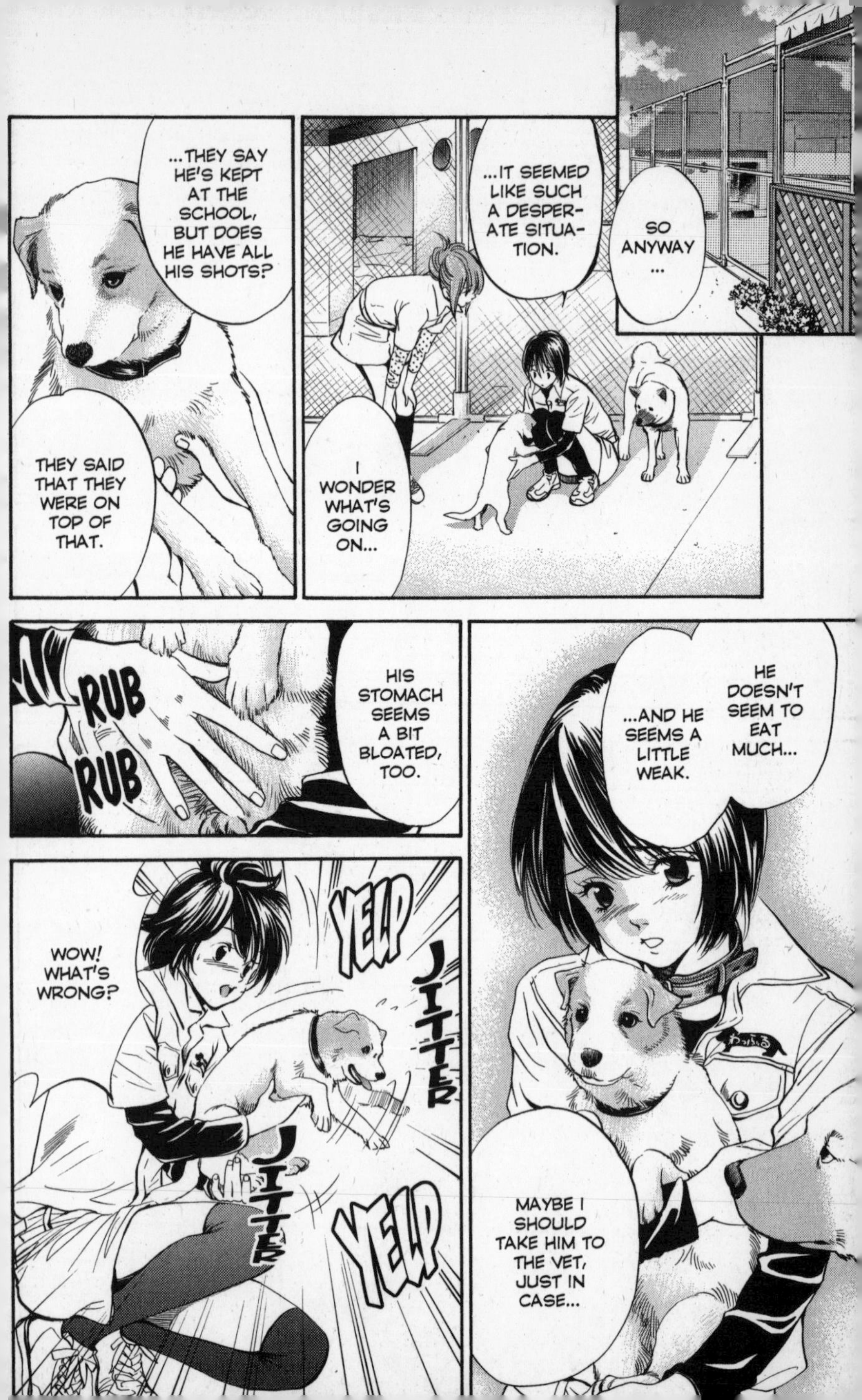
SO ANYWAY ...
...IT SEEMED LIKE SUCH A DESPERATE SITUATION.
I WONDER WHAT'S GOING ON...
...THEY SAY HE'S KEPT AT THE SCHOOL, BUT DOES HE HAVE ALL HIS SHOTS?
THEY SAID THAT THEY WERE ON TOP OF THAT.
HE DOESN'T SEEM TO EAT MUCH...
...AND HE SEEMS A LITTLE WEAK.
MAYBE I SHOULD TAKE HIM TO THE VET, JUST IN CASE...
HIS STOMACH SEEMS A BIT BLOATED, TOO.
RUB
RUB
YELP
JITTER
WOW! WHAT'S WRONG?
JITTER
YELP

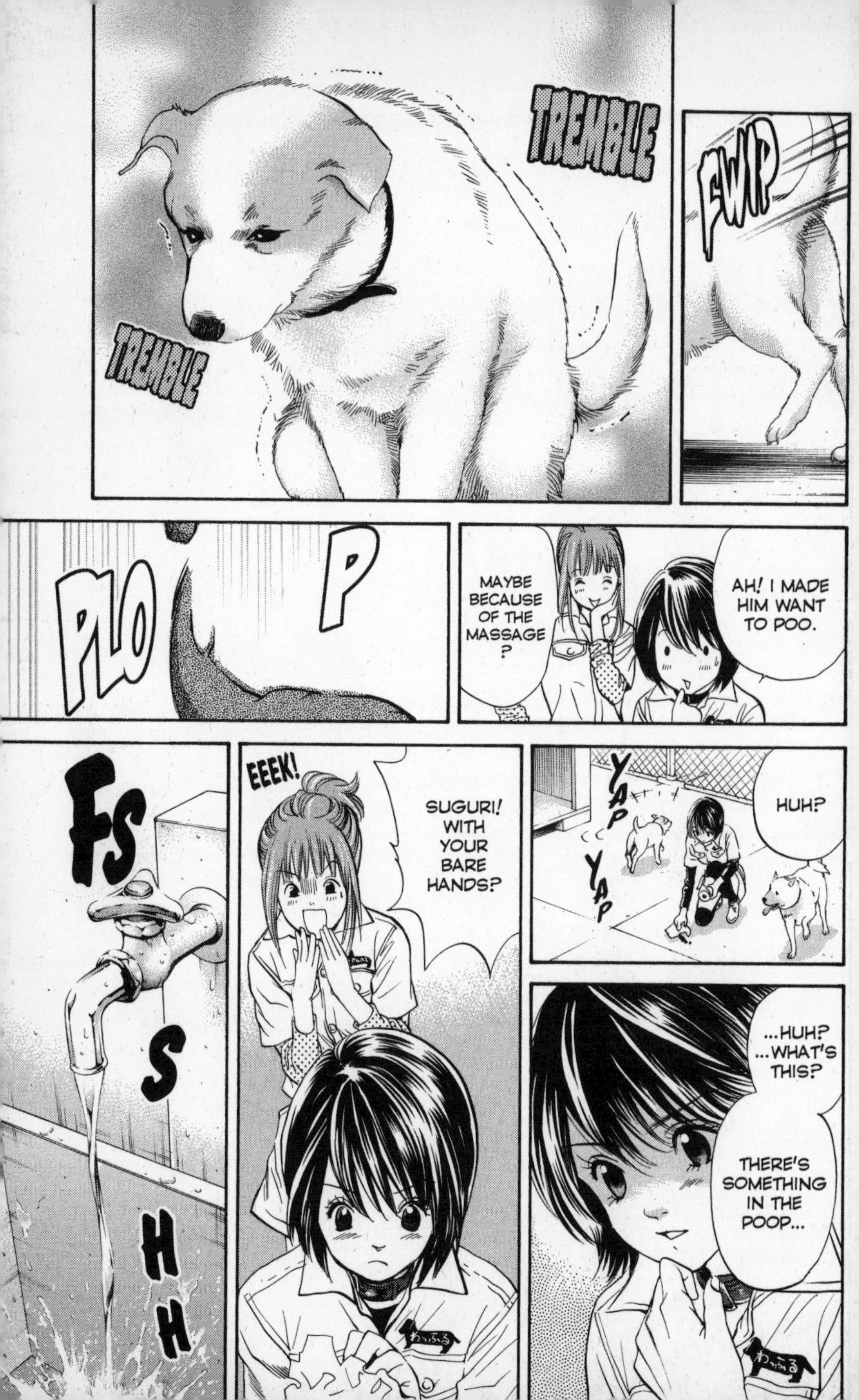
CWIP
TREMBLE
TREMBLE
AH! I MADE HIM WANT TO POO.
MAYBE BECAUSE OF THE MASSAGE?
PLOP
HUH?
YAP YAP
...HUH? ...WHAT'S THIS?
THERE'S SOMETHING IN THE POOP...
EEEK!
SUGURI! WITH YOUR BARE HANDS?
FSSHH

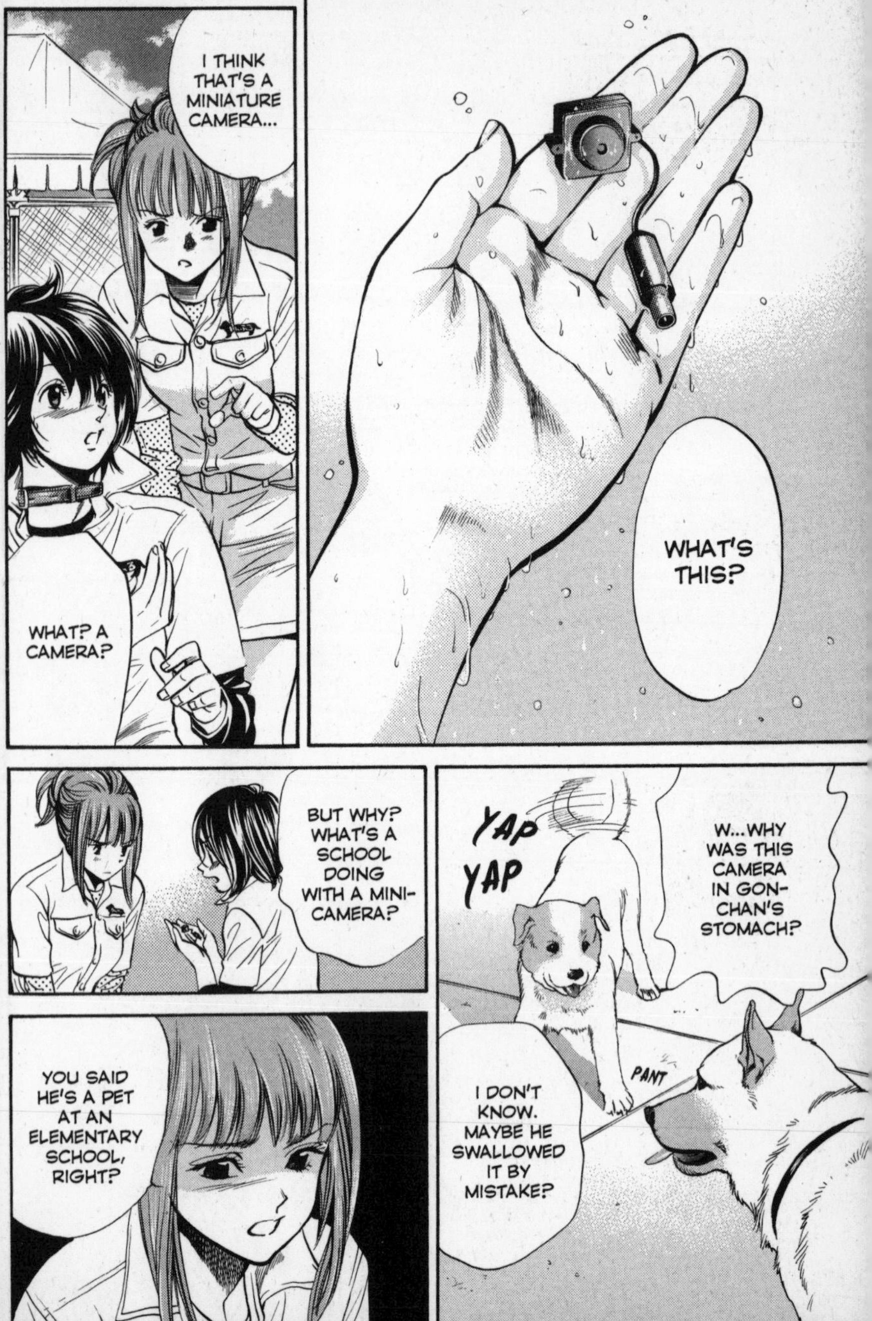
WHAT'S THIS?
I THINK THAT'S A MINIATURE CAMERA...
WHAT? A CAMERA?
W...WHY WAS THIS CAMERA IN GON-CHAN'S STOMACH?
YAP YAP
PANT
I DON'T KNOW. MAYBE HE SWALLOWED IT BY MISTAKE?
BUT WHY? WHAT'S A SCHOOL DOING WITH A MINI-CAMERA?
YOU SAID HE'S A PET AT AN ELEMENTARY SCHOOL, RIGHT?

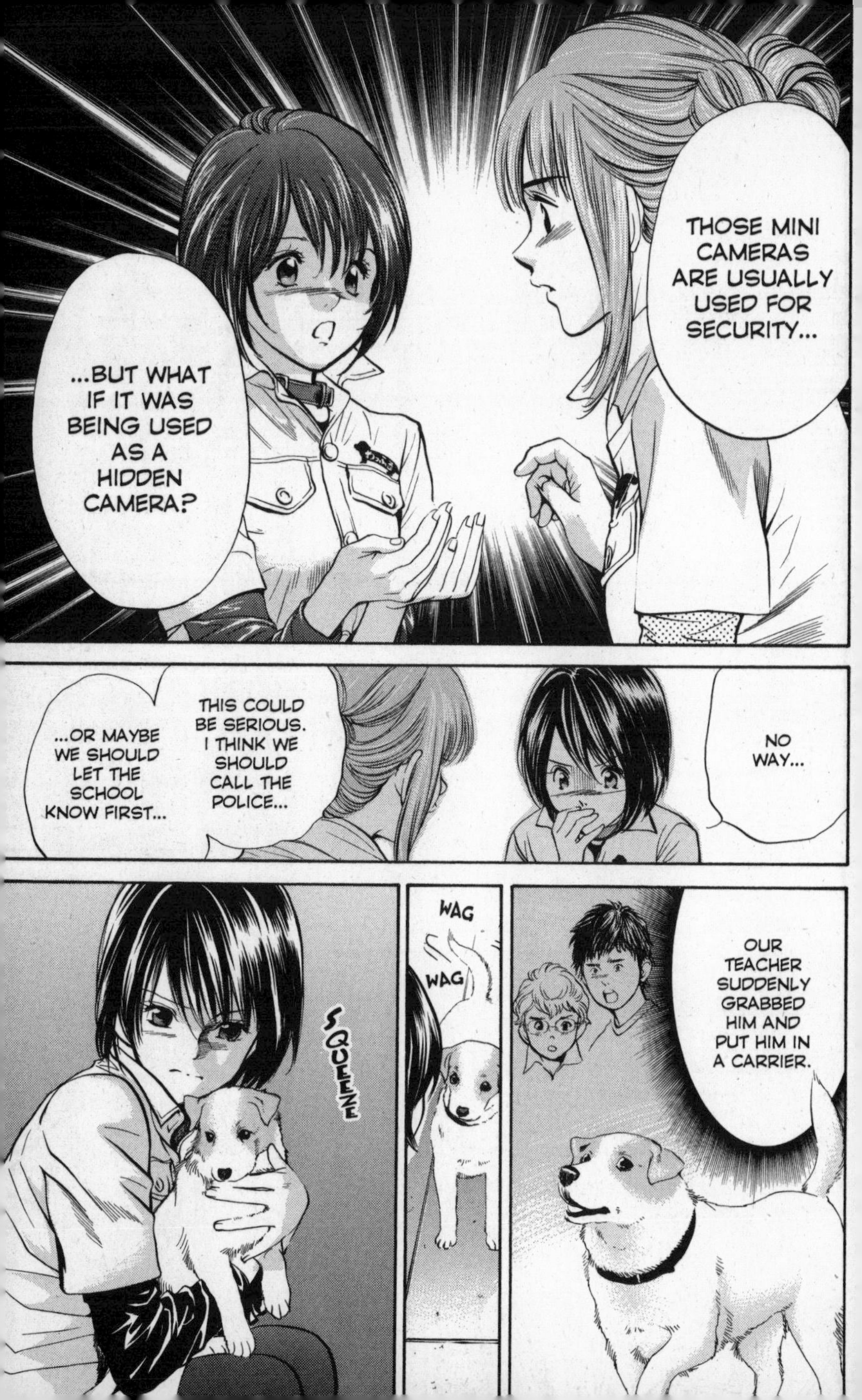
THOSE MINI CAMERAS ARE USUALLY USED FOR SECURITY...
...BUT WHAT IF IT WAS BEING USED AS A HIDDEN CAMERA?
NO WAY...
THIS COULD BE SERIOUS. I THINK WE SHOULD CALL THE POLICE...
...OR MAYBE WE SHOULD LET THE SCHOOL KNOW FIRST...
OUR TEACHER SUDDENLY GRABBED HIM AND PUT HIM IN A CARRIER.
WAG
WAG
SQUEEZE

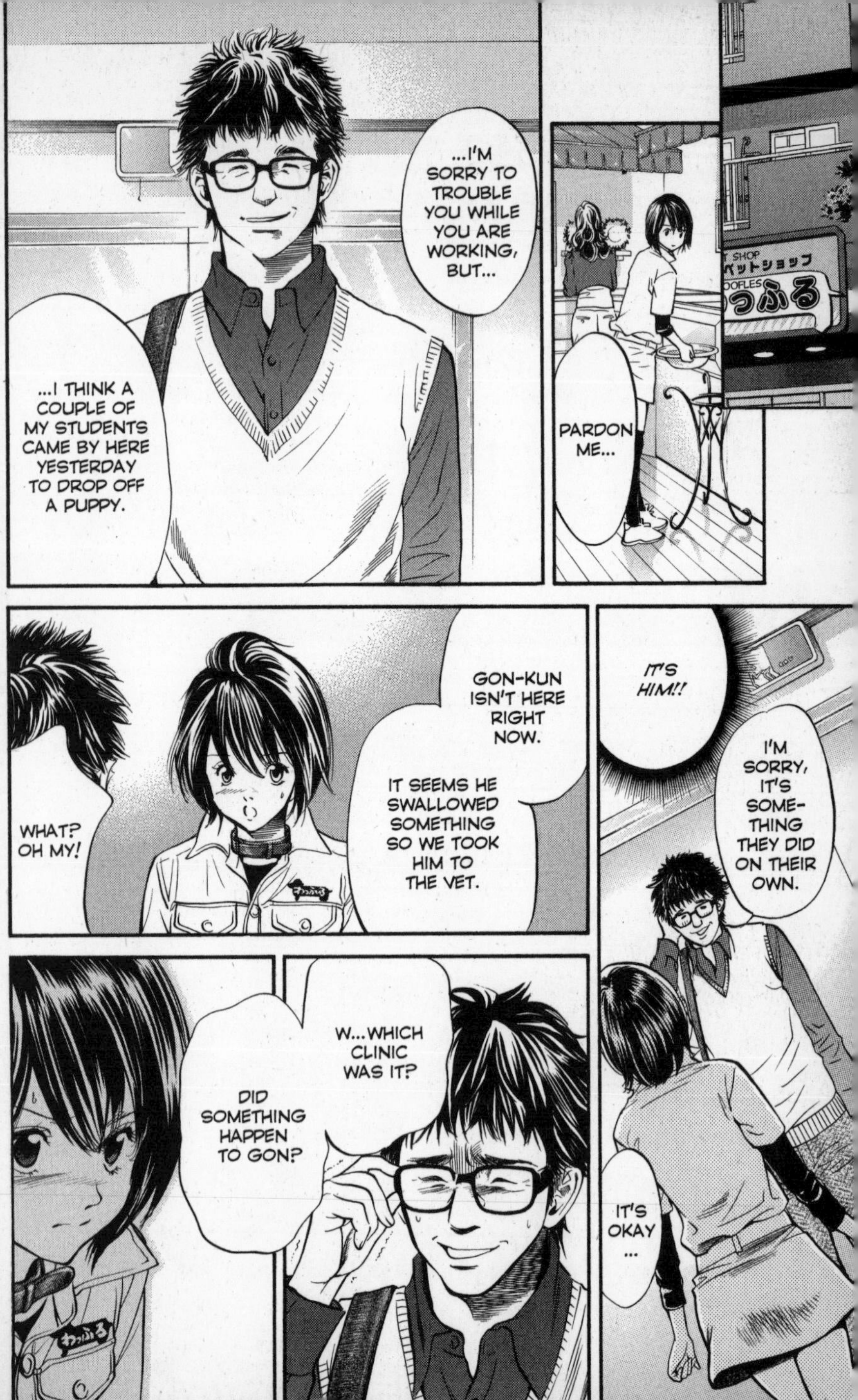
T SHOP
ペットショップ
OOFLES
っふる
PARDON ME...
...I'M SORRY TO TROUBLE YOU WHILE YOU ARE WORKING, BUT...
...I THINK A COUPLE OF MY STUDENTS CAME BY HERE YESTERDAY TO DROP OFF A PUPPY.
IT'S HIM!!
I'M SORRY, IT'S SOME-THING THEY DID ON THEIR OWN.
IT'S OKAY ...
GON-KUN ISN'T HERE RIGHT NOW.
IT SEEMS HE SWALLOWED SOMETHING SO WE TOOK HIM TO THE VET.
WHAT? OH MY!
W...WHICH CLINIC WAS IT?
DID SOMETHING HAPPEN TO GON?

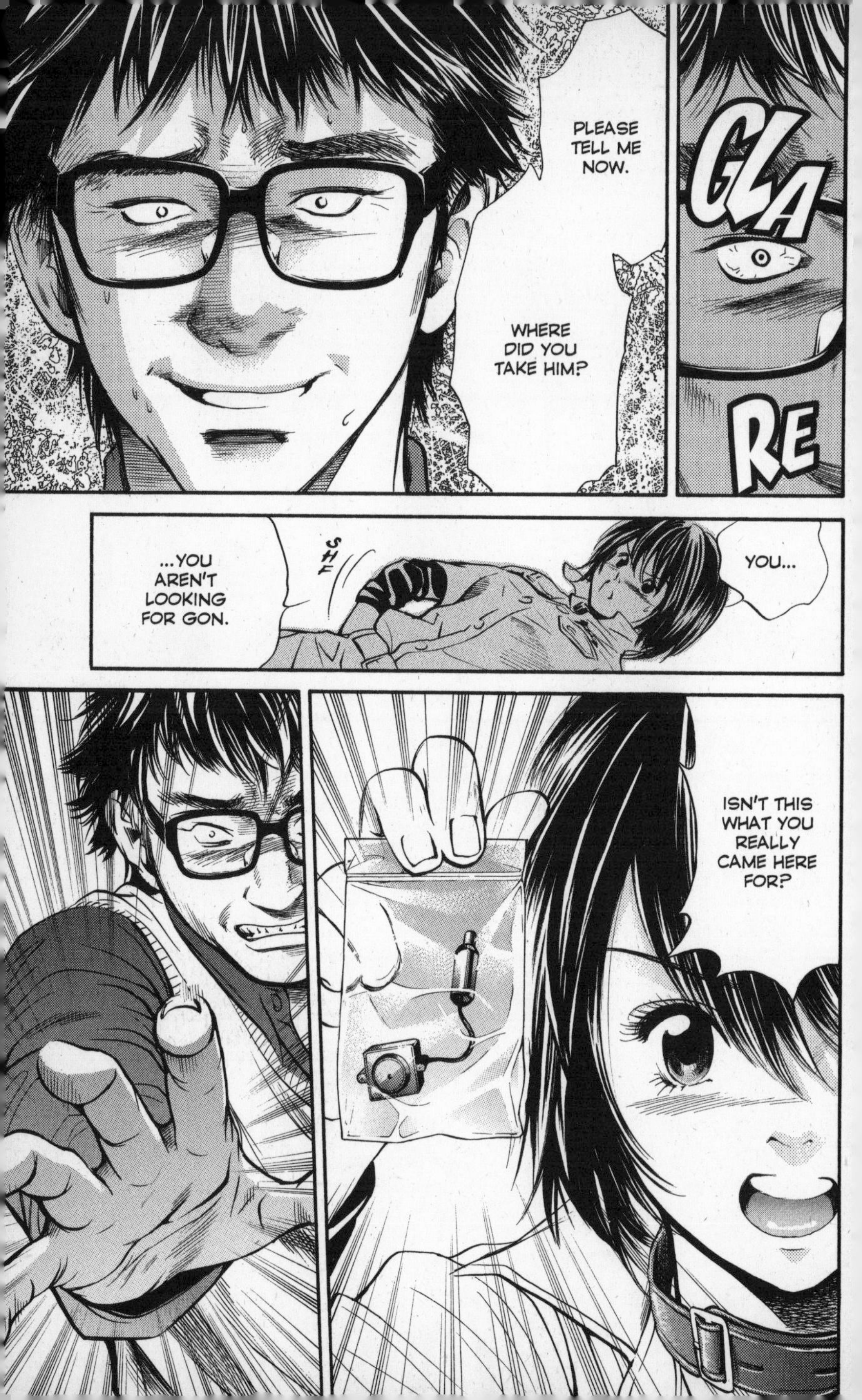
GLARE
PLEASE TELL ME NOW.
WHERE DID YOU TAKE HIM?
YOU...
SHF
...YOU AREN'T LOOKING FOR GON.
ISN'T THIS WHAT YOU REALLY CAME HERE FOR?

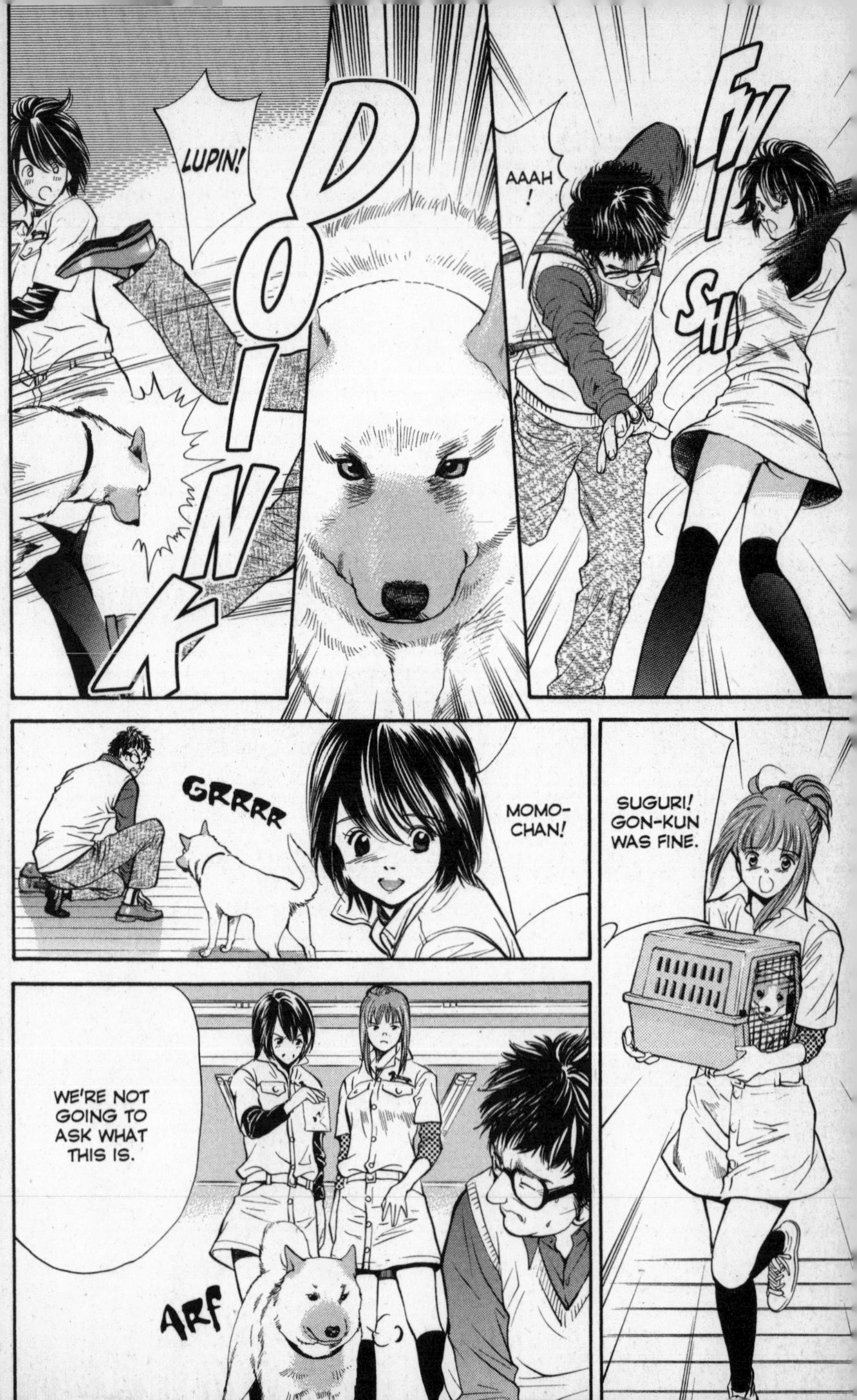
AAAH!
FWISH
DOINK
LUPIN!
SUGURI! GON-KUN WAS FINE.
MOMO-CHAN!
GRRRR
WE'RE NOT GOING TO ASK WHAT THIS IS.
ARF

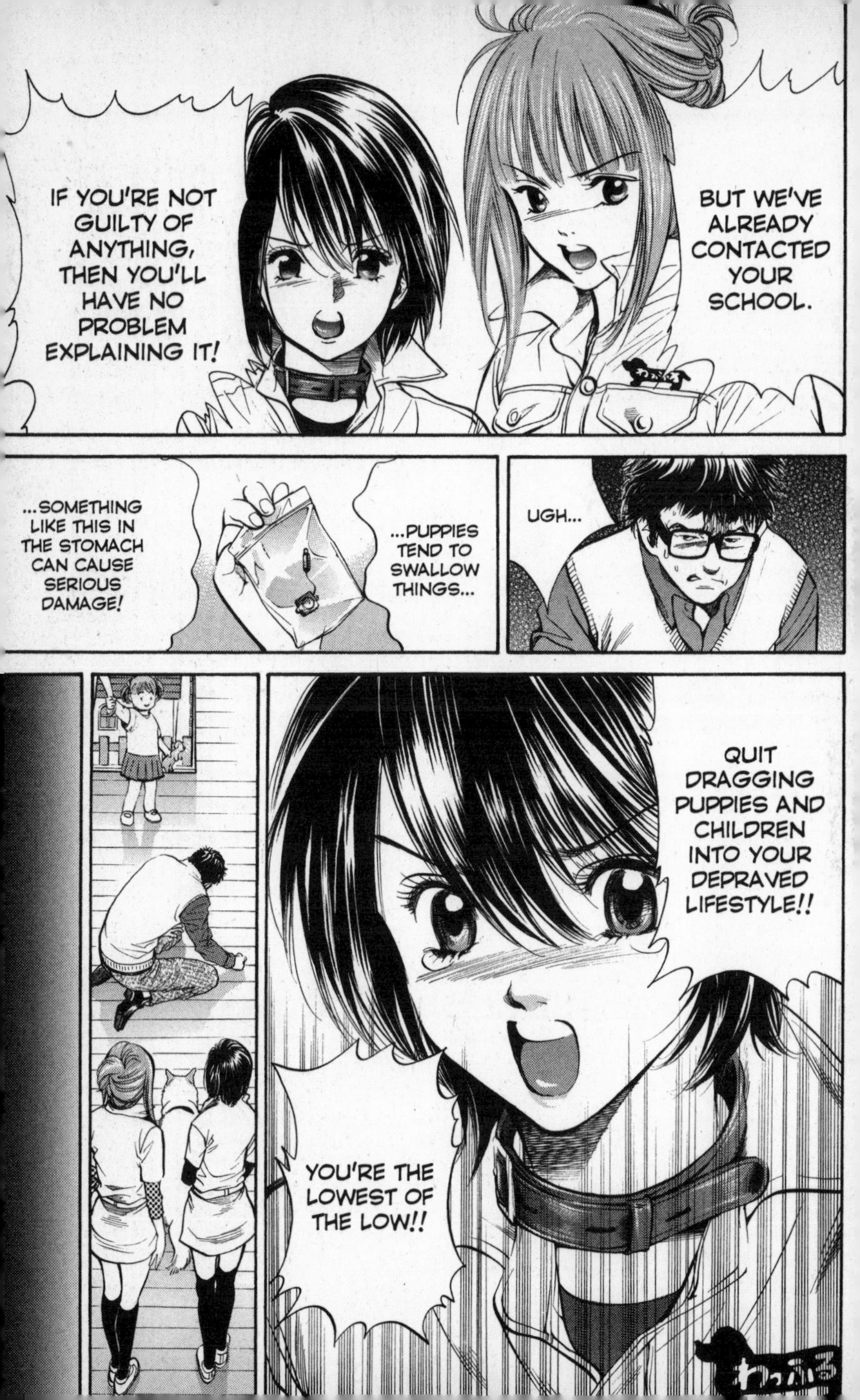
BUT WE'VE ALREADY CONTACTED YOUR SCHOOL.
IF YOU'RE NOT GUILTY OF ANYTHING, THEN YOU'LL HAVE NO PROBLEM EXPLAINING IT!
UGH...
...PUPPIES TEND TO SWALLOW THINGS...
...SOMETHING LIKE THIS IN THE STOMACH CAN CAUSE SERIOUS DAMAGE!
QUIT DRAGGING PUPPIES AND CHILDREN INTO YOUR DEPRAVED LIFESTYLE!!
YOU'RE THE LOWEST OF THE LOW!!

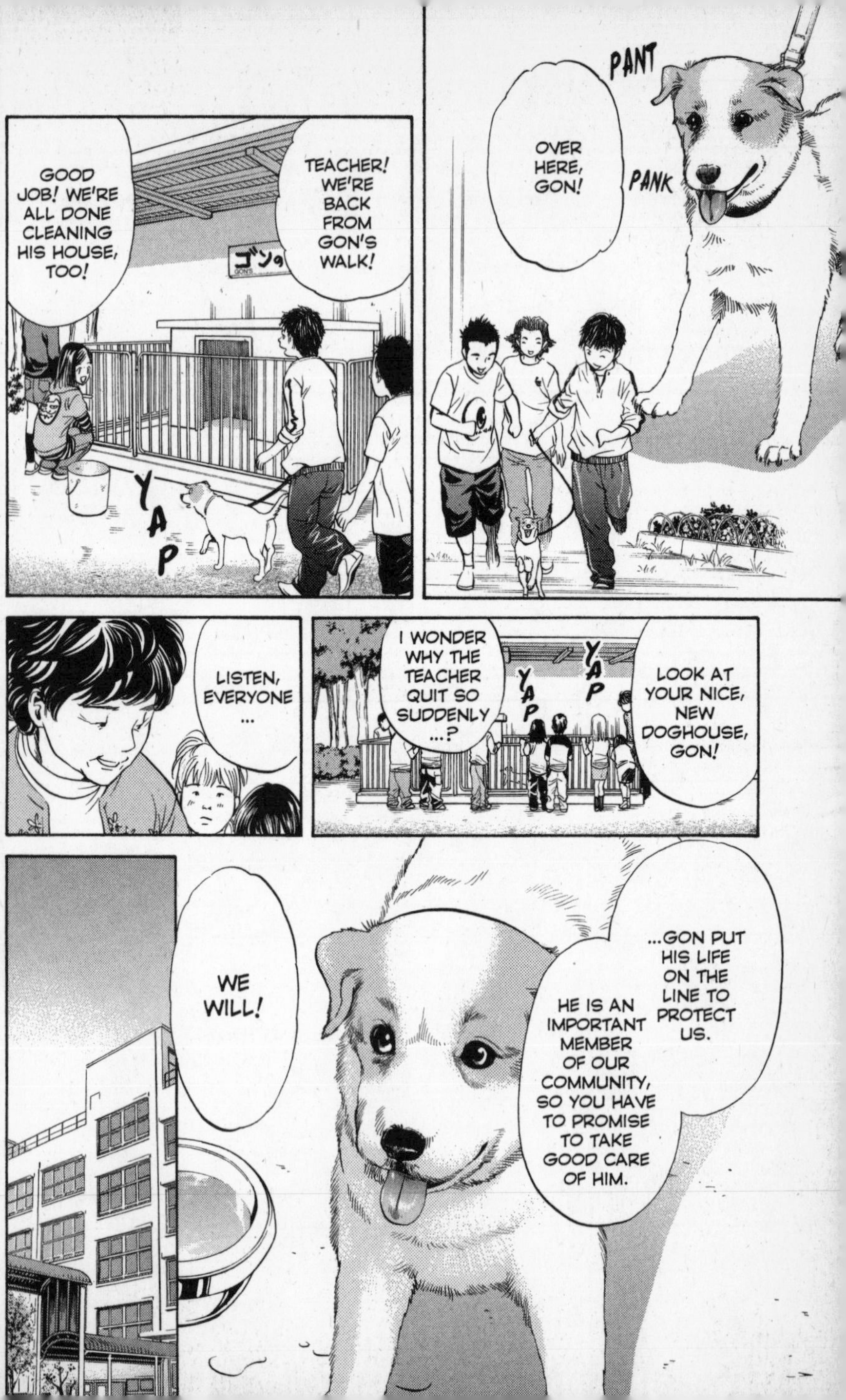
PANT
OVER HERE, GON!
PANK
TEACHER! WE'RE BACK FROM GON'S WALK!
GOOD JOB! WE'RE ALL DONE CLEANING HIS HOUSE, TOO!
ゴンの
YAP
LOOK AT YOUR NICE, NEW DOGHOUSE, GON!
YAP
YAP
I WONDER WHY THE TEACHER QUIT SO SUDDENLY ...?
LISTEN, EVERYONE ...
...GON PUT HIS LIFE ON THE LINE TO PROTECT US.
HE IS AN IMPORTANT MEMBER OF OUR COMMUNITY, SO YOU HAVE TO PROMISE TO TAKE GOOD CARE OF HIM.
WE WILL!

CHAPTER 115: WHAT'S K-9?

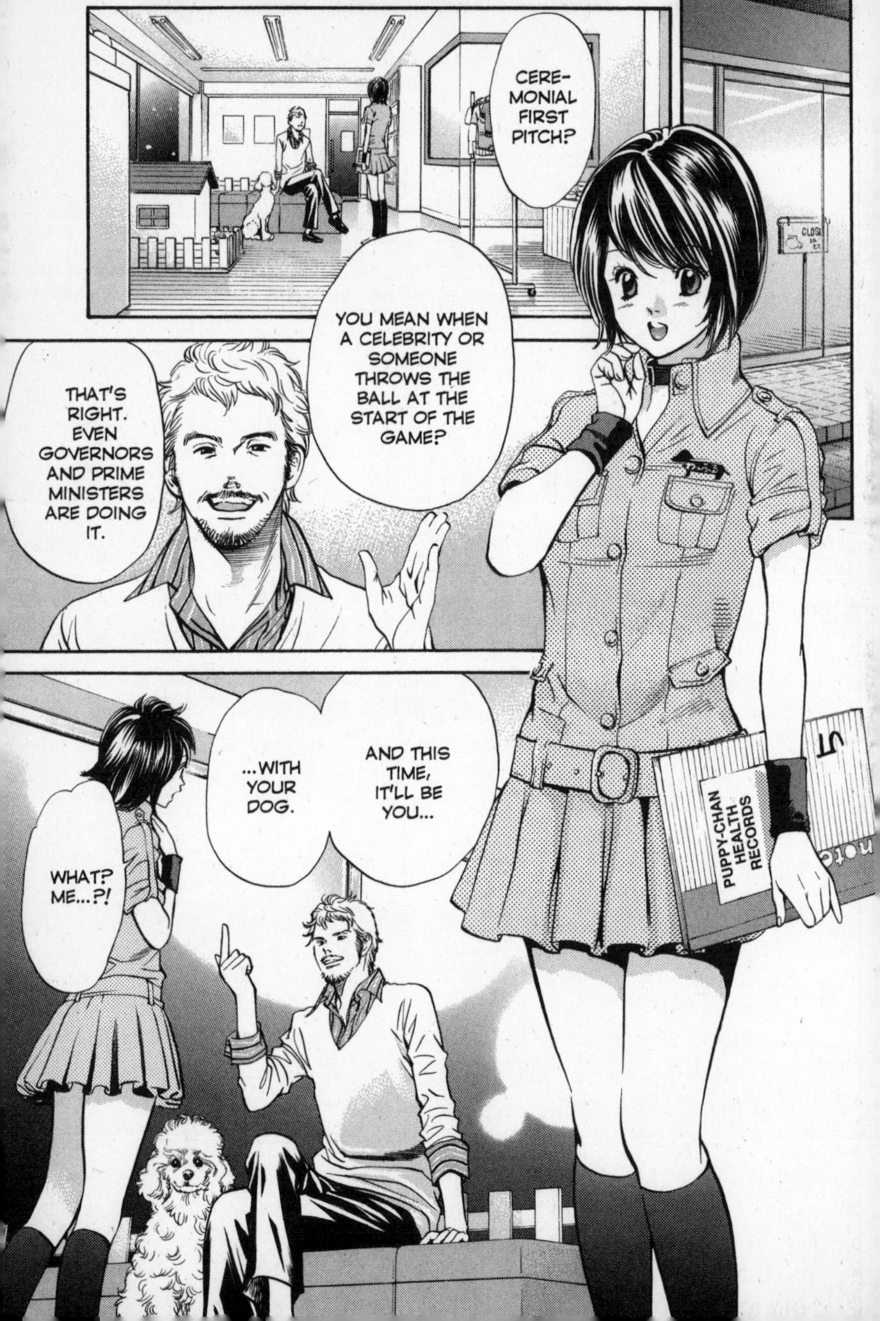
CERE-MONIAL FIRST PITCH?
YOU MEAN WHEN A CELEBRITY OR SOMEONE THROWS THE BALL AT THE START OF THE GAME?
THAT'S RIGHT. EVEN GOVERNORS AND PRIME MINISTERS ARE DOING IT.
PUPPY-CHAN HEALTH RECORDS
AND THIS TIME, IT'LL BE YOU...
...WITH YOUR DOG.
WHAT? ME...?!

CHAPTER 115: WHAT'S K-9?

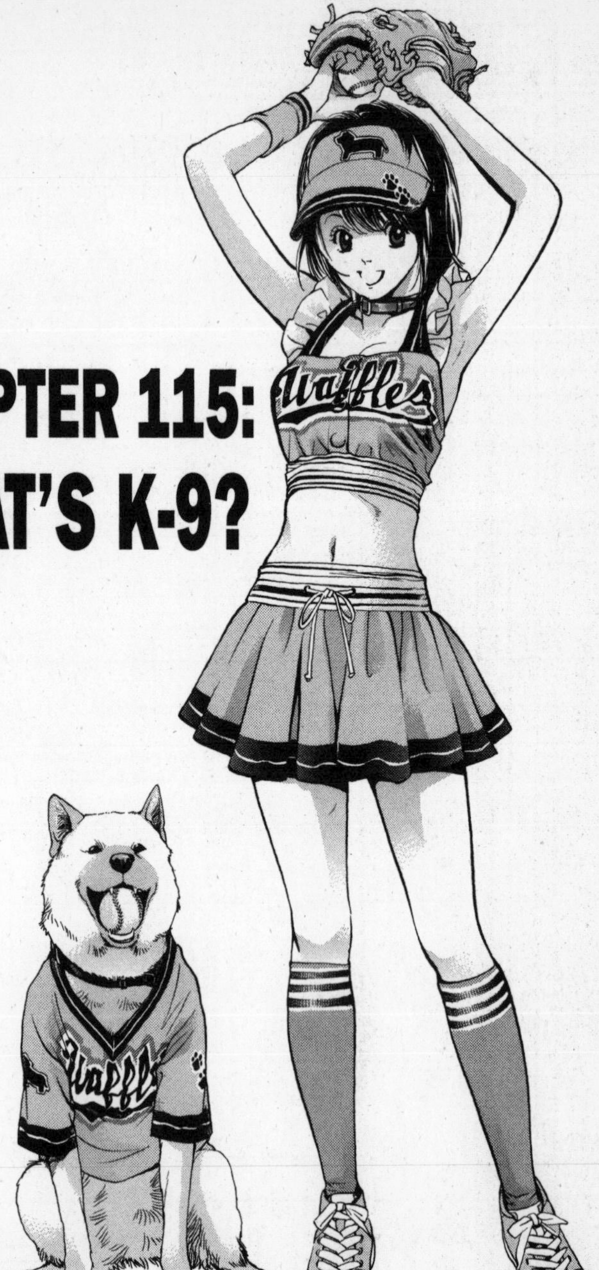
Waffles
Waffles

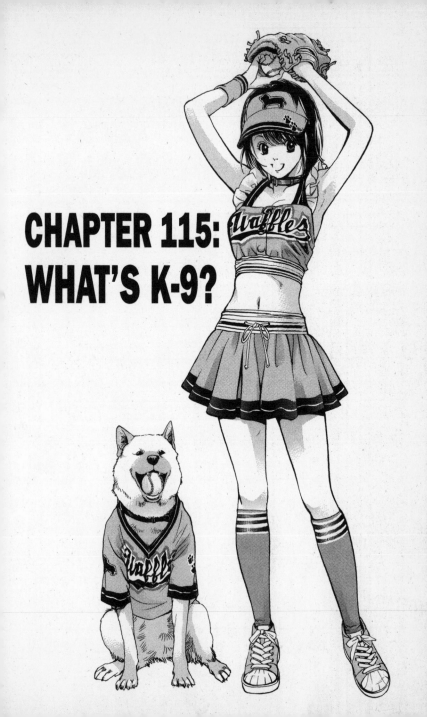

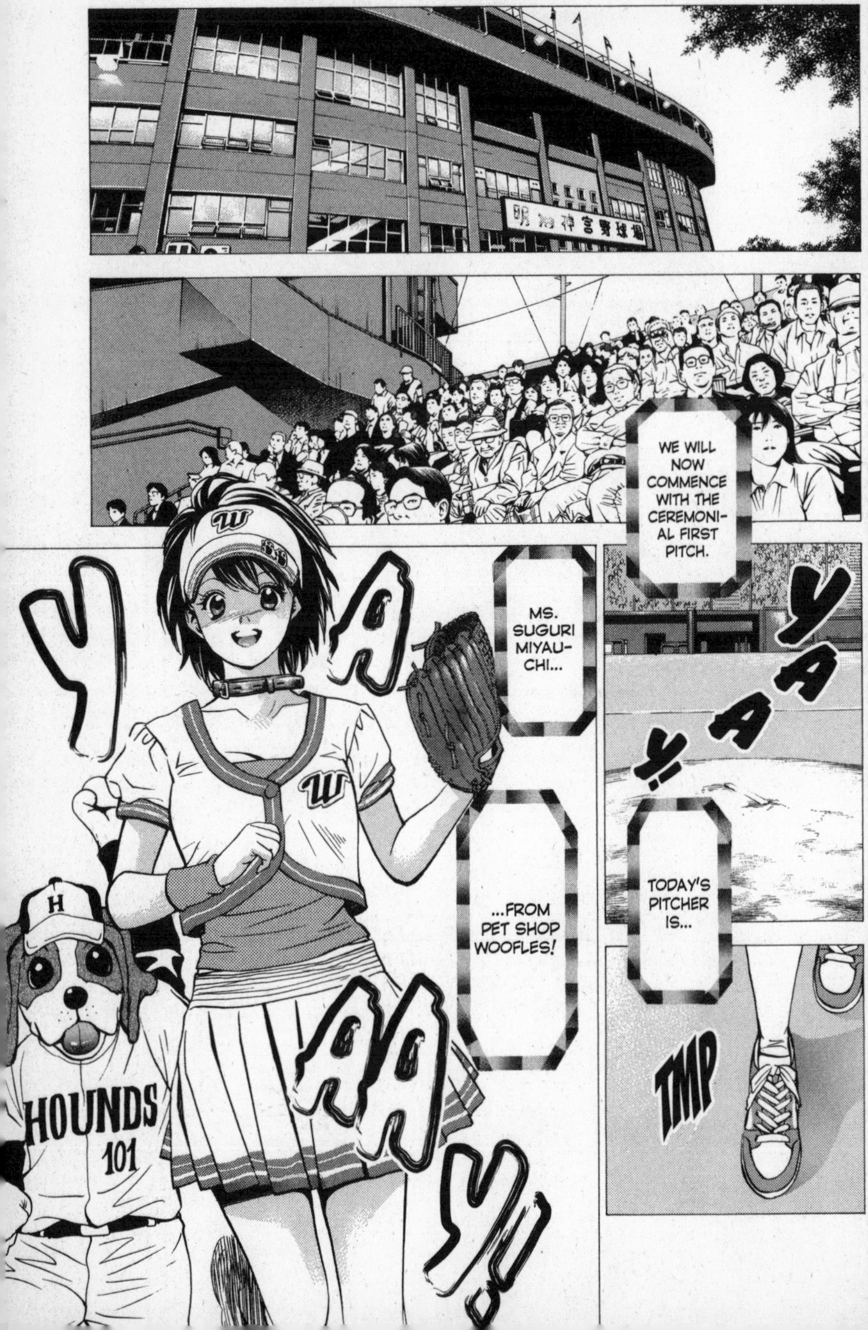
明治神宮野球場
WE WILL NOW COMMENCE WITH THE CEREMONIAL FIRST PITCH.
YAAY!
TODAY'S PITCHER IS...
TMP
MS. SUGURI MIYAUCHI...
...FROM PET SHOP WOOFLES!
YAAAAY!
HOUNDS
101

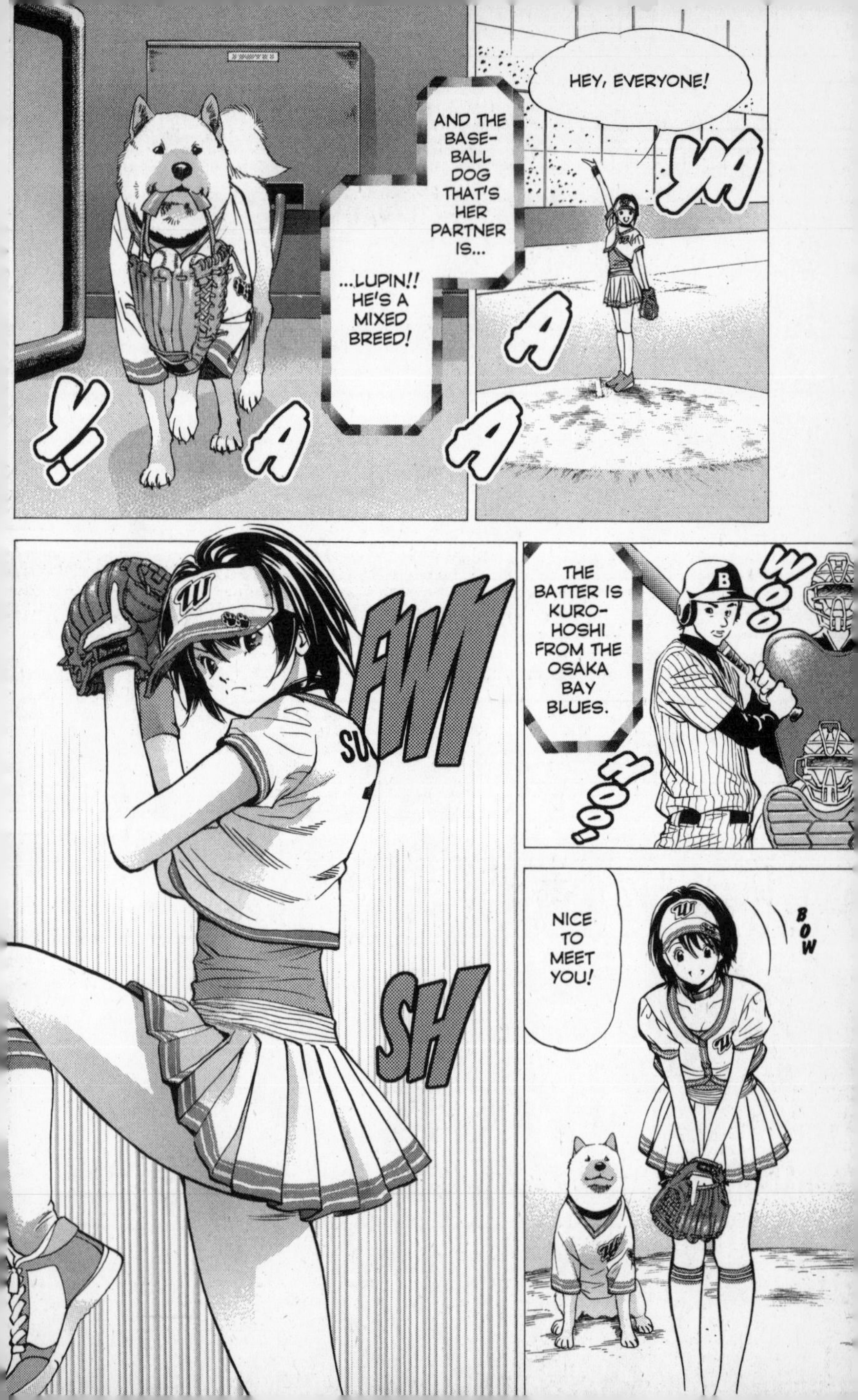
HEY, EVERYONE!
YA
A
A
AND THE BASE-BALL DOG THAT'S HER PARTNER IS...
...LUPIN!! HE'S A MIXED BREED!
A
Y!!
THE BATTER IS KURO-HOSHI FROM THE OSAKA BAY BLUES.
WOO
HOO!
NICE TO MEET YOU!
BOW
FWM
SH

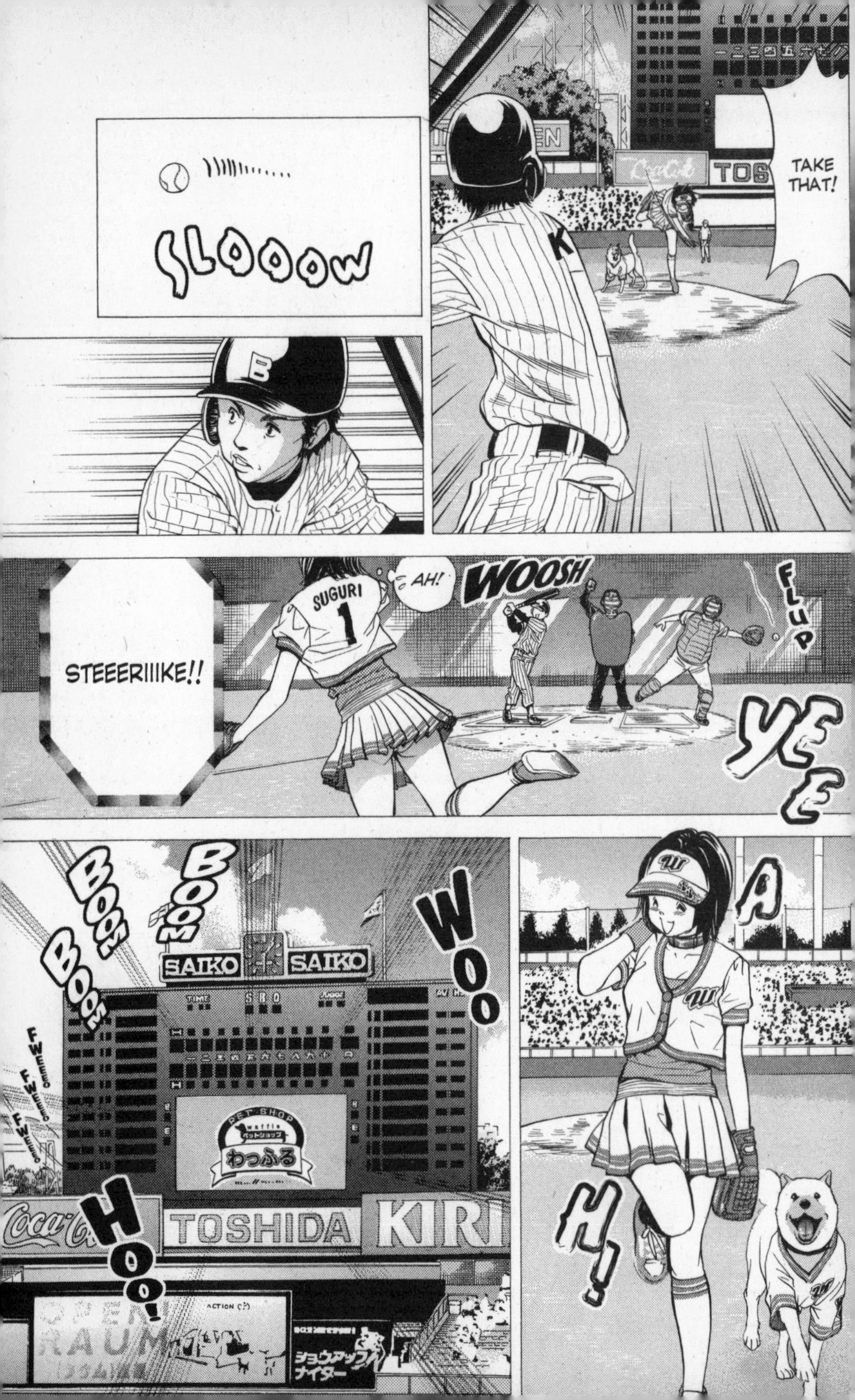

TAKE THAT!
)))))......
SLOOOW
FLUP
YEE
WOOSH
AH!
SUGURI 1
STEEERIIIKE!!
AH!
WOOO
BOOM
BOOO
BOOO
FWEEEO
FWEEEO
FWEEEO
SAIKO
SAIKO
TIME S B O
PET SHOP
waffle
ペットショップ
わっふる
TOSHIDA
KIRI
HOOO!
ACTION
ショウアップナイター

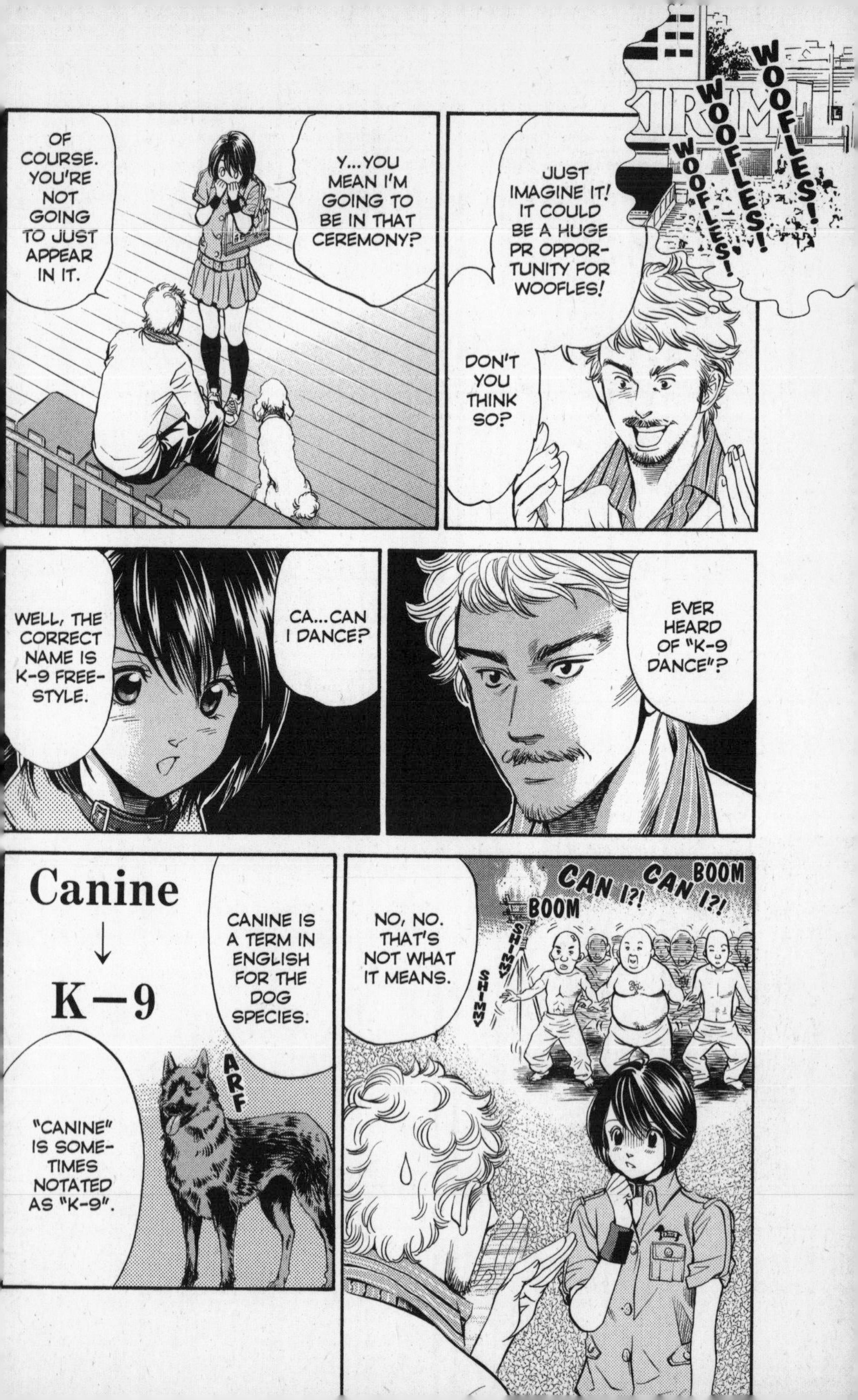
JUST IMAGINE IT! IT COULD BE A HUGE PR OPPORTUNITY FOR WOOFLES!
WOOFLES! WOOFLES! WOOFLES!
DON'T YOU THINK SO?
Y...YOU MEAN I'M GOING TO BE IN THAT CEREMONY?
OF COURSE. YOU'RE NOT GOING TO JUST APPEAR IN IT.
EVER HEARD OF "K-9 DANCE"?
CA...CAN I DANCE?
WELL, THE CORRECT NAME IS K-9 FREESTYLE.
CAN I?! CAN I?!
BOOM BOOM
SHIMMY SHIMMY
NO, NO. THAT'S NOT WHAT IT MEANS.
CANINE IS A TERM IN ENGLISH FOR THE DOG SPECIES.
Canine
↓
K−9
ARF
"CANINE" IS SOMETIMES NOTATED AS "K-9".

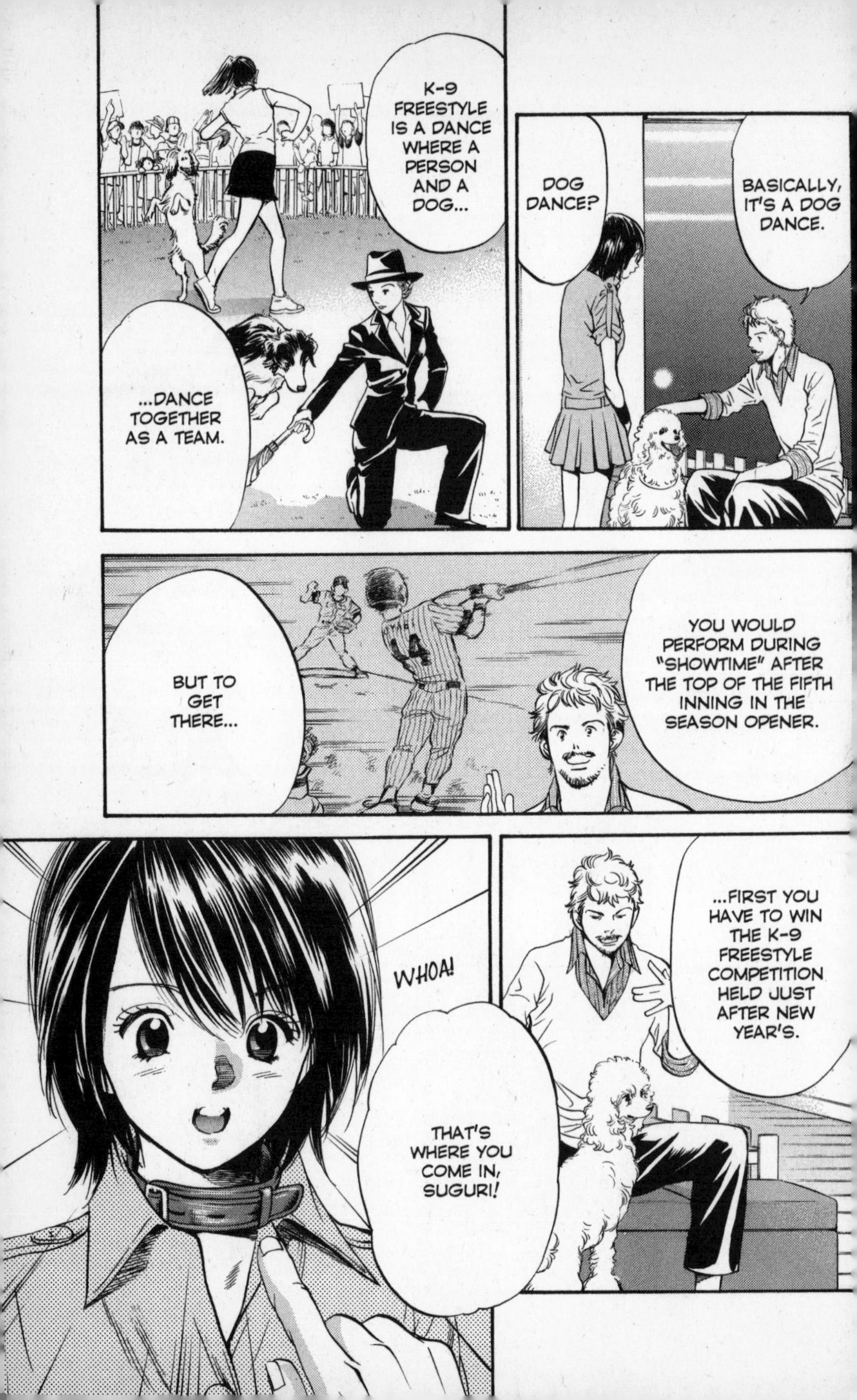
BASICALLY, IT'S A DOG DANCE.
DOG DANCE?
K-9 FREESTYLE IS A DANCE WHERE A PERSON AND A DOG...
...DANCE TOGETHER AS A TEAM.
YOU WOULD PERFORM DURING "SHOWTIME" AFTER THE TOP OF THE FIFTH INNING IN THE SEASON OPENER.
BUT TO GET THERE...
...FIRST YOU HAVE TO WIN THE K-9 FREESTYLE COMPETITION HELD JUST AFTER NEW YEAR'S.
WHOA!
THAT'S WHERE YOU COME IN, SUGURI!

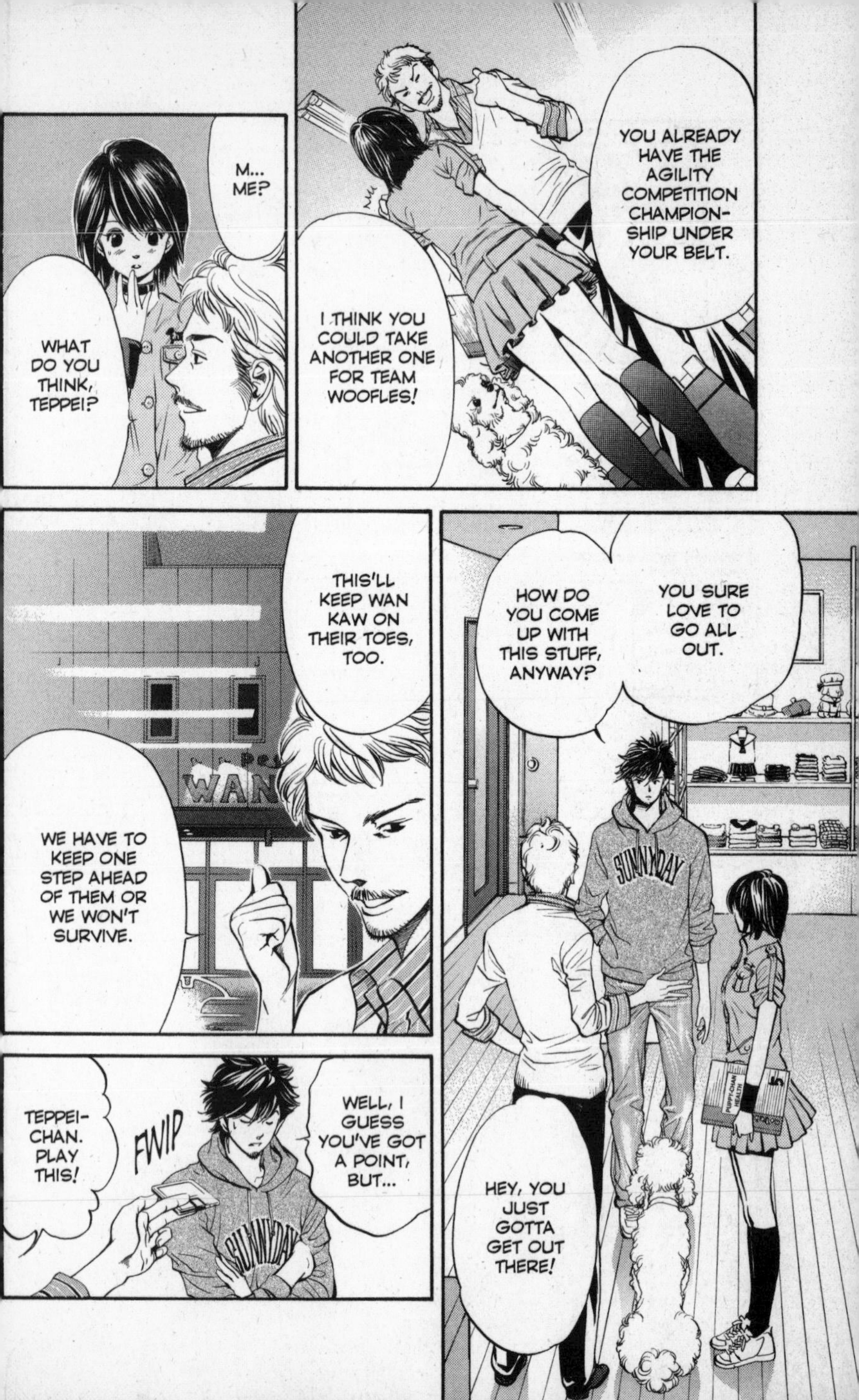
YOU ALREADY HAVE THE AGILITY COMPETITION CHAMPIONSHIP UNDER YOUR BELT.
I THINK YOU COULD TAKE ANOTHER ONE FOR TEAM WOOFLES!
M... ME?
WHAT DO YOU THINK, TEPPEI?
YOU SURE LOVE TO GO ALL OUT.
HOW DO YOU COME UP WITH THIS STUFF, ANYWAY?
HEY, YOU JUST GOTTA GET OUT THERE!
THIS'LL KEEP WAN KAW ON THEIR TOES, TOO.
WE HAVE TO KEEP ONE STEP AHEAD OF THEM OR WE WON'T SURVIVE.
WELL, I GUESS YOU'VE GOT A POINT, BUT...
FWIP
TEPPEI-CHAN. PLAY THIS!

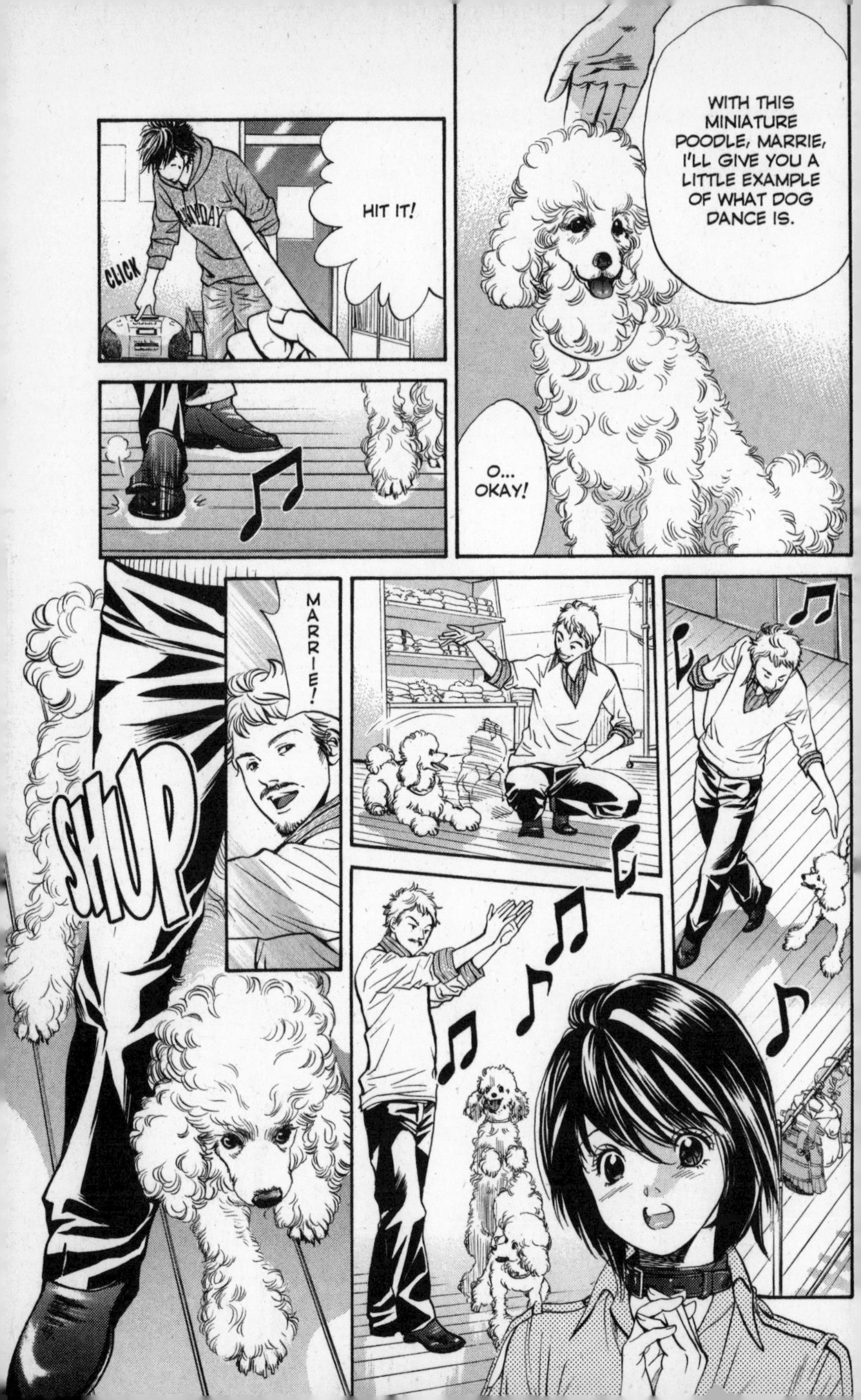
WITH THIS MINIATURE POODLE, MARRIE, I'LL GIVE YOU A LITTLE EXAMPLE OF WHAT DOG DANCE IS.
O... OKAY!
HIT IT!
CLICK
MARRIE!
SHUP

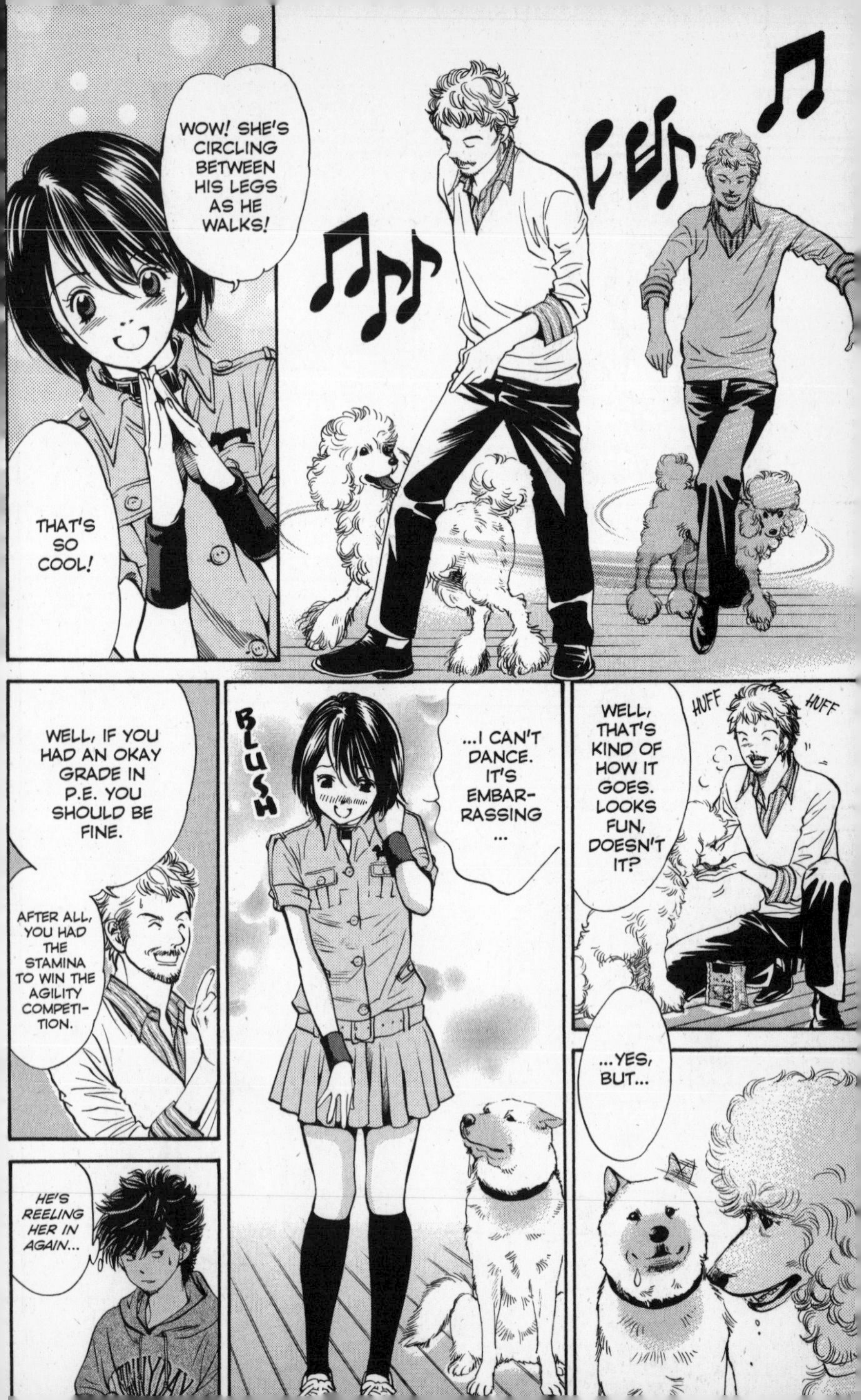
WOW! SHE'S CIRCLING BETWEEN HIS LEGS AS HE WALKS!
THAT'S SO COOL!
HUFF
HUFF
WELL, THAT'S KIND OF HOW IT GOES. LOOKS FUN, DOESN'T IT?
...YES, BUT...
BLUSH
...I CAN'T DANCE. IT'S EMBARRASSING...
WELL, IF YOU HAD AN OKAY GRADE IN P.E. YOU SHOULD BE FINE.
AFTER ALL, YOU HAD THE STAMINA TO WIN THE AGILITY COMPETITION.
HE'S REELING HER IN AGAIN...

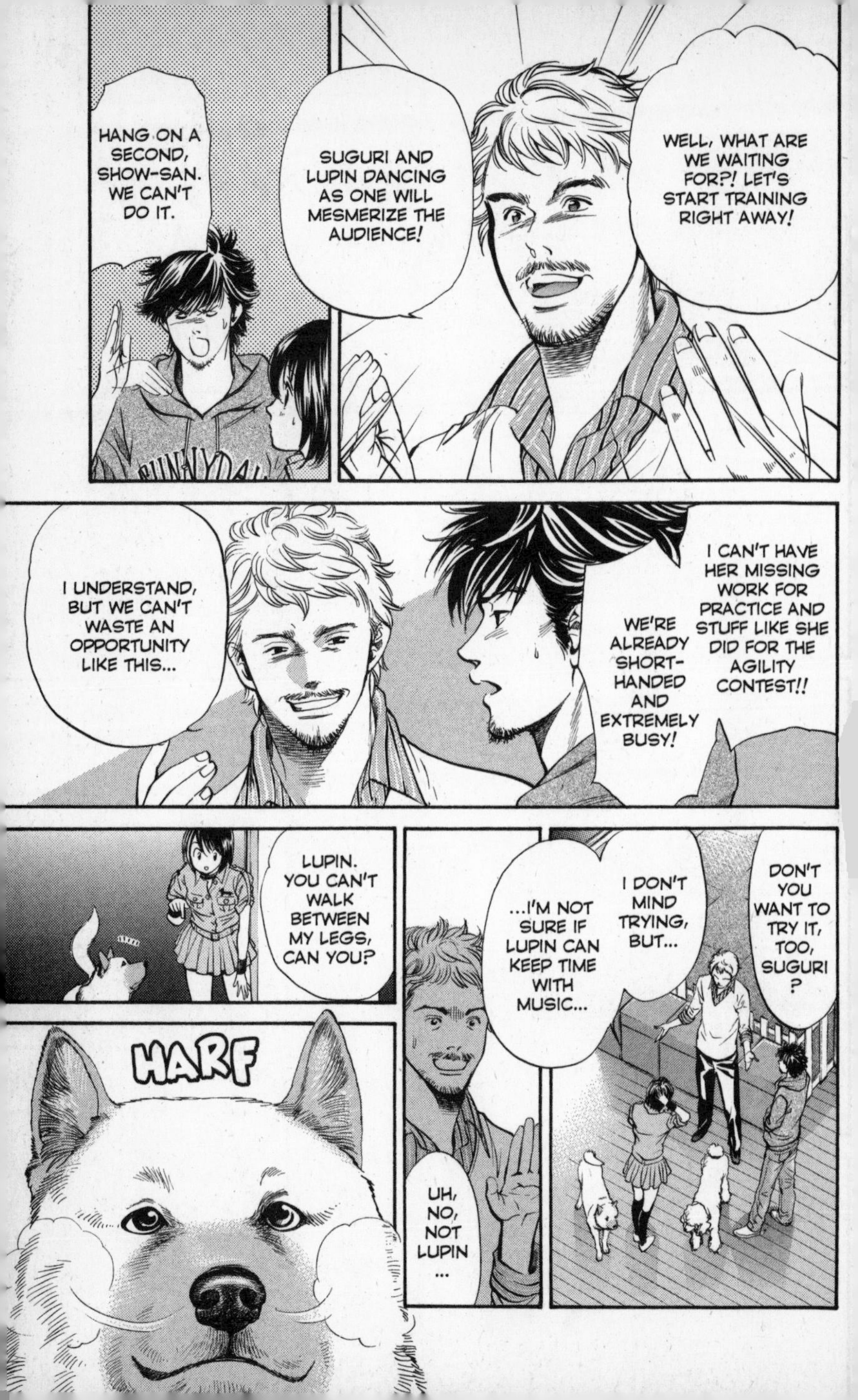
WELL, WHAT ARE WE WAITING FOR?! LET'S START TRAINING RIGHT AWAY!
SUGURI AND LUPIN DANCING AS ONE WILL MESMERIZE THE AUDIENCE!
HANG ON A SECOND, SHOW-SAN. WE CAN'T DO IT.
I CAN'T HAVE HER MISSING WORK FOR PRACTICE AND STUFF LIKE SHE DID FOR THE AGILITY CONTEST!!
WE'RE ALREADY SHORT-HANDED AND EXTREMELY BUSY!
I UNDERSTAND, BUT WE CAN'T WASTE AN OPPORTUNITY LIKE THIS...
DON'T YOU WANT TO TRY IT, TOO, SUGURI?
I DON'T MIND TRYING, BUT...
...I'M NOT SURE IF LUPIN CAN KEEP TIME WITH MUSIC...
UH, NO, NOT LUPIN...
LUPIN. YOU CAN'T WALK BETWEEN MY LEGS, CAN YOU?
HARF

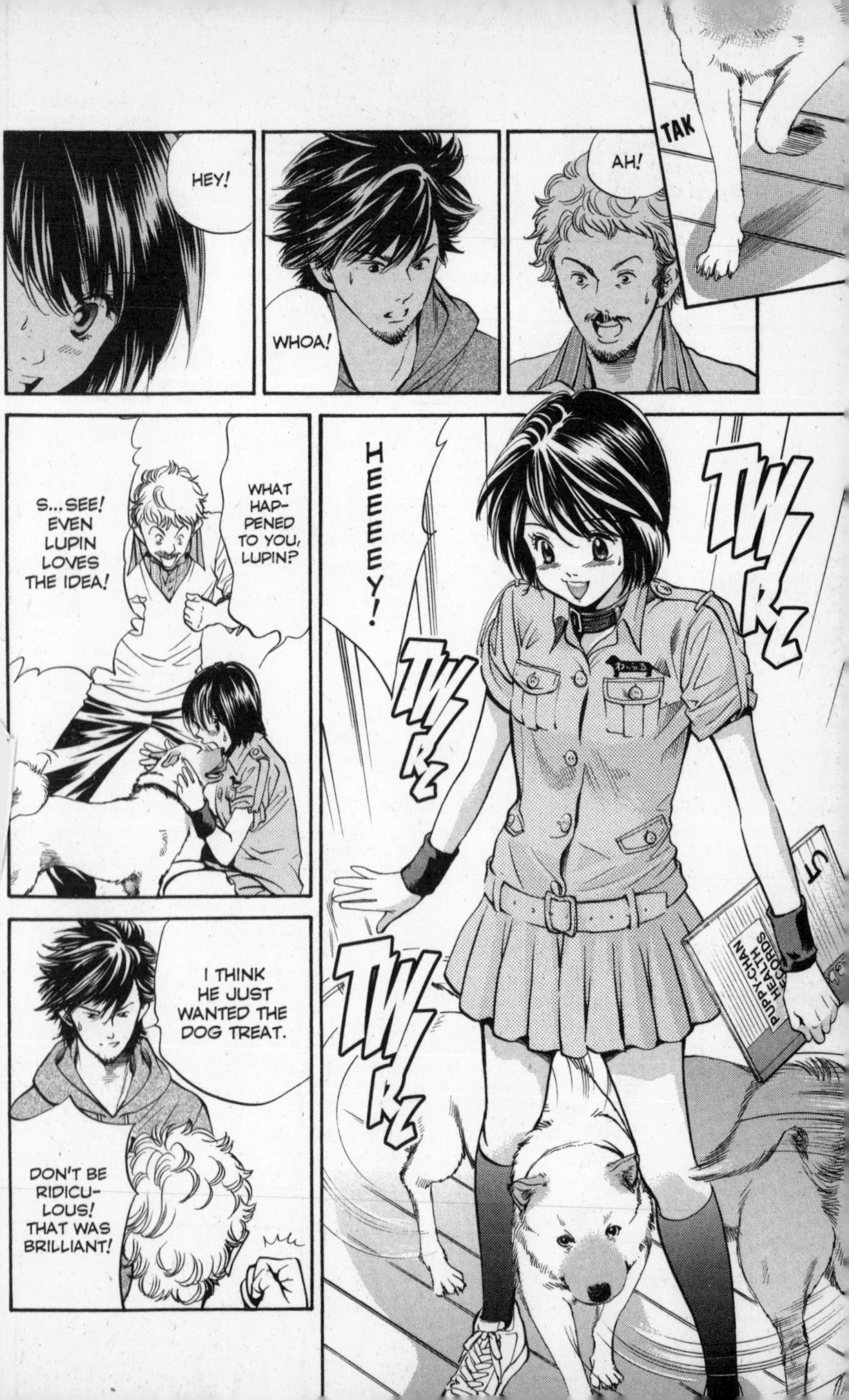
TAK
AH!
WHOA!
HEY!
HEEEEEY!
TWIRL
TWIRL
TWIRL
PUPPYCHAN HEALTH RECORDS
5
WHAT HAPPENED TO YOU, LUPIN?
S...SEE! EVEN LUPIN LOVES THE IDEA!
I THINK HE JUST WANTED THE DOG TREAT.
DON'T BE RIDICULOUS! THAT WAS BRILLIANT!

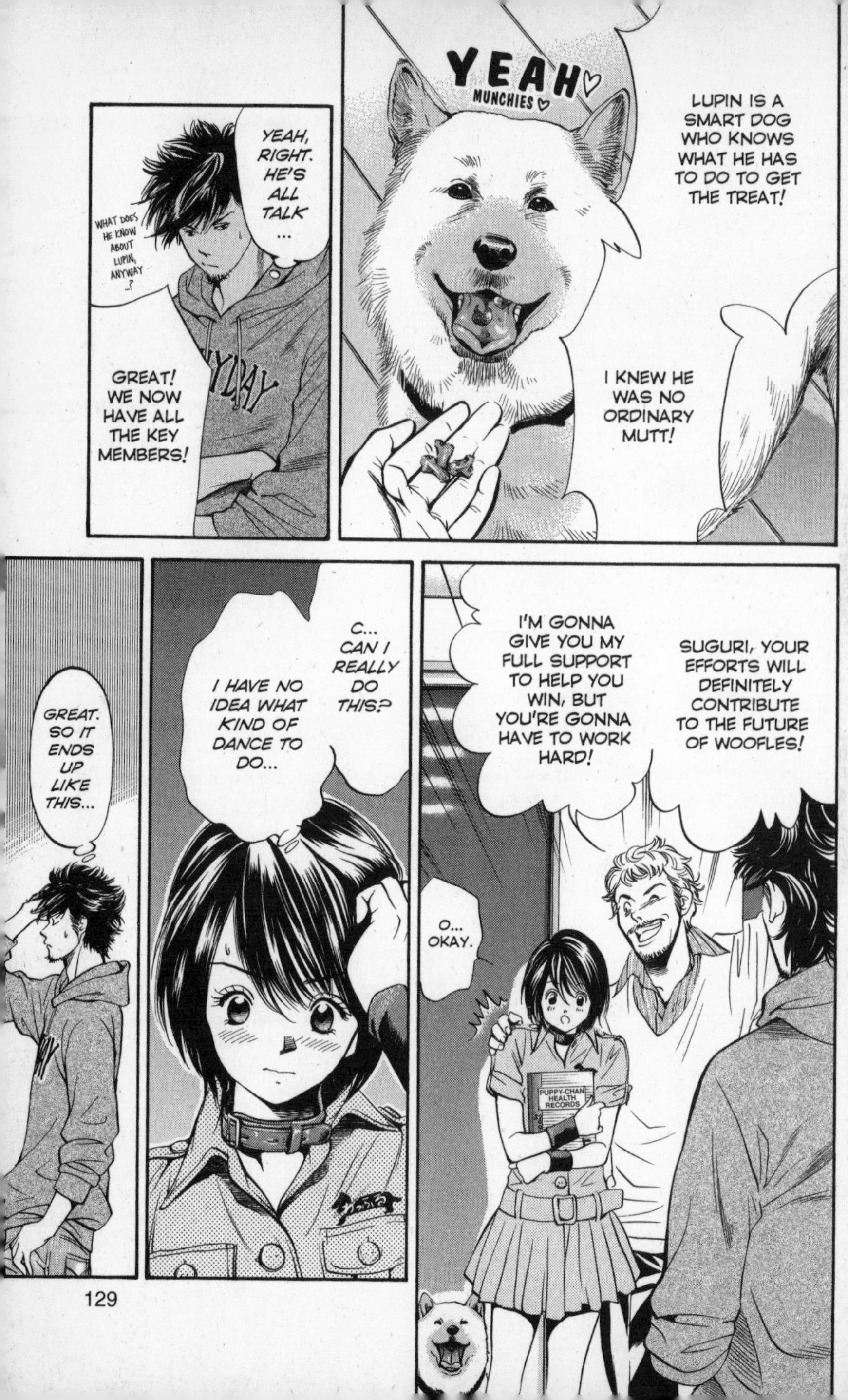
YEAH♡
MUNCHIES♡
LUPIN IS A SMART DOG WHO KNOWS WHAT HE HAS TO DO TO GET THE TREAT!
I KNEW HE WAS NO ORDINARY MUTT!
YEAH, RIGHT. HE'S ALL TALK ...
WHAT DOES HE KNOW ABOUT LUPIN, ANYWAY ...?
GREAT! WE NOW HAVE ALL THE KEY MEMBERS!
SUGURI, YOUR EFFORTS WILL DEFINITELY CONTRIBUTE TO THE FUTURE OF WOOFLES!
I'M GONNA GIVE YOU MY FULL SUPPORT TO HELP YOU WIN, BUT YOU'RE GONNA HAVE TO WORK HARD!
O... OKAY.
PUPPY-CHAN HEALTH RECORDS
C... CAN I REALLY DO THIS?
I HAVE NO IDEA WHAT KIND OF DANCE TO DO...
GREAT. SO IT ENDS UP LIKE THIS...

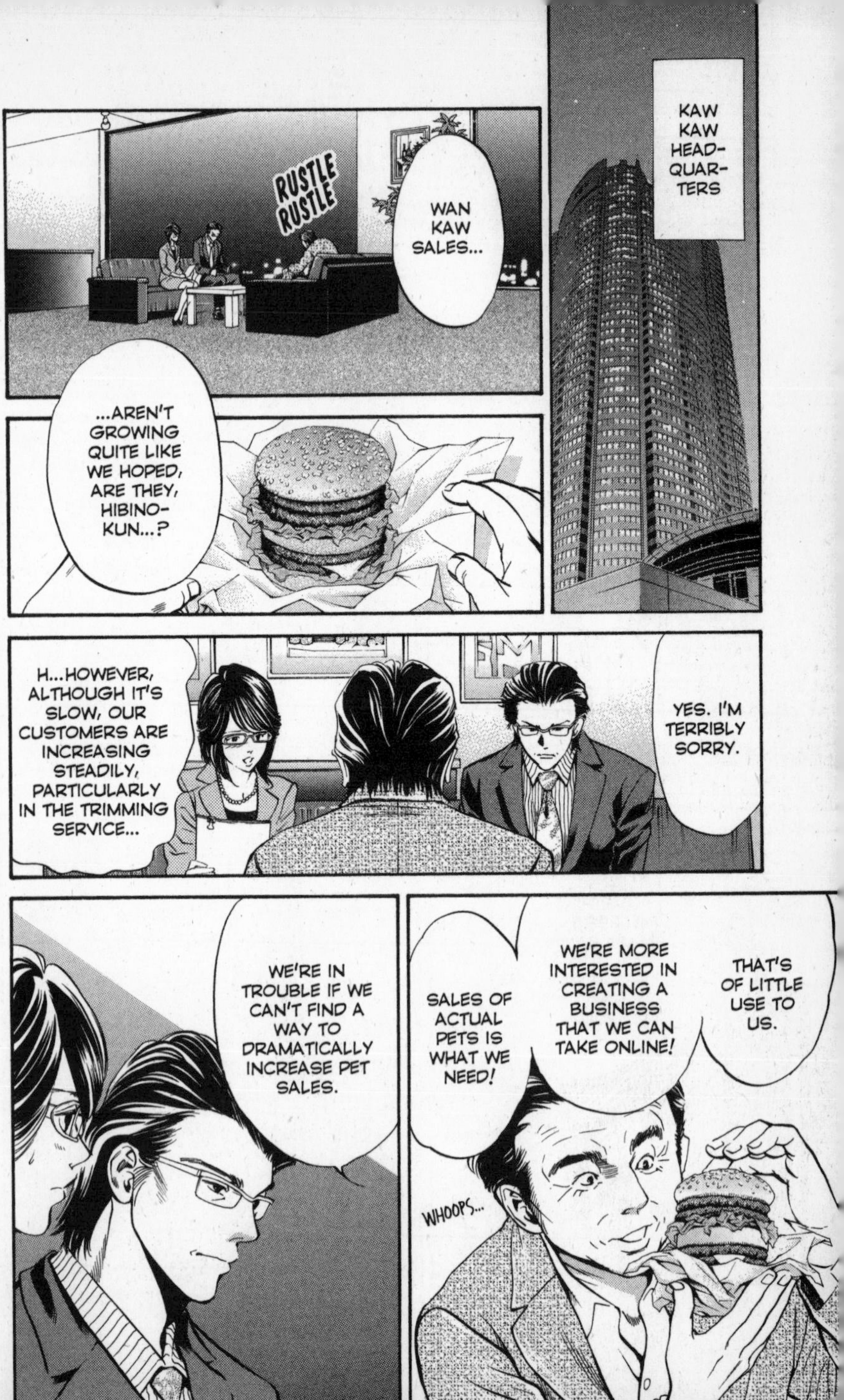
KAW KAW HEAD-QUARTERS
WAN KAW SALES...
RUSTLE RUSTLE
...AREN'T GROWING QUITE LIKE WE HOPED, ARE THEY, HIBINO-KUN...?
YES. I'M TERRIBLY SORRY.
H...HOWEVER, ALTHOUGH IT'S SLOW, OUR CUSTOMERS ARE INCREASING STEADILY, PARTICULARLY IN THE TRIMMING SERVICE...
THAT'S OF LITTLE USE TO US.
WE'RE MORE INTERESTED IN CREATING A BUSINESS THAT WE CAN TAKE ONLINE!
SALES OF ACTUAL PETS IS WHAT WE NEED!
WHOOPS...
WE'RE IN TROUBLE IF WE CAN'T FIND A WAY TO DRAMATICALLY INCREASE PET SALES.

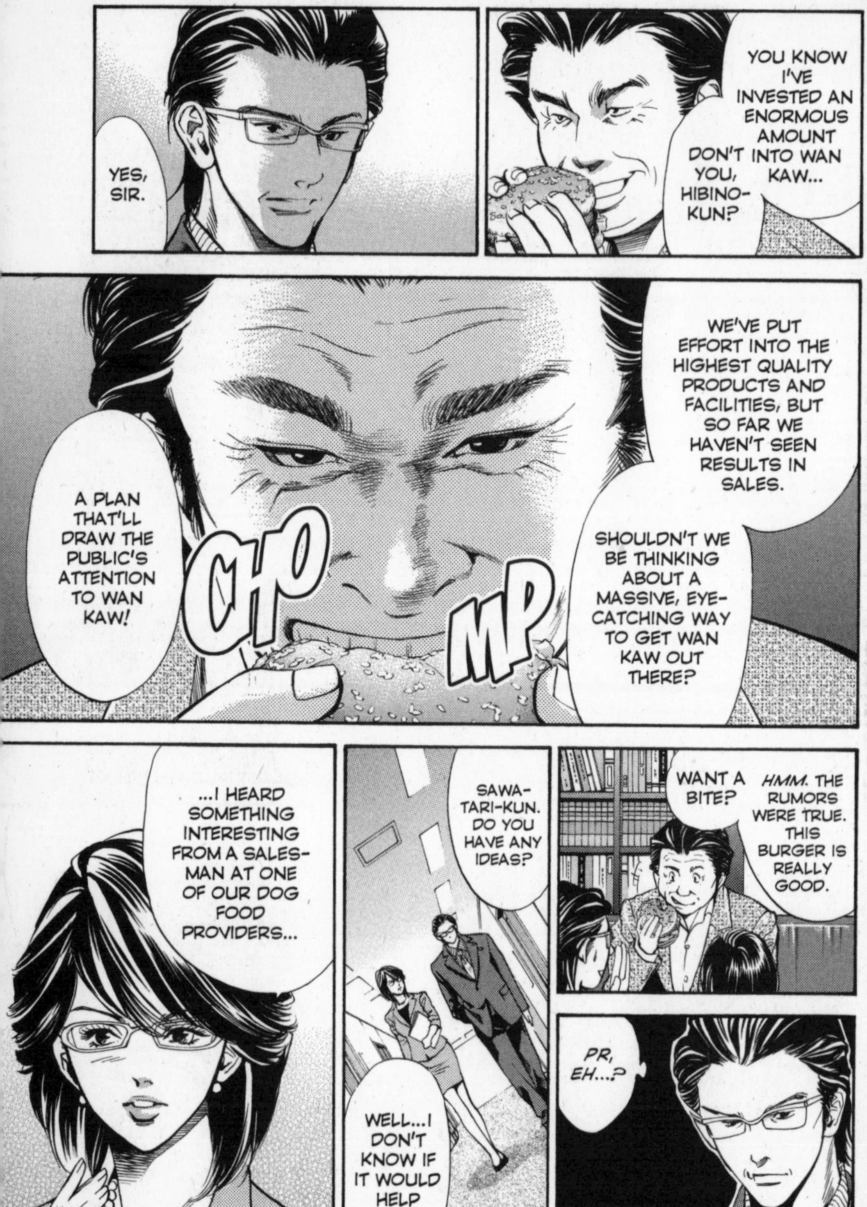
YOU KNOW I'VE INVESTED AN ENORMOUS AMOUNT INTO WAN KAW...
DON'T YOU, HIBINO-KUN?
YES, SIR.
WE'VE PUT EFFORT INTO THE HIGHEST QUALITY PRODUCTS AND FACILITIES, BUT SO FAR WE HAVEN'T SEEN RESULTS IN SALES.
SHOULDN'T WE BE THINKING ABOUT A MASSIVE, EYE-CATCHING WAY TO GET WAN KAW OUT THERE?
A PLAN THAT'LL DRAW THE PUBLIC'S ATTENTION TO WAN KAW!
CHOMP
HMM. THE RUMORS WERE TRUE. THIS BURGER IS REALLY GOOD.
WANT A BITE?
PR, EH...?
SAWA-TARI-KUN. DO YOU HAVE ANY IDEAS?
WELL...I DON'T KNOW IF IT WOULD HELP BUT...
...I HEARD SOMETHING INTERESTING FROM A SALES-MAN AT ONE OF OUR DOG FOOD PROVIDERS...

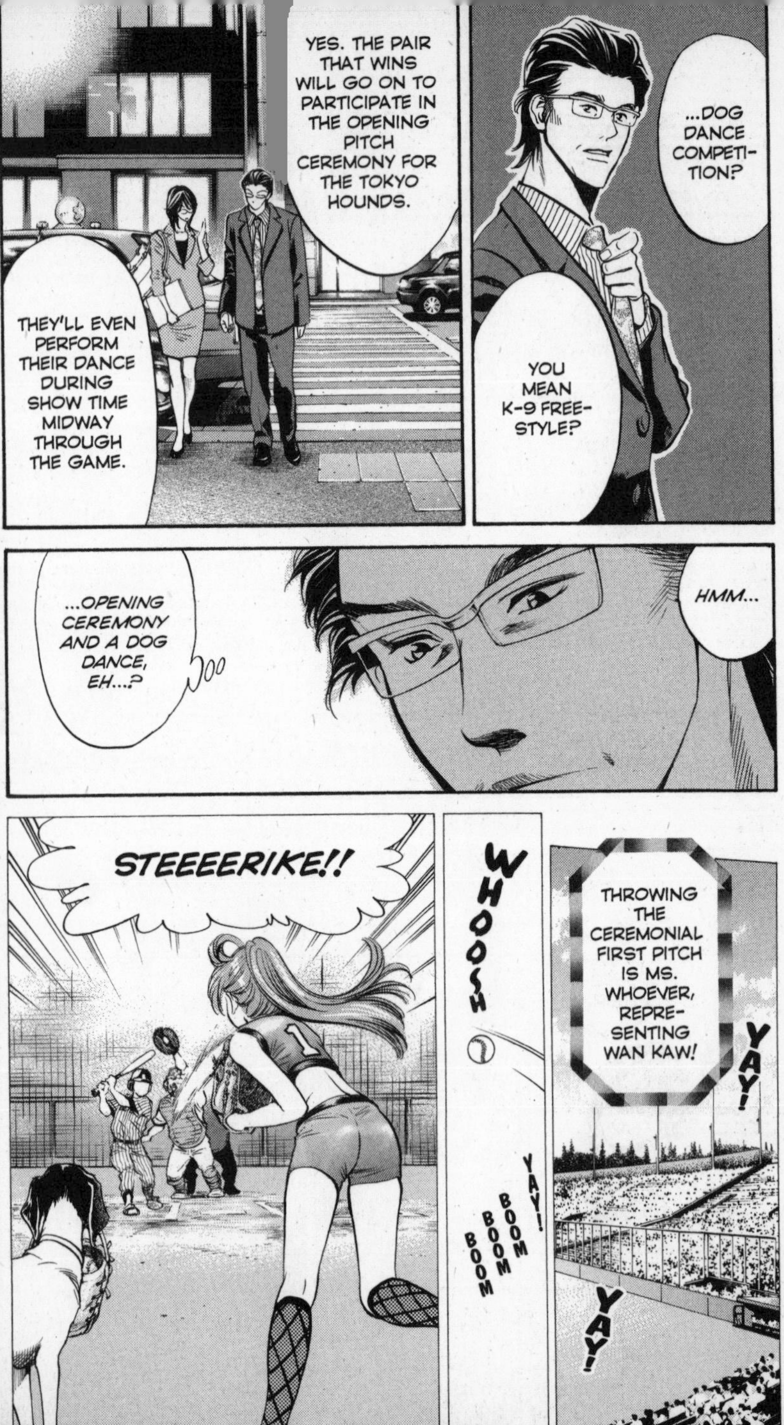
...DOG DANCE COMPETI-TION?
YOU MEAN K-9 FREE-STYLE?
YES. THE PAIR THAT WINS WILL GO ON TO PARTICIPATE IN THE OPENING PITCH CEREMONY FOR THE TOKYO HOUNDS.
THEY'LL EVEN PERFORM THEIR DANCE DURING SHOW TIME MIDWAY THROUGH THE GAME.
HMM...
...OPENING CEREMONY AND A DOG DANCE, EH...?
THROWING THE CEREMONIAL FIRST PITCH IS MS. WHOEVER, REPRE-SENTING WAN KAW!
YAY!
YAY!
WHOOSH
YAY!
BOOM BOOM BOOM
STEEEERIKE!!

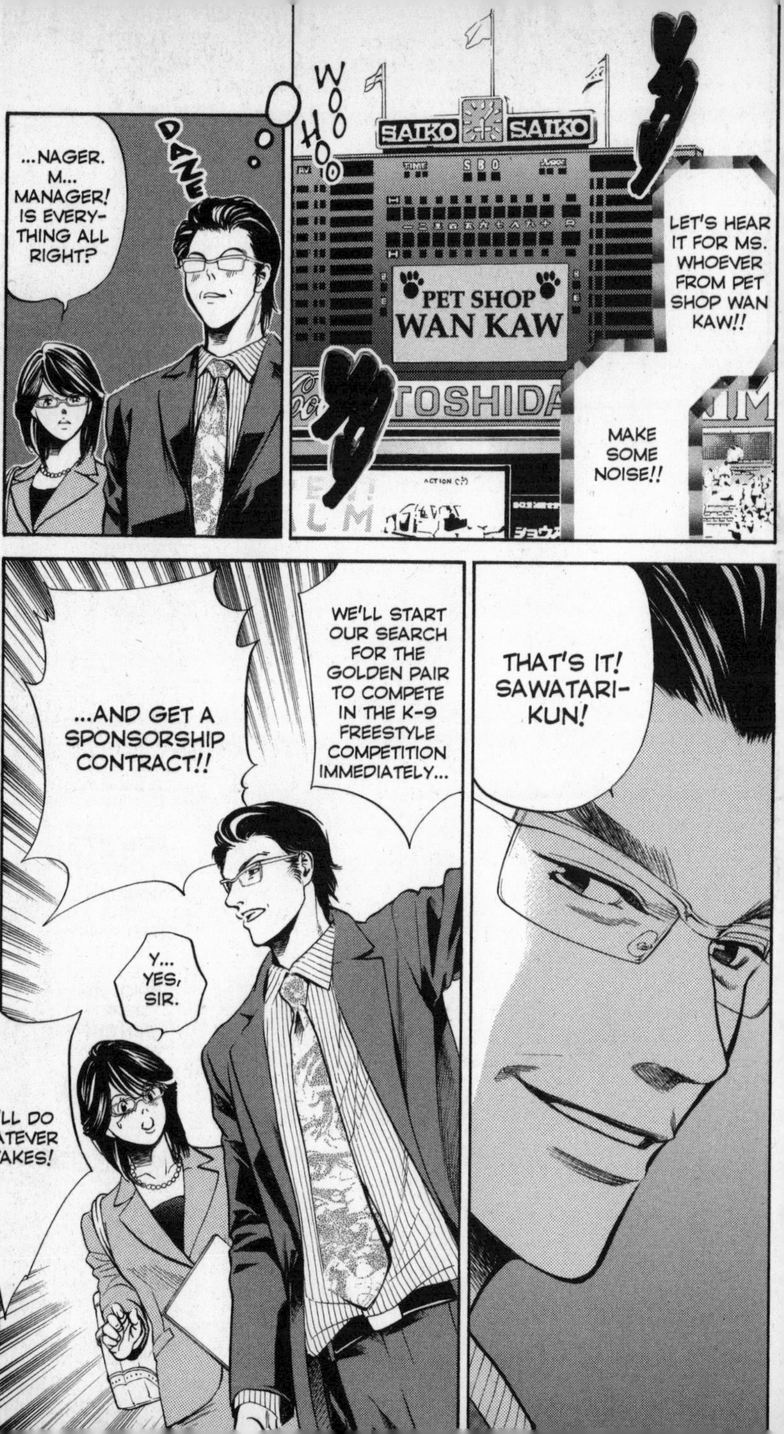
WOOHOO
SAIKO SAIKO
PET SHOP WAN KAW
TOSHIDA
LET'S HEAR IT FOR MS. WHOEVER FROM PET SHOP WAN KAW!!
MAKE SOME NOISE!!
DAZE
...NAGER. M... MANAGER! IS EVERYTHING ALL RIGHT?
THAT'S IT! SAWATARI-KUN!
WE'LL START OUR SEARCH FOR THE GOLDEN PAIR TO COMPETE IN THE K-9 FREESTYLE COMPETITION IMMEDIATELY...
...AND GET A SPONSORSHIP CONTRACT!!
Y... YES, SIR.
WE'LL DO WHATEVER IT TAKES!

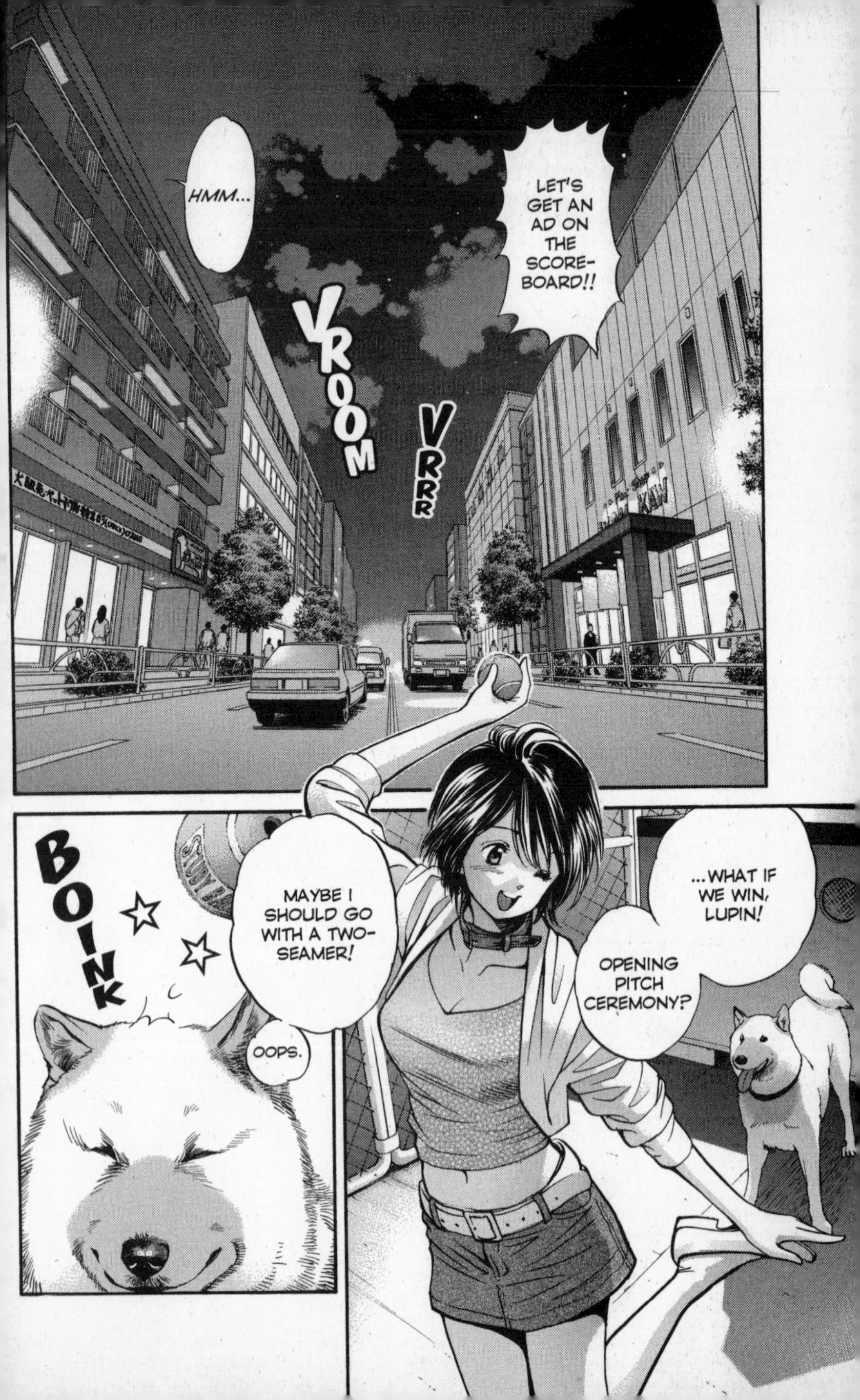
LET'S GET AN AD ON THE SCOREBOARD!!
HMM...
VROOM
VRRR
...WHAT IF WE WIN, LUPIN!
OPENING PITCH CEREMONY?
MAYBE I SHOULD GO WITH A TWO-SEAMER!
BOINK
OOPS.

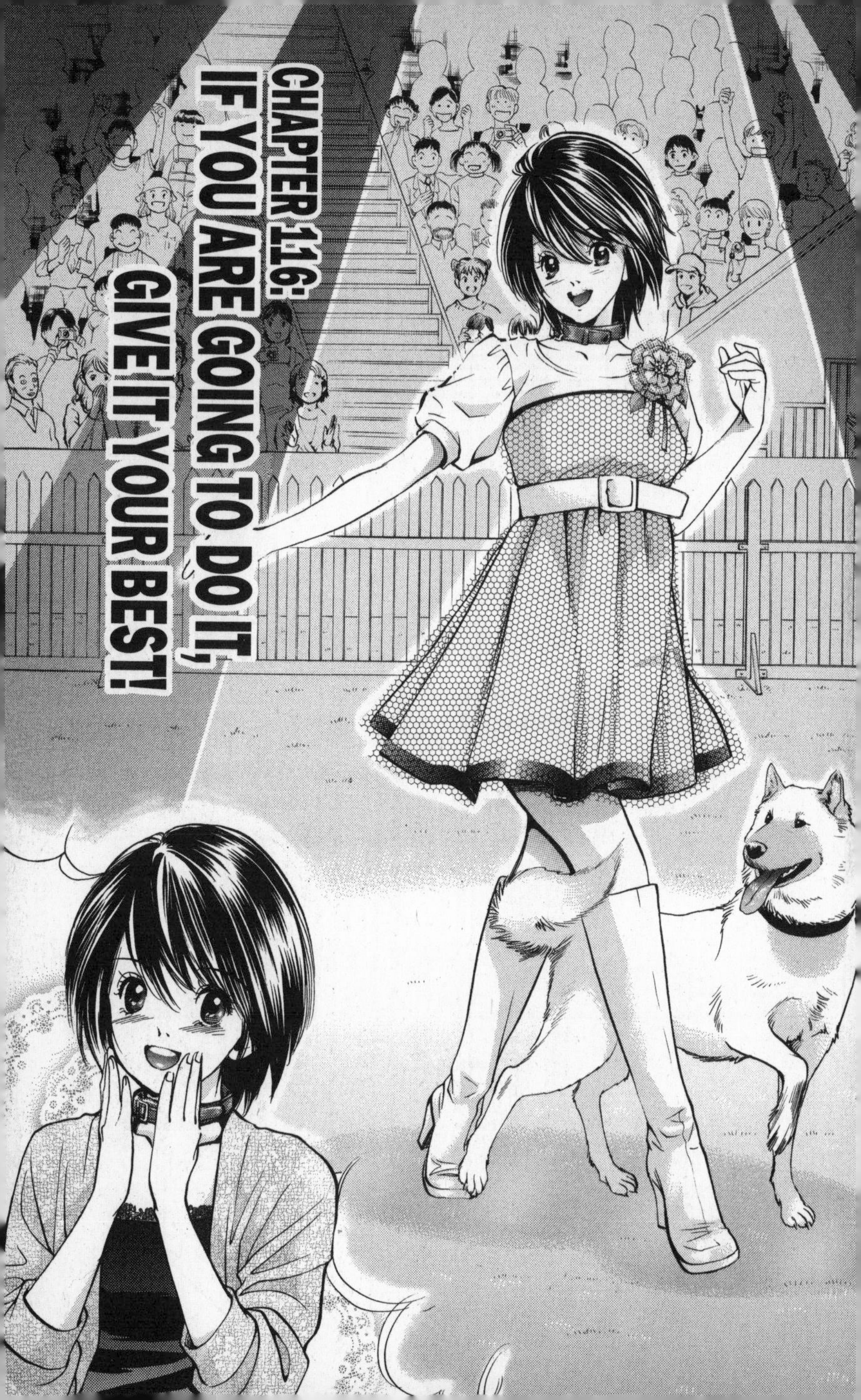
CHAPTER 116:
IF YOU ARE GOING TO DO IT,
GIVE IT YOUR BEST!

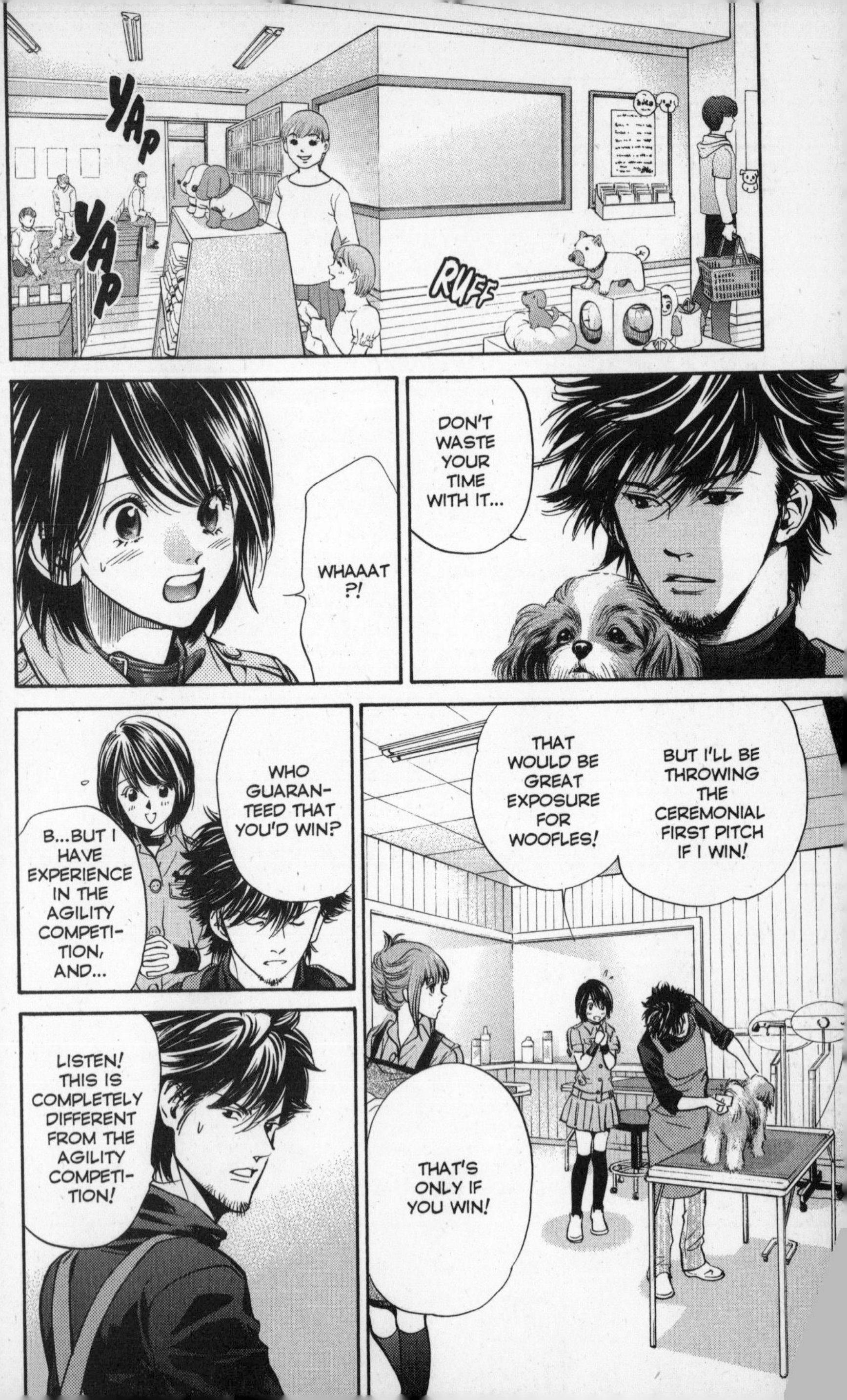
YAP
YAP
RUFF
DON'T WASTE YOUR TIME WITH IT...
WHAAAT?!
BUT I'LL BE THROWING THE CEREMONIAL FIRST PITCH IF I WIN!
THAT WOULD BE GREAT EXPOSURE FOR WOOFLES!
THAT'S ONLY IF YOU WIN!
WHO GUARAN-TEED THAT YOU'D WIN?
B...BUT I HAVE EXPERIENCE IN THE AGILITY COMPETI-TION, AND...
LISTEN! THIS IS COMPLETELY DIFFERENT FROM THE AGILITY COMPETI-TION!

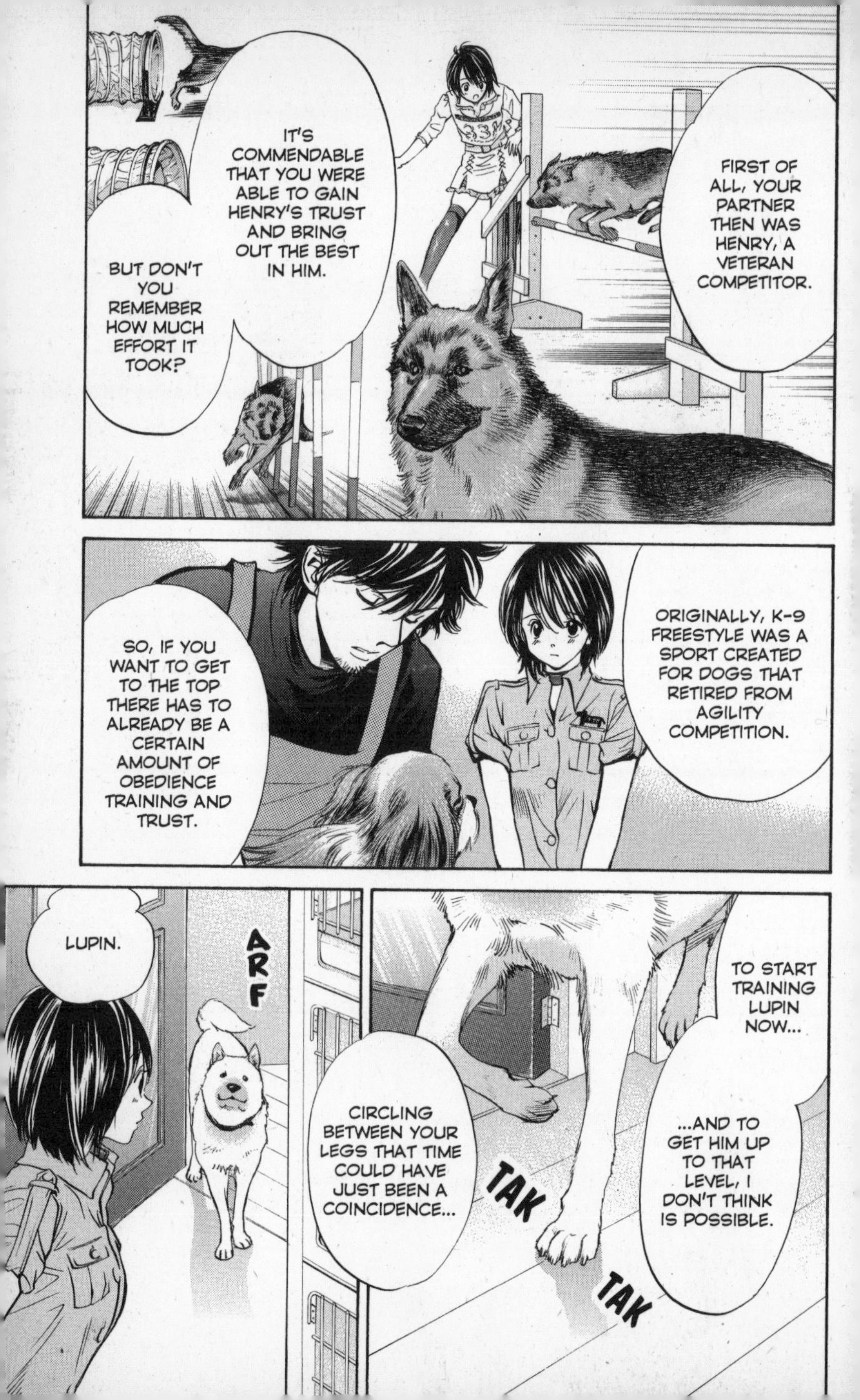
FIRST OF ALL, YOUR PARTNER THEN WAS HENRY, A VETERAN COMPETITOR.
IT'S COMMENDABLE THAT YOU WERE ABLE TO GAIN HENRY'S TRUST AND BRING OUT THE BEST IN HIM.
BUT DON'T YOU REMEMBER HOW MUCH EFFORT IT TOOK?
ORIGINALLY, K-9 FREESTYLE WAS A SPORT CREATED FOR DOGS THAT RETIRED FROM AGILITY COMPETITION.
SO, IF YOU WANT TO GET TO THE TOP THERE HAS TO ALREADY BE A CERTAIN AMOUNT OF OBEDIENCE TRAINING AND TRUST.
TO START TRAINING LUPIN NOW...
...AND TO GET HIM UP TO THAT LEVEL, I DON'T THINK IS POSSIBLE.
CIRCLING BETWEEN YOUR LEGS THAT TIME COULD HAVE JUST BEEN A COINCIDENCE...
TAK
TAK
ARF
LUPIN.

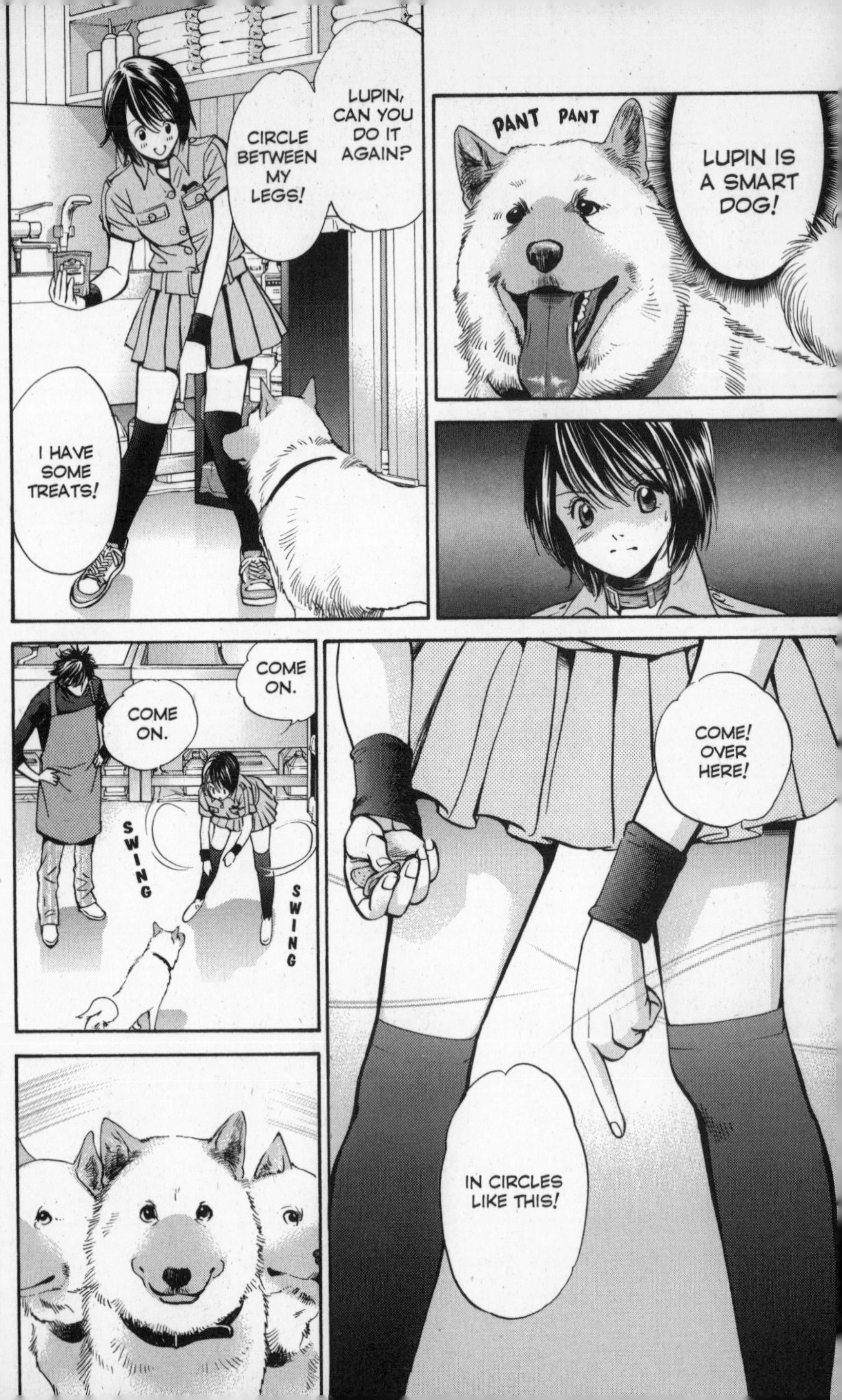
PANT PANT
LUPIN IS A SMART DOG!
LUPIN, CAN YOU DO IT AGAIN?
CIRCLE BETWEEN MY LEGS!
I HAVE SOME TREATS!
COME! OVER HERE!
IN CIRCLES LIKE THIS!
COME ON.
COME ON.
SWING
SWING

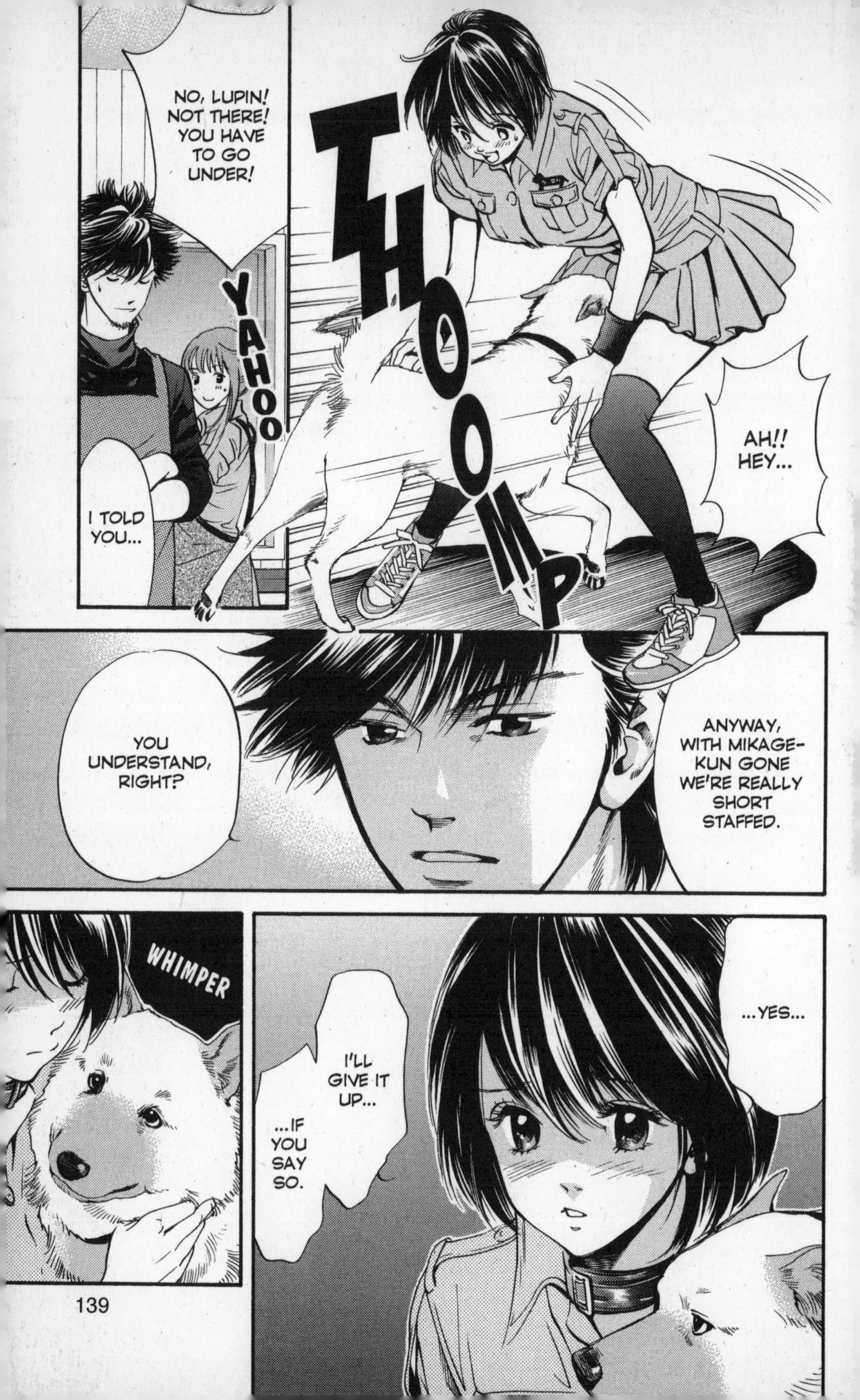
THOOOMP
AH!! HEY...
NO, LUPIN! NOT THERE! YOU HAVE TO GO UNDER!
YAHOO
I TOLD YOU...
ANYWAY, WITH MIKAGE-KUN GONE WE'RE REALLY SHORT STAFFED.
YOU UNDERSTAND, RIGHT?
...YES...
I'LL GIVE IT UP...
...IF YOU SAY SO.
WHIMPER

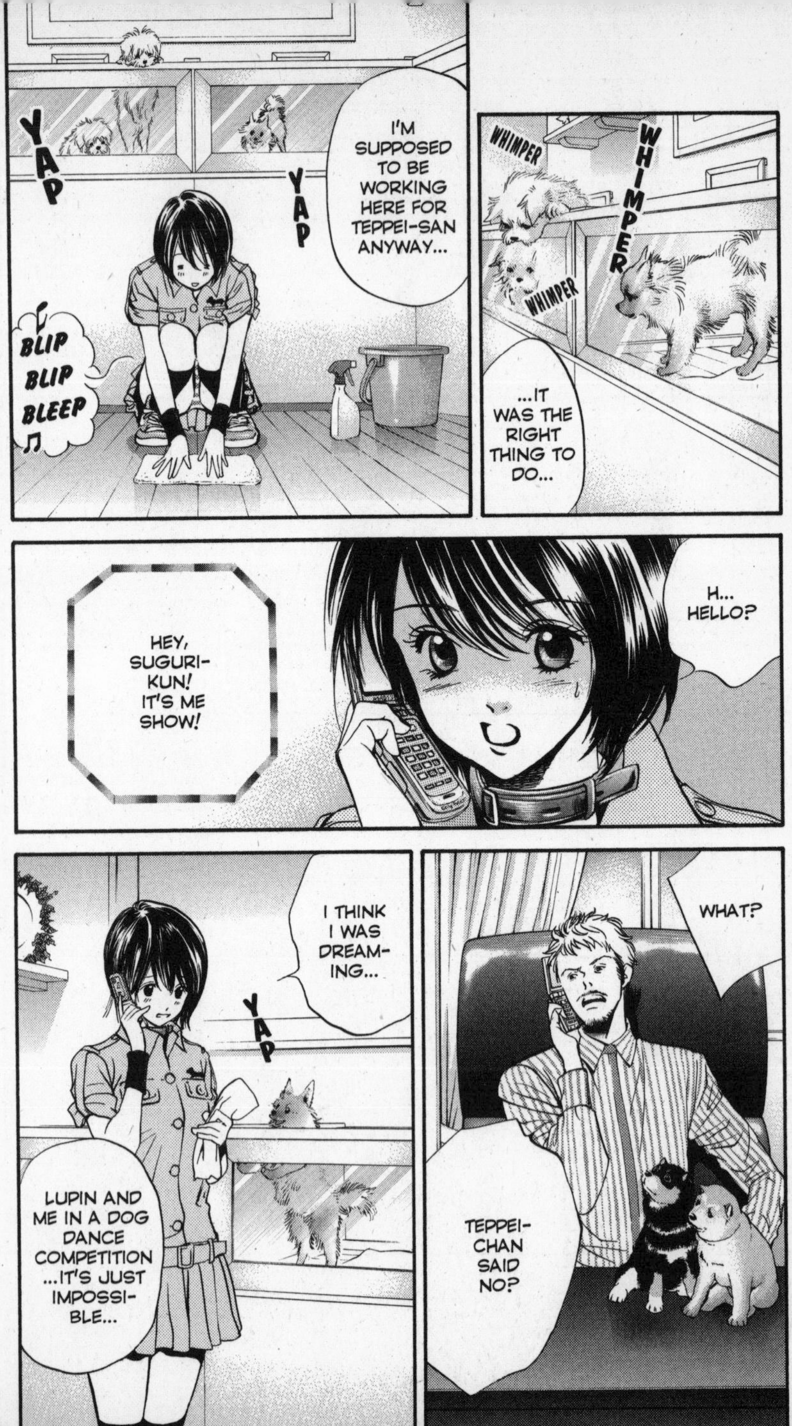
WHIMPER
WHIMPER
WHIMPER
...IT WAS THE RIGHT THING TO DO...
I'M SUPPOSED TO BE WORKING HERE FOR TEPPEI-SAN ANYWAY...
YAP
YAP
BLIP BLIP BLEEP ♫
H... HELLO?
HEY, SUGURI-KUN! IT'S ME SHOW!
WHAT?
TEPPEI-CHAN SAID NO?
I THINK I WAS DREAM-ING...
YAP
LUPIN AND ME IN A DOG DANCE COMPETITION ...IT'S JUST IMPOSSI-BLE...

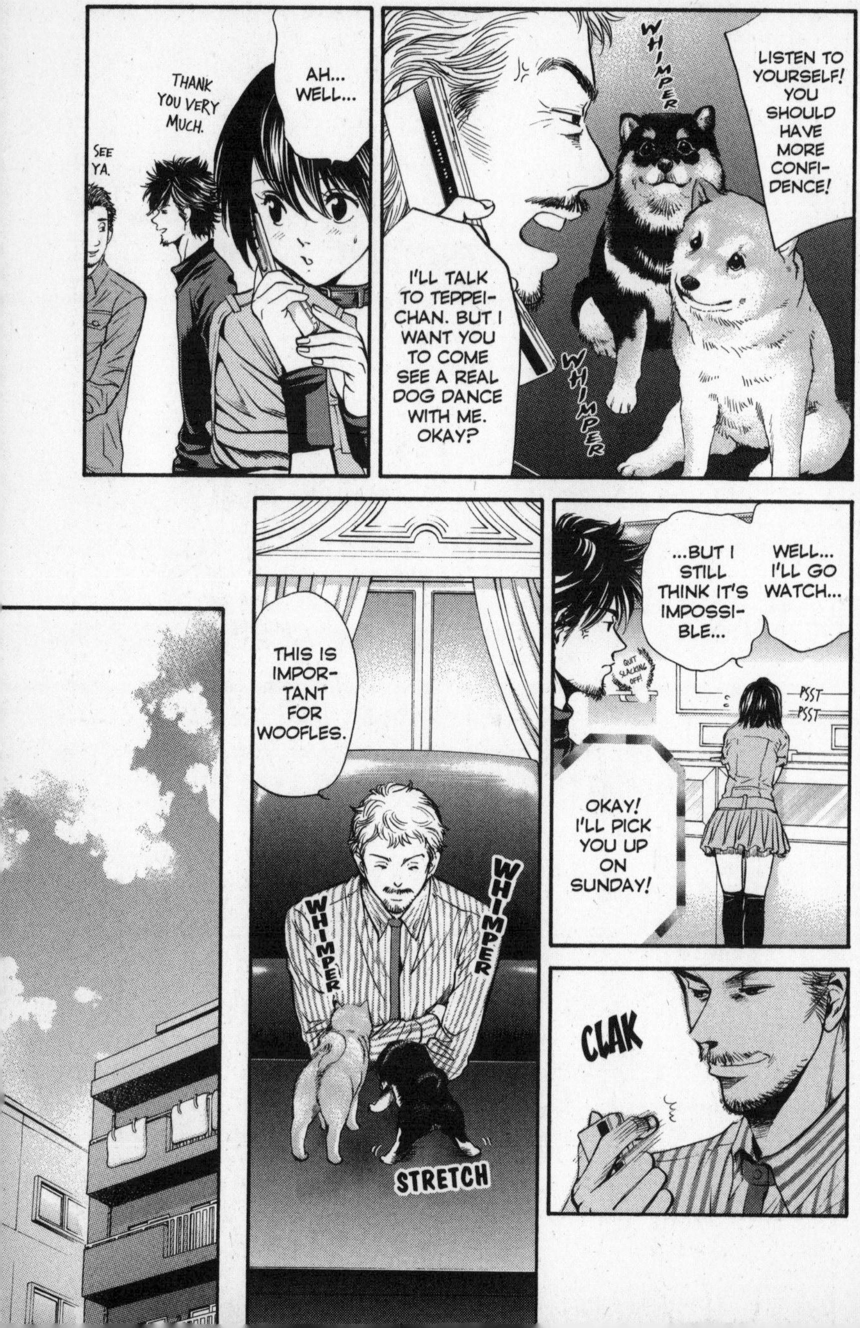
LISTEN TO YOURSELF! YOU SHOULD HAVE MORE CONFI-DENCE!
WHIMPER
I'LL TALK TO TEPPEI-CHAN. BUT I WANT YOU TO COME SEE A REAL DOG DANCE WITH ME. OKAY?
WHIMPER
AH... WELL...
THANK YOU VERY MUCH.
SEE YA.
WELL... I'LL GO WATCH...
...BUT I STILL THINK IT'S IMPOSSI-BLE...
QUIT SLACKING OFF!
PSST
PSST
OKAY! I'LL PICK YOU UP ON SUNDAY!
CLAK
THIS IS IMPOR-TANT FOR WOOFLES.
WHIMPER
WHIMPER
STRETCH

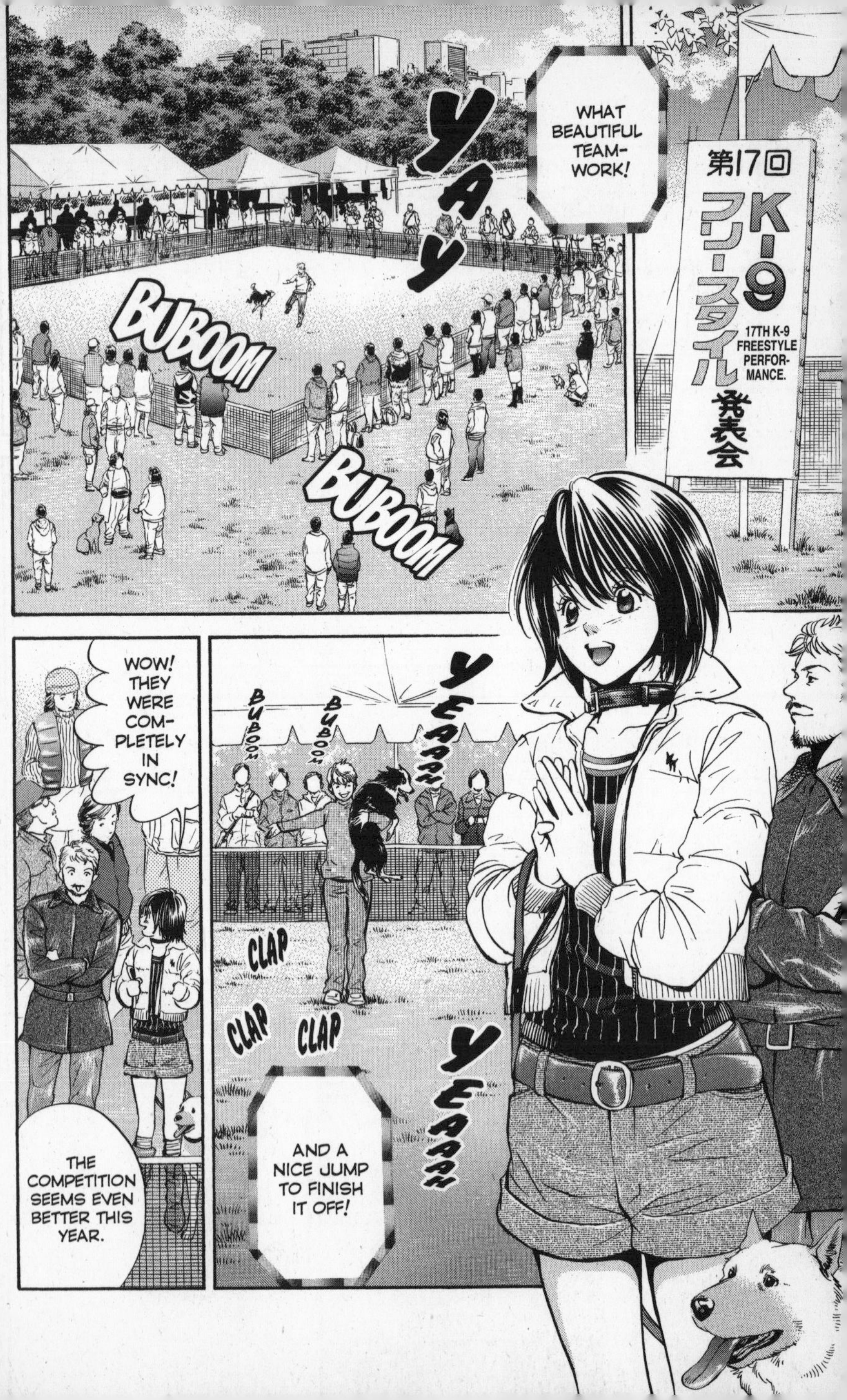
第17回 K-9 フリースタイル 発表会
17TH K-9 FREESTYLE PERFORMANCE.
WHAT BEAUTIFUL TEAMWORK!
YAY
BUBOOM
BUBOOM
YEAAAH
BUBOOM
BUBOOM
CLAP
CLAP
CLAP
YEAAAH
AND A NICE JUMP TO FINISH IT OFF!
WOW! THEY WERE COMPLETELY IN SYNC!
THE COMPETITION SEEMS EVEN BETTER THIS YEAR.

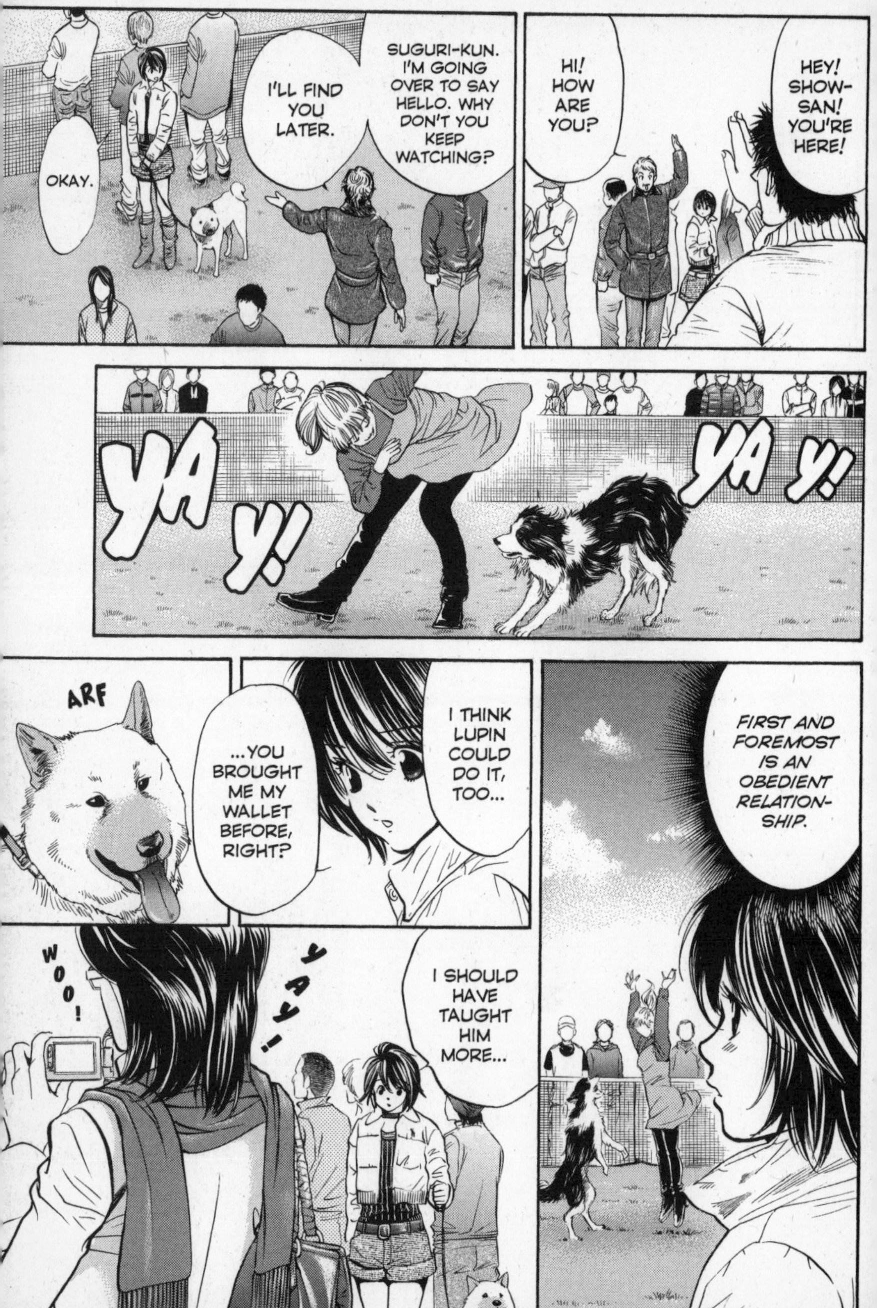
HEY! SHOW-SAN! YOU'RE HERE!
HI! HOW ARE YOU?
SUGURI-KUN. I'M GOING OVER TO SAY HELLO. WHY DON'T YOU KEEP WATCHING?
I'LL FIND YOU LATER.
OKAY.
YA Y!
YA Y!
FIRST AND FOREMOST IS AN OBEDIENT RELATIONSHIP.
I THINK LUPIN COULD DO IT, TOO...
...YOU BROUGHT ME MY WALLET BEFORE, RIGHT?
ARF
I SHOULD HAVE TAUGHT HIM MORE...
YAY!
WOO!

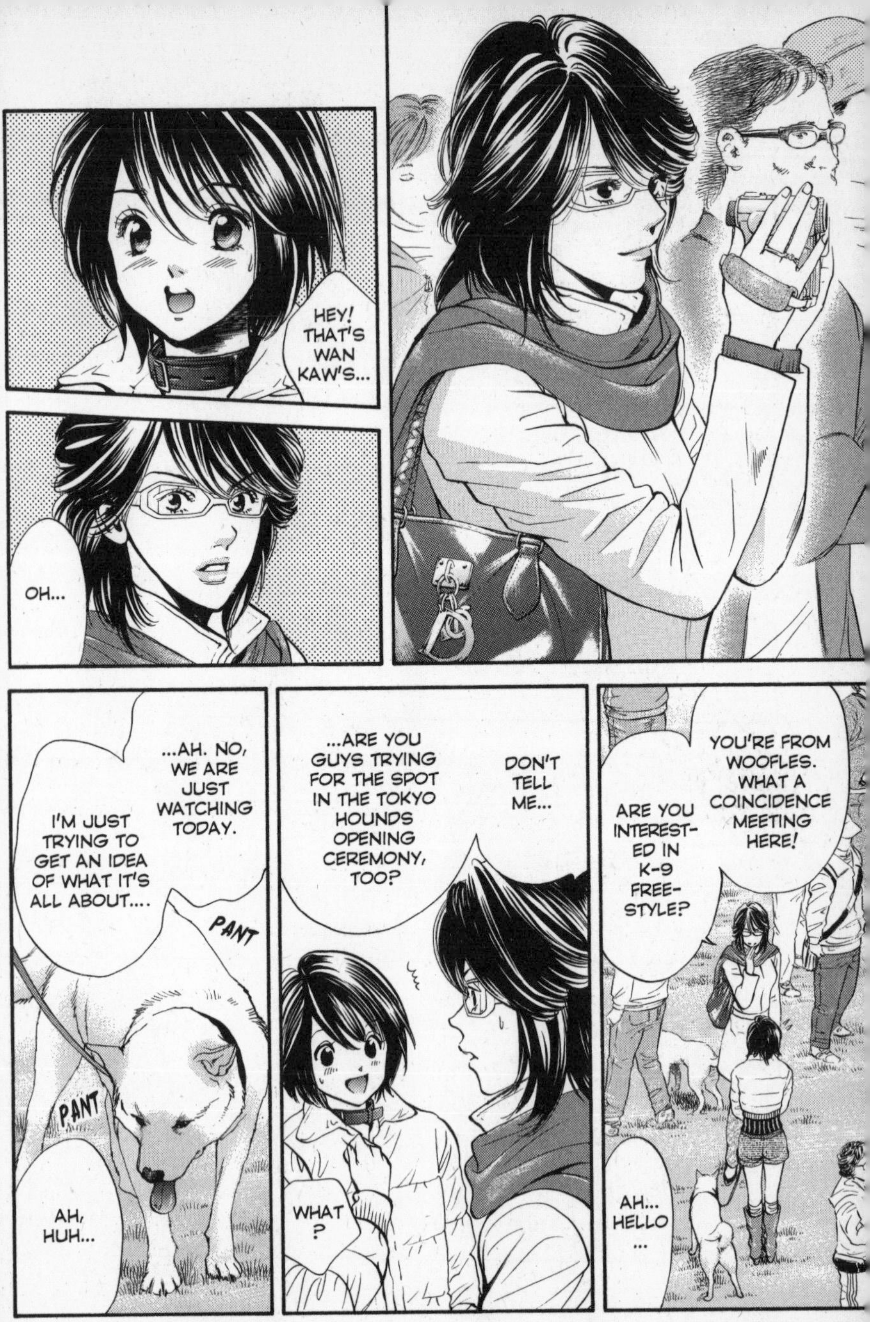
HEY! THAT'S WAN KAW'S...
OH...
YOU'RE FROM WOOFLES. WHAT A COINCIDENCE MEETING HERE!
ARE YOU INTEREST-ED IN K-9 FREE-STYLE?
AH... HELLO ...
DON'T TELL ME...
...ARE YOU GUYS TRYING FOR THE SPOT IN THE TOKYO HOUNDS OPENING CEREMONY, TOO?
WHAT?
...AH. NO, WE ARE JUST WATCHING TODAY.
I'M JUST TRYING TO GET AN IDEA OF WHAT IT'S ALL ABOUT....
PANT
PANT
AH, HUH...

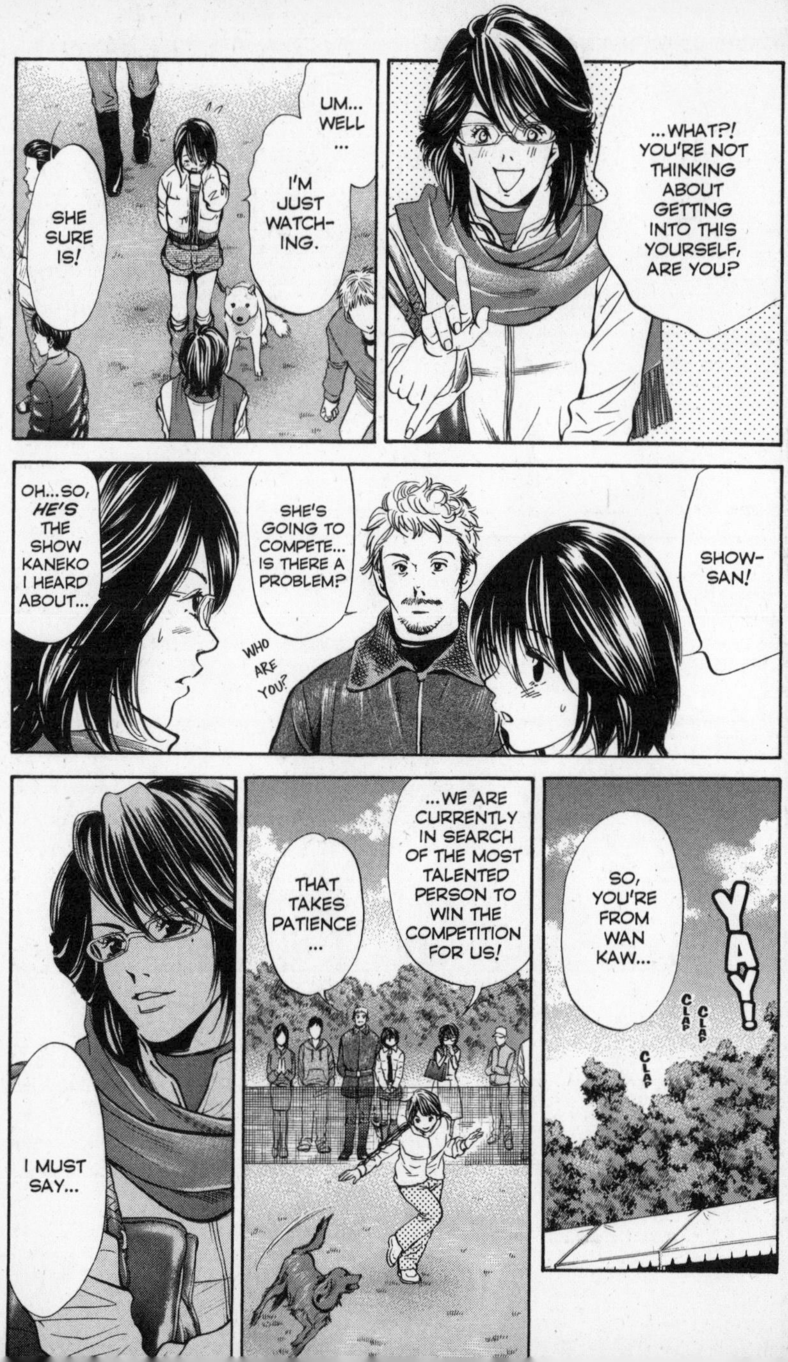
...WHAT?! YOU'RE NOT THINKING ABOUT GETTING INTO THIS YOURSELF, ARE YOU?
UM... WELL ...
I'M JUST WATCHING.
SHE SURE IS!
SHOW-SAN!
SHE'S GOING TO COMPETE... IS THERE A PROBLEM?
WHO ARE YOU?
OH...SO, *HE'S* THE SHOW KANEKO I HEARD ABOUT...
SO, YOU'RE FROM WAN KAW...
YAY!
CLAP CLAP
CLAP
...WE ARE CURRENTLY IN SEARCH OF THE MOST TALENTED PERSON TO WIN THE COMPETITION FOR US!
THAT TAKES PATIENCE ...
I MUST SAY...

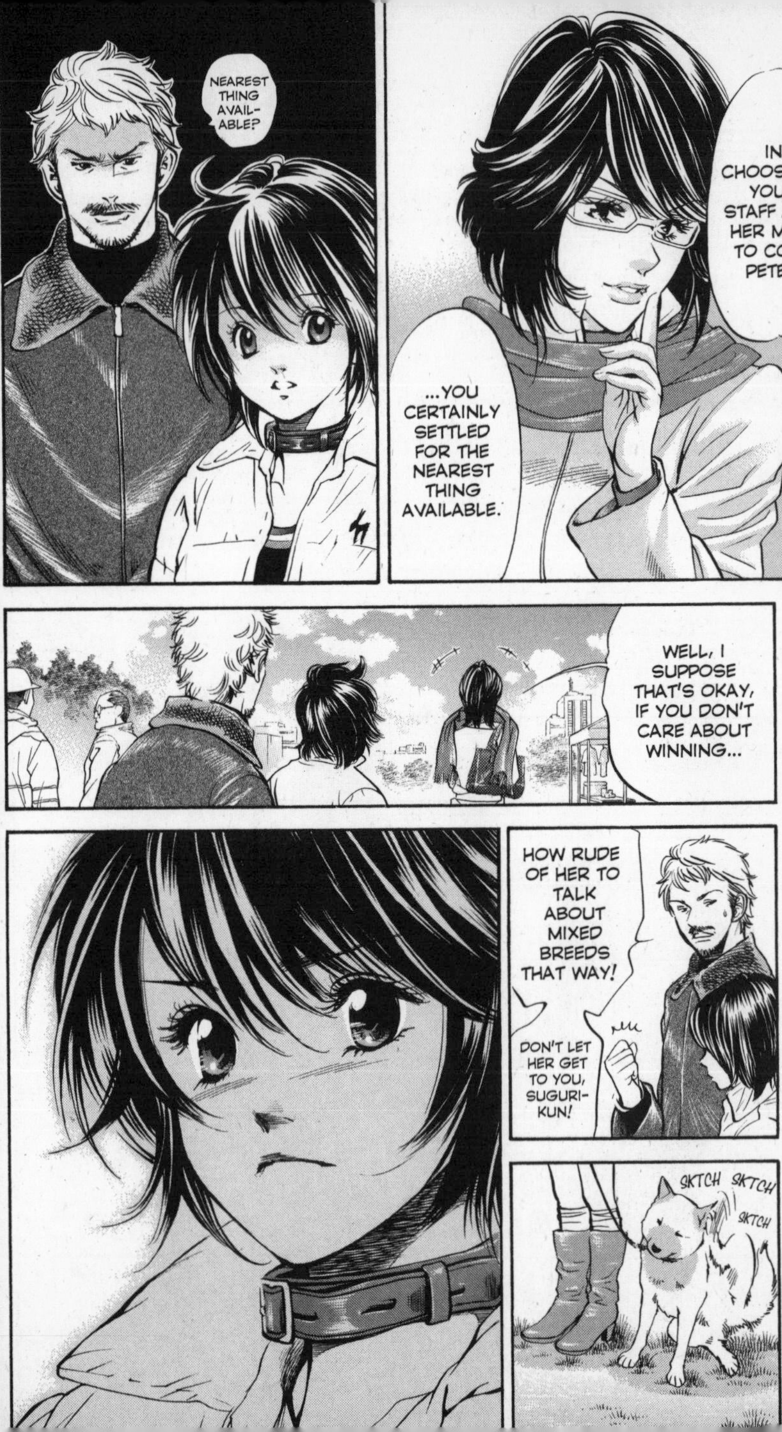
IN CHOOSING YOUR STAFF AND HER MUTT TO COMPETE...
...YOU CERTAINLY SETTLED FOR THE NEAREST THING AVAILABLE.
NEAREST THING AVAIL-ABLE?
WELL, I SUPPOSE THAT'S OKAY, IF YOU DON'T CARE ABOUT WINNING...
HOW RUDE OF HER TO TALK ABOUT MIXED BREEDS THAT WAY!
DON'T LET HER GET TO YOU, SUGURI-KUN!
SKTCH SKTCH
SKTCH

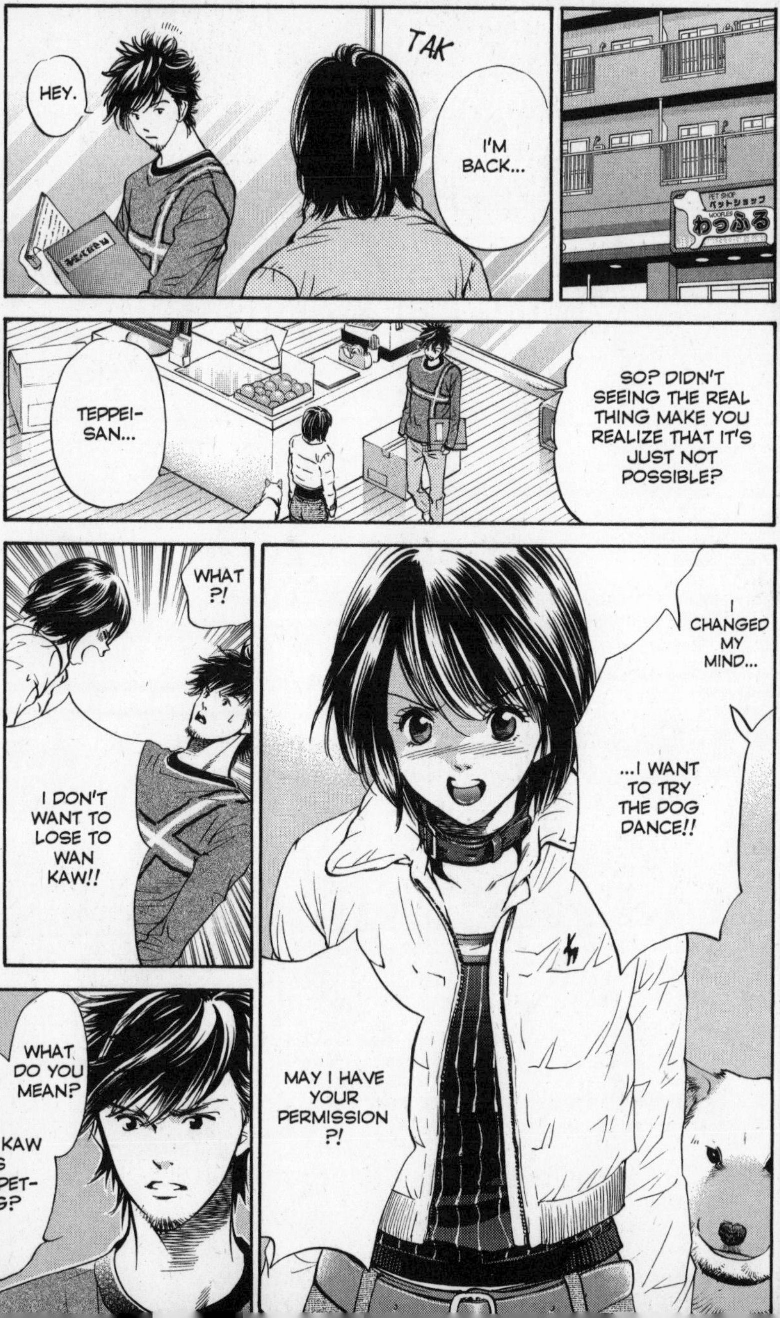
PET SHOP
ペットショップ
WOOFLES
わっふる
TAK
I'M BACK...
HEY.
SO? DIDN'T SEEING THE REAL THING MAKE YOU REALIZE THAT IT'S JUST NOT POSSIBLE?
TEPPEI-SAN...
I CHANGED MY MIND...
...I WANT TO TRY THE DOG DANCE!!
MAY I HAVE YOUR PERMISSION?!
WHAT?!
I DON'T WANT TO LOSE TO WAN KAW!!
WHAT DO YOU MEAN?
WAN KAW IS COMPETING?

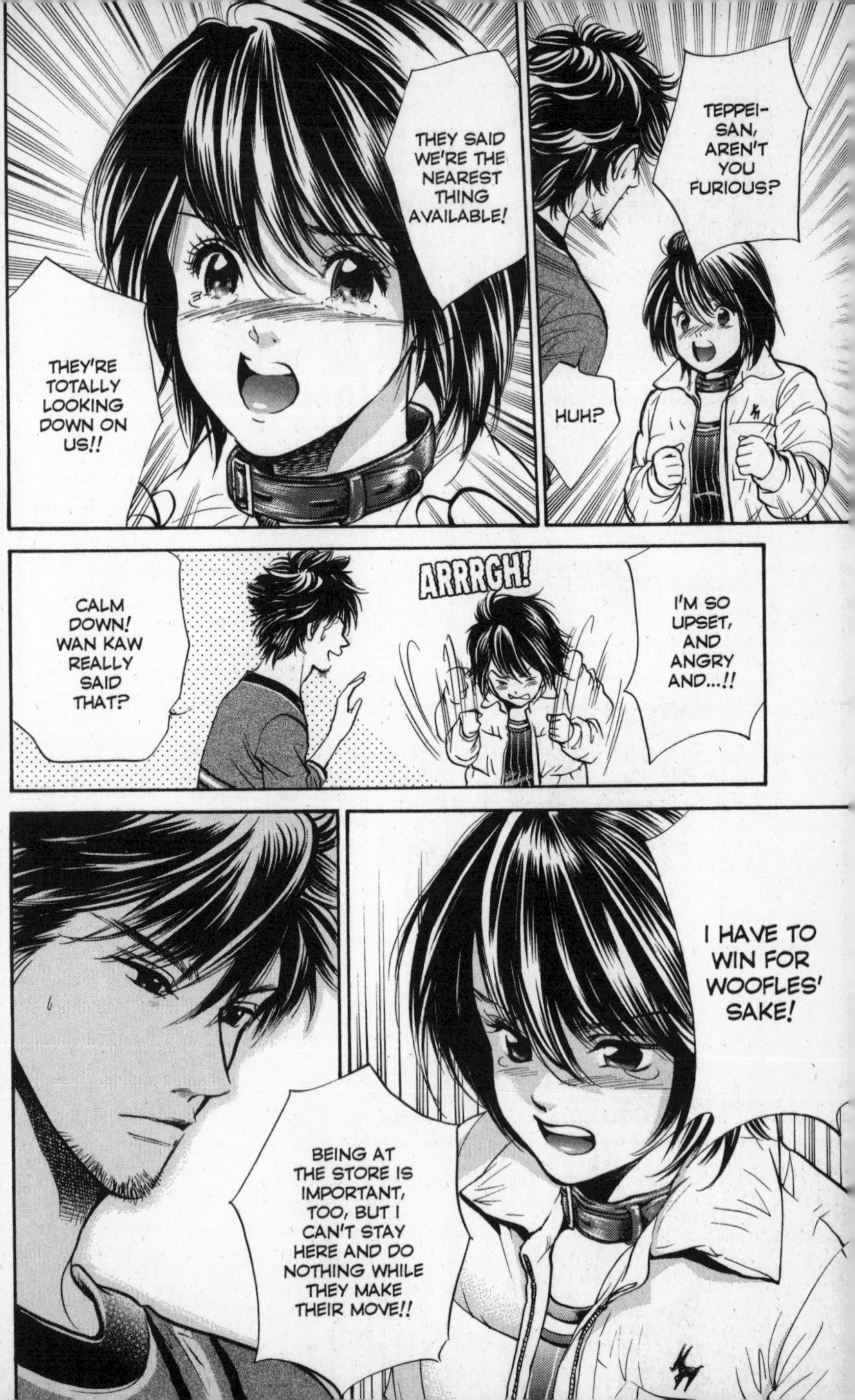
TEPPEI-SAN, AREN'T YOU FURIOUS?
HUH?
THEY SAID WE'RE THE NEAREST THING AVAILABLE!
THEY'RE TOTALLY LOOKING DOWN ON US!!
I'M SO UPSET, AND ANGRY AND...!!
ARRRGH!
CALM DOWN! WAN KAW REALLY SAID THAT?
I HAVE TO WIN FOR WOOFLES' SAKE!
BEING AT THE STORE IS IMPORTANT, TOO, BUT I CAN'T STAY HERE AND DO NOTHING WHILE THEY MAKE THEIR MOVE!!

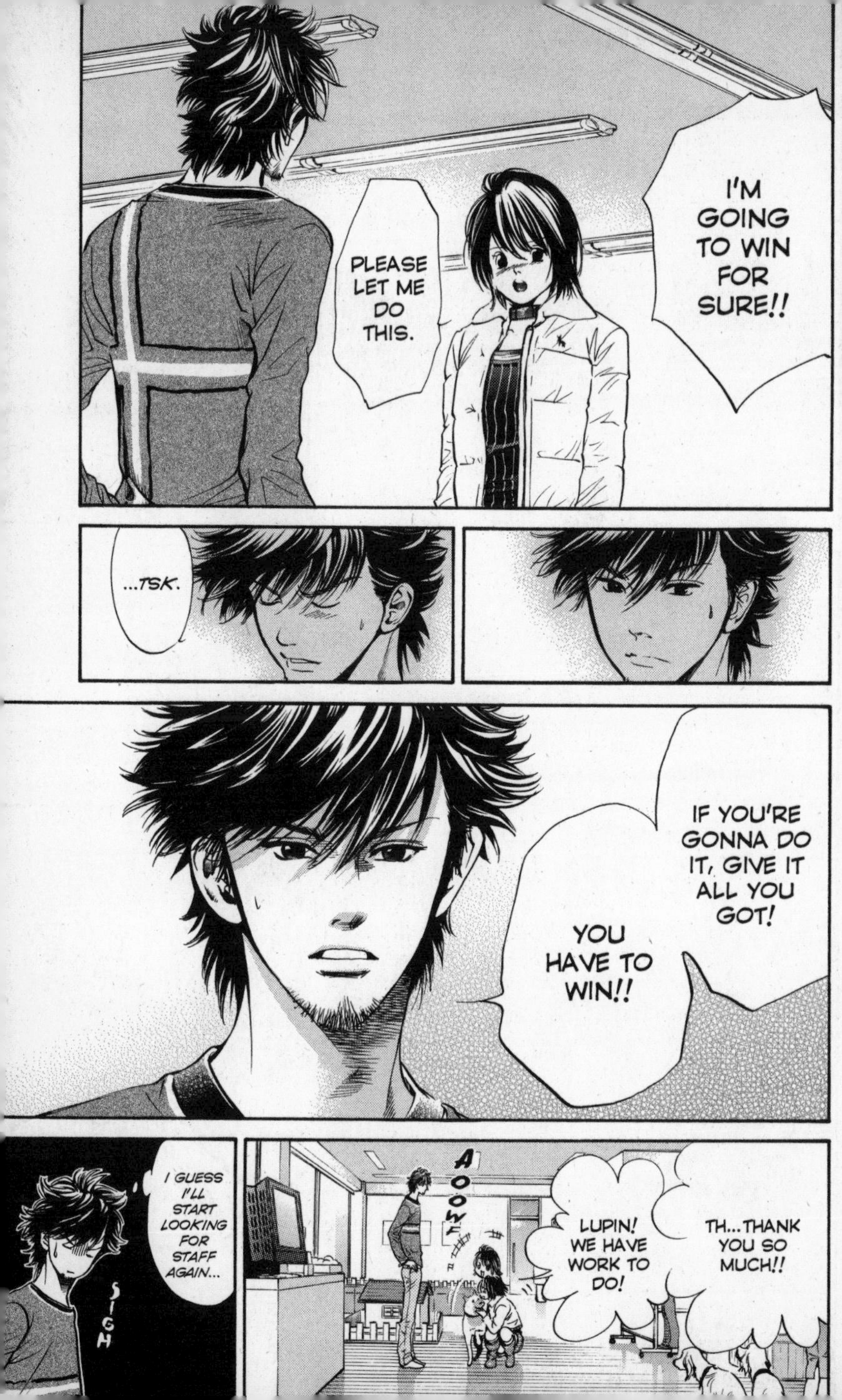

I'M GOING TO WIN FOR SURE!!
PLEASE LET ME DO THIS.
...TSK.
IF YOU'RE GONNA DO IT, GIVE IT ALL YOU GOT!
YOU HAVE TO WIN!!
TH...THANK YOU SO MUCH!!
LUPIN! WE HAVE WORK TO DO!
AOOWF
I GUESS I'LL START LOOKING FOR STAFF AGAIN...
SIGH

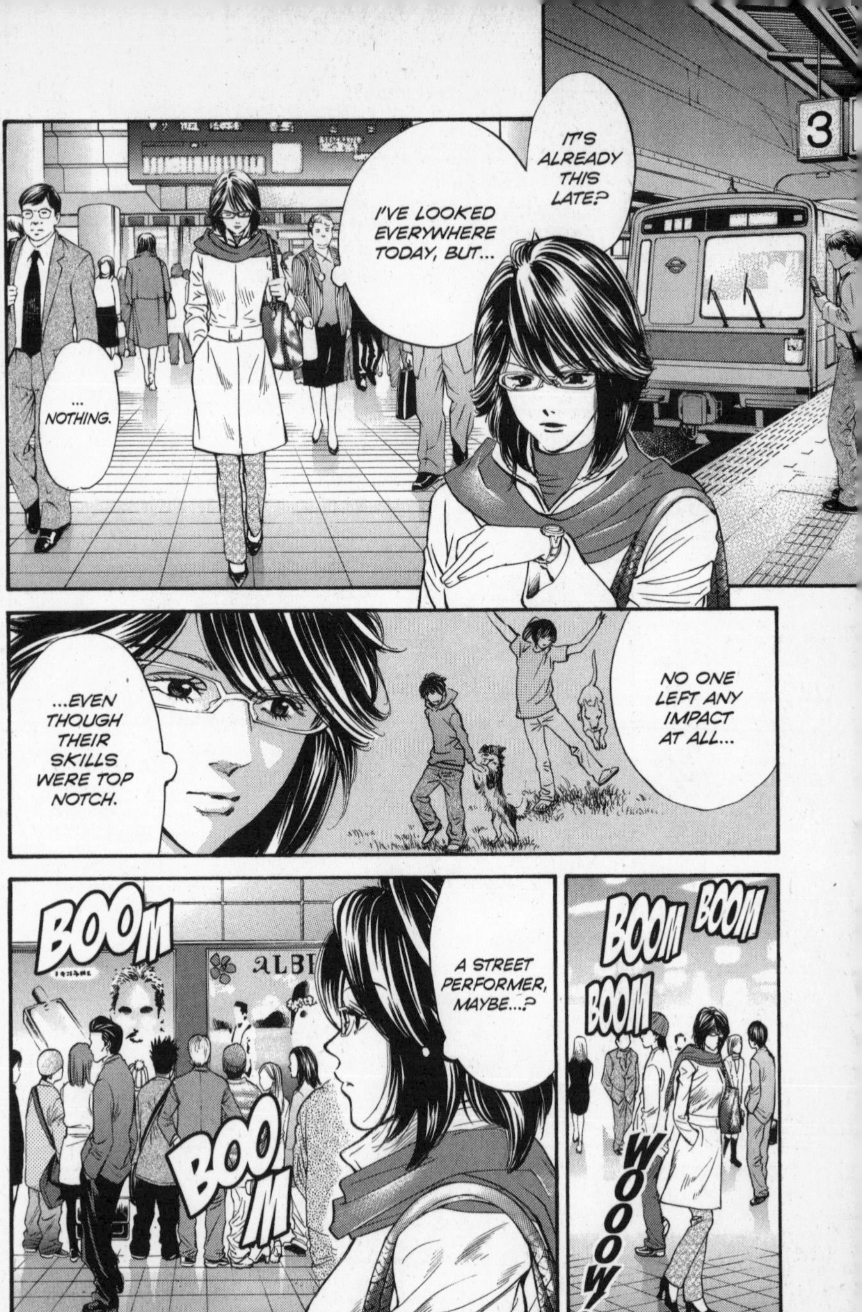

IT'S ALREADY THIS LATE?
I'VE LOOKED EVERYWHERE TODAY, BUT...
...NOTHING.
NO ONE LEFT ANY IMPACT AT ALL...
...EVEN THOUGH THEIR SKILLS WERE TOP NOTCH.
BOOM BOOM
BOOM
WOOOOW!
A STREET PERFORMER, MAYBE...?
BOOM
BOOM

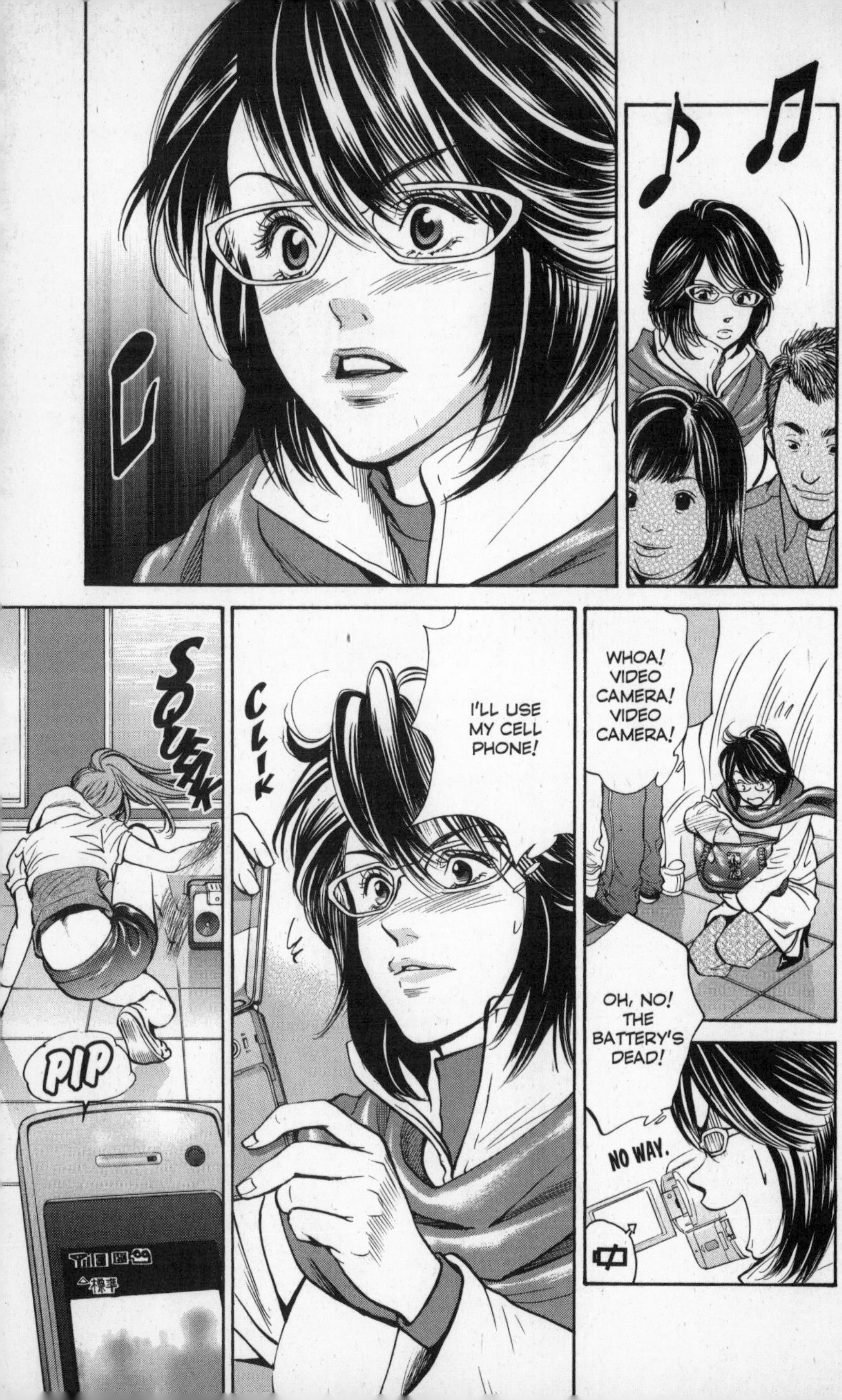
WHOA! VIDEO CAMERA! VIDEO CAMERA!
OH, NO! THE BATTERY'S DEAD!
NO WAY.
CLIK
I'LL USE MY CELL PHONE!
SQUEAK
PIP

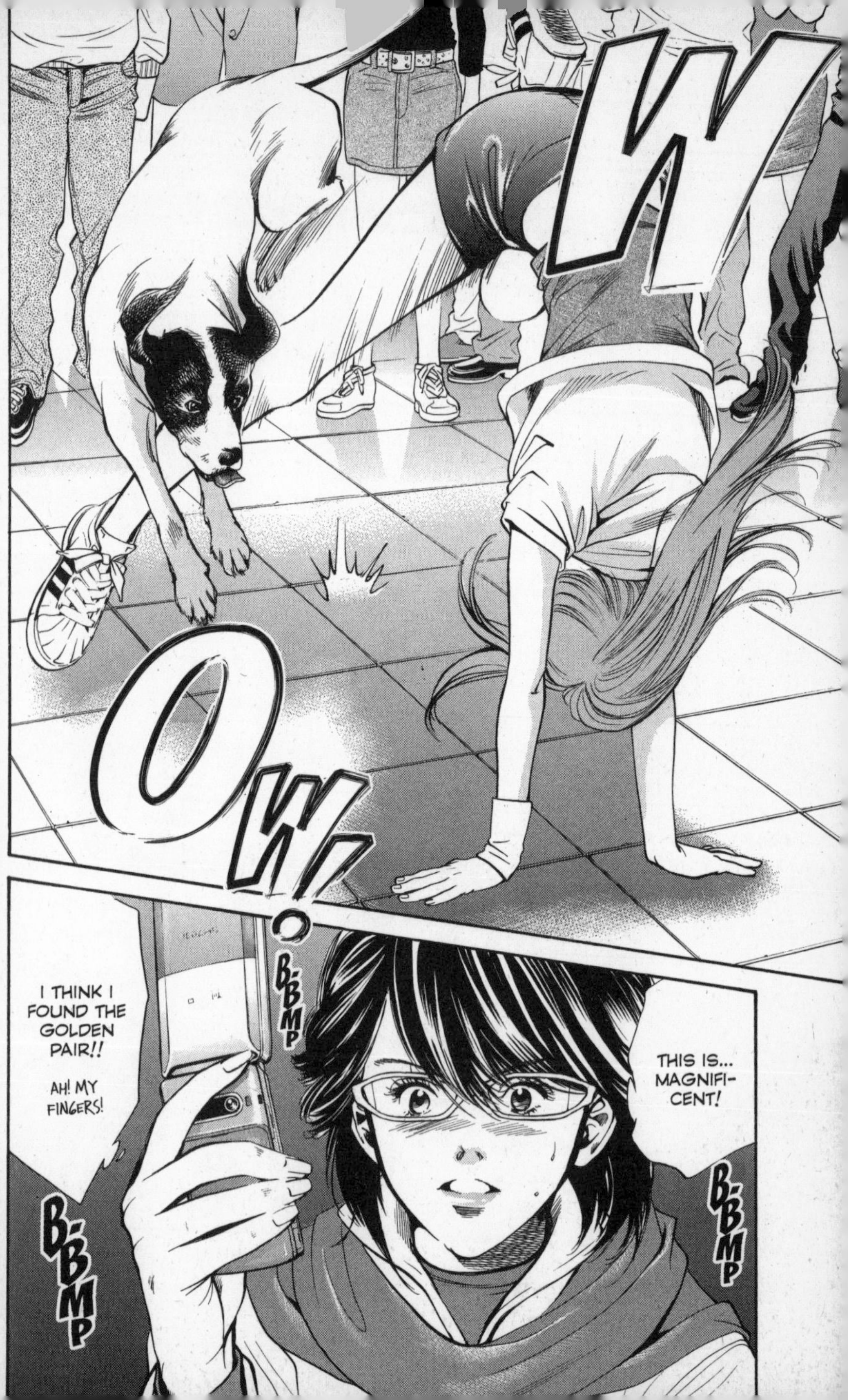
W
OW!
B-BMP
THIS IS... MAGNIFI-CENT!
I THINK I FOUND THE GOLDEN PAIR!!
AH! MY FINGERS!
B-BMP
B-BMP

CHAPTER 117: BLACK SHIP

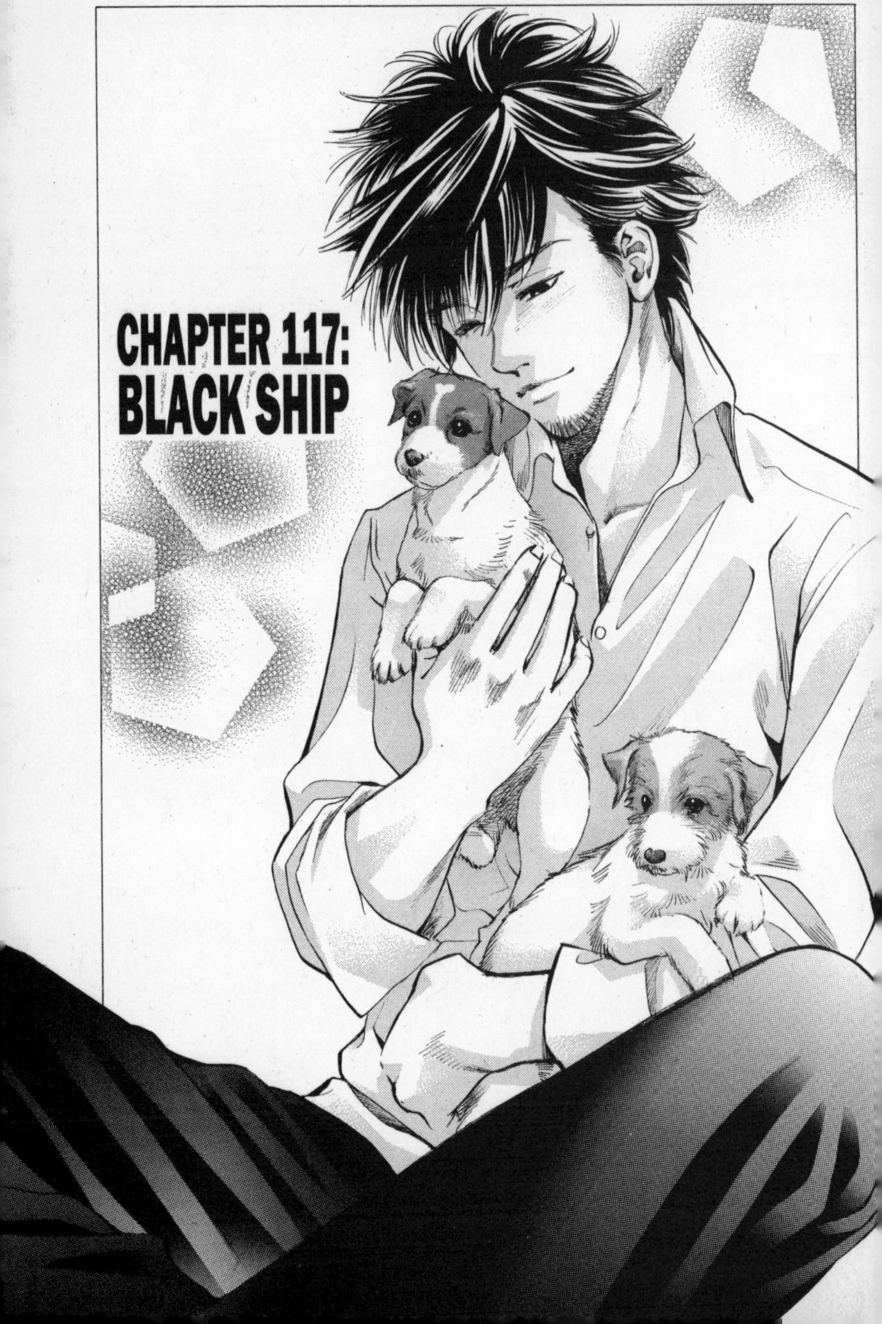

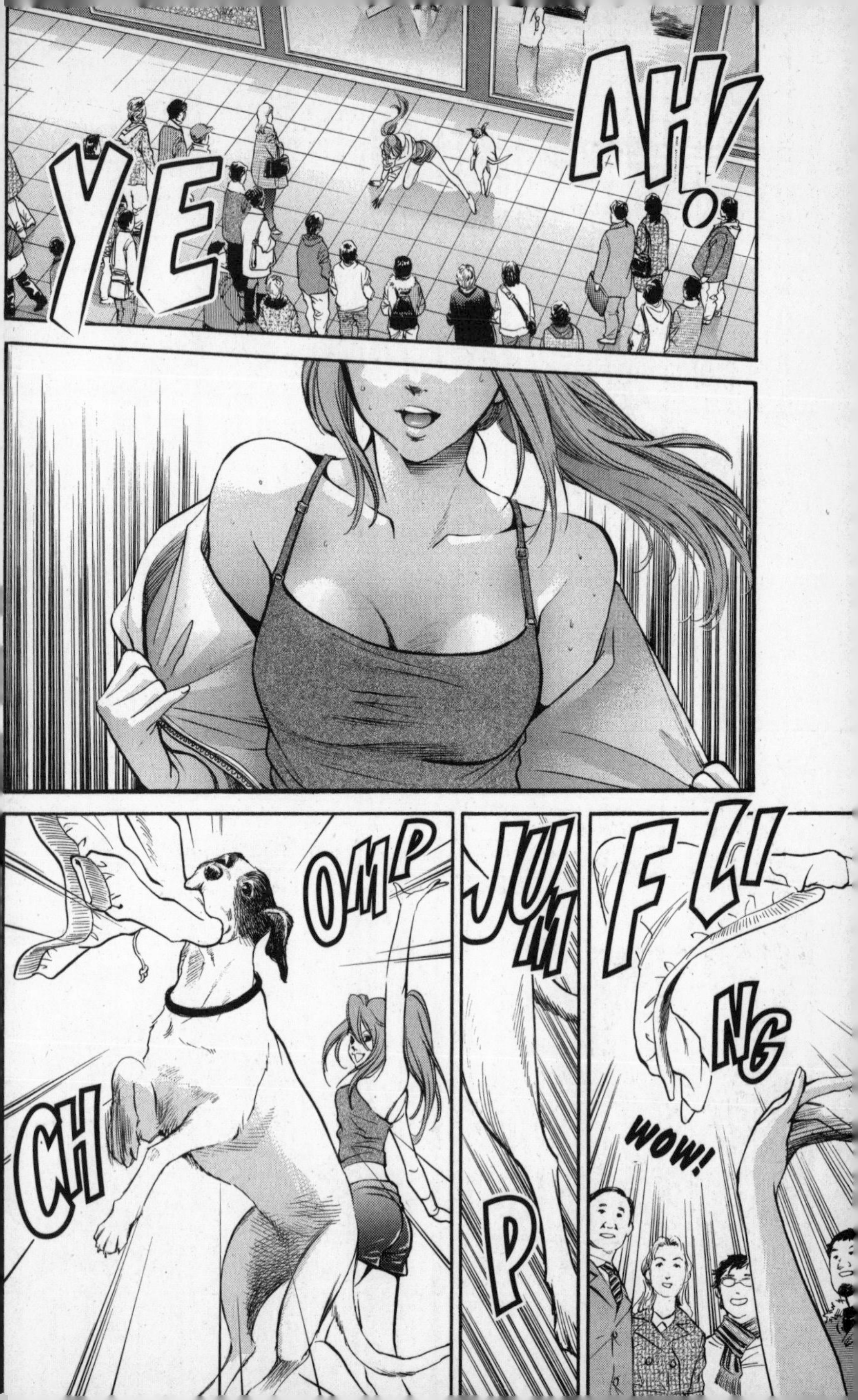
AH!
YE
FLING
WOW!
JUMP
CHOMP

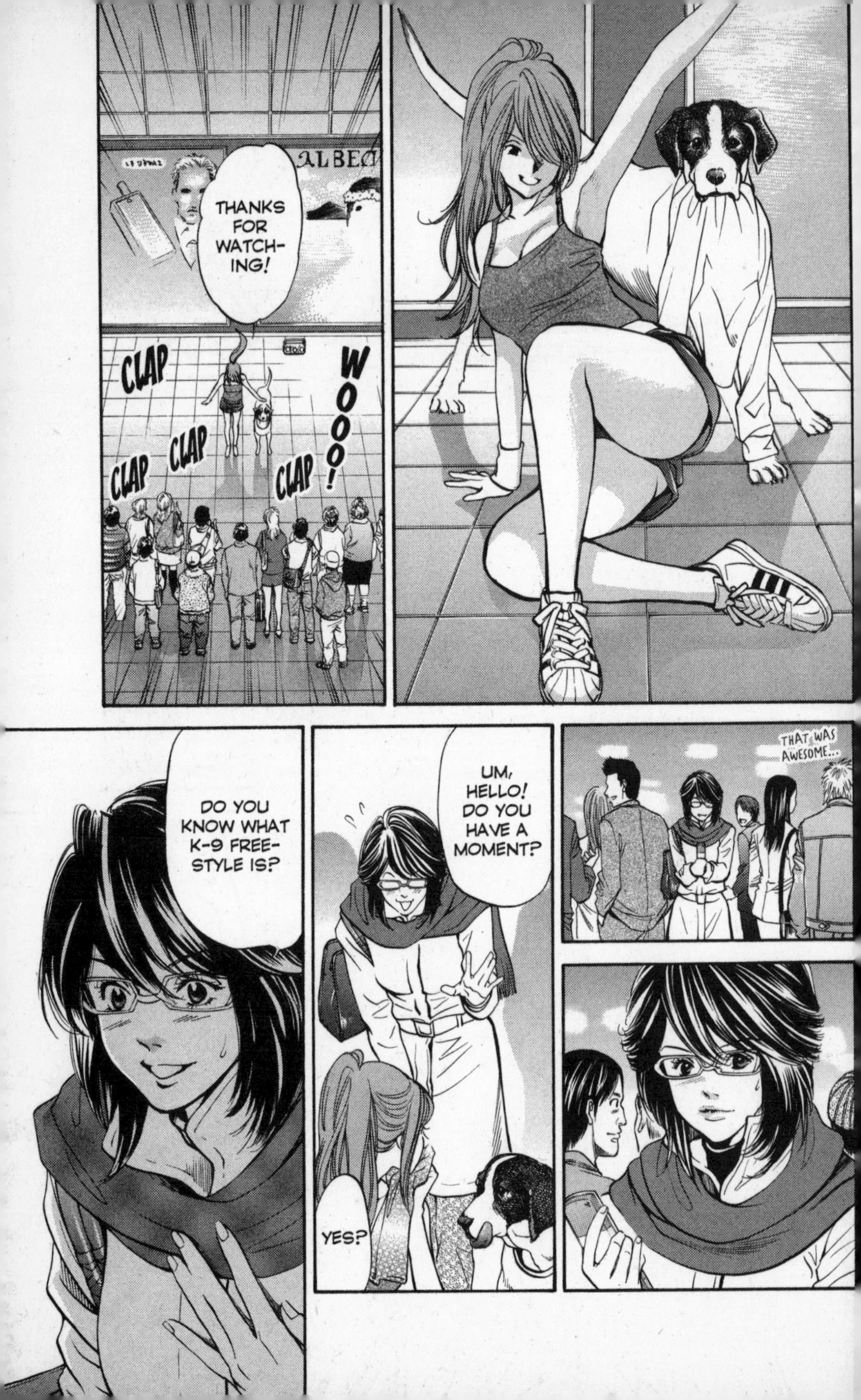
THANKS FOR WATCHING!
CLAP
WOOOO!
CLAP
CLAP
CLAP
THAT WAS AWESOME...
UM, HELLO! DO YOU HAVE A MOMENT?
YES?
DO YOU KNOW WHAT K-9 FREE-STYLE IS?

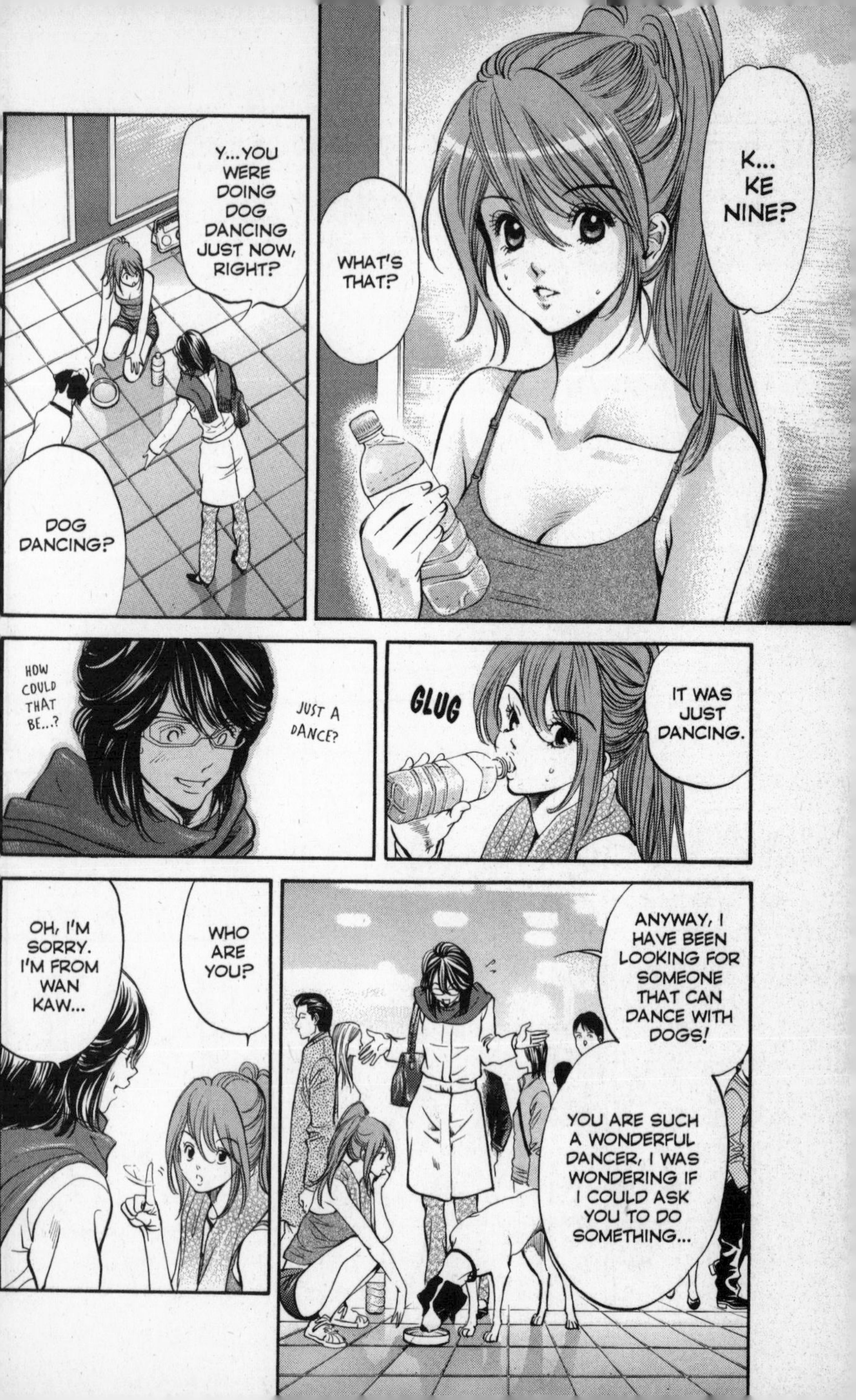
K... KE NINE?
WHAT'S THAT?
Y...YOU WERE DOING DOG DANCING JUST NOW, RIGHT?
DOG DANCING?
IT WAS JUST DANCING.
GLUG
JUST A DANCE?
HOW COULD THAT BE...?
ANYWAY, I HAVE BEEN LOOKING FOR SOMEONE THAT CAN DANCE WITH DOGS!
YOU ARE SUCH A WONDERFUL DANCER, I WAS WONDERING IF I COULD ASK YOU TO DO SOMETHING...
WHO ARE YOU?
OH, I'M SORRY. I'M FROM WAN KAW...

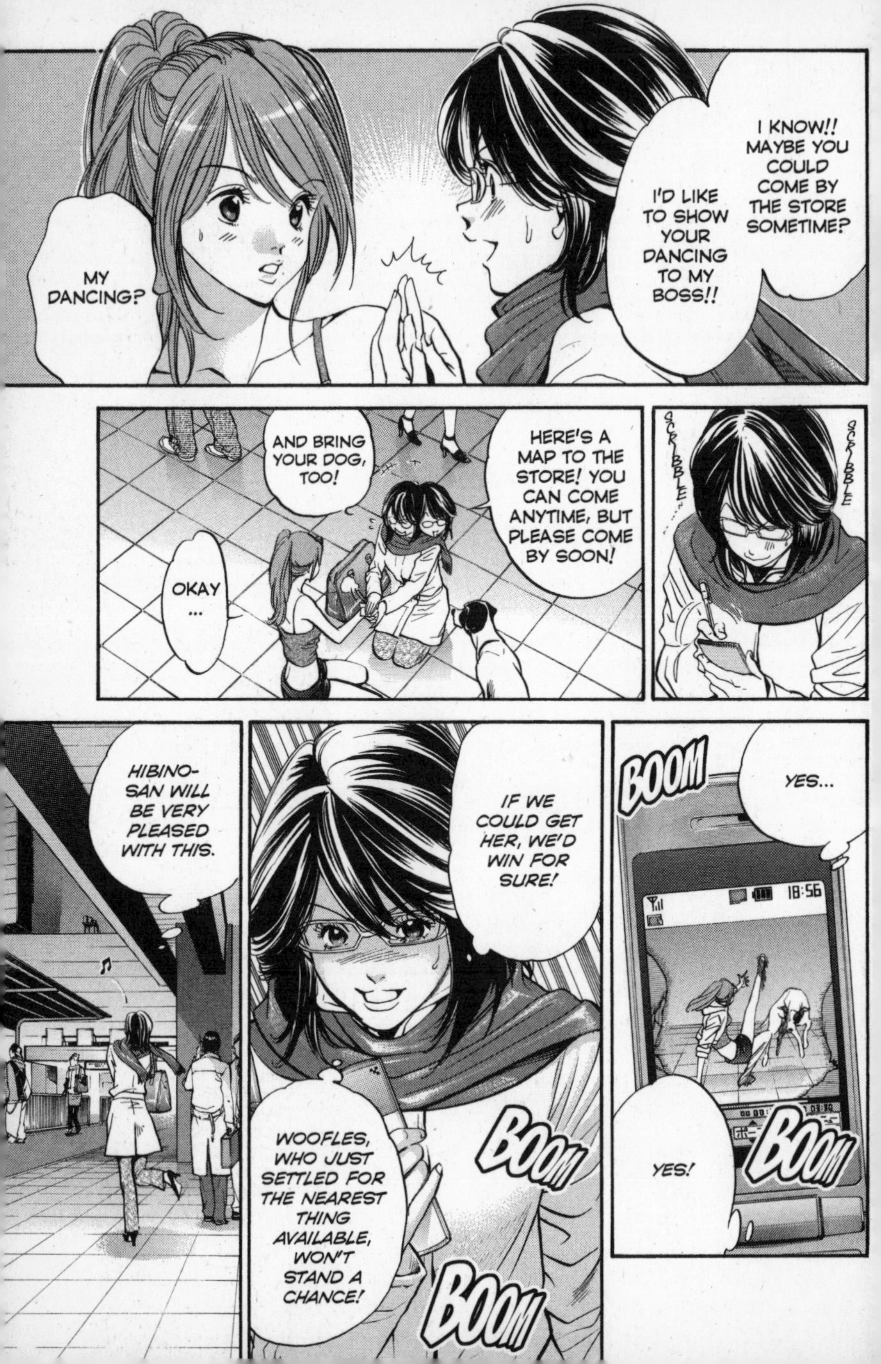
I KNOW!! MAYBE YOU COULD COME BY THE STORE SOMETIME?
I'D LIKE TO SHOW YOUR DANCING TO MY BOSS!!
MY DANCING?
SCRIBBLE
SCRIBBLE
HERE'S A MAP TO THE STORE! YOU CAN COME ANYTIME, BUT PLEASE COME BY SOON!
AND BRING YOUR DOG, TOO!
OKAY ...
BOOM
YES...
BOOM
YES!
18:56
IF WE COULD GET HER, WE'D WIN FOR SURE!
WOOFLES, WHO JUST SETTLED FOR THE NEAREST THING AVAILABLE, WON'T STAND A CHANCE!
BOOM
BOOM
HIBINO-SAN WILL BE VERY PLEASED WITH THIS.

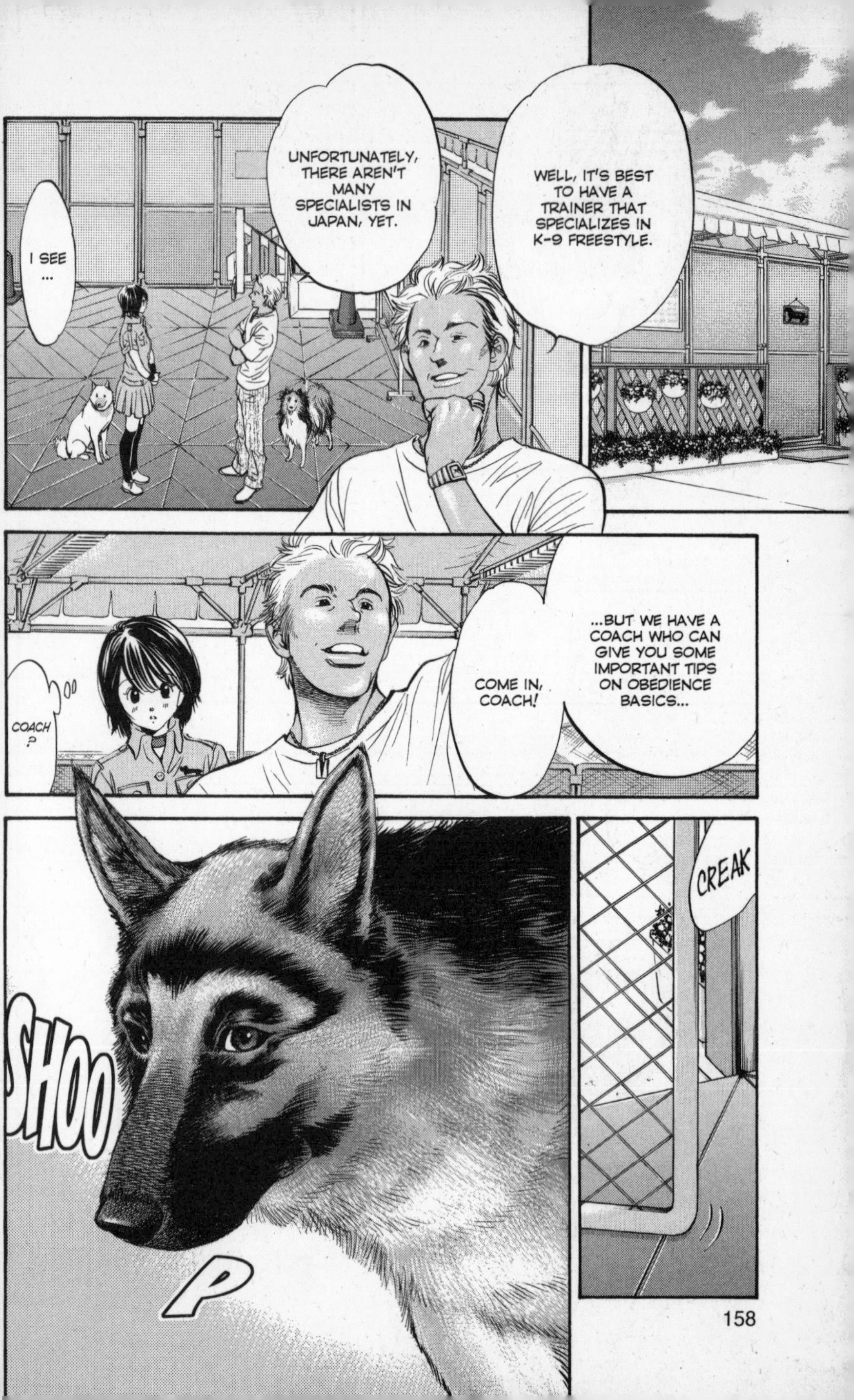
WELL, IT'S BEST TO HAVE A TRAINER THAT SPECIALIZES IN K-9 FREESTYLE.
UNFORTUNATELY, THERE AREN'T MANY SPECIALISTS IN JAPAN, YET.
I SEE ...
...BUT WE HAVE A COACH WHO CAN GIVE YOU SOME IMPORTANT TIPS ON OBEDIENCE BASICS...
COME IN, COACH!
COACH ?
CREAK
SHOO
P

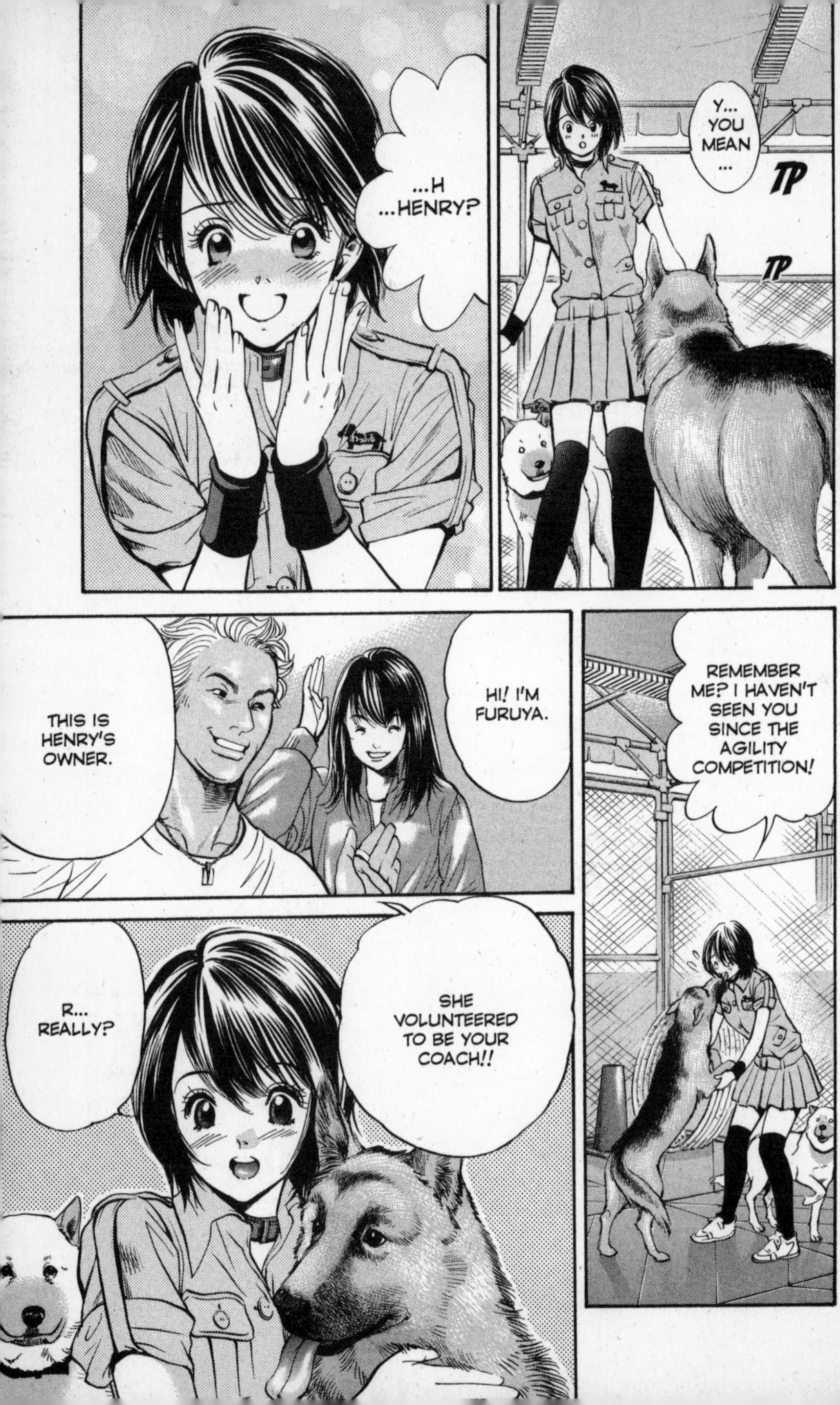
Y... YOU MEAN ...
TP
TP
...H ...HENRY?
REMEMBER ME? I HAVEN'T SEEN YOU SINCE THE AGILITY COMPETITION!
HI! I'M FURUYA.
THIS IS HENRY'S OWNER.
SHE VOLUNTEERED TO BE YOUR COACH!!
R... REALLY?

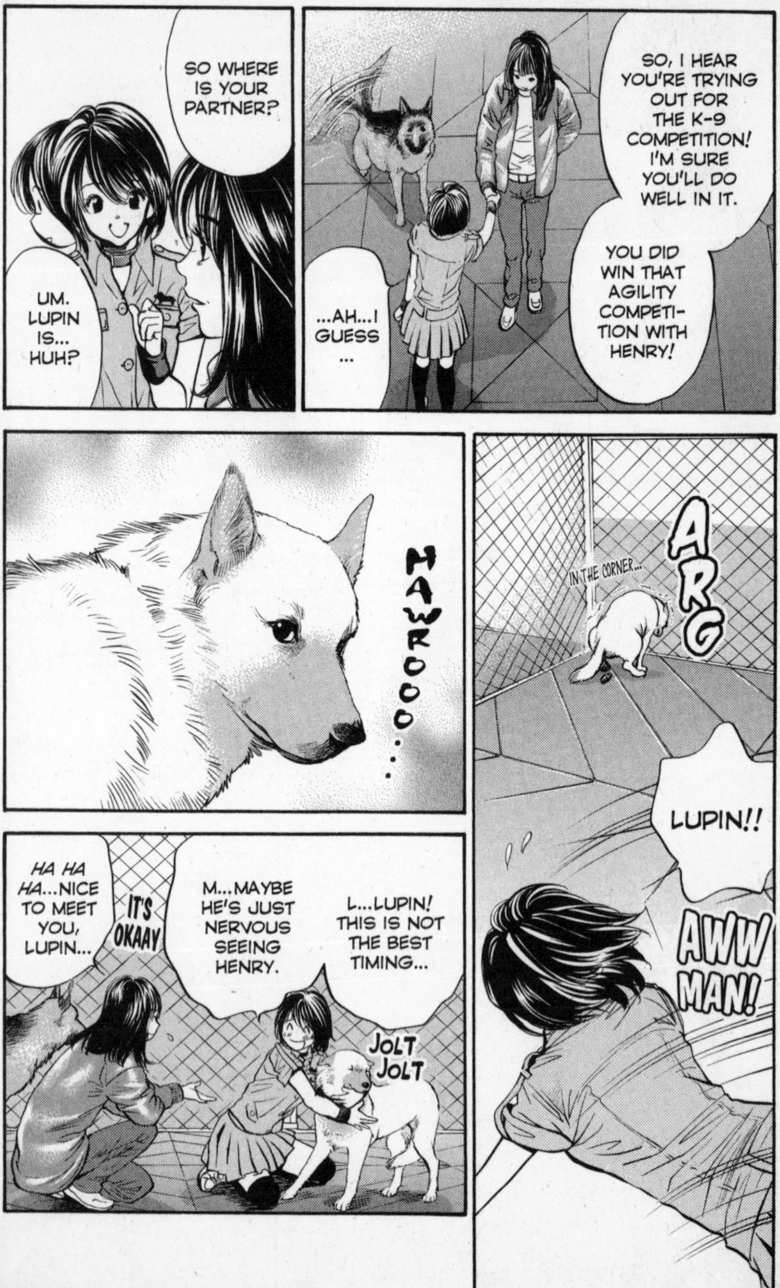
SO, I HEAR YOU'RE TRYING OUT FOR THE K-9 COMPETITION! I'M SURE YOU'LL DO WELL IN IT.
YOU DID WIN THAT AGILITY COMPETITION WITH HENRY!
...AH...I GUESS ...
SO WHERE IS YOUR PARTNER?
UM. LUPIN IS... HUH?
ARG
IN THE CORNER...
LUPIN!!
AWW MAN!
HAWROOO...
L...LUPIN! THIS IS NOT THE BEST TIMING...
M...MAYBE HE'S JUST NERVOUS SEEING HENRY.
IT'S OKAAY
HA HA HA...NICE TO MEET YOU, LUPIN...
JOLT JOLT

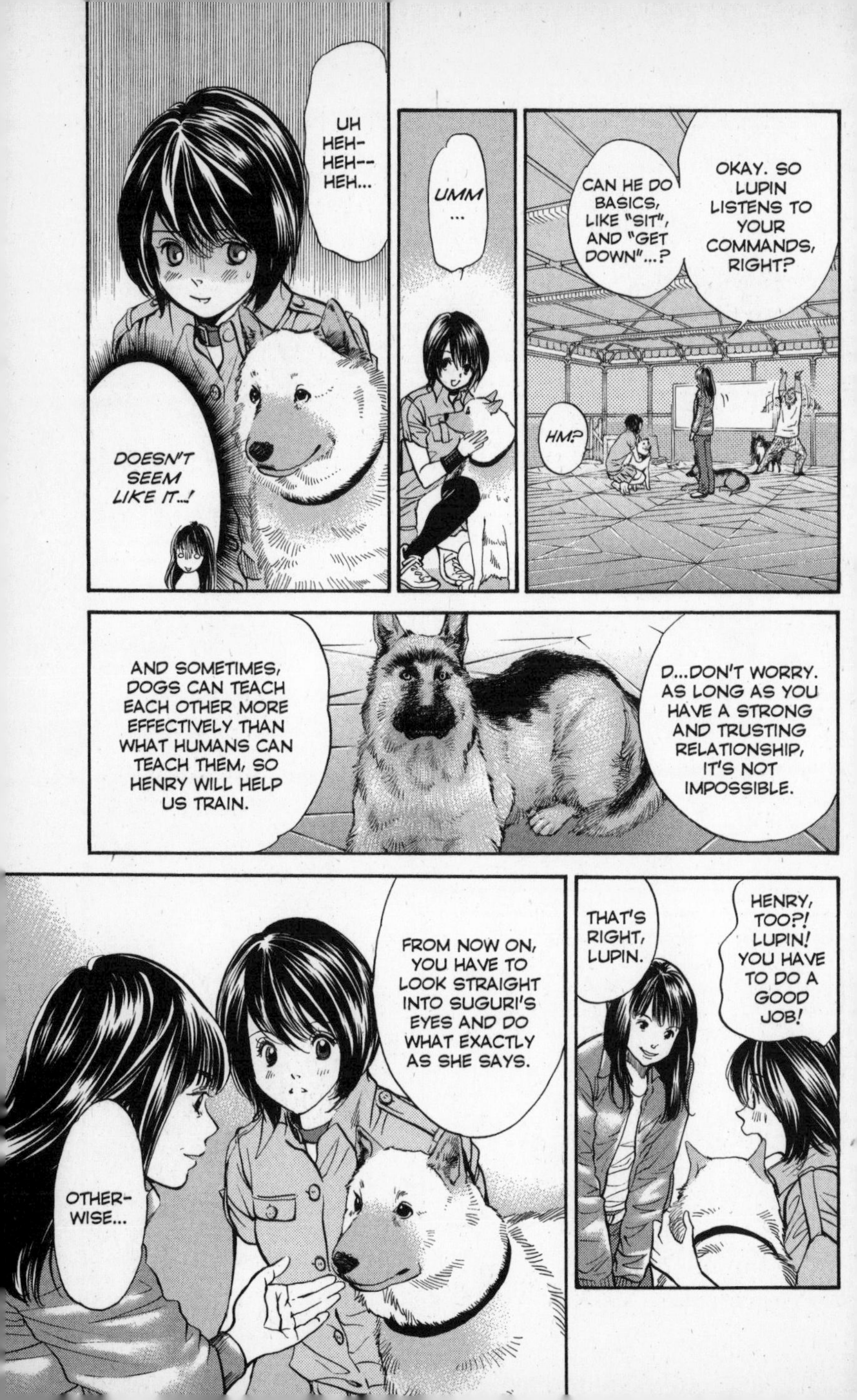
OKAY. SO LUPIN LISTENS TO YOUR COMMANDS, RIGHT?
CAN HE DO BASICS, LIKE "SIT", AND "GET DOWN"...?
HM?
UMM ...
UH HEH-HEH--HEH...
DOESN'T SEEM LIKE IT...!
D...DON'T WORRY. AS LONG AS YOU HAVE A STRONG AND TRUSTING RELATIONSHIP, IT'S NOT IMPOSSIBLE.
AND SOMETIMES, DOGS CAN TEACH EACH OTHER MORE EFFECTIVELY THAN WHAT HUMANS CAN TEACH THEM, SO HENRY WILL HELP US TRAIN.
HENRY, TOO?! LUPIN! YOU HAVE TO DO A GOOD JOB!
THAT'S RIGHT, LUPIN.
FROM NOW ON, YOU HAVE TO LOOK STRAIGHT INTO SUGURI'S EYES AND DO WHAT EXACTLY AS SHE SAYS.
OTHER-WISE...

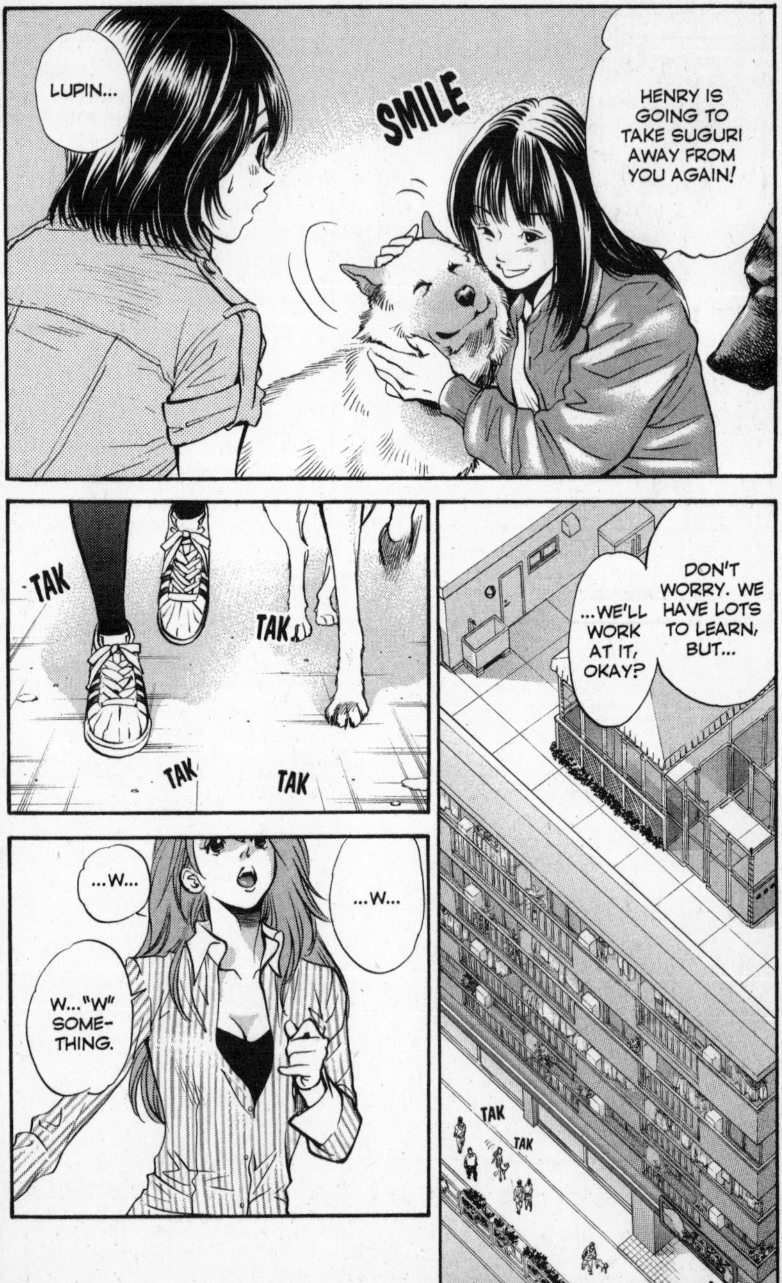
HENRY IS GOING TO TAKE SUGURI AWAY FROM YOU AGAIN!
SMILE
LUPIN...
DON'T WORRY. WE HAVE LOTS TO LEARN, BUT...
...WE'LL WORK AT IT, OKAY?
TAK
TAK
TAK
TAK
TAK
TAK
...W...
...W...
W..."W" SOME-THING.

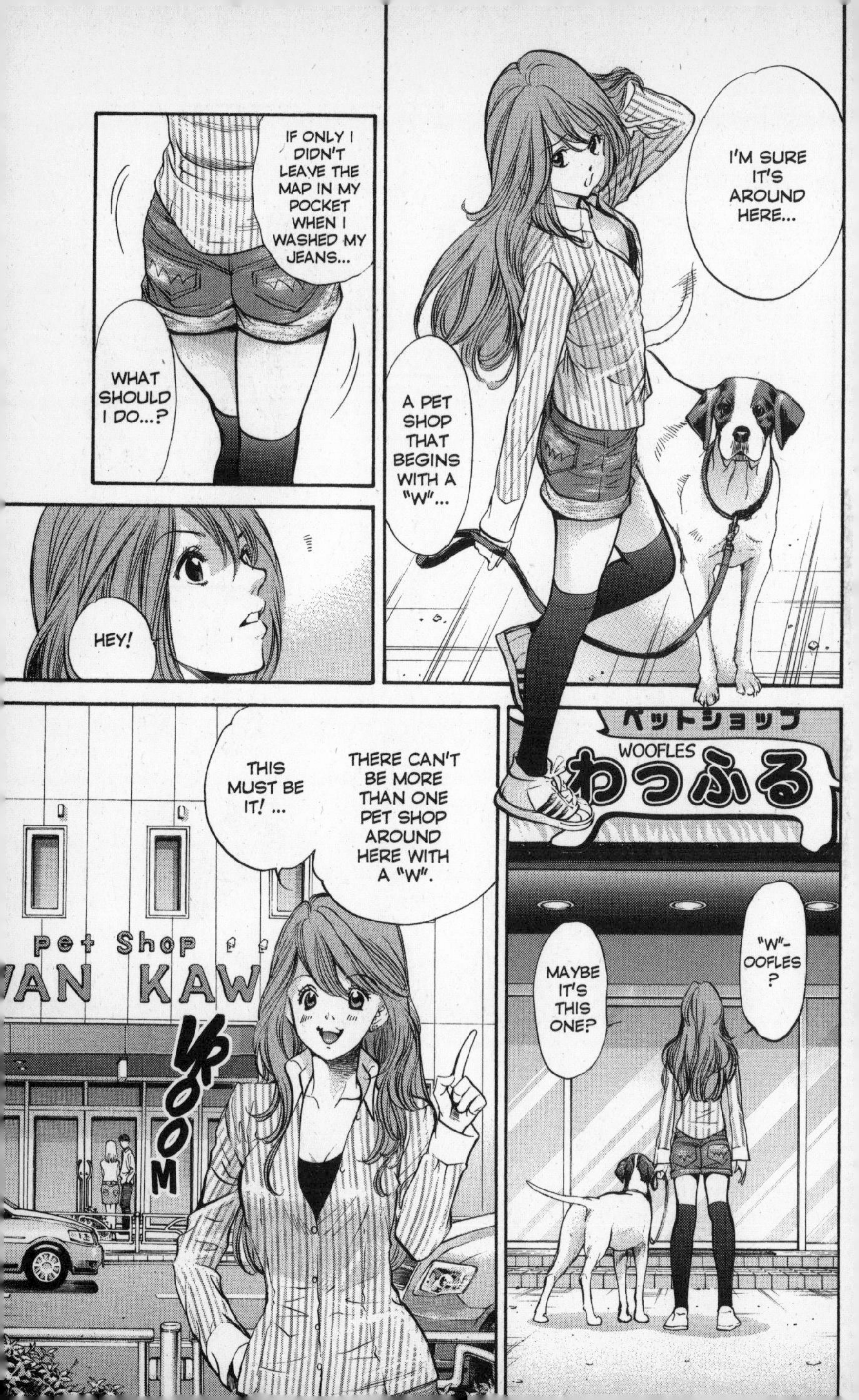
I'M SURE IT'S AROUND HERE...
A PET SHOP THAT BEGINS WITH A "W"...
IF ONLY I DIDN'T LEAVE THE MAP IN MY POCKET WHEN I WASHED MY JEANS...
WHAT SHOULD I DO...?
HEY!
ペットショップ
WOOFLES
わっふる
"W"-OOFLES?
MAYBE IT'S THIS ONE?
THERE CAN'T BE MORE THAN ONE PET SHOP AROUND HERE WITH A "W".
THIS MUST BE IT! ...
pet Shop
VAN KAW
VROOOM

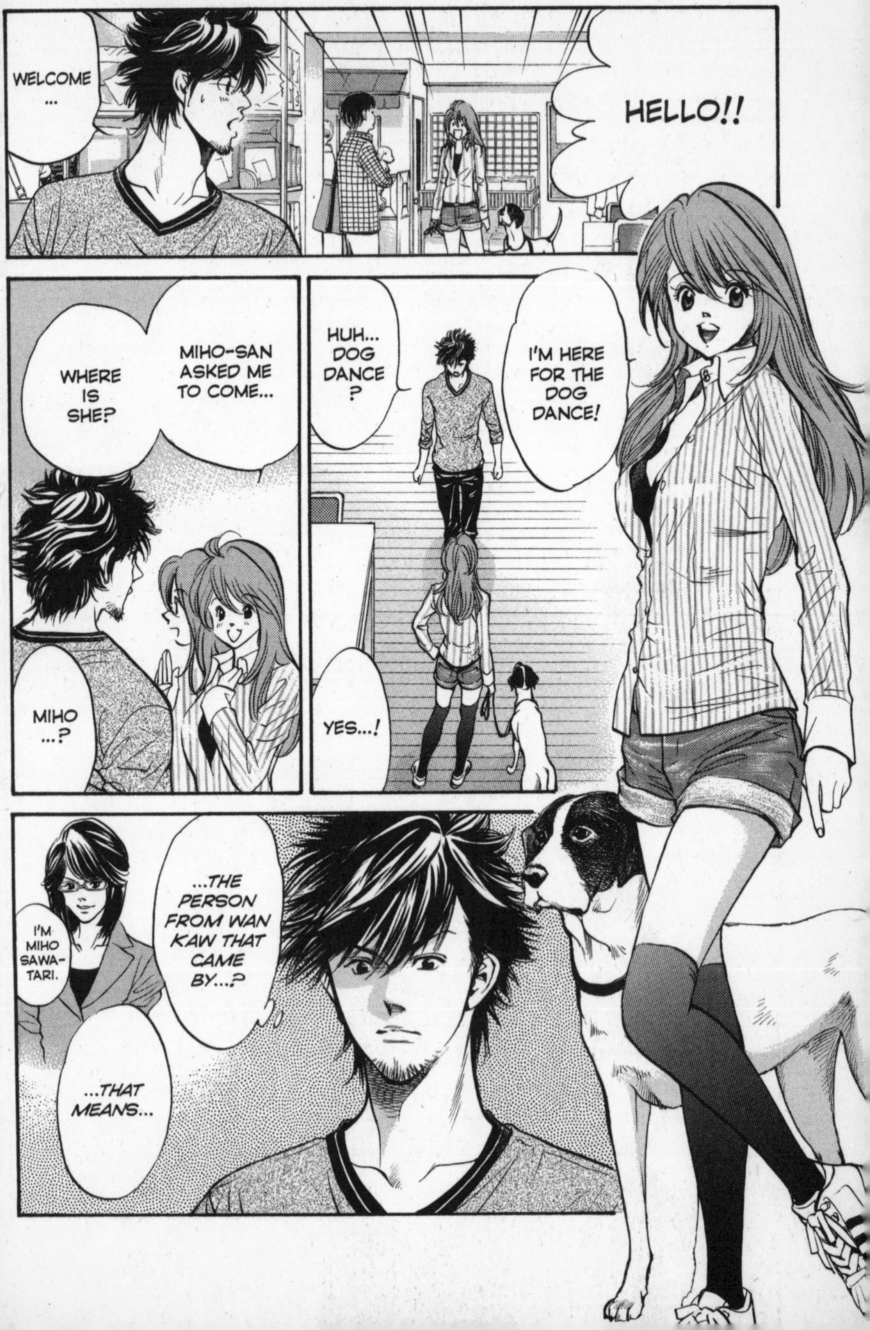
HELLO!!
WELCOME ...
I'M HERE FOR THE DOG DANCE!
HUH... DOG DANCE ?
YES...!
MIHO-SAN ASKED ME TO COME...
WHERE IS SHE?
MIHO ...?
...THE PERSON FROM WAN KAW THAT CAME BY...?
I'M MIHO SAWA-TARI.
...THAT MEANS...

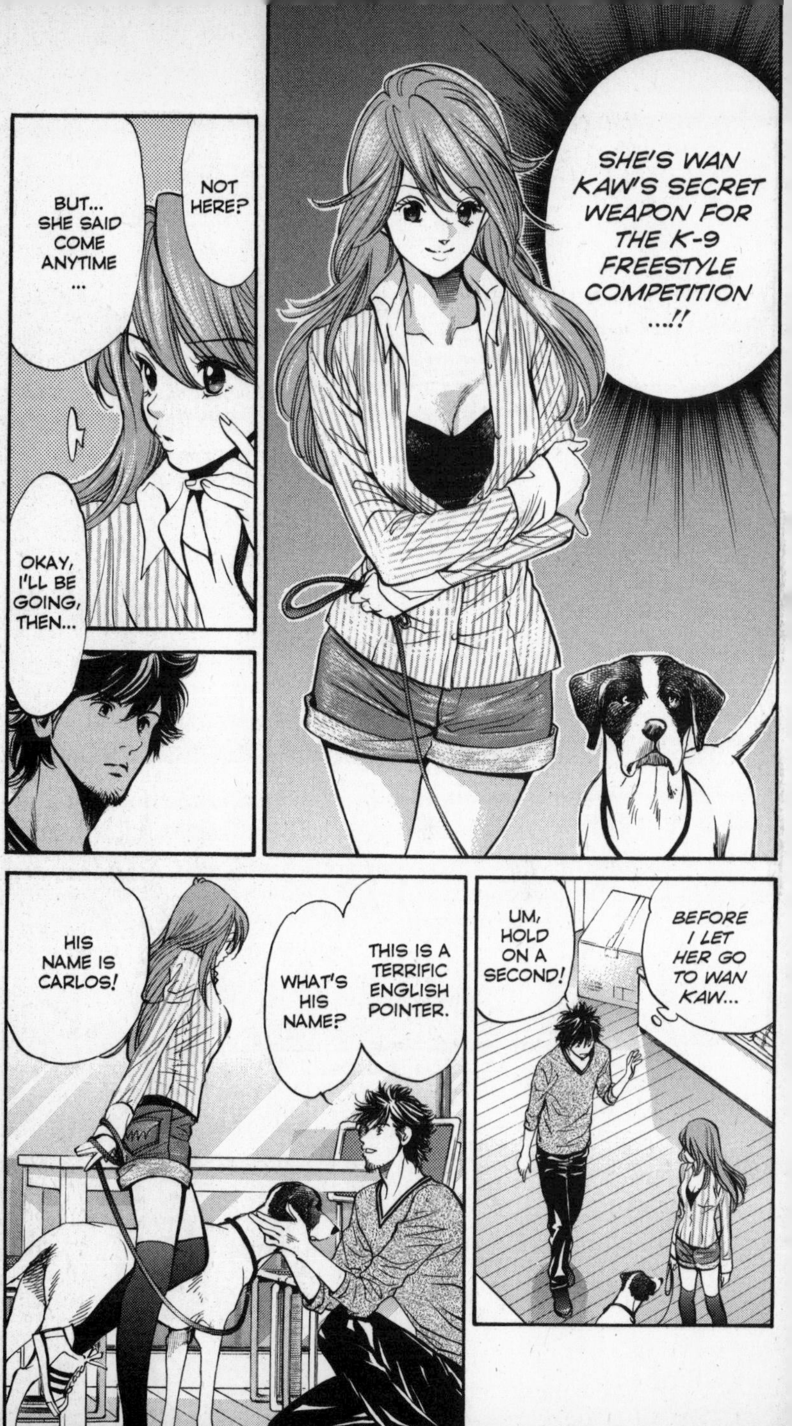
SHE'S WAN KAW'S SECRET WEAPON FOR THE K-9 FREESTYLE COMPETITION ...!!
NOT HERE?
BUT... SHE SAID COME ANYTIME ...
OKAY, I'LL BE GOING, THEN...
BEFORE I LET HER GO TO WAN KAW...
UM, HOLD ON A SECOND!
THIS IS A TERRIFIC ENGLISH POINTER.
WHAT'S HIS NAME?
HIS NAME IS CARLOS!

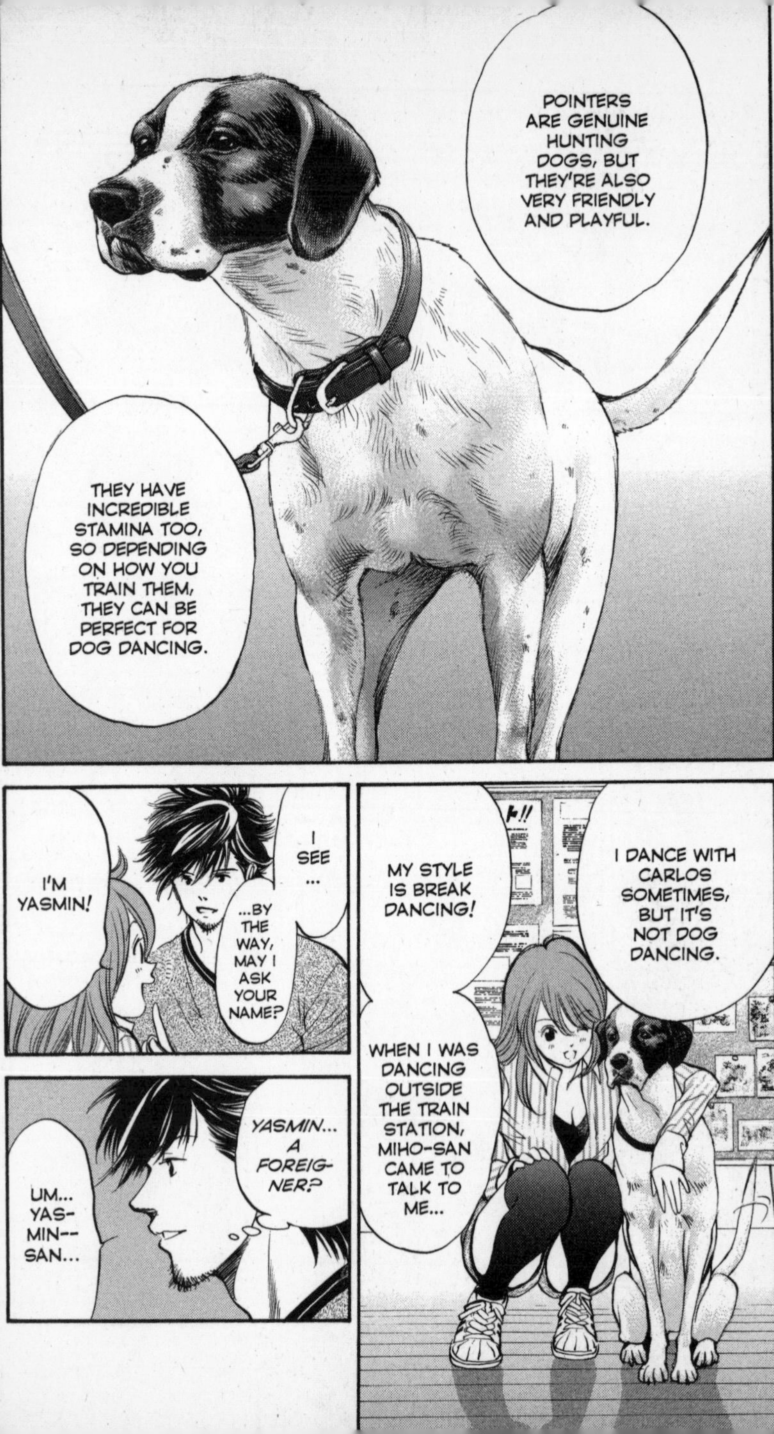
POINTERS ARE GENUINE HUNTING DOGS, BUT THEY'RE ALSO VERY FRIENDLY AND PLAYFUL.
THEY HAVE INCREDIBLE STAMINA TOO, SO DEPENDING ON HOW YOU TRAIN THEM, THEY CAN BE PERFECT FOR DOG DANCING.
I DANCE WITH CARLOS SOMETIMES, BUT IT'S NOT DOG DANCING.
MY STYLE IS BREAK DANCING!
WHEN I WAS DANCING OUTSIDE THE TRAIN STATION, MIHO-SAN CAME TO TALK TO ME...
I SEE...
...BY THE WAY, MAY I ASK YOUR NAME?
I'M YASMIN!
YASMIN... A FOREIG-NER?
UM... YAS-MIN--SAN...

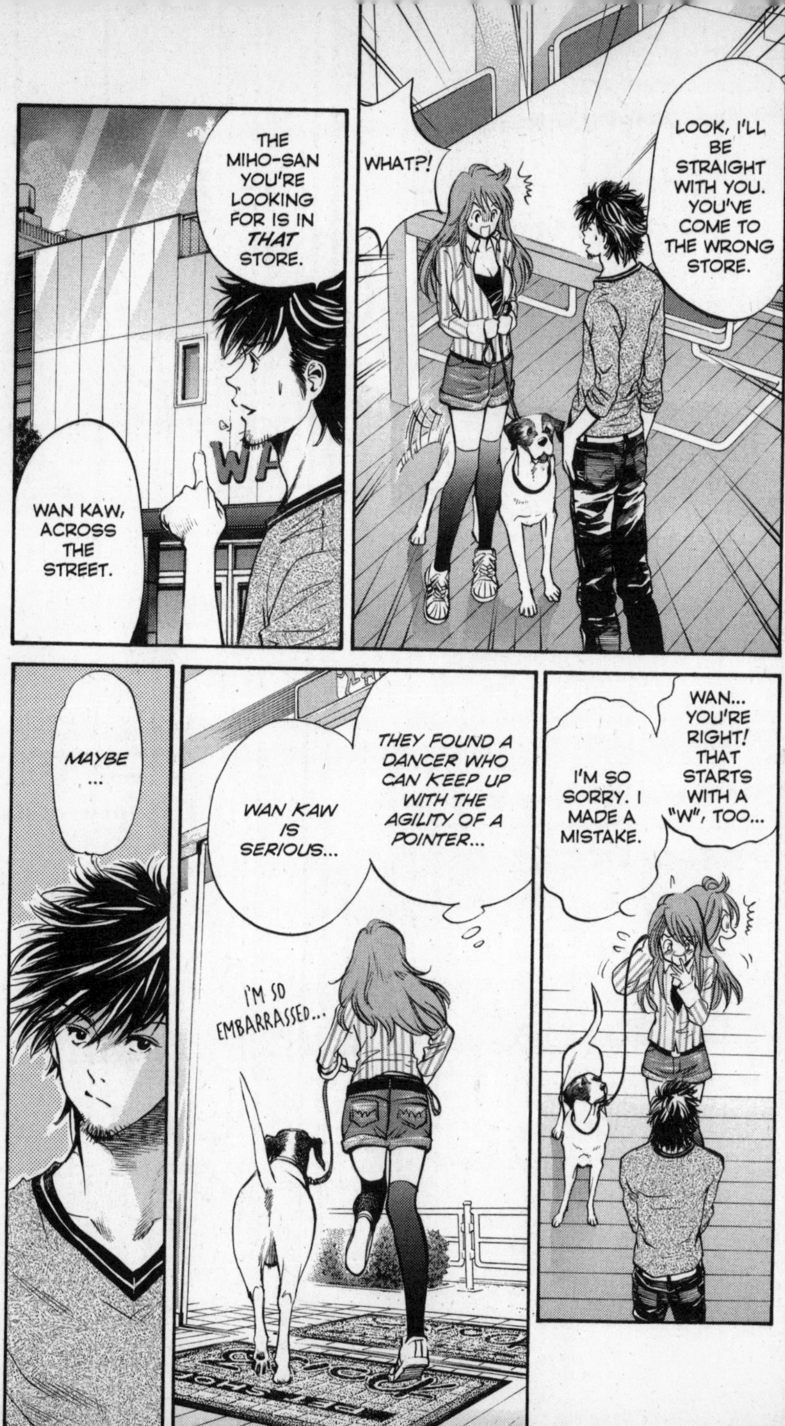
LOOK, I'LL BE STRAIGHT WITH YOU. YOU'VE COME TO THE WRONG STORE.
WHAT?!
THE MIHO-SAN YOU'RE LOOKING FOR IS IN *THAT* STORE.
WAN KAW, ACROSS THE STREET.
WAN... YOU'RE RIGHT! THAT STARTS WITH A "W", TOO...
I'M SO SORRY. I MADE A MISTAKE.
THEY FOUND A DANCER WHO CAN KEEP UP WITH THE AGILITY OF A POINTER...
WAN KAW IS SERIOUS...
I'M SO EMBARRASSED...
MAYBE ...

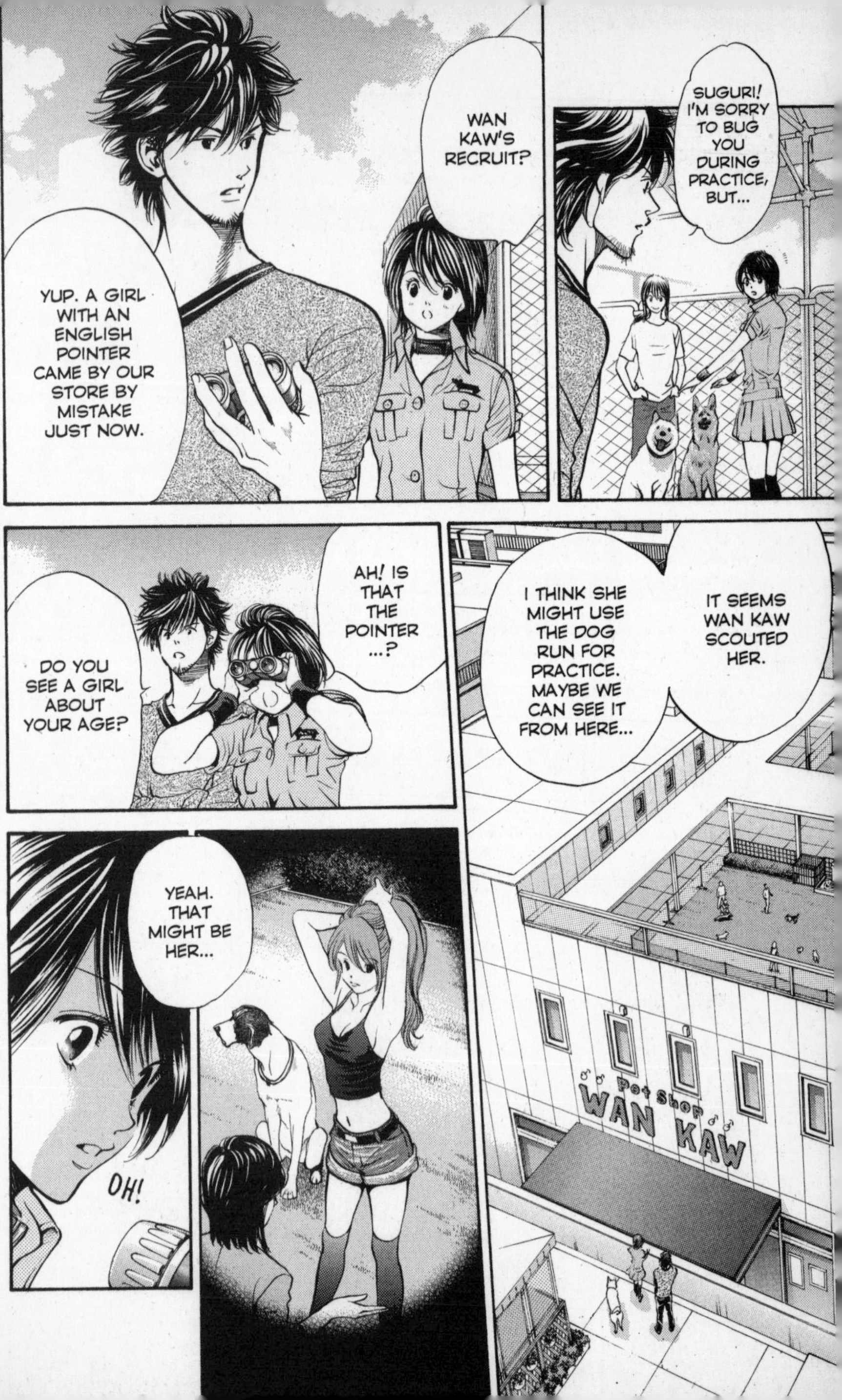
SUGURI! I'M SORRY TO BUG YOU DURING PRACTICE, BUT...
WAN KAW'S RECRUIT?
YUP. A GIRL WITH AN ENGLISH POINTER CAME BY OUR STORE BY MISTAKE JUST NOW.
IT SEEMS WAN KAW SCOUTED HER.
I THINK SHE MIGHT USE THE DOG RUN FOR PRACTICE. MAYBE WE CAN SEE IT FROM HERE...
Pet Shop WAN KAW
AH! IS THAT THE POINTER ...?
DO YOU SEE A GIRL ABOUT YOUR AGE?
YEAH. THAT MIGHT BE HER...
OH!

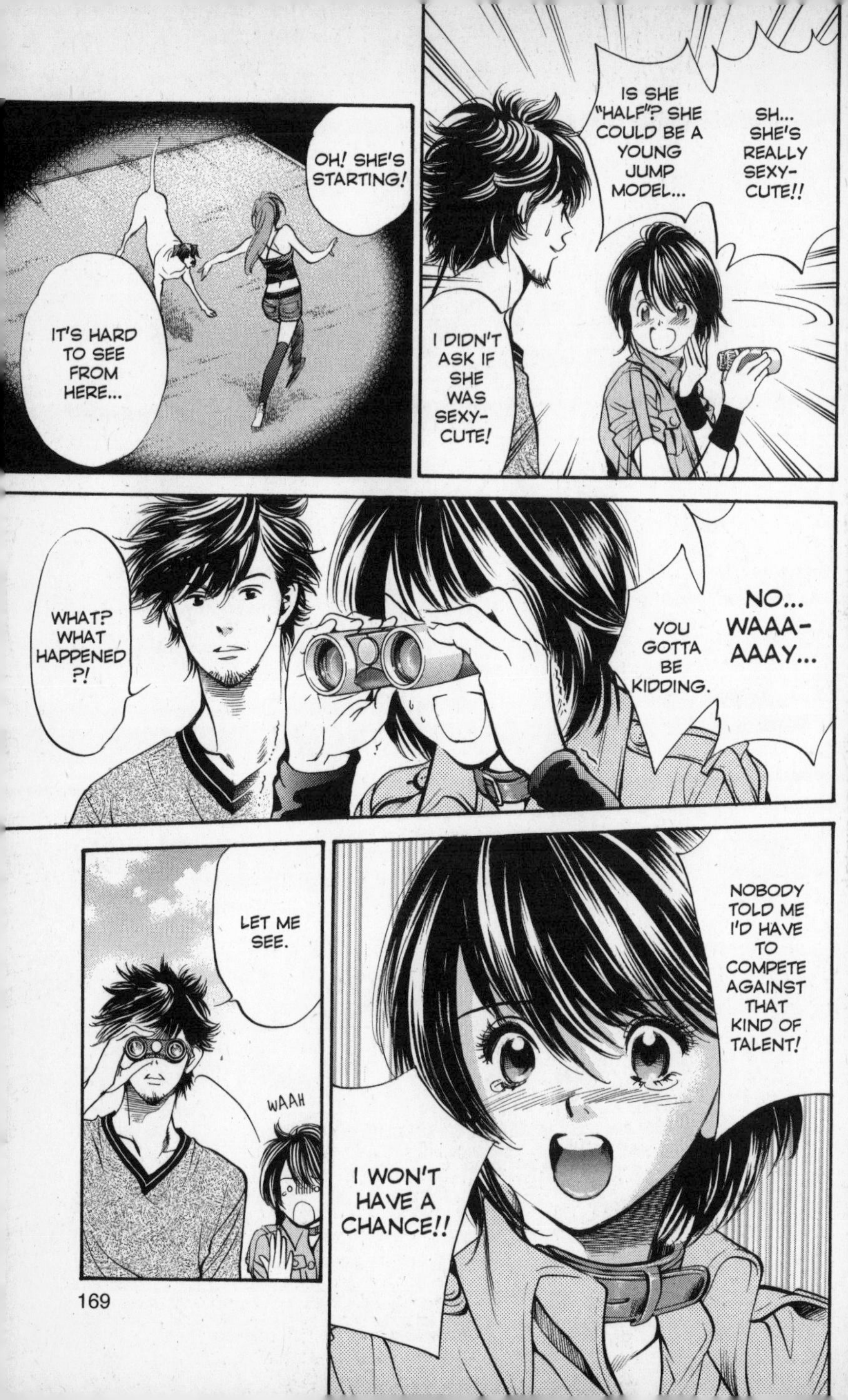

SH... SHE'S REALLY SEXY-CUTE!!
IS SHE "HALF"? SHE COULD BE A YOUNG JUMP MODEL...
I DIDN'T ASK IF SHE WAS SEXY-CUTE!
OH! SHE'S STARTING!
IT'S HARD TO SEE FROM HERE...
NO... WAAAA-AAAY...
YOU GOTTA BE KIDDING.
WHAT? WHAT HAPPENED?!
NOBODY TOLD ME I'D HAVE TO COMPETE AGAINST THAT KIND OF TALENT!
I WON'T HAVE A CHANCE!!
LET ME SEE.
WAAH

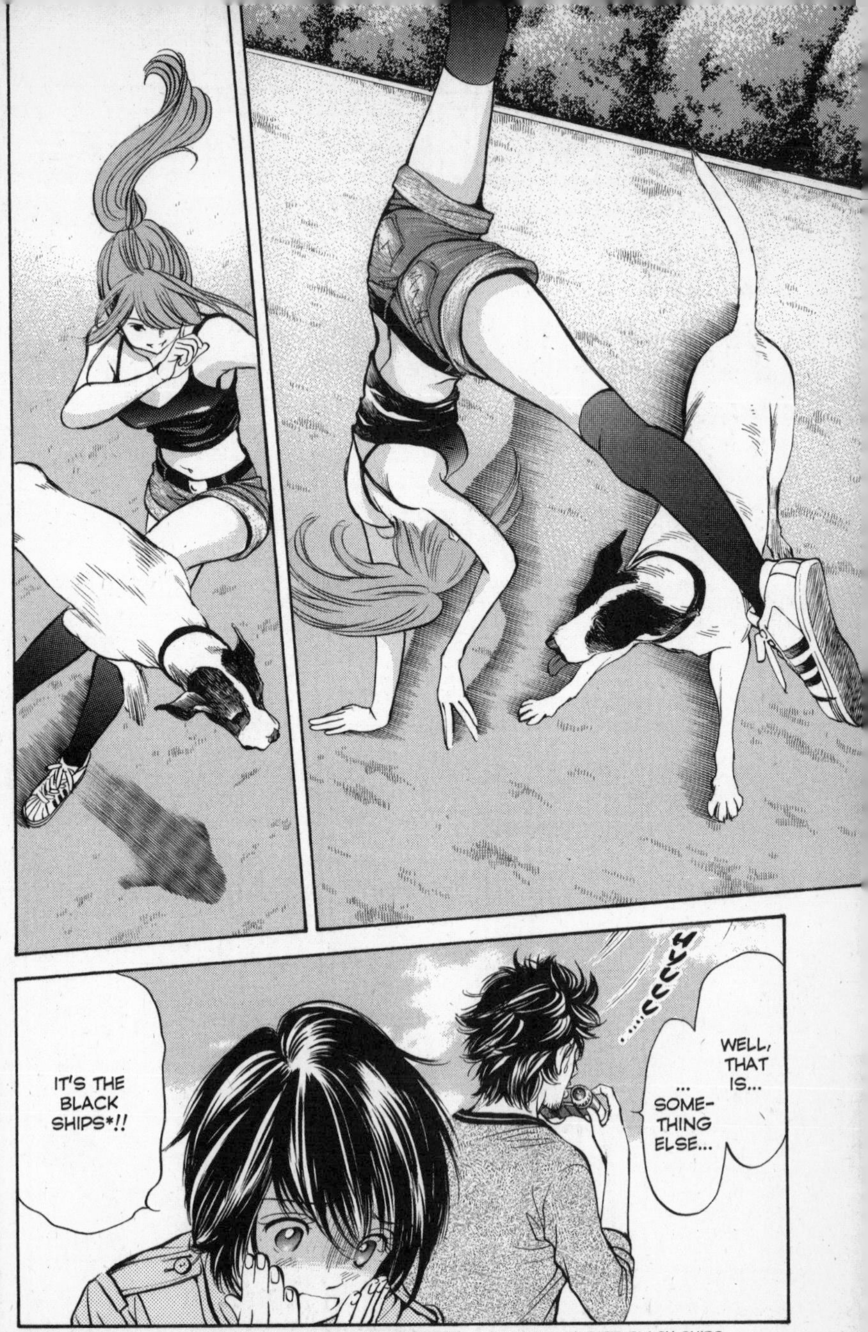
HYUUUU.....
WELL, THAT IS...
... SOME-THING ELSE...
IT'S THE BLACK SHIPS*!!

*THIS REFERS TO THE COMING OF COMMODORE PERRY OF THE U.S. NAVY AND THEIR BLACK SHIPS. IN 1845 THEY OPENED JAPAN, WHICH HAD BEEN A CLOSED COUNTRY TO THE WEST. THE TERM "BLACK SHIPS" IS ALSO SOMETIMES USED TO DESCRIBE OUTSIDE INTERFERENCE OR FOREIGN INTRUSION.

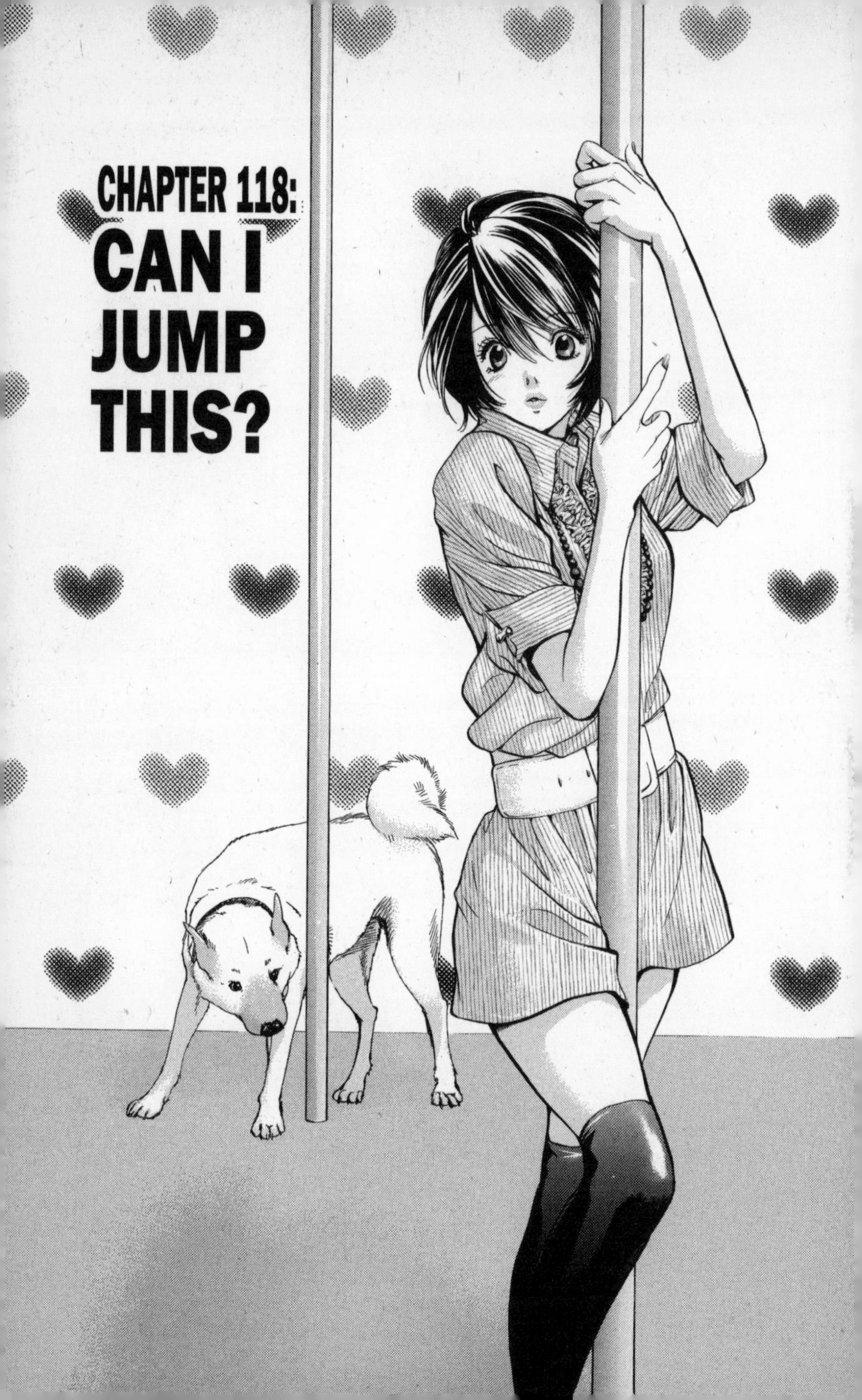
CHAPTER 118:
CAN I JUMP THIS?

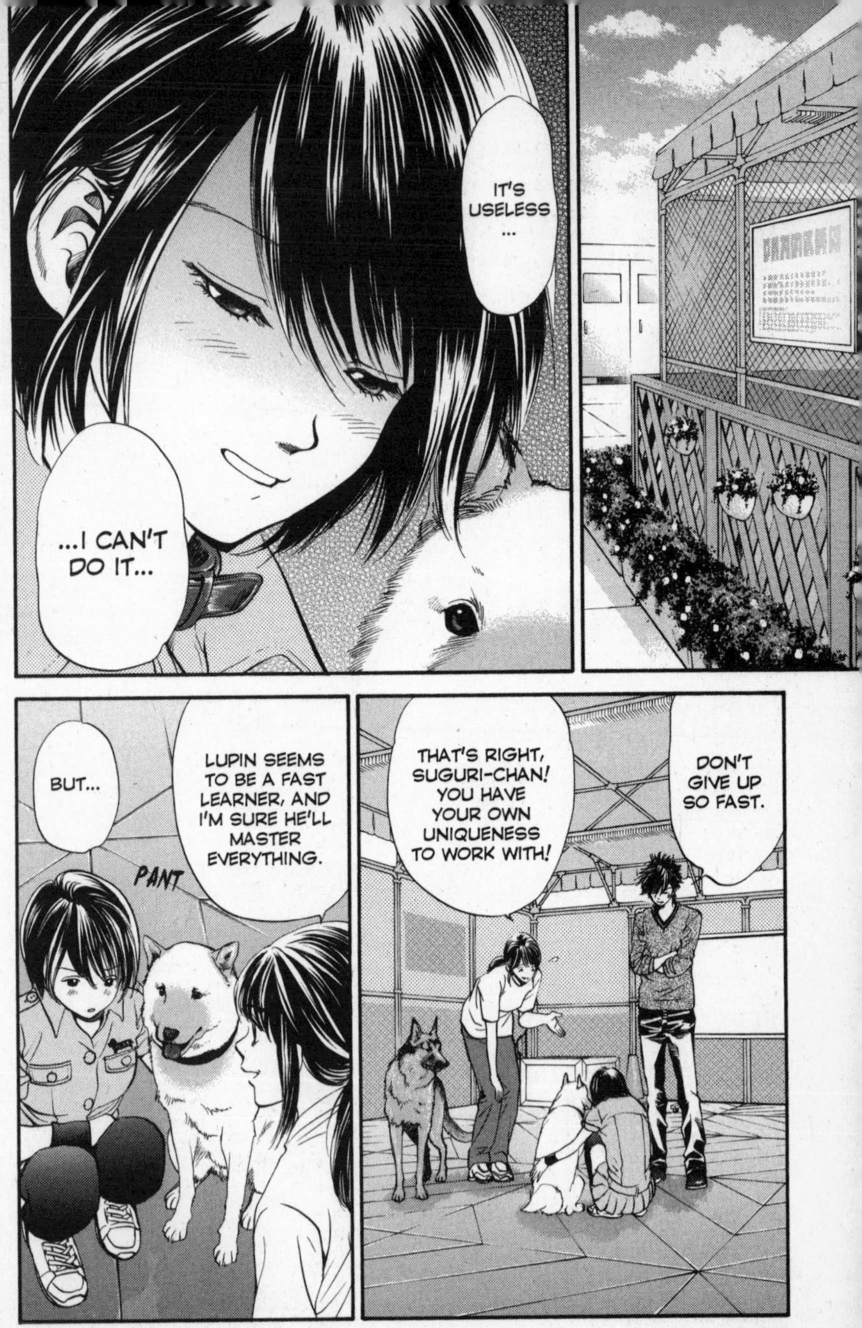
IT'S USELESS ...
...I CAN'T DO IT...
DON'T GIVE UP SO FAST.
THAT'S RIGHT, SUGURI-CHAN! YOU HAVE YOUR OWN UNIQUENESS TO WORK WITH!
LUPIN SEEMS TO BE A FAST LEARNER, AND I'M SURE HE'LL MASTER EVERYTHING.
BUT...
PANT

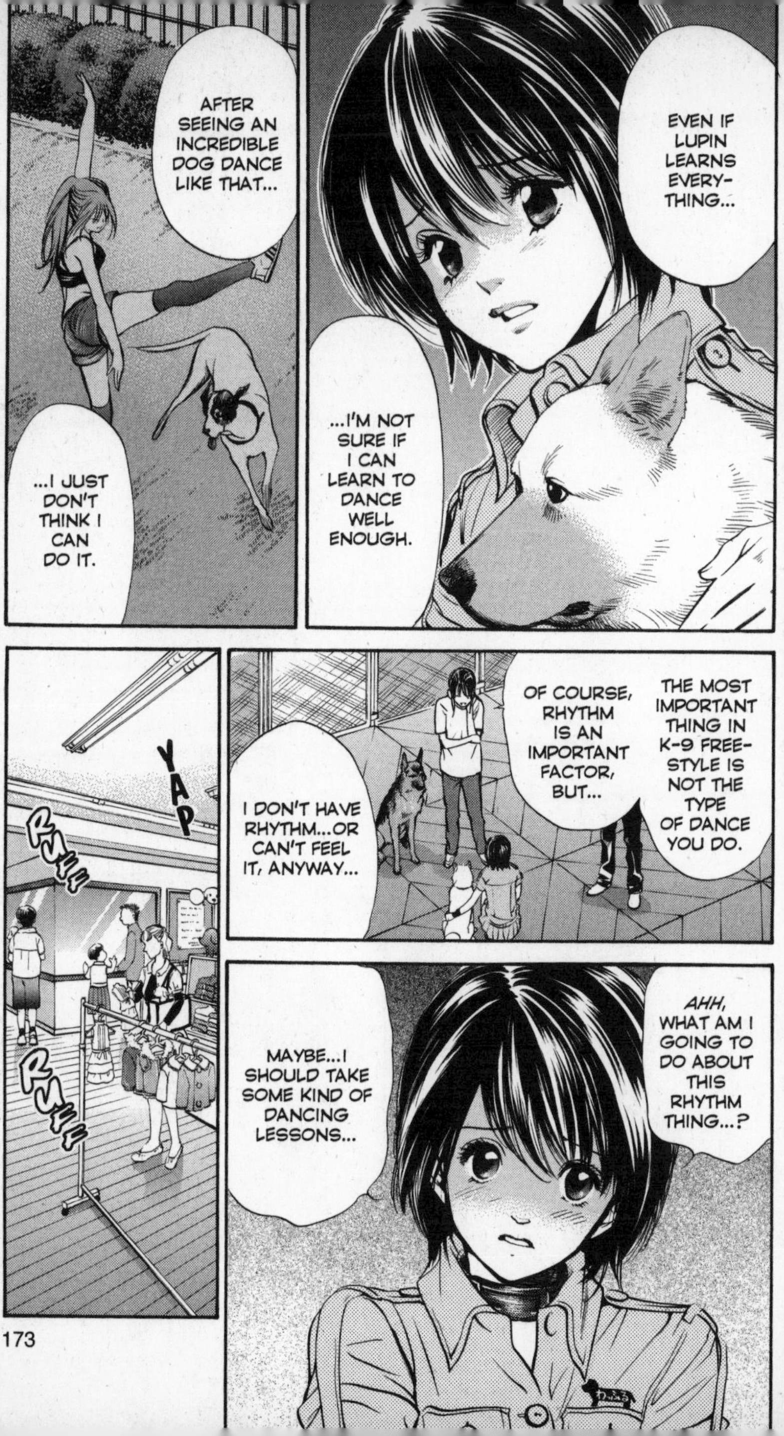
EVEN IF LUPIN LEARNS EVERYTHING...
...I'M NOT SURE IF I CAN LEARN TO DANCE WELL ENOUGH.
AFTER SEEING AN INCREDIBLE DOG DANCE LIKE THAT...
...I JUST DON'T THINK I CAN DO IT.
THE MOST IMPORTANT THING IN K-9 FREE-STYLE IS NOT THE TYPE OF DANCE YOU DO.
OF COURSE, RHYTHM IS AN IMPORTANT FACTOR, BUT...
I DON'T HAVE RHYTHM...OR CAN'T FEEL IT, ANYWAY...
AHH, WHAT AM I GOING TO DO ABOUT THIS RHYTHM THING...?
MAYBE...I SHOULD TAKE SOME KIND OF DANCING LESSONS...
YAP
RUFF
RUFF

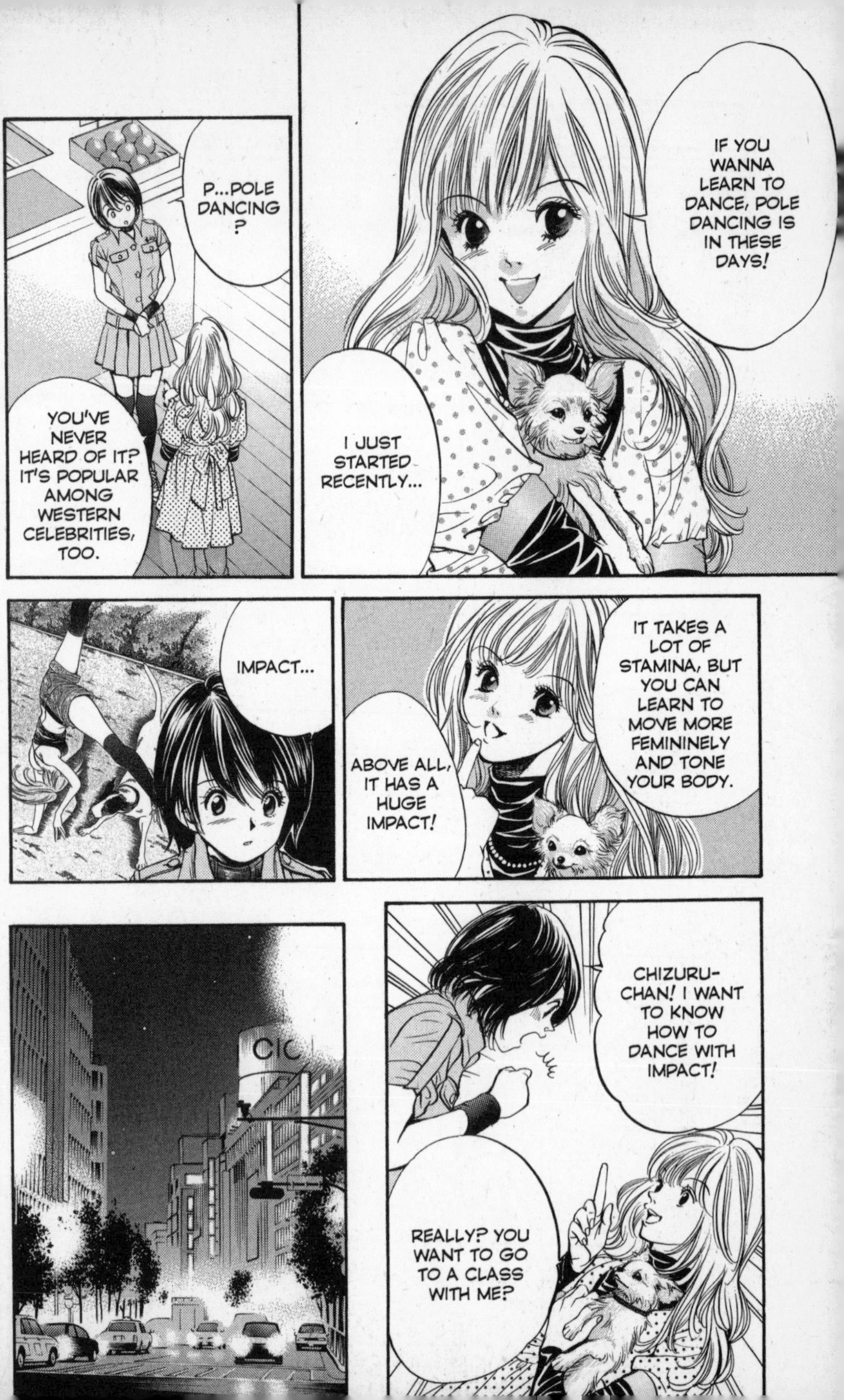
IF YOU WANNA LEARN TO DANCE, POLE DANCING IS IN THESE DAYS!
I JUST STARTED RECENTLY...
P...POLE DANCING?
YOU'VE NEVER HEARD OF IT? IT'S POPULAR AMONG WESTERN CELEBRITIES, TOO.
IT TAKES A LOT OF STAMINA, BUT YOU CAN LEARN TO MOVE MORE FEMININELY AND TONE YOUR BODY.
ABOVE ALL, IT HAS A HUGE IMPACT!
IMPACT...
CHIZURU-CHAN! I WANT TO KNOW HOW TO DANCE WITH IMPACT!
REALLY? YOU WANT TO GO TO A CLASS WITH ME?

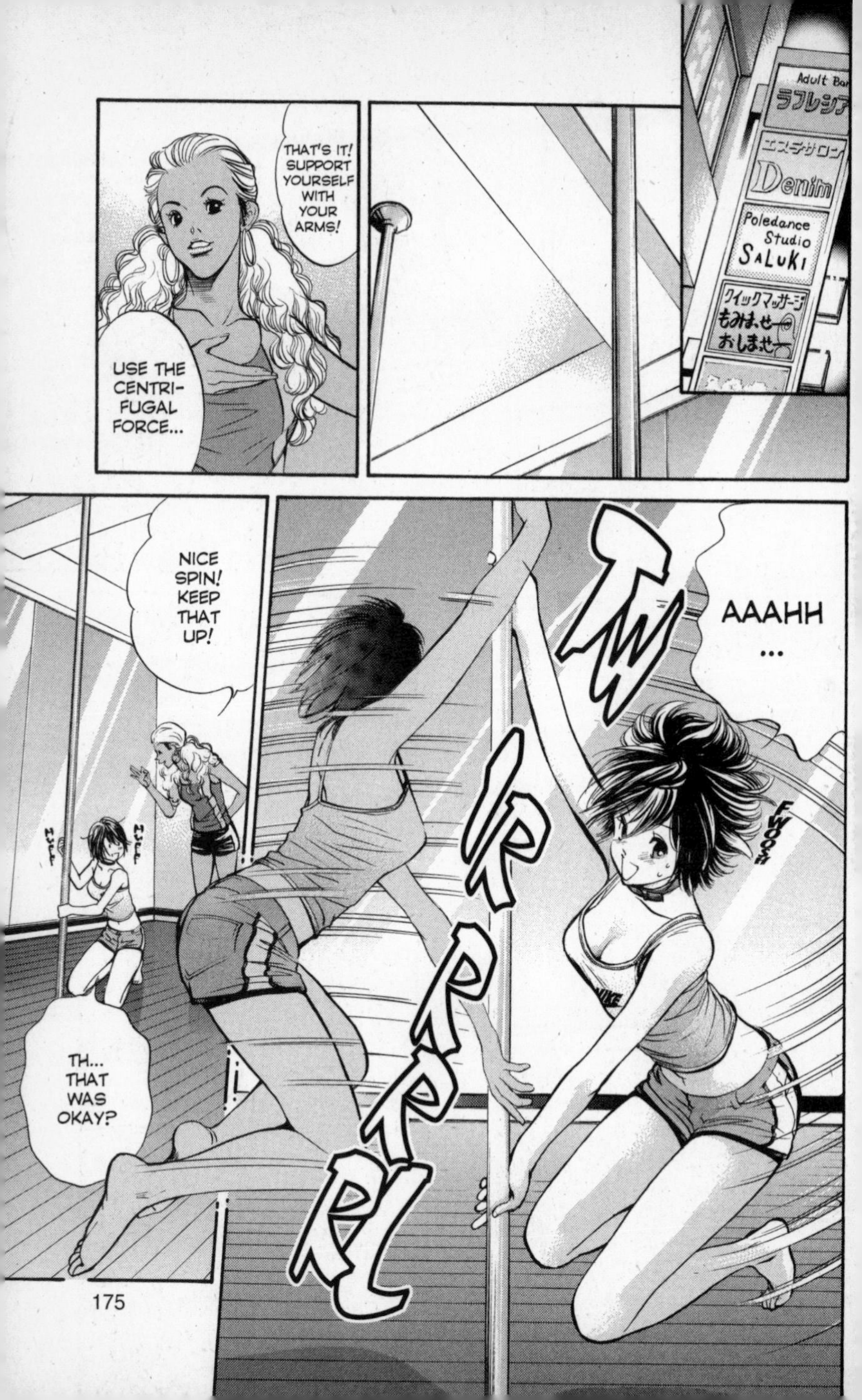
Adult Ba
エステサロン
Denim
Poledance Studio SALUKI
クイックマッサージ
もみませー
おしませー
THAT'S IT! SUPPORT YOURSELF WITH YOUR ARMS!
USE THE CENTRI-FUGAL FORCE...
AAAHH ...
TWIRRRRL
FWOOSH
NICE SPIN! KEEP THAT UP!
TH... THAT WAS OKAY?

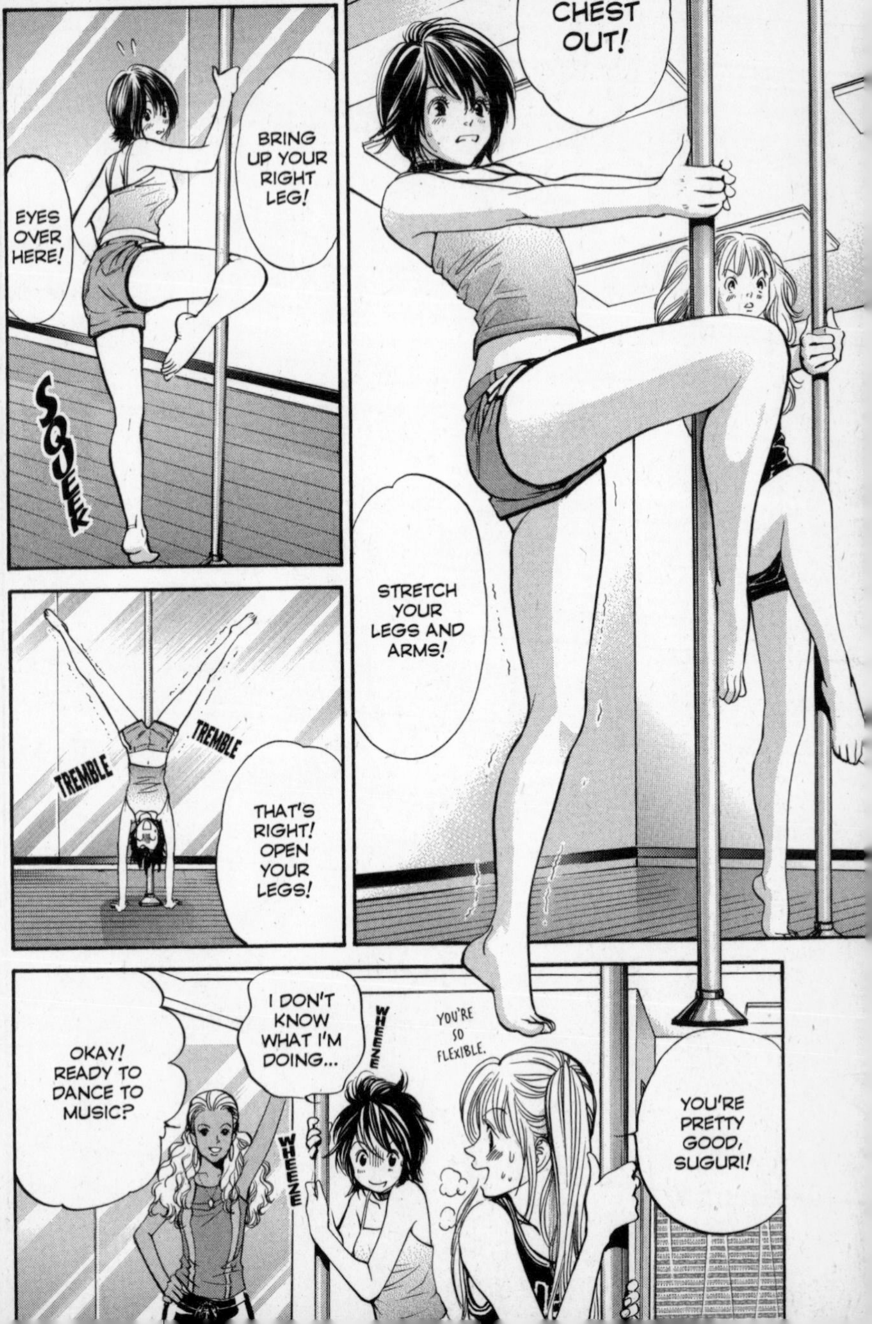
CHEST OUT!
STRETCH YOUR LEGS AND ARMS!
BRING UP YOUR RIGHT LEG!
EYES OVER HERE!
SQUEEK
TREMBLE
TREMBLE
THAT'S RIGHT! OPEN YOUR LEGS!
YOU'RE PRETTY GOOD, SUGURI!
YOU'RE SO FLEXIBLE.
I DON'T KNOW WHAT I'M DOING...
WHEEZE
WHEEZE
OKAY! READY TO DANCE TO MUSIC?

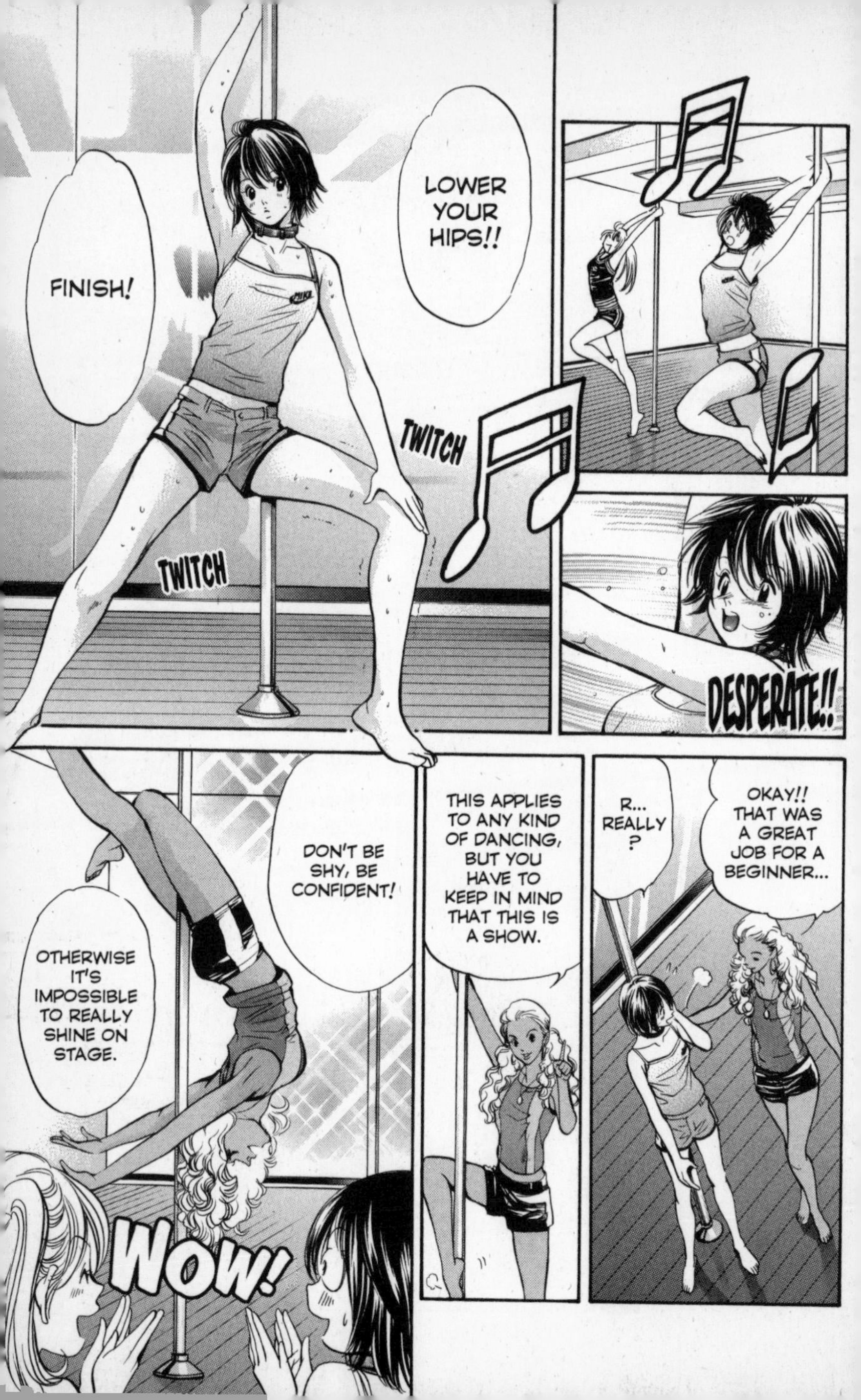
DESPERATE!!
LOWER YOUR HIPS!!
FINISH!
TWITCH
TWITCH
OKAY!! THAT WAS A GREAT JOB FOR A BEGINNER...
R... REALLY ?
THIS APPLIES TO ANY KIND OF DANCING, BUT YOU HAVE TO KEEP IN MIND THAT THIS IS A SHOW.
DON'T BE SHY, BE CONFIDENT!
OTHERWISE IT'S IMPOSSIBLE TO REALLY SHINE ON STAGE.
WOW!

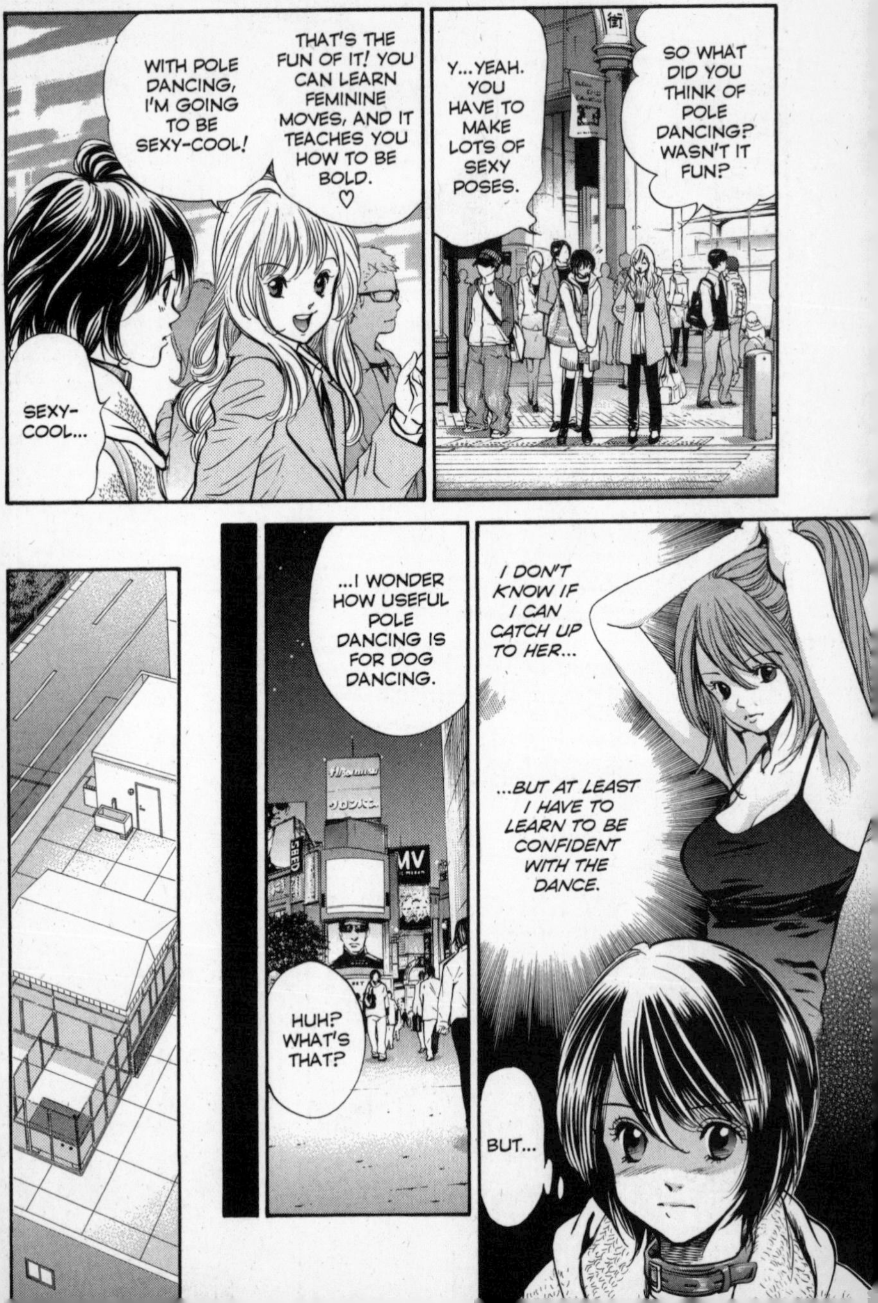
SO WHAT DID YOU THINK OF POLE DANCING? WASN'T IT FUN?
Y...YEAH. YOU HAVE TO MAKE LOTS OF SEXY POSES.
THAT'S THE FUN OF IT! YOU CAN LEARN FEMININE MOVES, AND IT TEACHES YOU HOW TO BE BOLD. ♡
WITH POLE DANCING, I'M GOING TO BE SEXY-COOL!
SEXY-COOL...
I DON'T KNOW IF I CAN CATCH UP TO HER...
...BUT AT LEAST I HAVE TO LEARN TO BE CONFIDENT WITH THE DANCE.
BUT...
...I WONDER HOW USEFUL POLE DANCING IS FOR DOG DANCING.
HUH? WHAT'S THAT?

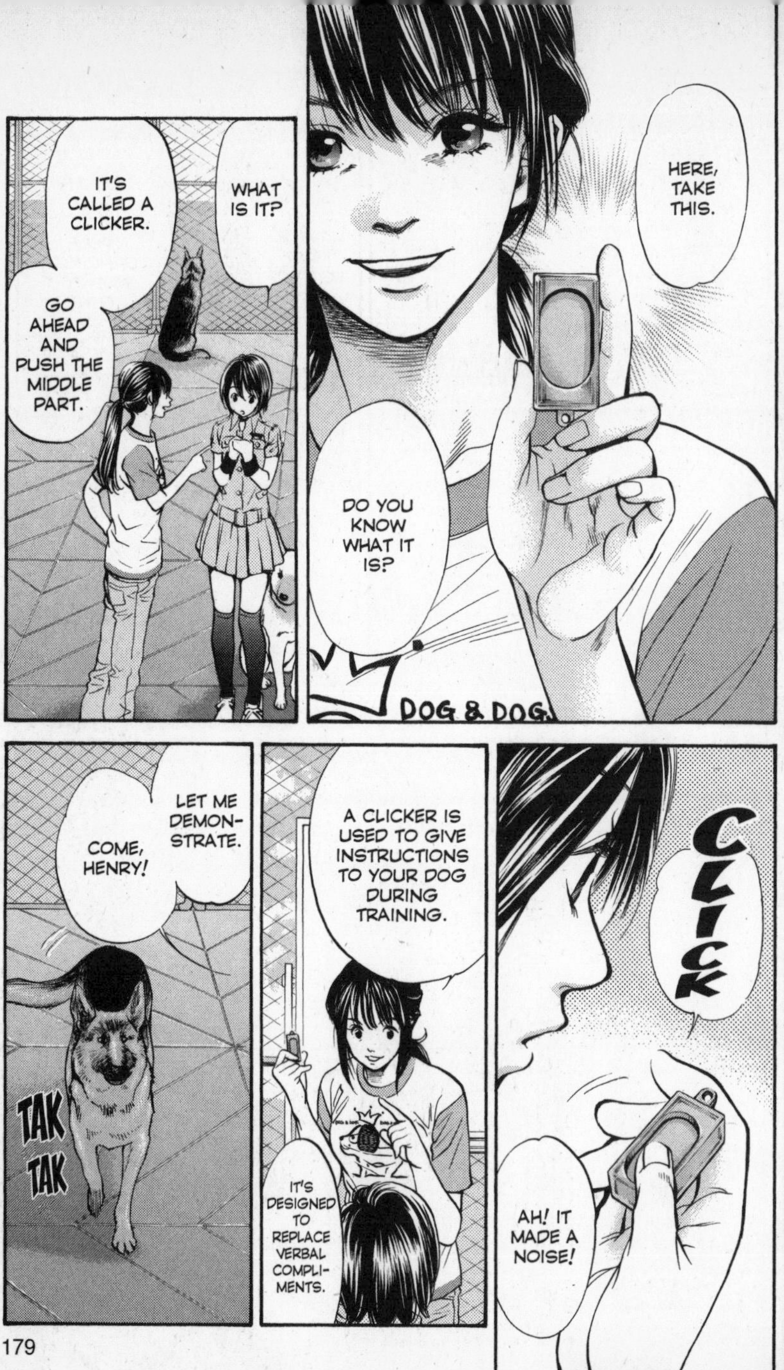
HERE, TAKE THIS.
DO YOU KNOW WHAT IT IS?
DOG & DOG
WHAT IS IT?
IT'S CALLED A CLICKER.
GO AHEAD AND PUSH THE MIDDLE PART.
CLICK
AH! IT MADE A NOISE!
A CLICKER IS USED TO GIVE INSTRUCTIONS TO YOUR DOG DURING TRAINING.
IT'S DESIGNED TO REPLACE VERBAL COMPLI-MENTS.
LET ME DEMON-STRATE.
COME, HENRY!
TAK TAK

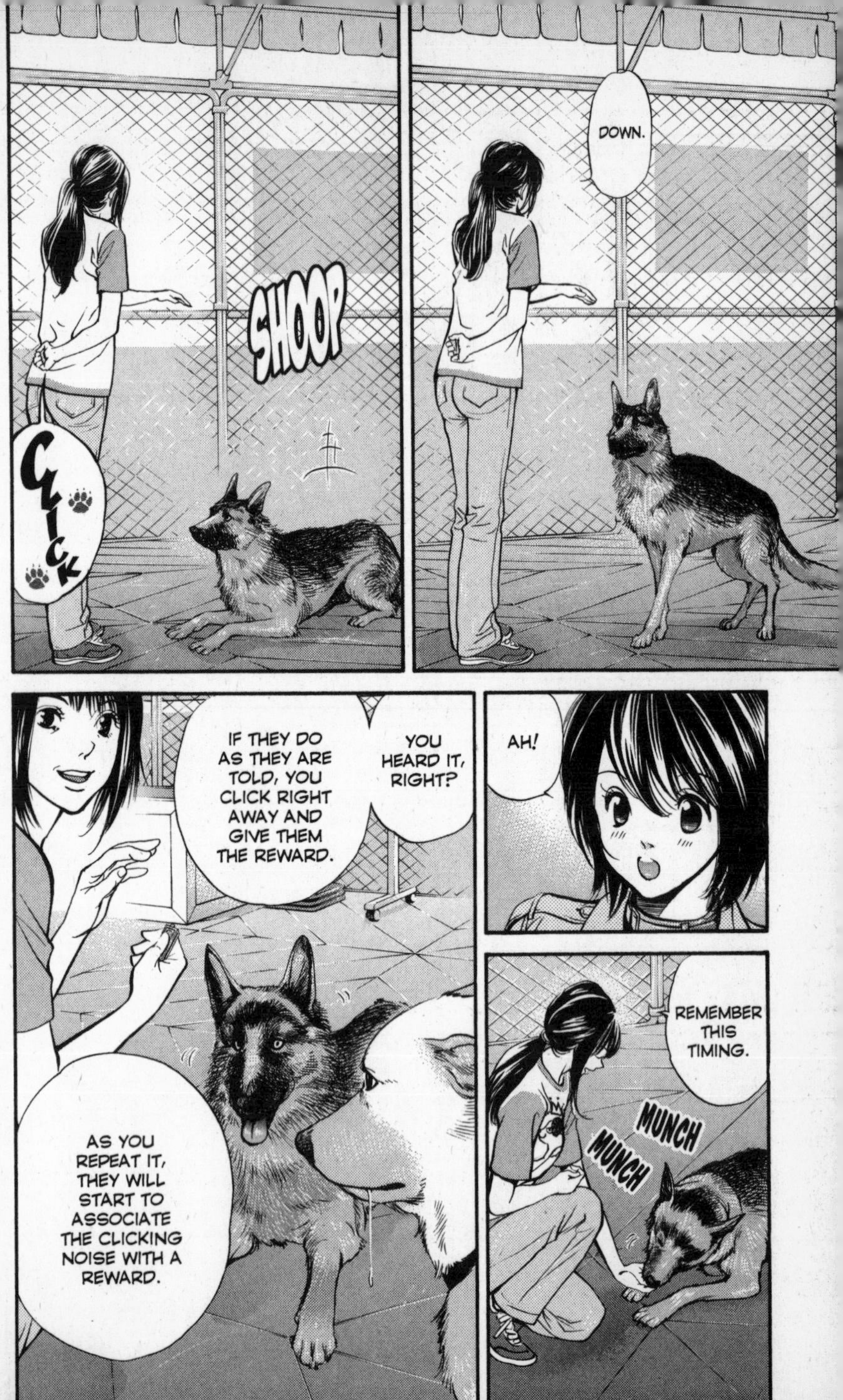
DOWN.
SHOOP
CLICK
AH!
REMEMBER THIS TIMING.
MUNCH
MUNCH
YOU HEARD IT, RIGHT?
IF THEY DO AS THEY ARE TOLD, YOU CLICK RIGHT AWAY AND GIVE THEM THE REWARD.
AS YOU REPEAT IT, THEY WILL START TO ASSOCIATE THE CLICKING NOISE WITH A REWARD.

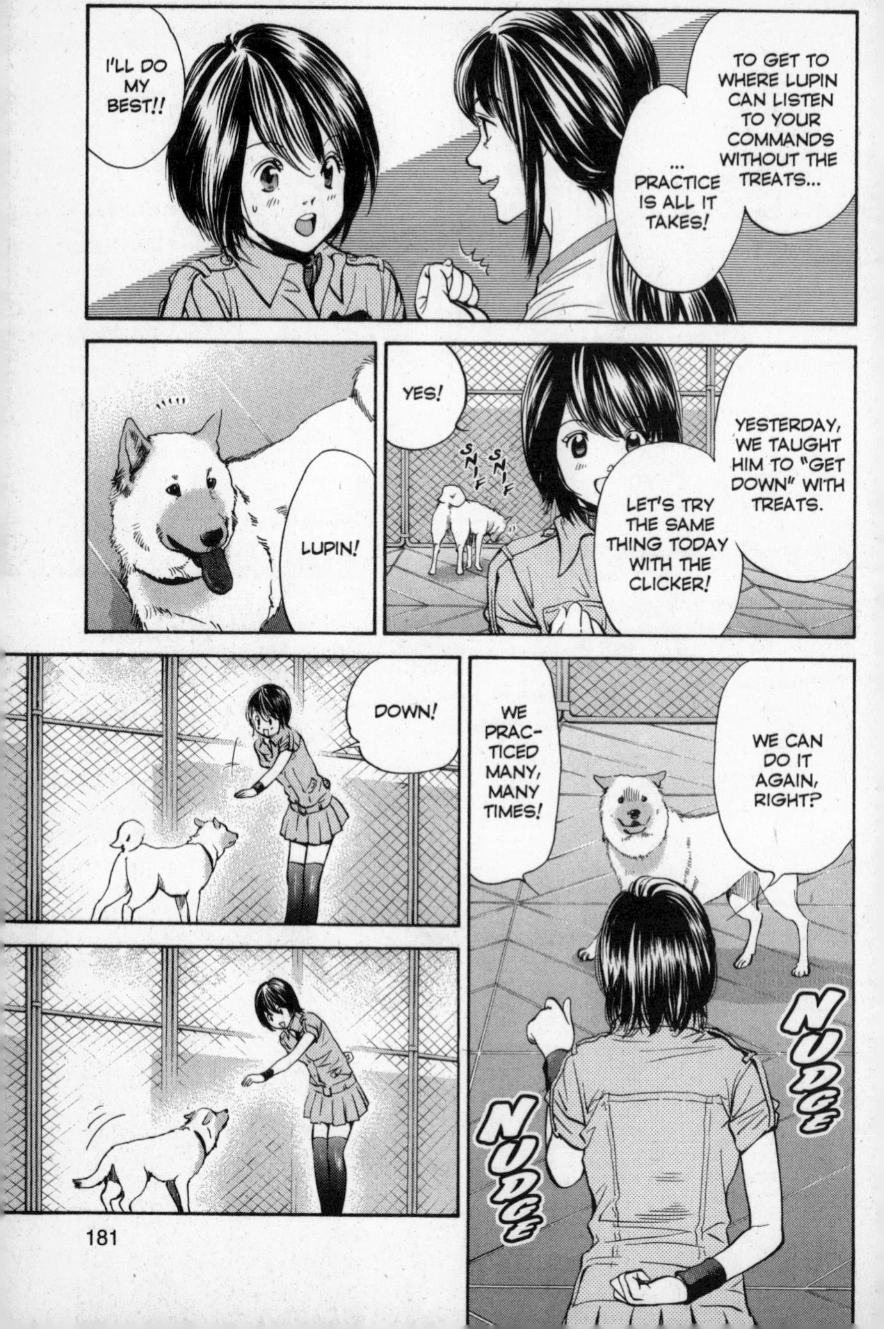
TO GET TO WHERE LUPIN CAN LISTEN TO YOUR COMMANDS WITHOUT THE TREATS...
... PRACTICE IS ALL IT TAKES!
I'LL DO MY BEST!!
YESTERDAY, WE TAUGHT HIM TO "GET DOWN" WITH TREATS.
LET'S TRY THE SAME THING TODAY WITH THE CLICKER!
YES!
SNIF SNIF
LUPIN!
WE CAN DO IT AGAIN, RIGHT?
WE PRACTICED MANY, MANY TIMES!
NUDGE
NUDGE
DOWN!

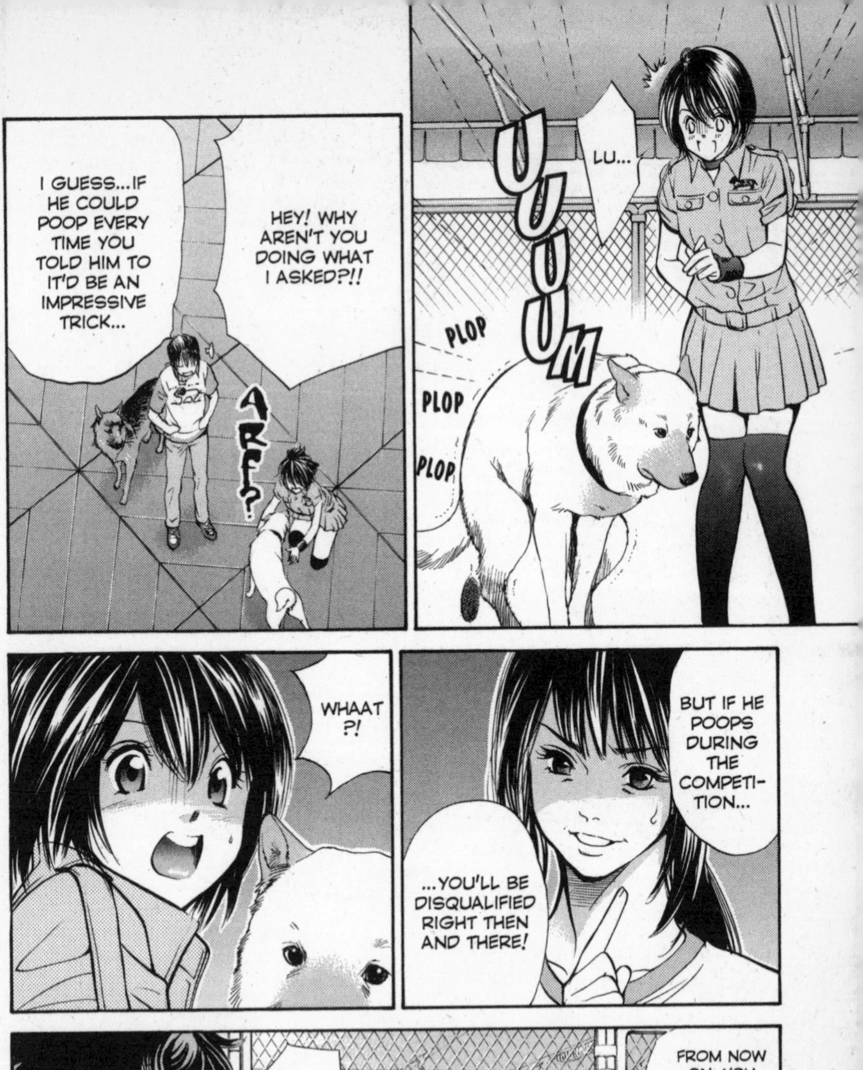
LU...
UUUUUM
PLOP
PLOP
PLOP
HEY! WHY AREN'T YOU DOING WHAT I ASKED?!!
I GUESS...IF HE COULD POOP EVERY TIME YOU TOLD HIM TO IT'D BE AN IMPRESSIVE TRICK...
ARF?
BUT IF HE POOPS DURING THE COMPETITION...
...YOU'LL BE DISQUALIFIED RIGHT THEN AND THERE!
WHAAT?!
FROM NOW ON, YOU SHOULD HAVE LUPIN GO TO THE BATHROOM BEFORE PRACTICE.
HE IS POTTY-TRAINED, RIGHT?
YES. I'M SO SORRY.

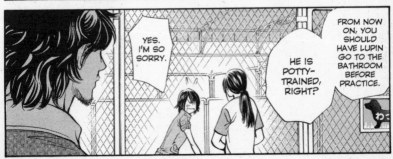

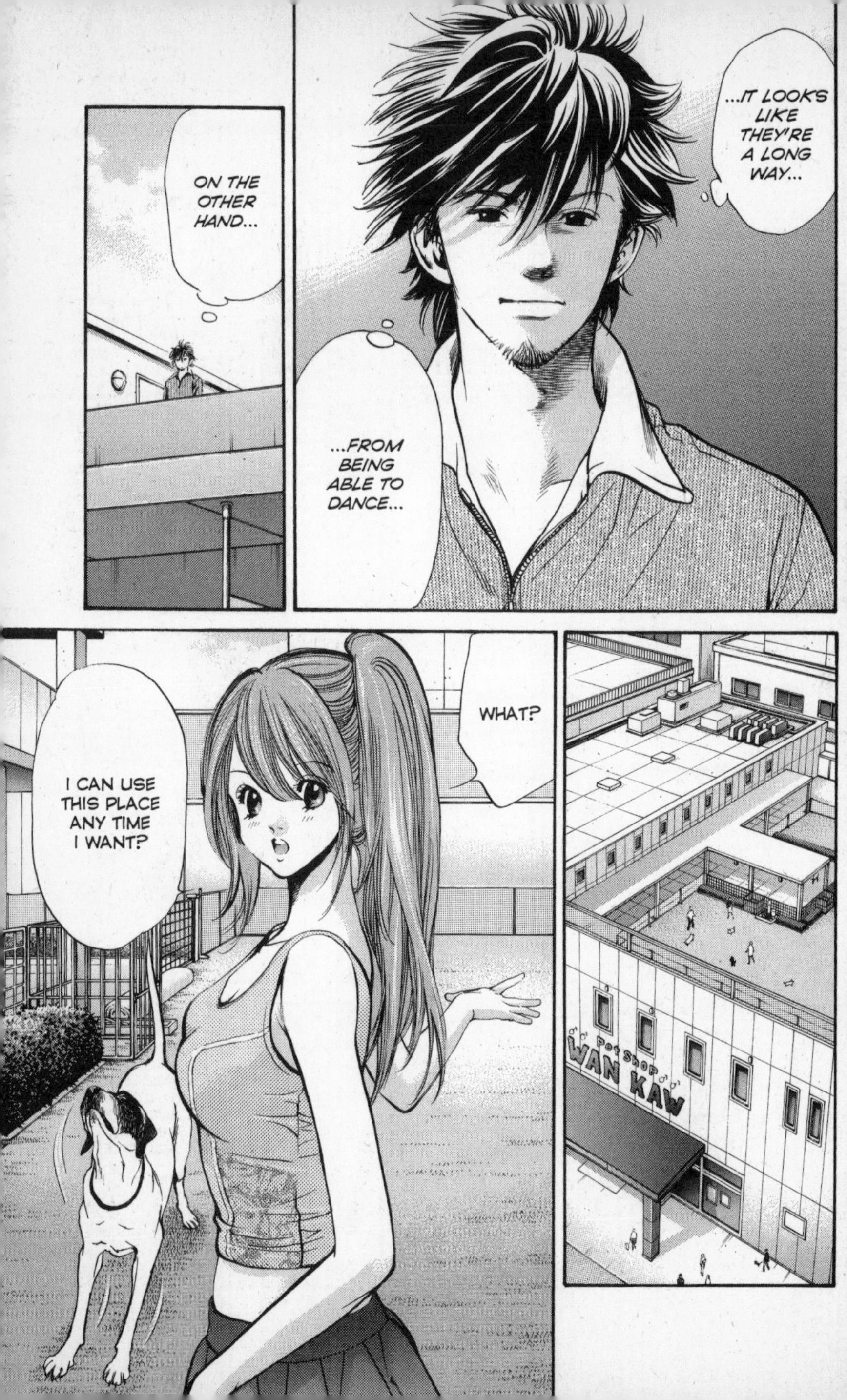
...IT LOOKS LIKE THEY'RE A LONG WAY...
...FROM BEING ABLE TO DANCE...
ON THE OTHER HAND...
Pet SHOP WAN KAW
WHAT?
I CAN USE THIS PLACE ANY TIME I WANT?

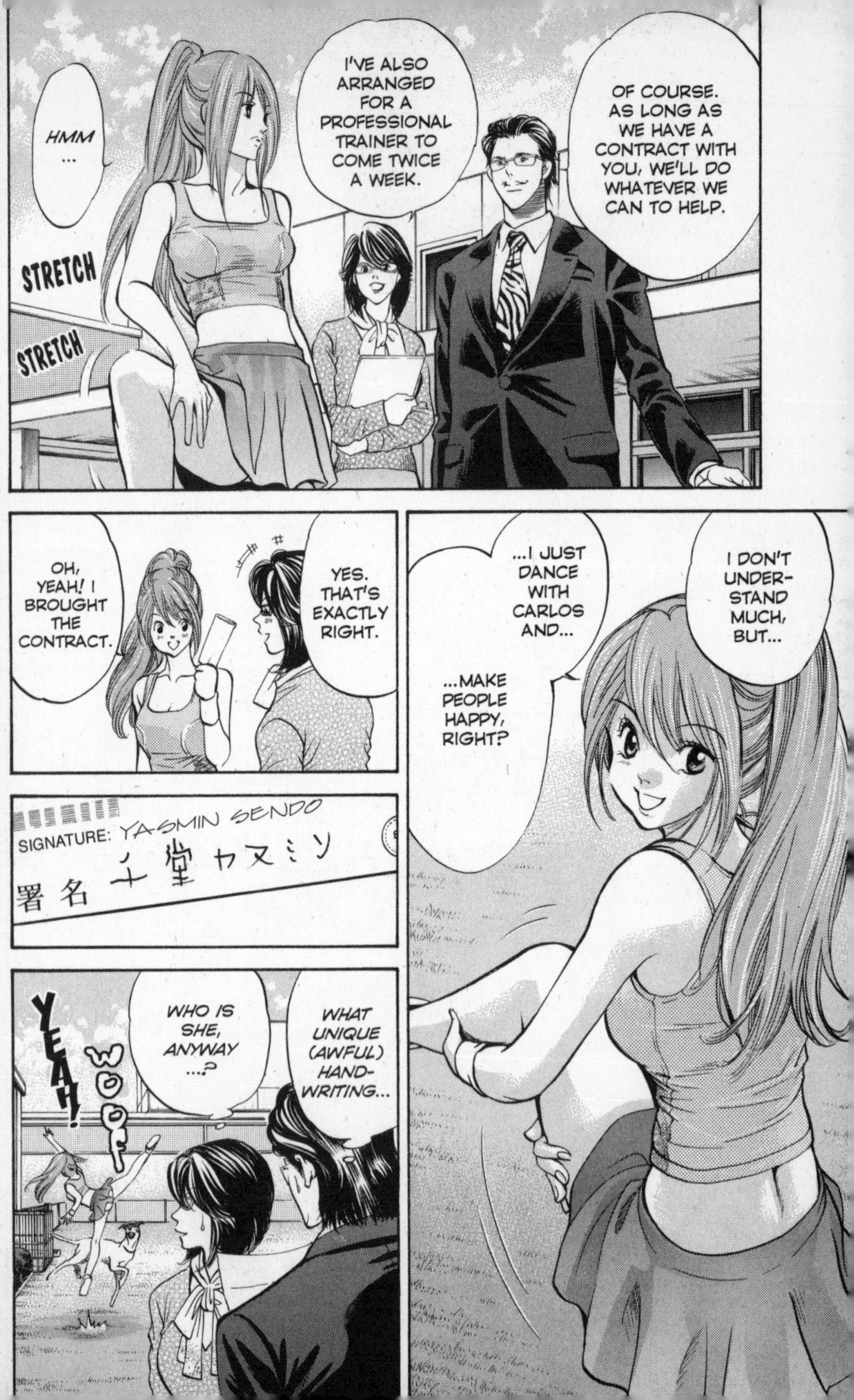
OF COURSE. AS LONG AS WE HAVE A CONTRACT WITH YOU, WE'LL DO WHATEVER WE CAN TO HELP.
I'VE ALSO ARRANGED FOR A PROFESSIONAL TRAINER TO COME TWICE A WEEK.
HMM ...
STRETCH
STRETCH
I DON'T UNDER-STAND MUCH, BUT...
...I JUST DANCE WITH CARLOS AND...
...MAKE PEOPLE HAPPY, RIGHT?
YES. THAT'S EXACTLY RIGHT.
OH, YEAH! I BROUGHT THE CONTRACT.
SIGNATURE: YASMIN SENDO
署名 千堂ヤヌミソ
WHAT UNIQUE (AWFUL) HAND-WRITING...
WHO IS SHE, ANYWAY ...?
YEAH!
WOOF

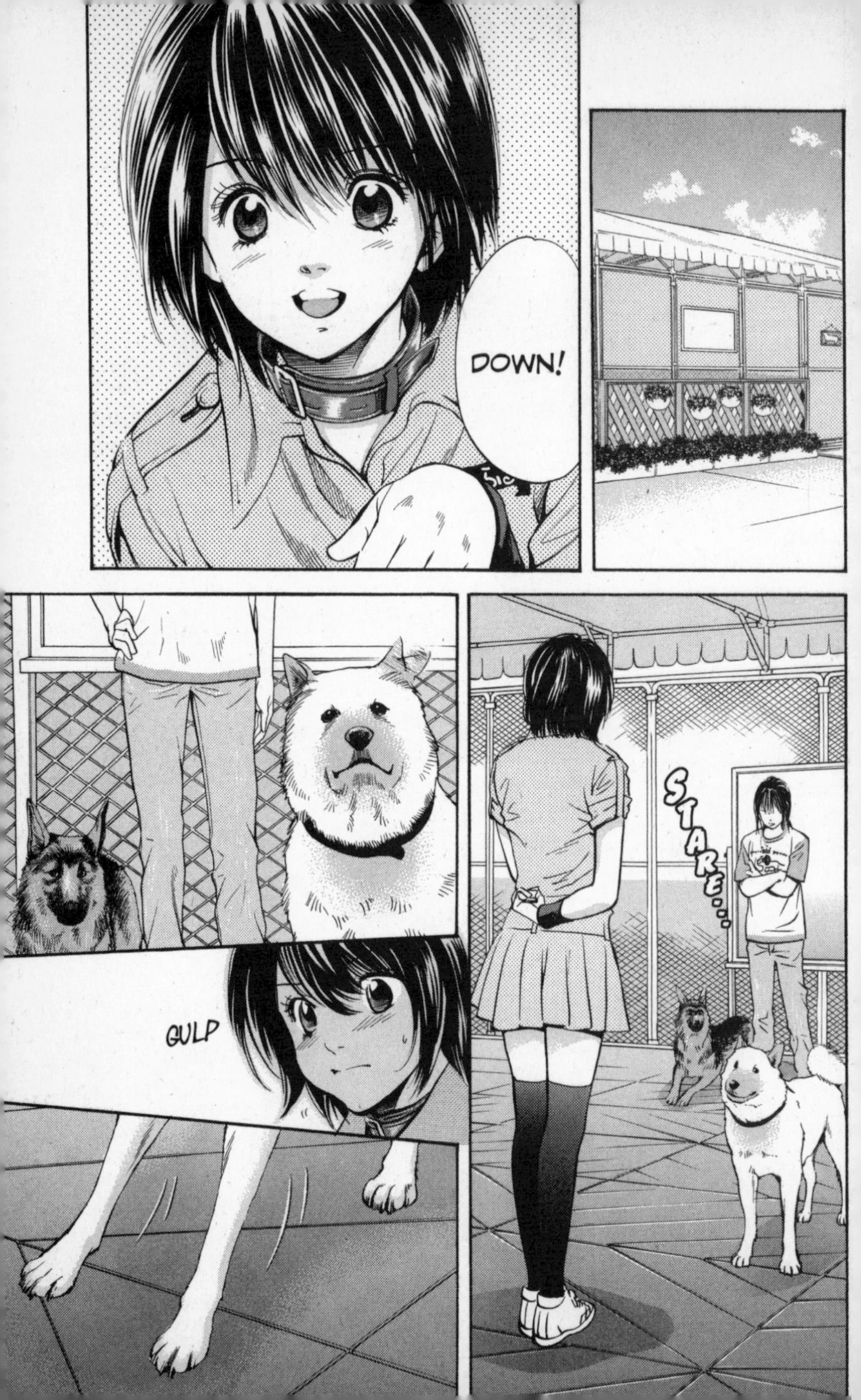
DOWN!
STARE...
GULP

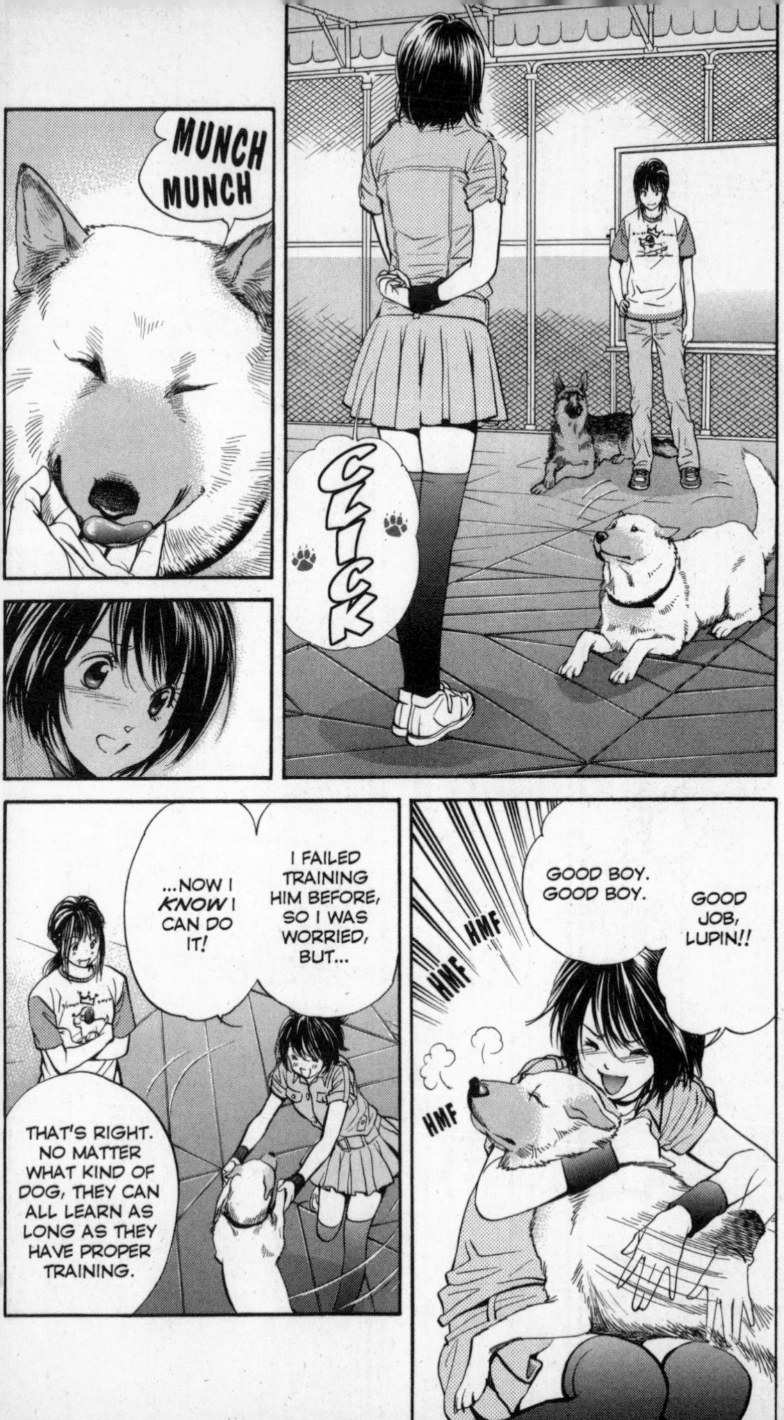
CLICK
MUNCH MUNCH
GOOD JOB, LUPIN!!
GOOD BOY. GOOD BOY.
HMF HMF
HMF
I FAILED TRAINING HIM BEFORE, SO I WAS WORRIED, BUT...
...NOW I *KNOW* I CAN DO IT!
THAT'S RIGHT. NO MATTER WHAT KIND OF DOG, THEY CAN ALL LEARN AS LONG AS THEY HAVE PROPER TRAINING.

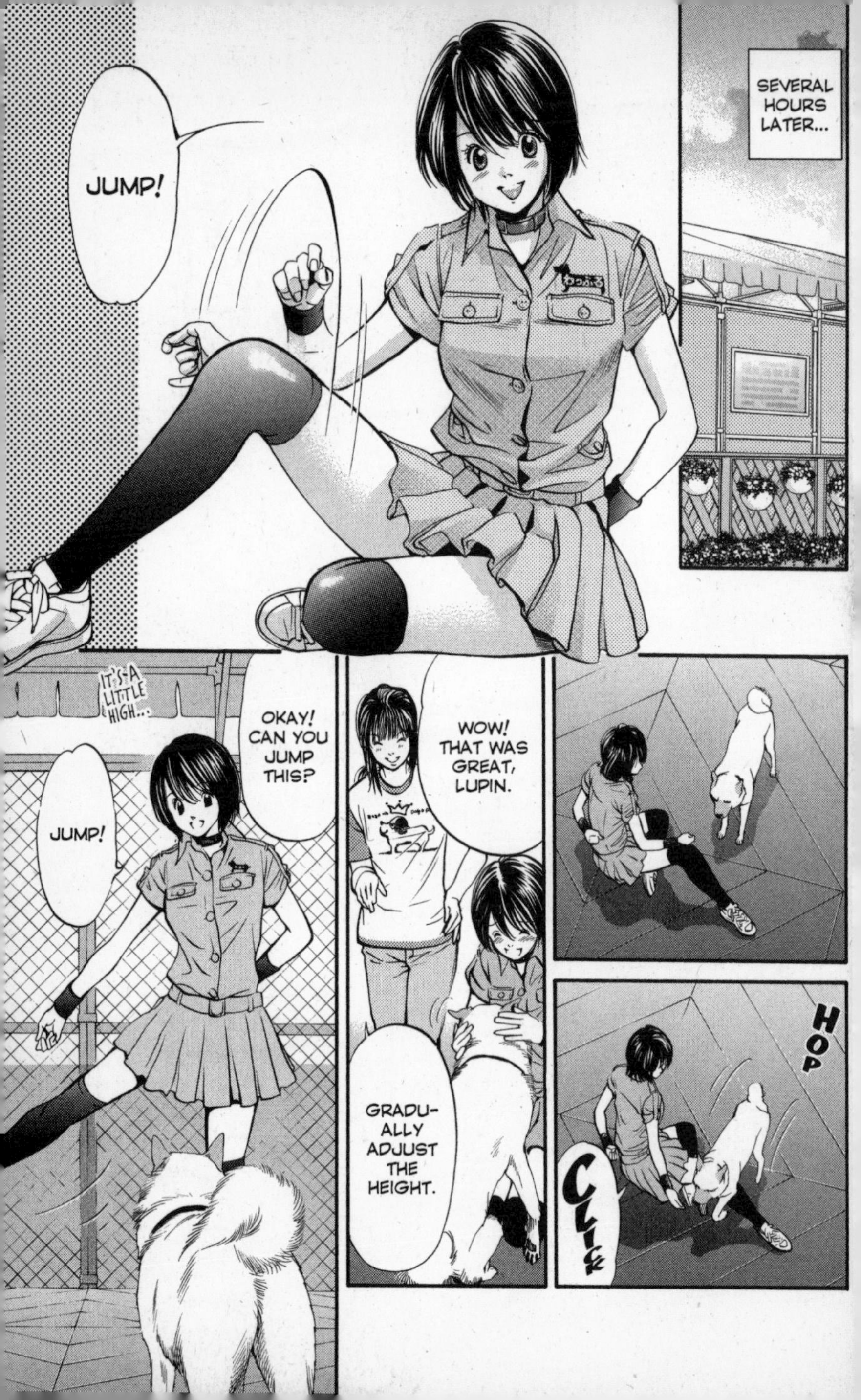
SEVERAL HOURS LATER...
JUMP!
HOP
CLICK
WOW! THAT WAS GREAT, LUPIN.
GRADU-ALLY ADJUST THE HEIGHT.
OKAY! CAN YOU JUMP THIS?
IT'S A LITTLE HIGH...
JUMP!

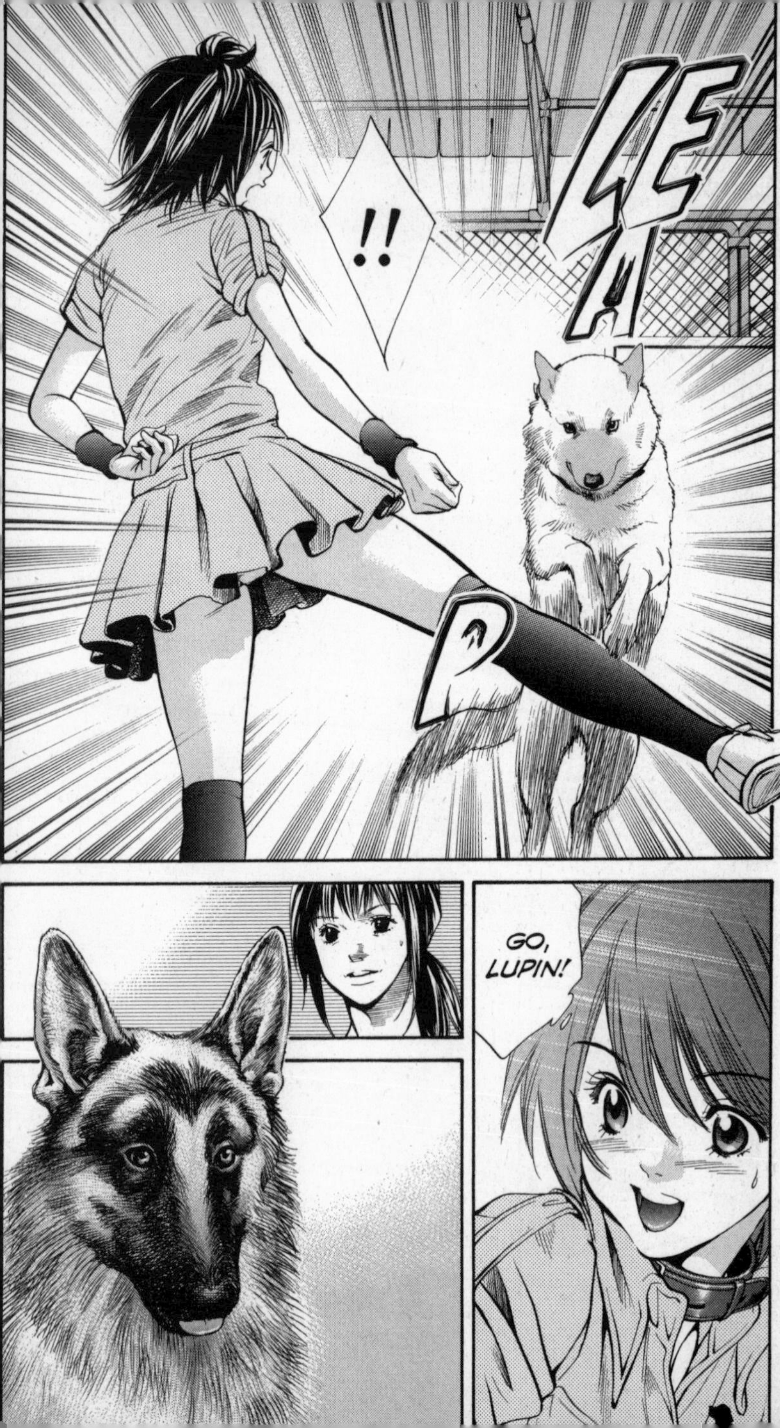
!!
GO, LUPIN!

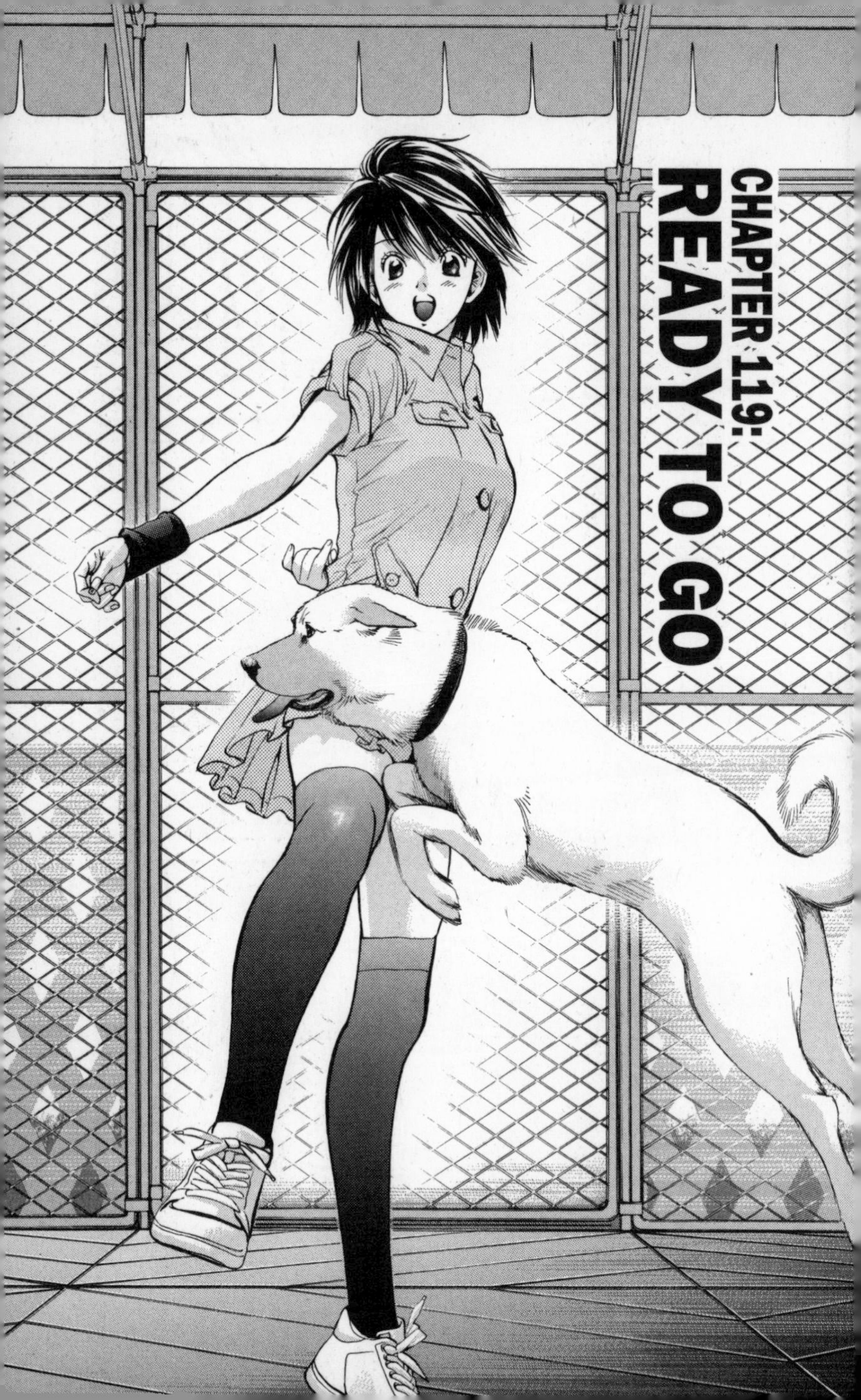
CHAPTER 119:
READY TO GO

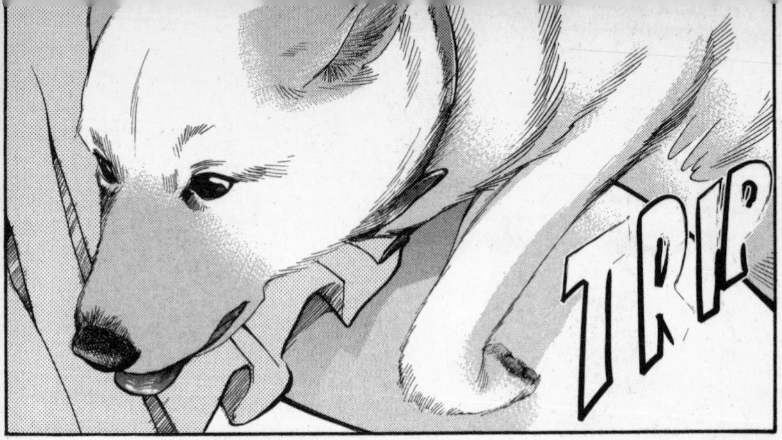
TRIP
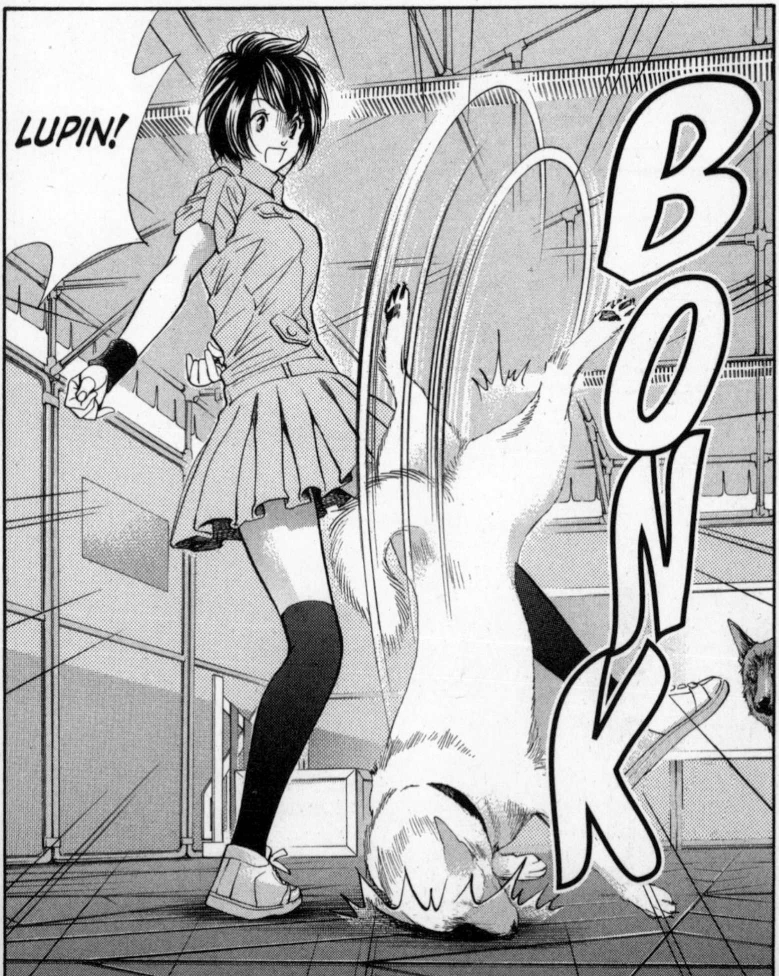
BONK
LUPIN!

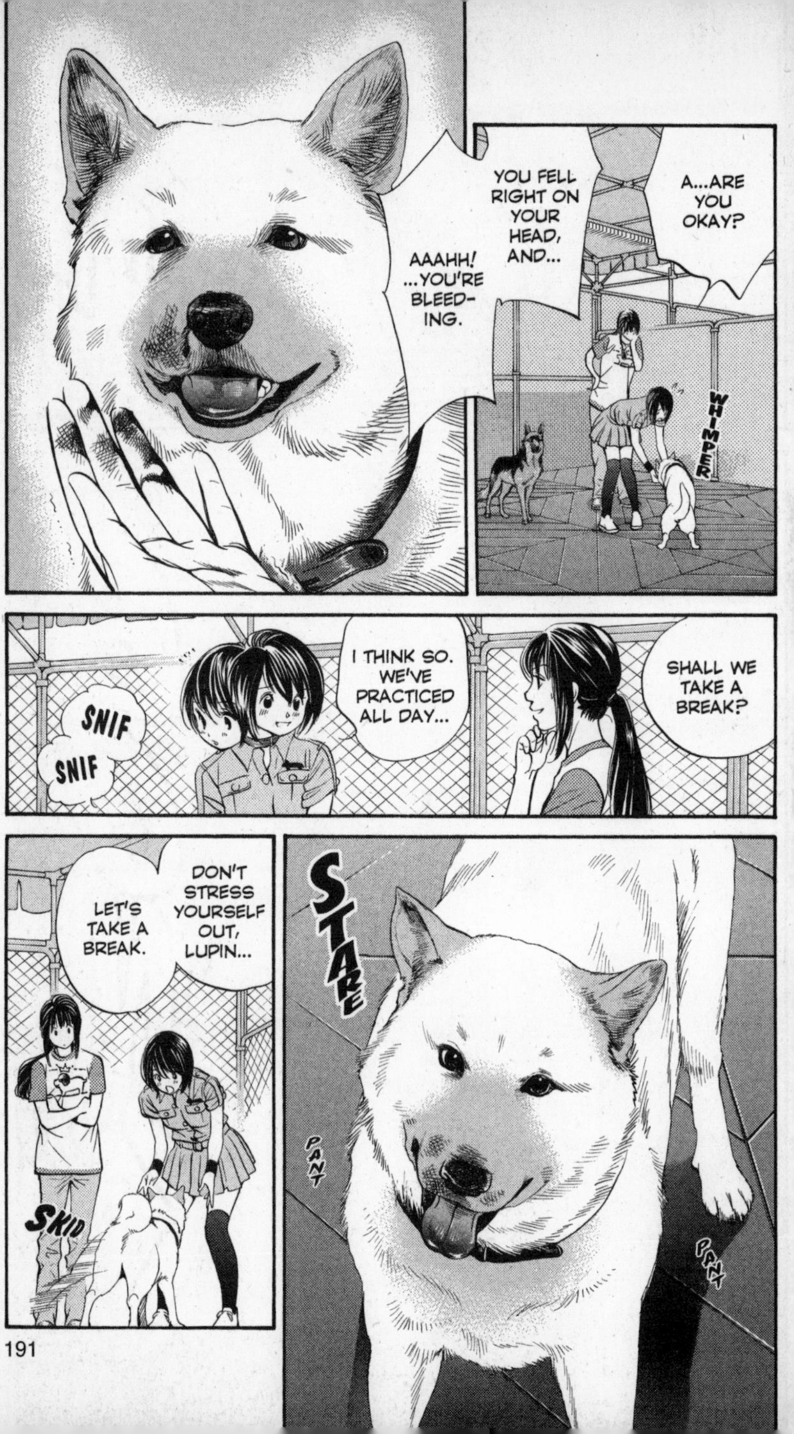
A...ARE YOU OKAY?
YOU FELL RIGHT ON YOUR HEAD, AND...
AAAHH! ...YOU'RE BLEED-ING.
WHIMPER
SHALL WE TAKE A BREAK?
I THINK SO. WE'VE PRACTICED ALL DAY...
SNIF
SNIF
STARE
PANT
PANT
DON'T STRESS YOURSELF OUT, LUPIN...
LET'S TAKE A BREAK.
SKID

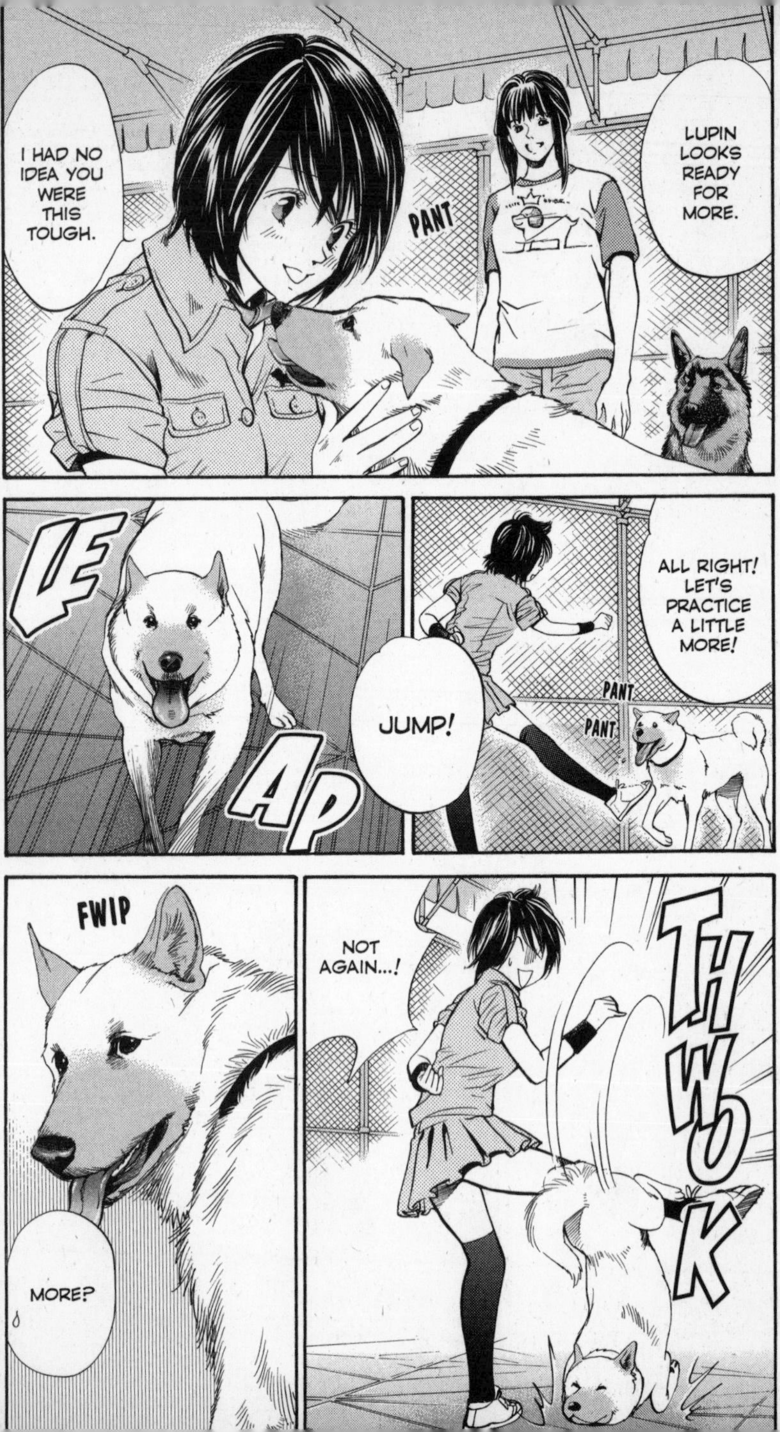

LUPIN LOOKS READY FOR MORE.
PANT
I HAD NO IDEA YOU WERE THIS TOUGH.
ALL RIGHT! LET'S PRACTICE A LITTLE MORE!
PANT
PANT
JUMP!
LEAP
THWOK
NOT AGAIN...!
FWIP
MORE?

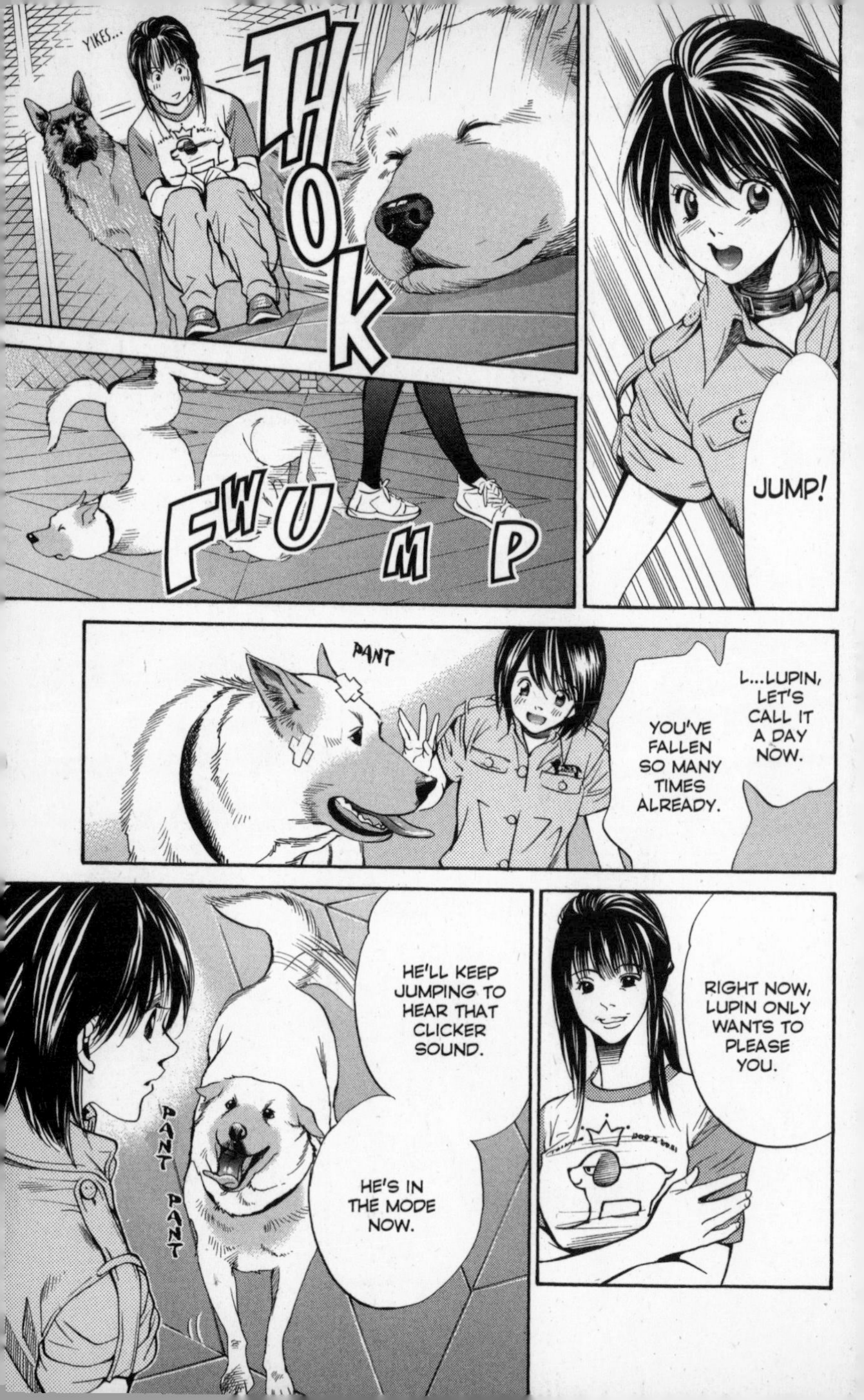
JUMP!
YIKES...
THOK
FWUMP
L...LUPIN, LET'S CALL IT A DAY NOW.
YOU'VE FALLEN SO MANY TIMES ALREADY.
PANT
RIGHT NOW, LUPIN ONLY WANTS TO PLEASE YOU.
HE'LL KEEP JUMPING TO HEAR THAT CLICKER SOUND.
HE'S IN THE MODE NOW.
PANT PANT PANT

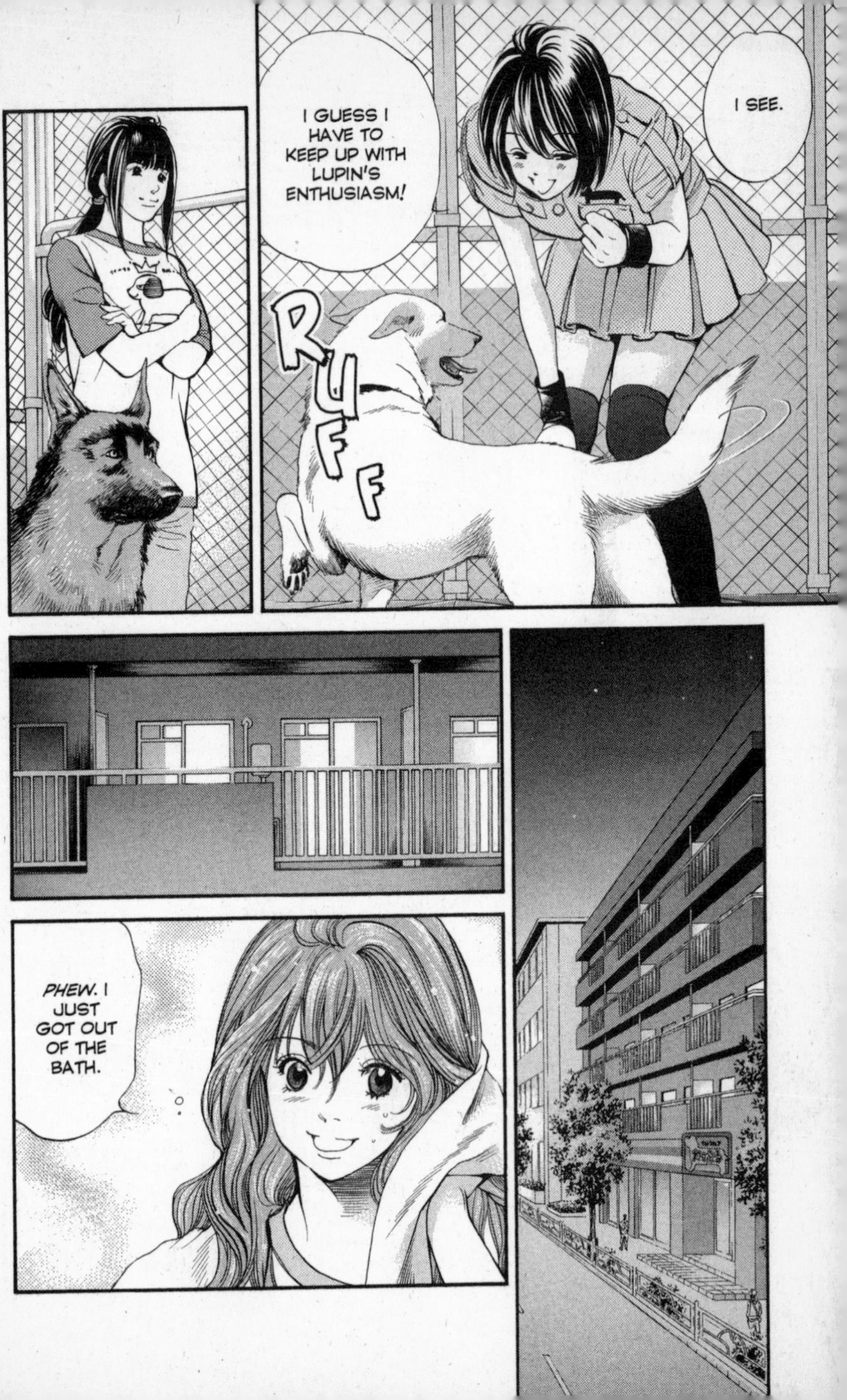
I SEE.
I GUESS I HAVE TO KEEP UP WITH LUPIN'S ENTHUSIASM!
RUFF
PHEW. I JUST GOT OUT OF THE BATH.

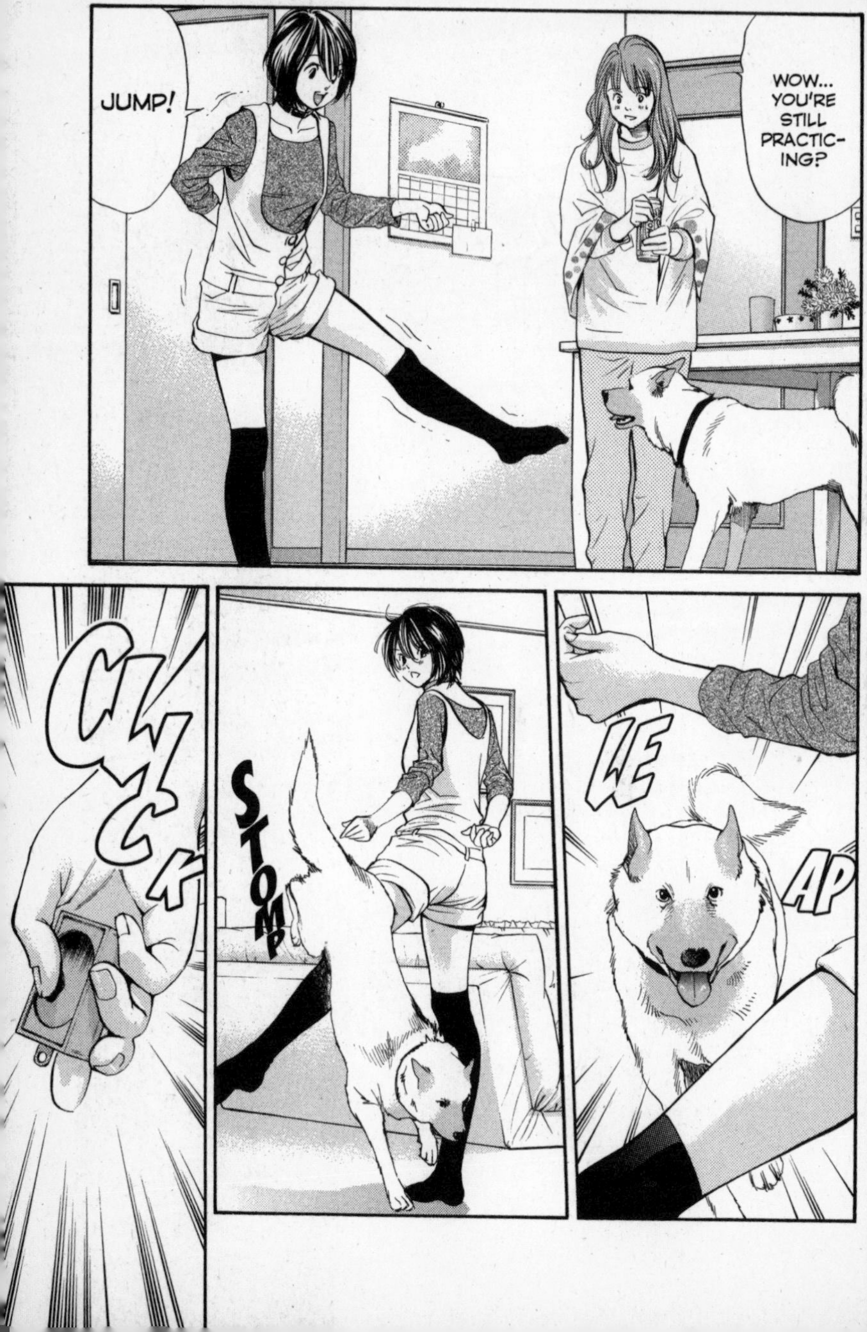
WOW... YOU'RE STILL PRACTIC- ING?
JUMP!
LE
AP
STOMP
CLICK

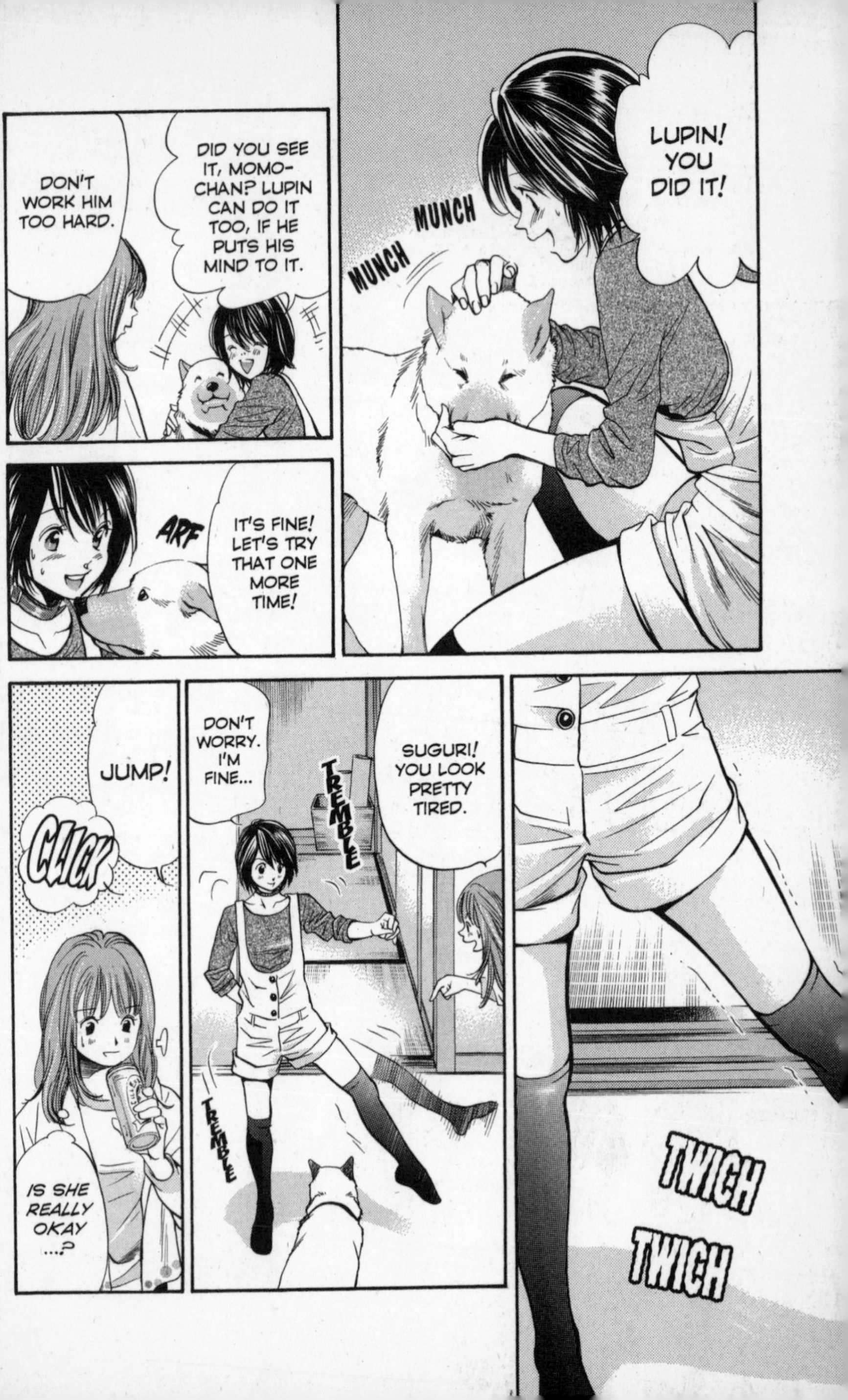
LUPIN! YOU DID IT!
MUNCH
MUNCH
DID YOU SEE IT, MOMO-CHAN? LUPIN CAN DO IT TOO, IF HE PUTS HIS MIND TO IT.
DON'T WORK HIM TOO HARD.
IT'S FINE! LET'S TRY THAT ONE MORE TIME!
ARF
TWICH
TWICH
SUGURI! YOU LOOK PRETTY TIRED.
DON'T WORRY. I'M FINE...
TREMBLE
TREMBLE
JUMP!
CLICK
IS SHE REALLY OKAY ...?

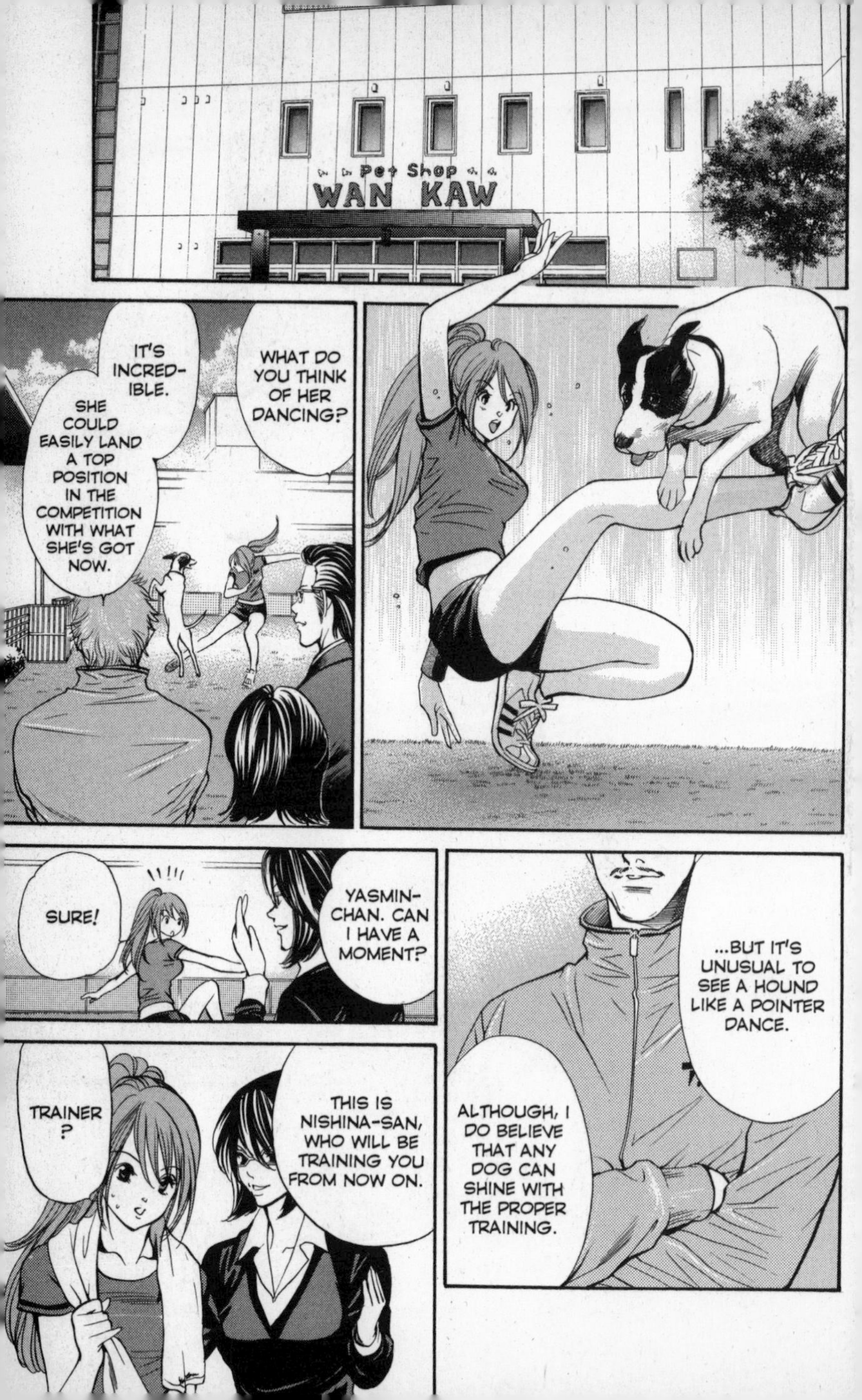
Pet Shop
WAN KAW
WHAT DO YOU THINK OF HER DANCING?
IT'S INCRED-IBLE.
SHE COULD EASILY LAND A TOP POSITION IN THE COMPETITION WITH WHAT SHE'S GOT NOW.
...BUT IT'S UNUSUAL TO SEE A HOUND LIKE A POINTER DANCE.
ALTHOUGH, I DO BELIEVE THAT ANY DOG CAN SHINE WITH THE PROPER TRAINING.
YASMIN-CHAN. CAN I HAVE A MOMENT?
SURE!
THIS IS NISHINA-SAN, WHO WILL BE TRAINING YOU FROM NOW ON.
TRAINER?

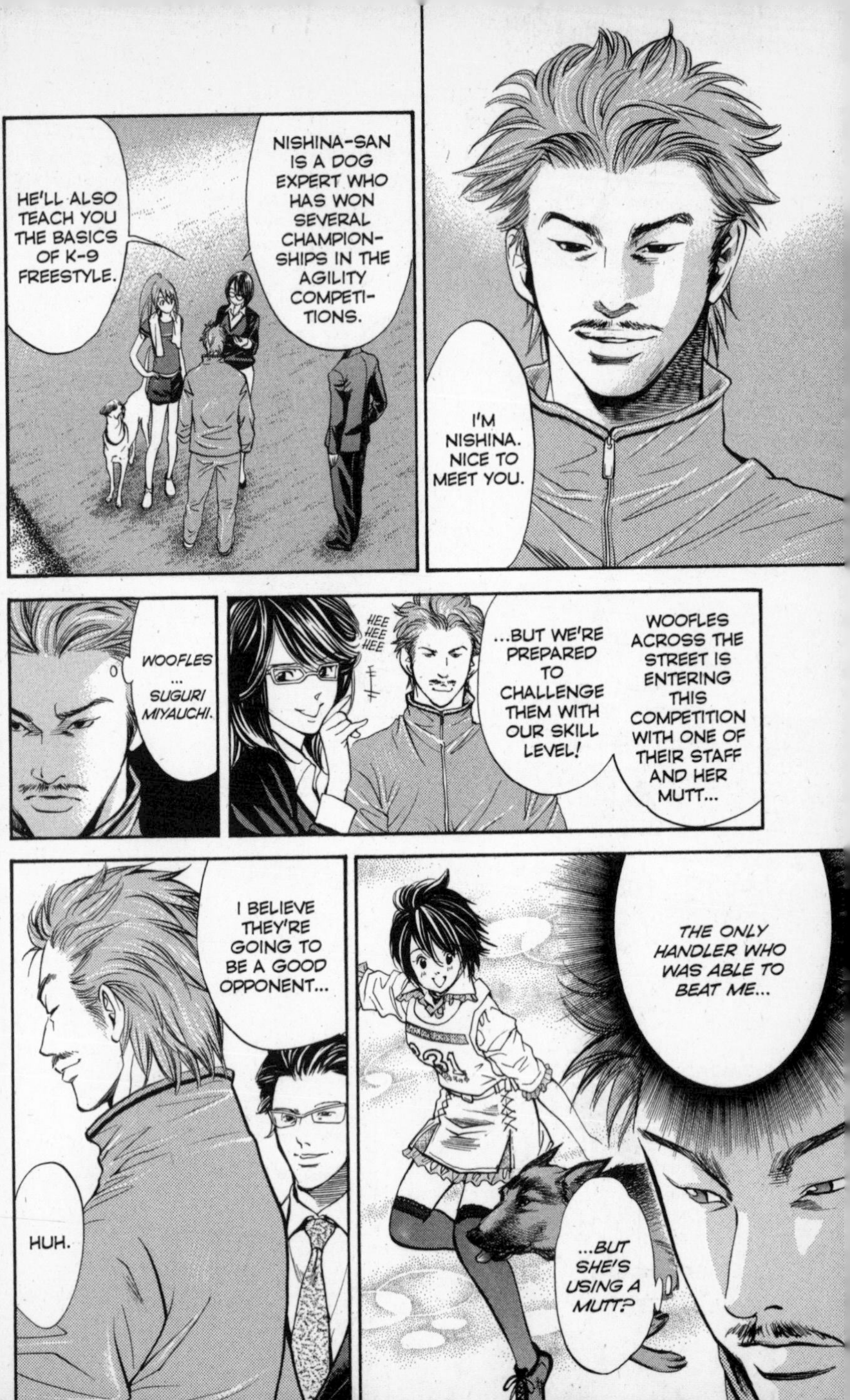
I'M NISHINA. NICE TO MEET YOU.
NISHINA-SAN IS A DOG EXPERT WHO HAS WON SEVERAL CHAMPION-SHIPS IN THE AGILITY COMPETI-TIONS.
HE'LL ALSO TEACH YOU THE BASICS OF K-9 FREESTYLE.
WOOFLES ACROSS THE STREET IS ENTERING THIS COMPETITION WITH ONE OF THEIR STAFF AND HER MUTT...
...BUT WE'RE PREPARED TO CHALLENGE THEM WITH OUR SKILL LEVEL!
HEE HEE HEE
WOOFLES ... SUGURI MIYAUCHI.
THE ONLY HANDLER WHO WAS ABLE TO BEAT ME...
...BUT SHE'S USING A MUTT?
I BELIEVE THEY'RE GOING TO BE A GOOD OPPONENT...
HUH.

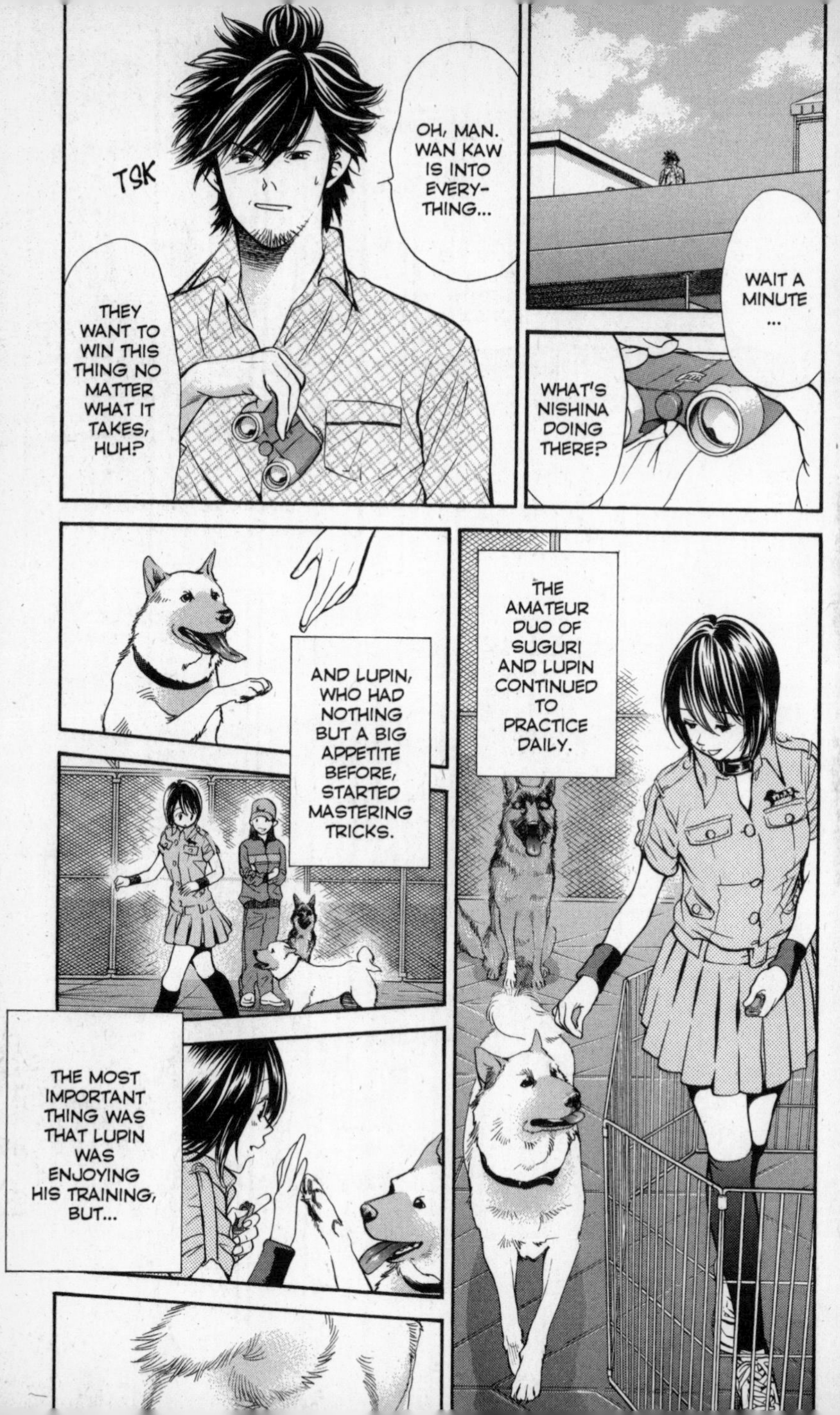
WAIT A MINUTE ...
WHAT'S NISHINA DOING THERE?
OH, MAN. WAN KAW IS INTO EVERYTHING...
TSK
THEY WANT TO WIN THIS THING NO MATTER WHAT IT TAKES, HUH?
THE AMATEUR DUO OF SUGURI AND LUPIN CONTINUED TO PRACTICE DAILY.
AND LUPIN, WHO HAD NOTHING BUT A BIG APPETITE BEFORE, STARTED MASTERING TRICKS.
THE MOST IMPORTANT THING WAS THAT LUPIN WAS ENJOYING HIS TRAINING, BUT...

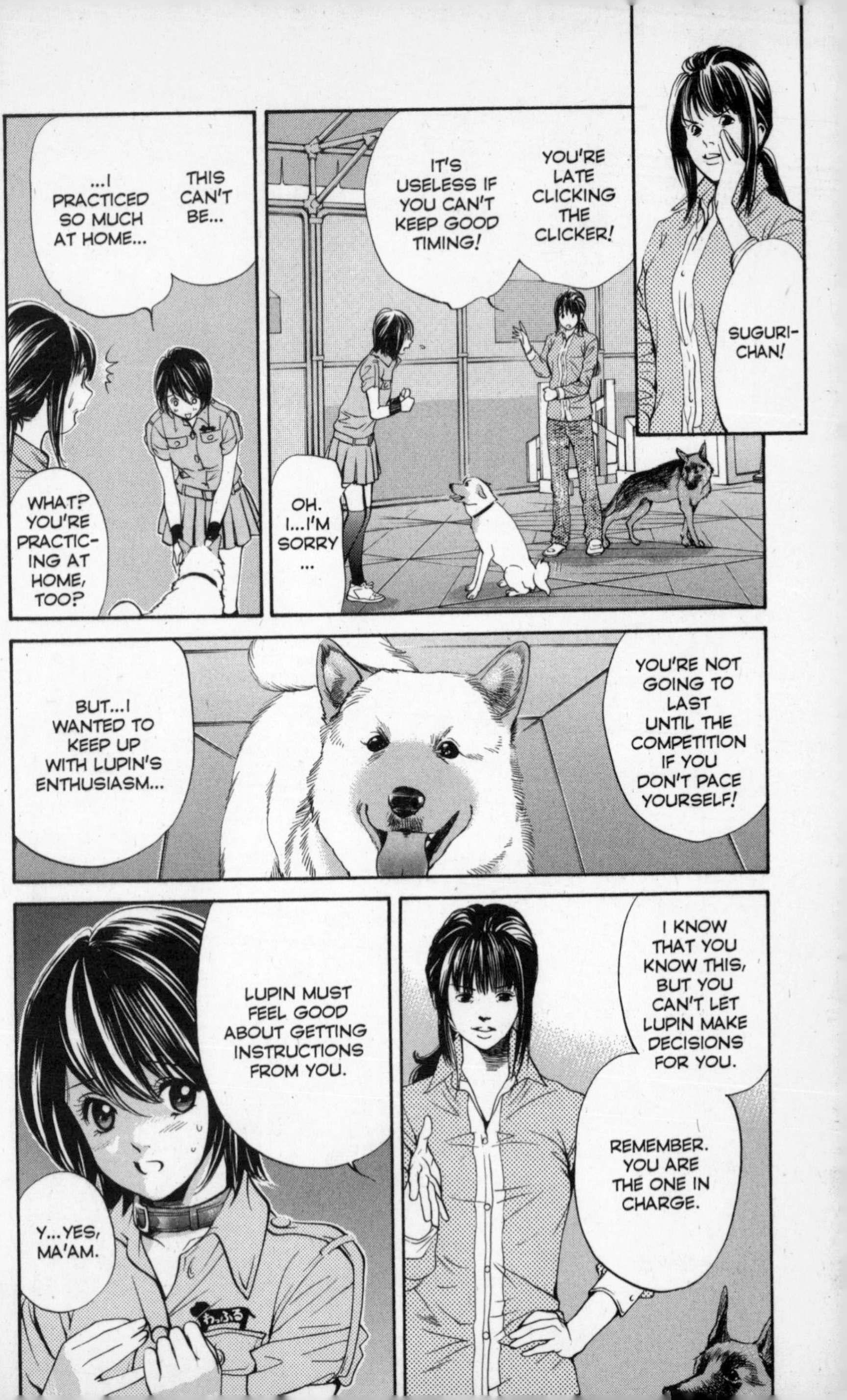
SUGURI-CHAN!
YOU'RE LATE CLICKING THE CLICKER!
IT'S USELESS IF YOU CAN'T KEEP GOOD TIMING!
OH. I...I'M SORRY ...
THIS CAN'T BE...
...I PRACTICED SO MUCH AT HOME...
WHAT? YOU'RE PRACTICING AT HOME, TOO?
YOU'RE NOT GOING TO LAST UNTIL THE COMPETITION IF YOU DON'T PACE YOURSELF!
BUT...I WANTED TO KEEP UP WITH LUPIN'S ENTHUSIASM...
I KNOW THAT YOU KNOW THIS, BUT YOU CAN'T LET LUPIN MAKE DECISIONS FOR YOU.
REMEMBER. YOU ARE THE ONE IN CHARGE.
LUPIN MUST FEEL GOOD ABOUT GETTING INSTRUCTIONS FROM YOU.
Y...YES, MA'AM.
わっふる

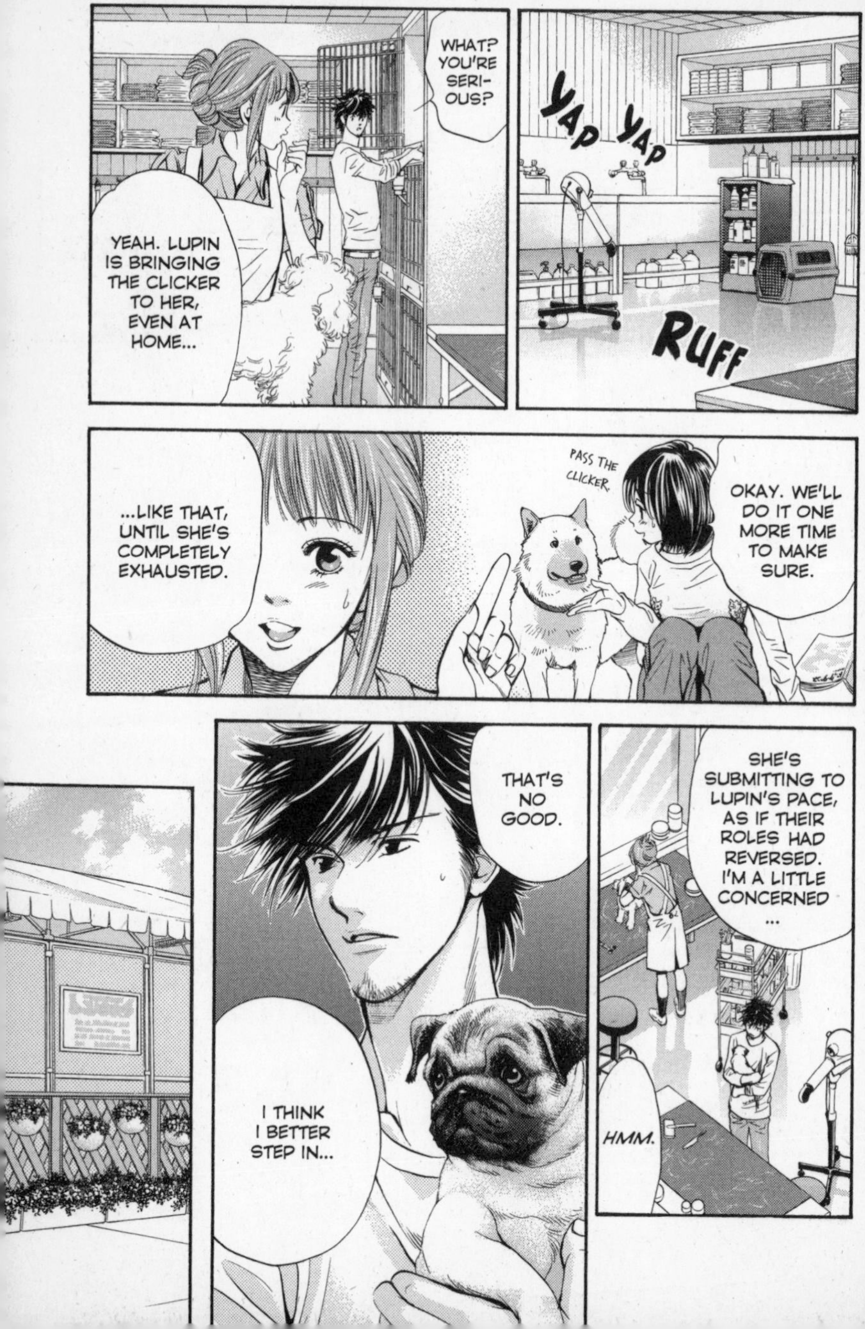
YAP YAP
RUFF
WHAT? YOU'RE SERI-OUS?
YEAH. LUPIN IS BRINGING THE CLICKER TO HER, EVEN AT HOME...
OKAY. WE'LL DO IT ONE MORE TIME TO MAKE SURE.
PASS THE CLICKER.
...LIKE THAT, UNTIL SHE'S COMPLETELY EXHAUSTED.
SHE'S SUBMITTING TO LUPIN'S PACE, AS IF THEIR ROLES HAD REVERSED. I'M A LITTLE CONCERNED ...
HMM.
THAT'S NO GOOD.
I THINK I BETTER STEP IN...

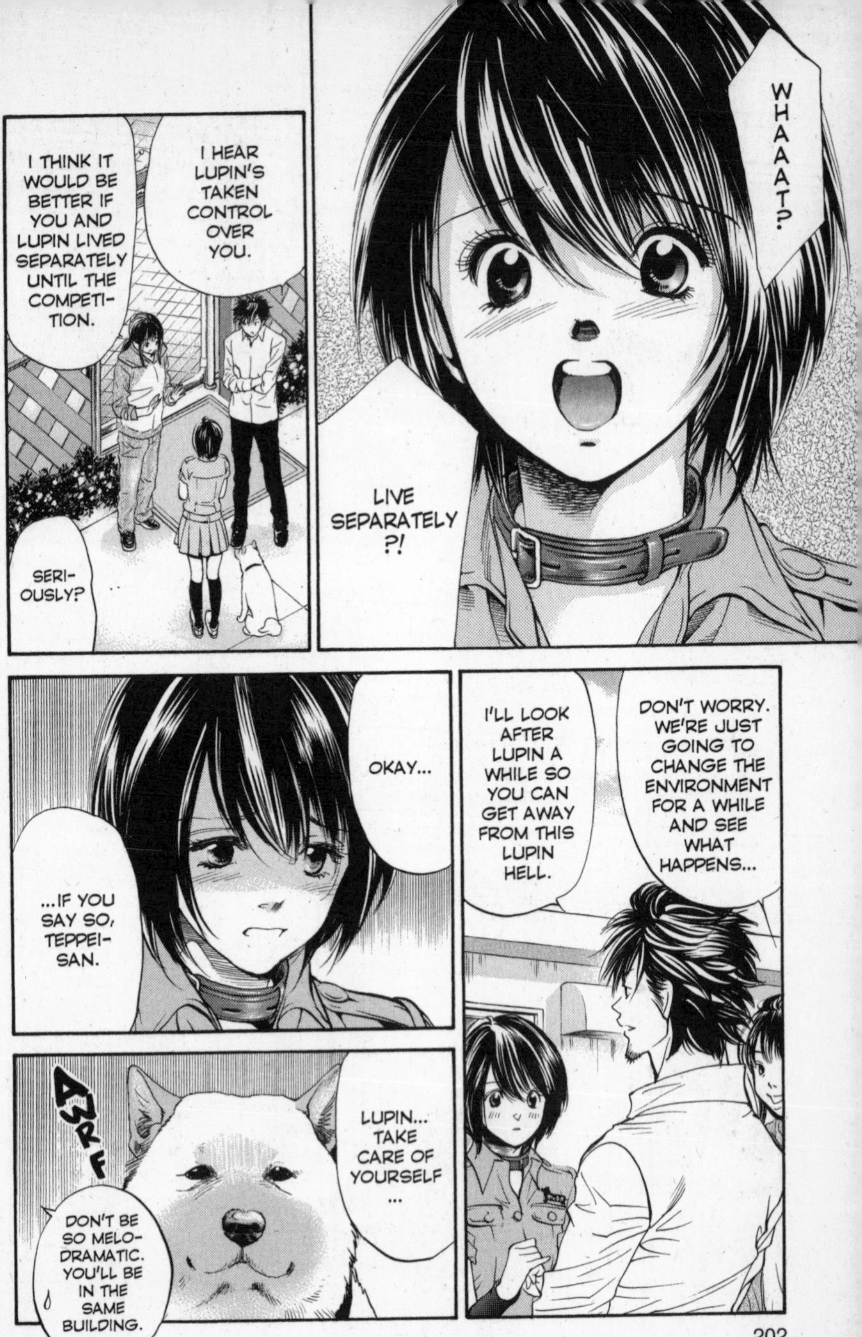
WHAAAT?
LIVE SEPARATELY ?!
I HEAR LUPIN'S TAKEN CONTROL OVER YOU.
I THINK IT WOULD BE BETTER IF YOU AND LUPIN LIVED SEPARATELY UNTIL THE COMPETI-TION.
SERI-OUSLY?
DON'T WORRY. WE'RE JUST GOING TO CHANGE THE ENVIRONMENT FOR A WHILE AND SEE WHAT HAPPENS...
I'LL LOOK AFTER LUPIN A WHILE SO YOU CAN GET AWAY FROM THIS LUPIN HELL.
OKAY...
...IF YOU SAY SO, TEPPEI-SAN.
LUPIN... TAKE CARE OF YOURSELF ...
AWRF
DON'T BE SO MELO-DRAMATIC. YOU'LL BE IN THE SAME BUILDING.

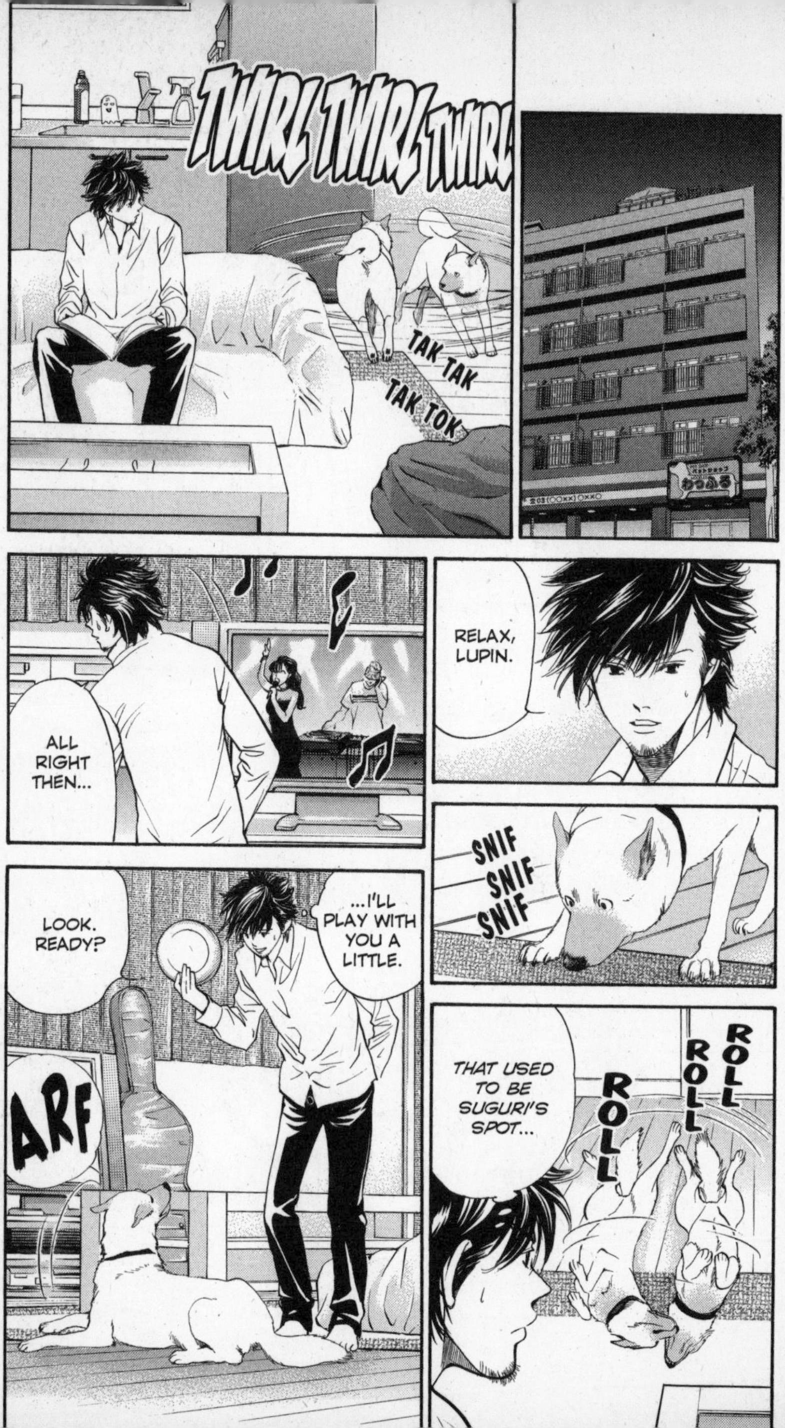

TWIRL TWIRL TWIRL
TAK TAK
TAK TOK
RELAX, LUPIN.
ALL RIGHT THEN...
SNIF SNIF SNIF
...I'LL PLAY WITH YOU A LITTLE.
LOOK. READY?
ARF
THAT USED TO BE SUGURI'S SPOT...
ROLL ROLL ROLL

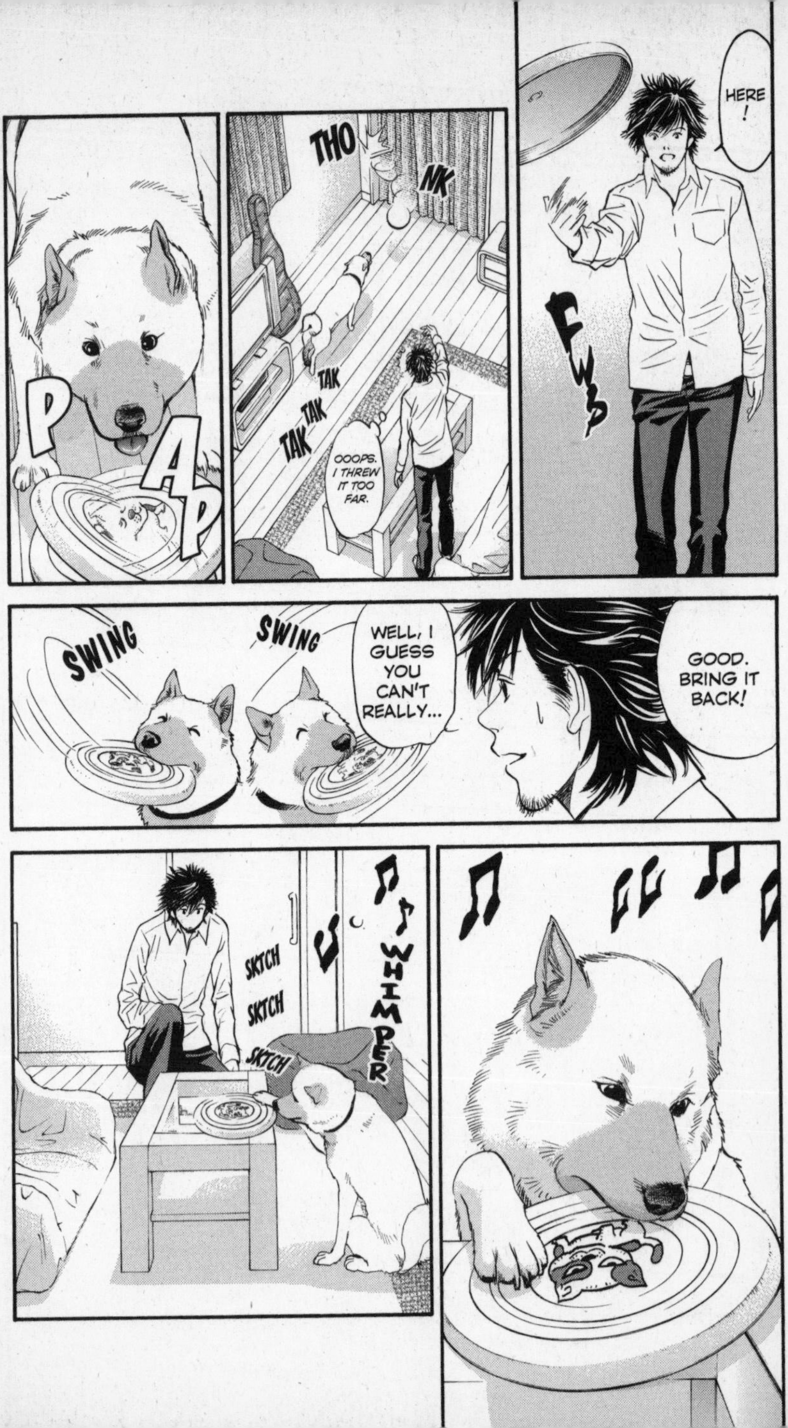
HERE!
FWP
THONK
TAK
TAK
TAK
OOOPS. I THREW IT TOO FAR.
PAP
GOOD. BRING IT BACK!
WELL, I GUESS YOU CAN'T REALLY...
SWING
SWING
WHIMPER
SKTCH
SKTCH
SKTCH

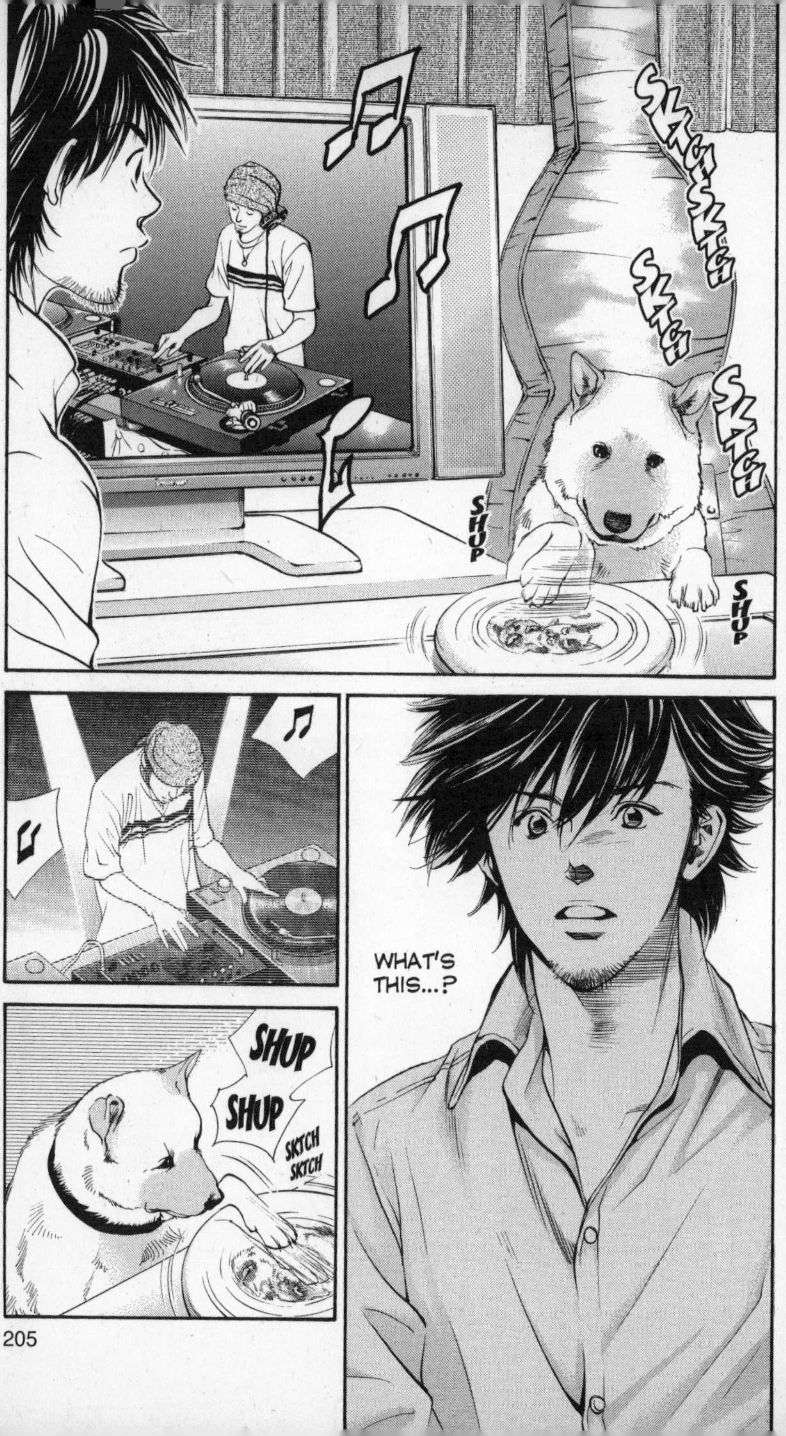
SKTCHSKTCH
SKTCH
SKTCH
SHUP
SHUP
WHAT'S THIS...?
SHUP
SHUP
SKTCH SKTCH

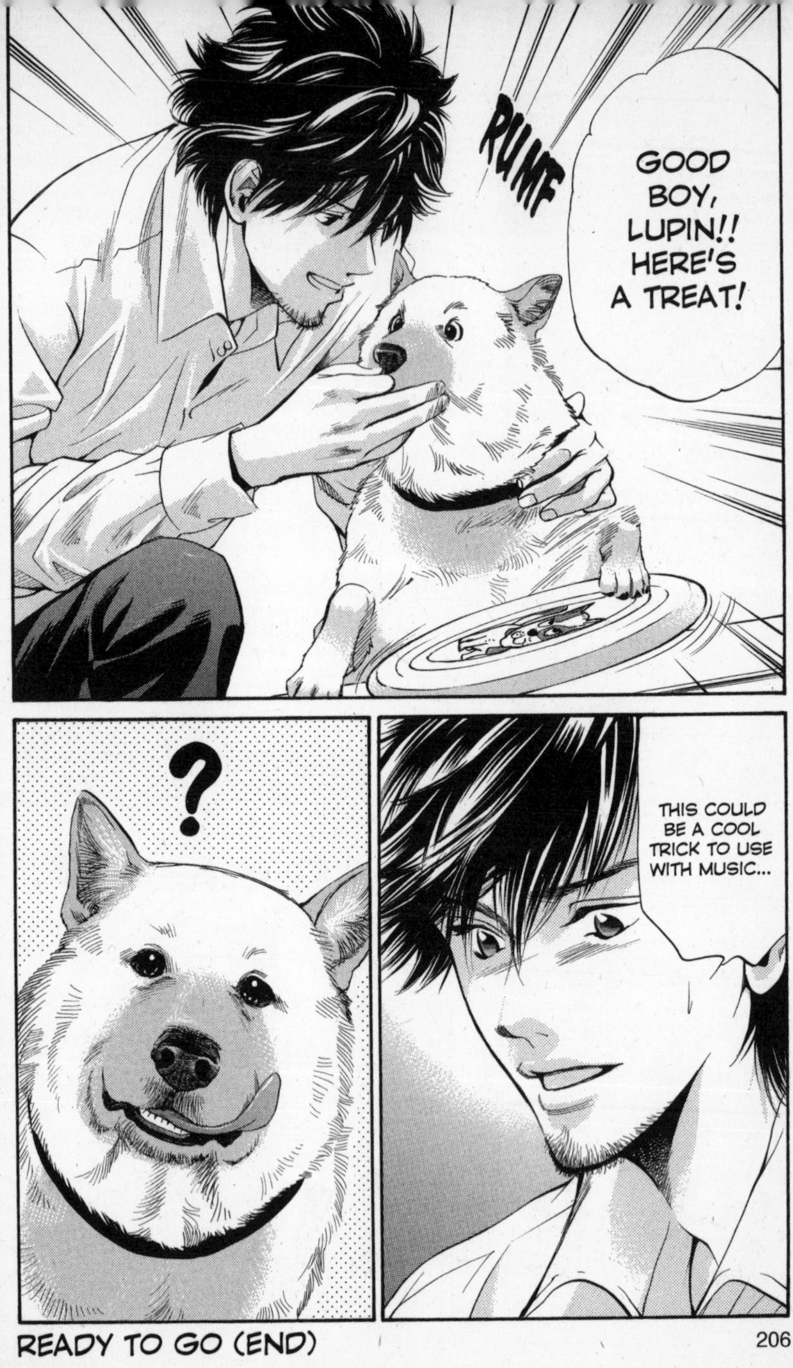
RUMF
GOOD BOY, LUPIN!! HERE'S A TREAT!
THIS COULD BE A COOL TRICK TO USE WITH MUSIC...
?

READY TO GO (END)

INUBA*KA

INUBAKA

Everybody's Crazy for Dogs!

From Ooya-san in Tokyo Prefecture

🐾 Riku-kun (Shiba)

Riku-kun is all about learning new tricks these days. He can now walk a little on his hind legs, shake hands, and then shake the other hand, etc. The picture was taken while he was training to wait with food on his nose. (Same as Aru in vol. 2) I wonder if he was successful?

Yukiya Sakuragi

He looks very smart for a puppy. He must be learning so many tricks so that he can spend lots of happy moments with his owner. I see a "Crazy for Dogs" lifestyle for years to come.

From Nakata-san in Hyogo Prefecture

🐾 Chappie-chan (Shih tzu)

She loves the cart so much that once she's in it she's there for a while. She must have been happy this day, enjoying the cherry blossoms.

Yukiya Sakuragi

So her favorite place to be is the cart. Her looking right into the camera is so cute! We've just welcomed a shih tzu into our home. He's a very rambunctious boy. Chappie-chan seems so calm and sweet…

From Kang Hee Jin-san in Korea

🐾 Poi-kun (Miniature schnauzer)

*We've received a photo
from a dog maniac from
our neighboring country, Ko-
rea! He smiles as soon as he
sees a camera. His loveliness
comes through the picture,
and he looks pretty cool in his
outfit too!*

Yukiya Sakuragi

Wow! What a great schnauzer photo
from a reader of the Korean version
of *Inubaka*! His excellent posture along with the awesome outfit makes him look
so sharp! This confirms that "Crazy for Dogs" is universal! (lol)

From Yoshida-san in Tokyo Prefecture

🐾 Takko-chan (Welsh corgi)

*Born in Hokkaido, Takko-chan has
only recently moved to Tokyo.
Perhaps she misses the cold air in
Hokkaido because she loves eating
ice cubes and taking naps on the
cool wooden floors. Takko-chan, I
hope you had a good summer in
Tokyo. Stay well!*

Yukiya Sakuragi

Welcome to Tokyo all the way from the northern land! The summers in Tokyo
can be pretty brutal. Dogs have a higher body temperature to begin with, so it's
important to take precautions. My dogs love ice cubes too. They eat a ton of
them during the summer. But as long as she gets through this summer, she'll be
fine for summers to come.

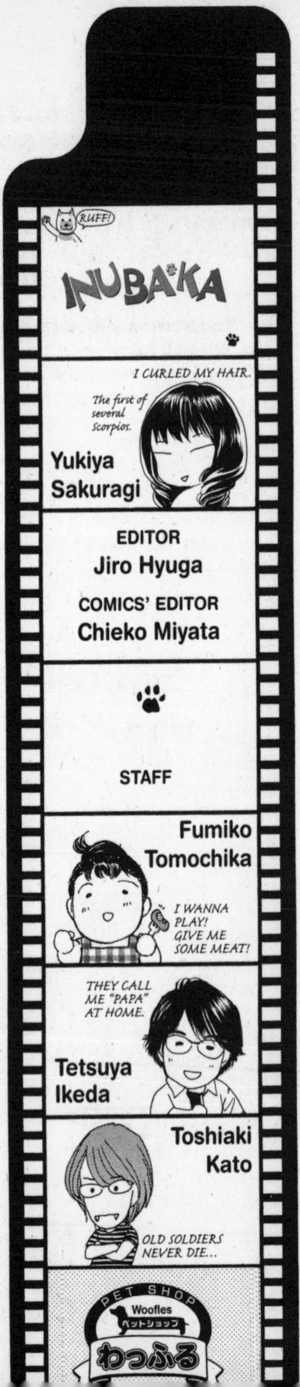
RUFF!
INUBAKA
I CURLED MY HAIR.
The first of several Scorpios.
Yukiya Sakuragi
EDITOR
Jiro Hyuga
COMICS' EDITOR
Chieko Miyata
STAFF
Fumiko Tomochika
I WANNA PLAY! GIVE ME SOME MEAT!
THEY CALL ME "PAPA" AT HOME.
Tetsuya Ikeda
Toshiaki Kato
OLD SOLDIERS NEVER DIE...
PET SHOP
Woofles
ペットショップ
わっふる

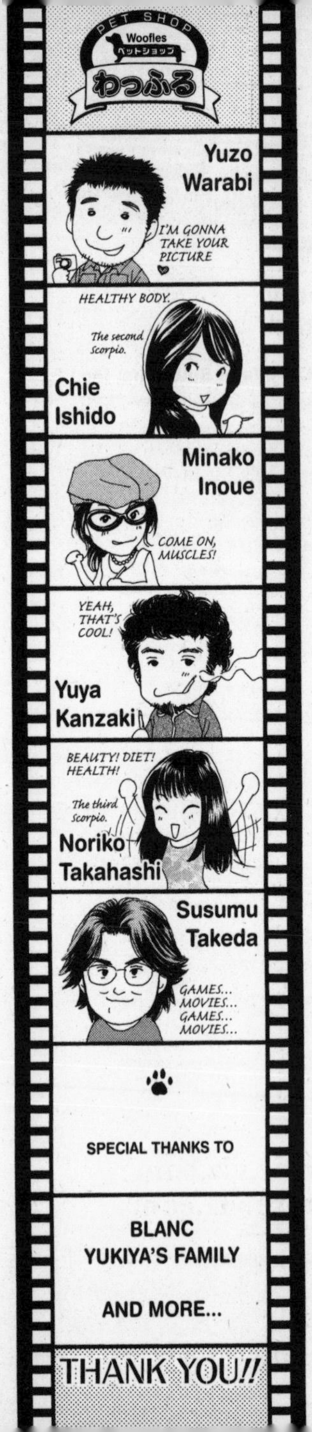
PET SHOP
Woofles
ペットショップ
わっふる
Yuzo Warabi
I'M GONNA TAKE YOUR PICTURE
HEALTHY BODY.
The second Scorpio.
Chie Ishido
Minako Inoue
COME ON, MUSCLES!
YEAH, THAT'S COOL!
Yuya Kanzaki
BEAUTY! DIET! HEALTH!
The third Scorpio.
Noriko Takahashi
Susumu Takeda
GAMES... MOVIES... GAMES... MOVIES...
SPECIAL THANKS TO
BLANC
YUKIYA'S FAMILY
AND MORE...
THANK YOU!!

Inubaka
Crazy for Dogs
Vol. #11
VIZ Media Edition

Story and Art by
Yukiya Sakuragi

Translation/Hidemi Hachitori, HC Language Solutions, Inc.
English Adaptation/Ian Reid, HC Language Solutions, Inc.
Touch-up Art & Lettering/Kelle Hahn
Cover and Interior Design/Hidemi Sahara
Editor/Ian Robertson

Editor in Chief, Books/Alvin Lu
Editor in Chief, Magazines/Marc Weidenbaum
VP, Publishing Licensing/Rika Inouye
VP, Sales and Product Marketing/Gonzalo Ferreyra
VP, Creative/Linda Espinosa
Publisher/Hyoe Narita

Published by VIZ Media, LLC
P.O. Box 77010
San Francisco, CA 94107

10 9 8 7 6 5 4 3 2 1
First printing, October 2008

www.viz.com
store.viz.com

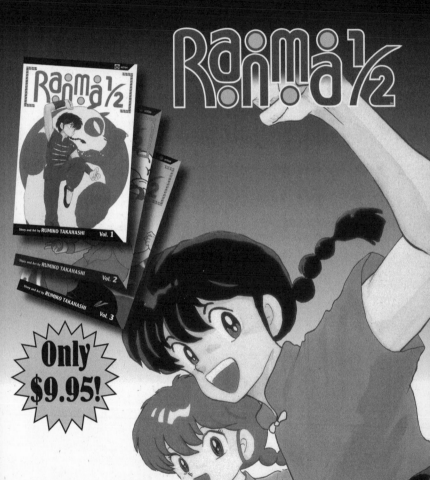

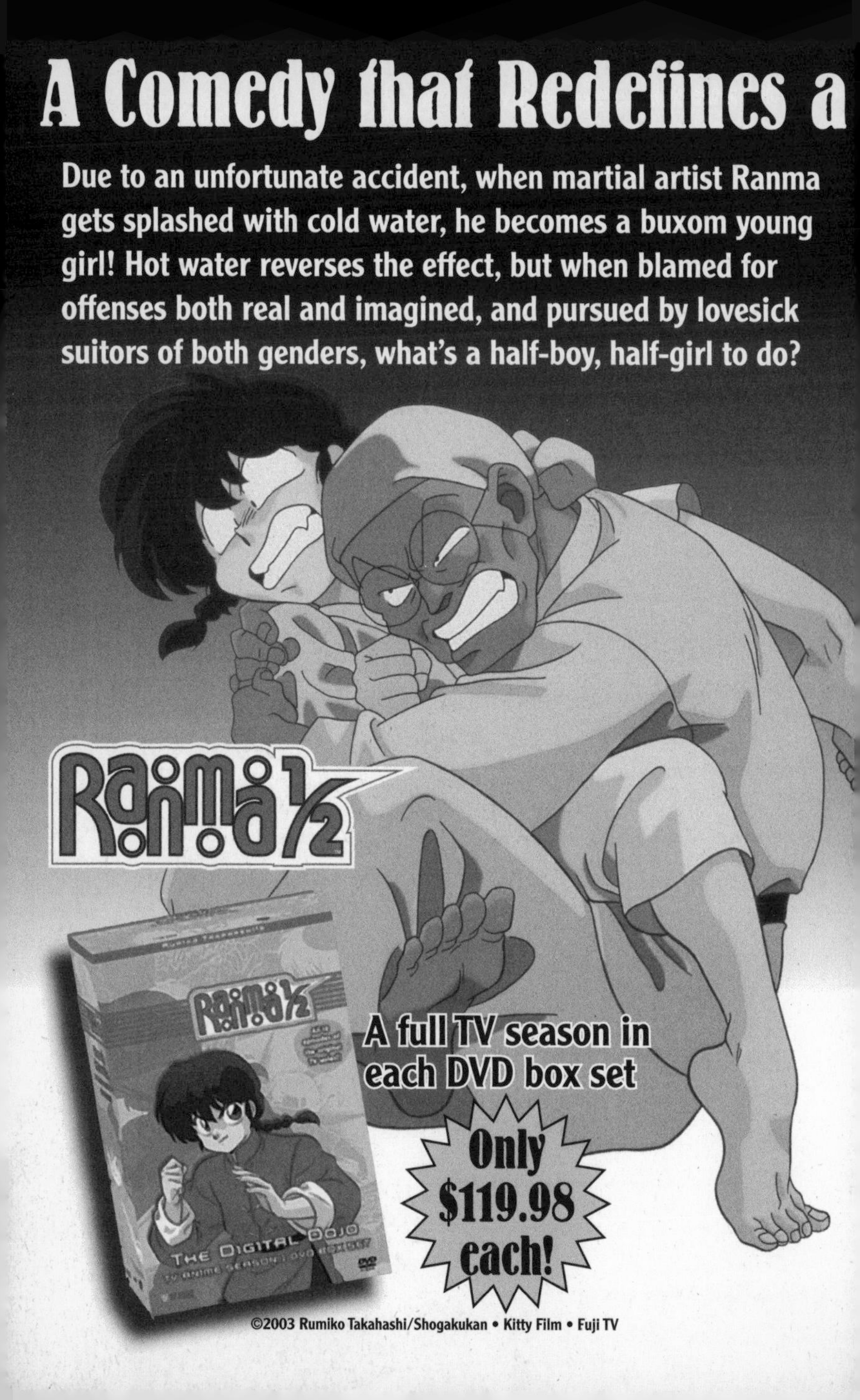

A Comedy that Redefines a
Due to an unfortunate accident, when martial artist Ranma gets splashed with cold water, he becomes a buxom young girl! Hot water reverses the effect, but when blamed for offenses both real and imagined, and pursued by lovesick suitors of both genders, what's a half-boy, half-girl to do?
Ranma ½
Ranma ½
THE DIGITAL DOJO
A full TV season in each DVD box set
Only $119.98 each!
©2003 Rumiko Takahashi/Shogakukan • Kitty Film • Fuji TV

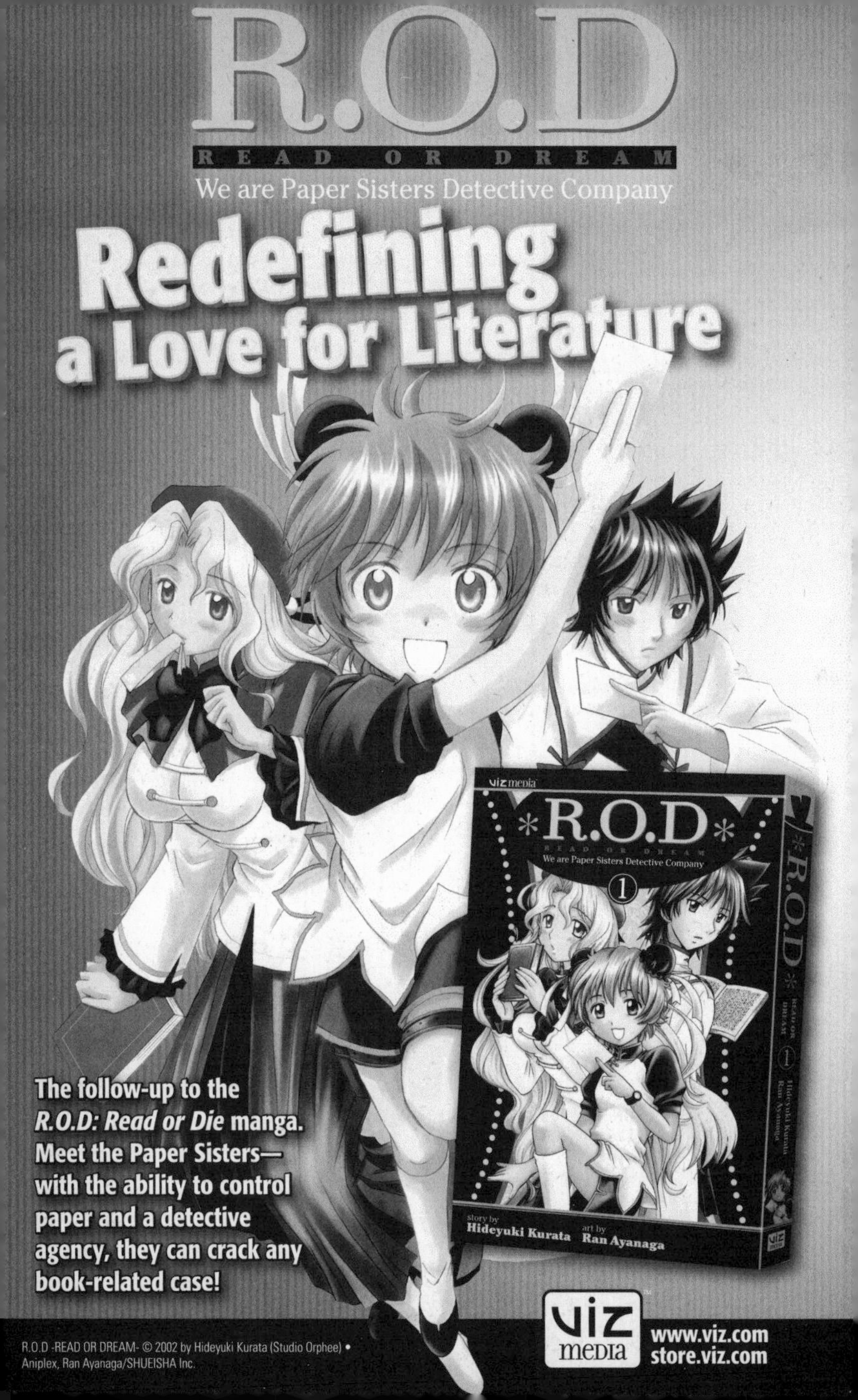
R.O.D
READ OR DREAM
We are Paper Sisters Detective Company
Redefining a Love for Literature
viz media
R.O.D
READ OR DREAM
We are Paper Sisters Detective Company
1
story by Hideyuki Kurata
art by Ran Ayanaga
The follow-up to the R.O.D: Read or Die manga. Meet the Paper Sisters—with the ability to control paper and a detective agency, they can crack any book-related case!
viz media
www.viz.com
store.viz.com
R.O.D -READ OR DREAM- © 2002 by Hideyuki Kurata (Studio Orphee) • Aniplex, Ran Ayanaga/SHUEISHA Inc.

LOVE MANGA?
LET US KNOW WHAT YOU THINK!

OUR MANGA SURVEY IS NOW
AVAILABLE ONLINE. PLEASE VISIT:
VIZ.COM/MANGASURVEY

HELP US MAKE THE MANGA
YOU LOVE BETTER!